NeWest

Profiles in Dissent

Profiles in Dissent

The Shaping of Radical Thought
in the Canadian West

Harry Gutkin
and
Mildred Gutkin

NeWest

First Edition

Canadian Cataloguing in Publication Data

Gutkin, Harry, 1915-
Profiles in Dissent

Includes bibliographical references.
ISBN 1-896300-08-1

1. General Strike, Winnipeg, Man., 1919. 2. Labor movement—Canada—Biography. 3. Canada, Western—Biography. I. Gutkin, Mildred. II. Title.
HD5330.W46G87 1996 331.89′25′09712743 C95-911118-2

Editor for the Press: Don Kerr
Editorial Coordinator: Eva Radford
Cover and book design: John Luckhurst/GDL
Photo Credits: Helen Armstrong, Winnipeg *Tribune*; William Pritchard, Burnaby Historical Society; George Armstrong, Francis Beynon, Robert Bray, Fred Dixon, A. A. Heaps, E. Cora Hind, William Ivens, Gertrude Richardson, Robert Russell, Provincial Archives of Manitoba; R. J. Johns, Katherine Queen (Winnipeg *Tribune* Photo Collection), Department of Archives and Special Collections, the University of Manitoba; Nellie McClung, Lillian Beynon Thomas, James S. Woodsworth, National Archives of Canada; Dr. Amelia Yeomans, Western Canada Pictorial Index.

NeWest Press gratefully acknowledges the financial assistance of The Canada Council and The Alberta Foundation for the Arts.

Printed and bound in Canada

NeWest Publishers Limited
Box 60632
U of A Postal Outlet
Edmonton, Alberta T6G 2S8

To the memory of our parents

Etta and Louis Gutkin
Sara and Alex Shanas

who were part of these events
in their adopted city

NeWest Press wishes to thank the following
for financial support of this book:

The Boag Foundation
Douglas – Coldwell Foundation

Contents

Acknowledgments

The basic materials for the account of the Winnipeg General Strike and for many of the biographical sketches in this book are lodged primarily in several public and academic archives across Canada. Beyond these generally available sources, we have mined a rich miscellany of information ranging from the official records of the trial to the publications of the Strikers' Defence Committee and other memorabilia in our own possession, and to the fragmentary reminiscences of a number of individuals in interviews and correspondence specifically conducted for purposes of this book with the descendants of our subjects or their surviving acquaintances. Given the overlapping nature of all this material, detailed and specific attribution has proved impossible; instead, in this present section we have attempted to indicate for the interest of our readers the major sources of information, and to acknowledge our enormous debt to a number of most helpful people.

For the Manitoba labour scene in general during the period covered in this book and the Winnipeg General Strike in particular, the primary sources are *The Voice* and the *Western Labor News*, and the mainstream local newspapers, the *Manitoba Free Press* (after 1931, the *Winnipeg Free Press*), the *Winnipeg Telegram*, and the *Winnipeg Tribune*; these files are housed, variously, in the National Archives of Canada, the Provincial Archives of Manitoba, the Legislative Library of Manitoba, and the archives of the University of Manitoba. Information on British Columbia and on Bill Pritchard is stored in the respective archives of the Province of British Columbia, the City of Vancouver, the Corporation and District of Burnaby, the Burnaby Public Library, and the archives of the University of British Columbia and Simon Fraser University. In addition to the various accounts that have been published on the watershed Manitoba event, some of them in the reading list at the end of the book, the 1970 doctoral thesis of Frederick David Millar for Carleton University provides a comprehensive and illuminating perspective.

Both the national and the Manitoba provincial archives have collections on Dixon, Ivens, Russell, Woodsworth, and Heaps, among others; material on George Armstrong is in the Manitoba archives; the University of Manitoba has the more extensive collections on Queen and Johns. The Woodsworth and Heaps papers, in Ottawa, are a primary source, and there are further details on the interaction of the parliamentary group in the papers of Agnes Macphail, Grace MacInnis and Angus MacInnis, and on the immigration problem in the Sam Factor and the S. W. Jacobs files. Of central interest are the reports of the RNWMP and of Military District No. 10, Winnipeg, and there is additional documentation in the papers of prime ministers Arthur Meighen, W. L. Mackenzie King, and R. B. Bennett.

Many of the prominent women who appear in our pages are represented in National Archives collections: Nellie McClung, E. Cora Hind, Amelia Yeomans, Lillian Beynon Thomas, Lucy Staples Woodsworth. In Ottawa are also the records of the Women's Christian Temperance Union, the National Council of Women, and the Canadian Women's Press Club; the Political Equality League records are in the Manitoba provincial archives. Information on Gertrude Richardson is to be found in the Manitoba archives, including some of her letters, articles, and poems in various publications; a most appreciative acknowledgement is also due to Professor Barbara Roberts of Athabasca University for her generosity with her own research on Richardson. Francis Beynon was women's editor of the Grain Growers' Guide; these files are in the Manitoba archives and legislative library, as are Beatrice Brigden's papers, with their pertinent observations on the events and the people of the period.

Much less satisfactorily recorded, information on the labour women — Helen Armstrong, Katherine Queen, Ada Muir, and others — must be gleaned from local newspapers and from passing references in other documents. As well, among the many researchers, archivists, librarians, and other professionals whom we have come to know, as an additional pleasure in the arduous process of composition, we must single out Anne Molgat, of Ottawa and Toronto. Not only did Ms. Molgat respond promptly and efficiently to our requests for a variety of specific and often obscure pieces of information, but she turned over to us the massive files on labour women which she herself had accumulated for her 1988 University of Ottawa Ph.D. thesis, "*The Voice* and the Women of Winnipeg, 1894–1918."

As biographers seeking an intimate glimpse of our subjects beyond the data of historical record, we have found a most valuable mirror in letters and interviews in the several archival collections, now including copies of our own recent acquisitions. Most noteworthy in this group is a three-hour memoir by Bill Pritchard, in his own voice, taped in 1975 at the age of eighty-seven, and now in the collections of both the provincial archives of British Columbia and the University of British Columbia. Available at Simon Fraser University are three separate sets of taped interviews with Pritchard, by David Millar, by Norman Penner and others, and by Bettina Bradbury and George Cook; and still another Pritchard tape, recorded by Ross McCormack, is located in the British Columbia provincial archives. For our own part, we have had the benefit of communication with R. A. Williams, the grandson of Bill Pritchard and resources minister in the CCF government of British Columbia under David Barrett.

Most illuminating also among the documents shelved at the National Archives are the papers of people who were involved, as participants or observers, in the events with which we are concerned. Alex Shepherd's correspondence with David Bercuson offers a contemporary's insight into the labour struggles of the day, as well as Shepherd's assessments of several of his colleagues and some vivid details of their personal lives. Professor Bercuson has also filed interviews with Eric McKinnon, Les Paulley, and Fred Tipping; Lionel Orlikow has contributed interviews with Bob Russell, Fred Tipping, James Aiken, Mrs. James Aiken, and C. A. Tanner; Paul Barber has also interviewed Bob

Russell; Brian McKillop has interviewed Marshall Gauvin, Mitch Sago, and Stanley Knowles. The soldiers' story is further reflected in the reminiscences of Graham Spry, as interviewed by David Bercuson, and of F. G. Thompson, as interviewed by David Millar. At the University of Manitoba are two interviews with Gloria Queen-Hughes, by Vera Pybus and Paul Barber.

We also appreciate the courtesy of David Heaps and Leo Heaps, who responded to our inquiries about their father, A. A. Heaps, in letters and in personal interviews, and of Saul Cherniack, Q. C., for a conversation with us on Heaps. As well, we offer a general recognition of the countless people whose recollections and observations have helped shape our story.

From the outset of our project we have been most fortunate in having the warm interest and cooperation of Allen Mills, the author of a recent critical biography of J. S. Woodsworth, *Fool for Christ*. Not only did Professor Mills make available to us his extensive research on Woodsworth, on the labour movement and its leaders, and on recent Canadian political history in general, but he was an active participant in the initial stages of this book's development, in the discussion of its context and controlling ideas. In the express interests of this endeavour, he conducted a number of engaging interviews on relevant events and people: with Don Aiken, Art Coulter, Magnus Eliasson, and Harry Monroe, and with Margaret Sykes, the daughter of Bob Russell. Finally, he read and commented most cogently on the manuscript at a late stage of its completion. We must add, of course, a requisite disclaimer: any remaining error or misuse of material is of our own making, and in no way reflects on the integrity of Professor Mills's contribution.

Many other people responded in many different ways to our requests for assistance in the course of this book's composition. A partial list of all these people must include the following: in British Columbia, Sue M. Baptie, George Brandak, Caroline Christie, Susan Hart, S. Norton, Mary Ellen Pennington, Jim Ross, Allen Specht, C. A. Turpin, and Ann Yandle; in Manitoba, Zenon Gawron, Kevin Ginter, Barry Hyman, Chris Kotecki, and Henry Trachtenberg; in Ottawa, John Armstrong, David Fraser, Berne R. Joyal, Antonio Lechasseur, Roy Maddocks, Walter Neutel, John Smart, Lawrence

Tapper, and George D. Zwaan. To others whom we may have inadvertently failed to mention, an assurance, nevertheless, of our appreciation and our sincere thanks.

Finally, our project has benefited greatly from the careful attention of our NeWest editor, Professor Don Kerr of the University of Saskatchewan. Professor Kerr's knowledgeable and sensitive suggestions and his constant insistence on "focus" have guided us in some vital surgery, clarifying the meaning of these lives, perhaps for the reader but certainly for ourselves.

For readers who may wish to explore this period and its issues further, the appended suggestions at the back of the book may be of interest.

Introduction

In the perspective of time, the lasting interest of a historic event often lies in the lives of the people who played a role in that event, men and women who came to a brief prominence, and then faded into obscurity. This book explores the human element in the Winnipeg General Strike of May and June 1919 in a series of profiles of the ten arrested strike leaders and in a corollary sketch of some of the women whose struggles and concerns became an integral part of the labour battle. In the shifting uncertainties of a rapidly changing world at the end of the twentieth century, the convictions of 1919 in all their contradictory variety may prove illuminating.

The general strike began as an attempt to achieve trade union rights, making only two basic demands: a living wage and recognition of the principle of collective bargaining. Six weeks of upheaval ensued, involving as many as 35,000 workers, both unionized and non-unionized, in a city whose population then totalled only 175,000. Winnipeg's commercial and industrial activity came virtually to a standstill, sending shock waves to other cities in Canada and beyond.

This wholly unprecedented occurrence was widely regarded in its time as an outrageous disruption of civic order, and even as a fortunate containment of a potential national disaster. The magnitude of the challenge to the traditional structures of authority can be measured by the intensity of the legal measures directed against the strikers, by the armed squads hired from out-of-province to break up meetings, and the use of the military and the Royal North-West Mounted Police to enforce order.

Far beyond the sensation it initially created, however, the Winnipeg General Strike can now be recognized for its full and lasting impact on the very character of Canadian life. A landmark event in the development of Canada's political party structure, it is acknowledged as the wellspring of Canadian social legislation. In its stand against mainstream authority, it defines a distinctively western sense of identity, nonconforming and generally left of centre. Even further, its conflict of personalities mirrors the characteristically diverse dissent at the heart of radical thought.

At the climax of the labour action ten men were apprehended as ringleaders. Charged with offences ranging from seditious conspiracy and inciting to riot down to common nuisance, nine eventually had their day in court: Robert B. Russell, George Armstrong, Roger Bray, Frederick J. Dixon, Abraham A. Heaps, William Ivens, Richard J. Johns, William A. Pritchard, and John Queen. The tenth man and the best-known today, James S. Woodsworth, was charged but never tried. All were socialists of various shadings, or liberal social reformers. In the end the strikers capitulated, having apparently achieved nothing.

Shadowing the very visible battle of the men, a determined women's movement fought its own campaign for recognition and empowerment, contributing in no small measure to the social upheaval that the general strike reflected. By 1919 many women were engaged in paid employment. Organization among female workers had been slow, but at least one predominantly female union, the telephone operators', was fully as militant as any of the longer-established locals in the male occupations. Moreover, women were disconcertingly aggressive in backing the strikers in the 1919 action, as recent reexaminations of the records have shown, and one woman, Helen Armstrong, both participated in the decisions of the Central Strike Committee and single-handedly organized a number of women's unions.

All of these people, men and women, took issue with the existing order at considerable cost to themselves, essentially defying the ruling establishment in an effort to achieve a more humane existence. With the city police themselves offering to join the strikers, the issue quickly became a confrontation between ordinary citizens, who had seemed powerless up to this point, and the established government — civic, provincial, federal — augmented by the business-organized Citizens' Committee of One Thousand.

Among the people in the labour ranks, what emerges vividly is the extent of disagreement and open conflict that marked their interaction throughout the entire period. Coming together only briefly under stress, they fought each other bitterly in the zeal of their dissent. The accused strike leaders were targeted together by the authorities as conspirators in a plot to destroy civil order, but they continued their dissent behind bars, and beyond.

Years later, when the passions of the moment had subsided, Bill Pritchard could repeat with amusement the comment of a young, newly arrived Scottish guard at the prison farm where he and the others convicted with him served their sentences. "Conspiracy?" the guard exclaimed, as they all enjoyed a forbidden smoke together, with Pritchard, John Queen, Dick Johns, and some of the others vehemently arguing politics, "Seditious conspiracy? My god, you fellows can't agree on any one point!"

After two decades or more of shifting party alignments, the first stable left-of-centre party to emerge on the Canadian scene was the Independent Labor Party, founded even as the convicted strike dissidents served out their sentences. Led by the widely respected Fred Dixon, the ILP brought together a fairly cohesive group of moderate socialists and reformers. Dixon himself was primarily dedicated to the land and tax principles of Henry George, and drawn into the labour movement by a moral concern for the equitable distribution of the world's goods. Willing to cooperate with politicians of whatever stripe to gain a practical end, he was only marginally if at all a socialist.

The extreme left in the labour spectrum would have no part of a movement unprepared to abide by the precepts of Karl Marx. With *Das Kapital* and the *Communist Manifesto* as the fixed foundation of their belief, absolute Marxists such as Jacob Penner made the class struggle their central preoccupation, and their primary goal the overthrowing of capitalism by direct force, by violence if necessary — at least in theory.

A member of the Socialist Party of Canada in the early 1900s,

3

Penner joined the Social Democrats for a time, but became a Communist, like a number of the leftists associated with Bob Russell in the creation of the One Big Union. Penner remained loyal to Moscow all his life, but was elected year after year to the city council and, paradoxically, became something of a legend in Winnipeg for his gentle and unflagging attention to the needs of his impoverished constituents.

Russell was primarily a union man, battling the bosses and therefore the entire capitalist system on behalf of working people. Regarded by the authorities as the king-pin of the labour movement, his radicalism seems to have had little theoretical foundation. He was initially scornful of what he considered the half-hearted moderation of Dixon's new party, but ran for office under the ILP banner a few years later, when he had been virtually betrayed by his own far-left colleagues. But he resisted party discipline and party decisions, and fought an increasingly virulent battle with party leaders, notably John Queen.

Avowedly Marxist in their analysis of the world's economic problems, socialists such as George and Helen Armstrong and British Columbia's Bill Pritchard advocated as a foundation for meaningful change in the social order the collective ownership of the means of production and distribution of goods, and thereby an end to the pervasive inequities of the existing system. Often as passionate as the Marxist left in their total denunciation of capitalism and capitalists, they pulled back from the pursuit of revolution by violence, insisting that the education of the masses was the path to a new, enlightened era of working-class supremacy.

For social democrats such as John Queen and Abe Heaps, the economic and social changes necessary for worldwide justice and peace were to be achieved by the gradual transformation of society through the institutions of democratic government. Often derided as mere reformers by the more radical socialists, and as "capitalist lackeys" in the inflammatory vocabulary of the extreme Marxists, they pursued their aims step by pragmatic step, making common cause with other reformers and socialist reformers such as Dixon and Woodsworth.

Added to the volatile political mix in early twentieth-century Winnipeg was the element of ethical Christianity, as exemplified by William Ivens and the Social Gospel, and even more in the deeply spiritual devotion of James Woodsworth to the cause of suffering humanity. This Christian socialism preached the practical goals of an end to hunger and want, but it partnered uneasily with the secular anticlericalism of most socialists and social democrats. In the high drama of the general strike, William Ivens was an outstanding performer, but eventually the ILP and its successor the Co-operative Commonwealth Federation (CCF) had no use for his pious and unfocused sincerity, and discarded him.

Common to all these related but divergent ideologies was a deepdyed pacifism, particularly pronounced in the heightened political climate of Winnipeg. It meant a total rejection of the European militarism that led to the Great War of 1914–18. Radical Marxists, many of whose origins were in the revolutionary movements of eastern Europe, denounced the war as a struggle between imperialistic powers, and all the more so when Britain and the Allies turned against the successful Bolsheviks in the Russian Revolution. Socialists and social democrats embraced pacifism, protesting the price that the common people paid for the greed and folly of their masters; and for devout believers in the compassionate wisdom of Jesus, such as Ivens and Woodsworth and Gertrude Richardson, the horrors of war were unequivocally an offence against the soul as well as the body.

Contributing to the climate of dissent and social disruption, the issue of woman suffrage provoked outrage on every level of society. Generally, the suffragists found support among many — though by no means all — male reformers and progressive thinkers, but the rank and file of male workers were as wary of women's demands as the rest of the population, particularly when those demands appeared to compete with the interests of men in the labour market. For their part, the pronouncements by the relatively few prominent women leaders were often scathing in their contempt for the folly of male legislators. Women must use the vote, said Nellie McClung, to strengthen family life and improve rural and urban living conditions, "to shape the world nearest to our heart's desire."

The drive for the franchise was the most visible aspect of the women's movement in the second decade of the twentieth century, but across the country women's organizations were pursuing a complex of concerns closely related to labour's ongoing struggle. As labourites and union men fought their public wars for empowerment, for the oft-repeated goals of "higher wages and better working conditions," women in scattered farm groups and church groups and temperance unions turned their sights directly on the havoc that poverty inflicted on the anonymous lives of ordinary people. Sweat shops, slum housing, child labour, malnutrition, disease, alcoholism, and prostitution: these were the daily realities that lay behind labour's demand for a greater share of the world's wealth, and these were the direct concerns of women's organizations, large and small; and before women's voices could be clearly heard in the labour movement, suffragists were vociferously demanding attention to the problems of women workers.

The lives of the people in the pages that follow intersect at the dramatic moment of the labour action, but they have arrived at that prominence from different directions, almost inadvertently, and frequently at odds with others whose battles parallel and complement their own. Each of the protagonists experiences the unfolding events differently, setting out a personal version of what constitutes human justice and well-being, so that each chapter, retelling the tale, highlights a different aspect of the period's history. In sum, what emerges is a composite portrait of an era in our recent past and an anatomy of human aspirations.

Decades later, the aims and the conflicts of some of these men and women retain their interest. Here, in this counterpoint of passions and principles, of theories the actors in the drama embraced but only partly understood, of idealism and self-interest intermixed, can be found a multilayered reflection of an enduring discontent with the status quo. Beyond the specific political and economic developments that can be traced to the 1919 Winnipeg General Strike, dissent is the key to its significance, a timeless common denominator of unsatisfied human needs.

The Inalienable Rights of the Individual

Frederick John Dixon

The Mobius Circle

By the early 1900s Winnipeg's Main Street was lined with enterprises of every sort, as artisans and shopkeepers, many of them only recently arrived, staked their claims to a place in the burgeoning community. Near William Avenue, a few doors down from the splendid city hall, Ryan's Shoe Store was located, and above, in two rooms on the second floor, were the offices of the Manitoba Institute of Mental Sciences, Professor R. M. Mobius, Principal. A notice in the 1905 Henderson's Directory set forth the institute's credentials: Madame Adeline Mobius was "Vice-Principal" and "Professor of Phrenology and Scientific Palmistry," and the proprietor himself offered his services as a "Consulting Hygienist, Medical Electrician, Naturopath, and Phrenologist." In addition, "Books, magazines, and literature" were advertised for sale, and there was a "Lending Library in connection."

Like a number of other people who gravitated to the raw, new western towns, Professor Mobius was a curious figure, seemingly out of step with conventional society. He had apparently taught at a German university, but had to leave, it was said, because he was a pacifist and because he insisted on the freedom to express his views publicly. He was understood to speak several languages and to be proficient in higher mathematics; he had read widely in literature, history, economics, philosophy, and in the more esoteric branches of inquiry; and he had become keenly interested in the teaching of Henry George, whose "single tax" principles offered a direct solution to a variety of society's ills.

Not surprisingly Mobius's library and bookstore attracted a group of serious-minded citizens concerned with the social issues of the day and intent on investigating theories of radical change to established government. Seymour James Farmer and Lewis St. George Stubbs met here, both already prominent in the movement for electoral and economic reform. Farmer's future path was to take him to the office of mayor of the city of Winnipeg and a seat in the Manitoba legislature as leader of the ILP and the CCF parties; Stubbs, who had studied law in Winnipeg after a restless career at Cambridge University, action in the Boer War, and work on a Manitoba farm, rose eventually to the office of senior county court judge. A pugnacious jurist, as controversial as he was humane, he was finally removed from the bench for his unorthodox decisions. D. W. Buchanan, a florist, enjoyed a congenial audience here for his single tax explorations. The group included John W. Ward, later a prominent figure in the cooperative movement, and William Ivens, who was ordained in 1909 as a Methodist minister and became the leading advocate of the Social Gospel, the church movement for social justice. All of these men met regularly in Professor Mobius's rooms, to read, to argue, to discuss.

It was here also that Fred Dixon found his political direction, although the nonconforming pattern seems to have been set in his childhood. The youngest in a family of nine, Frederick John Dixon was born in January 1881, in the small village of Englefield, near Reading, England. His father was a coachman on a large estate, and neither parent had received much formal education, but in the tradition-bound society of rural England their yeoman ancestry gave them a certain distinction, with all the sturdy self-reliance of that class. There was very little money, and yet, with their parents' encouragement, several of the Dixon children pushed beyond the limitations of the village school to achieve a higher education on scholarship.

When young Fred's turn came, however, he balked. At the age of thirteen he declared that he was through with being shut up in a schoolroom and would now make his own way in the world. Telling the story in his later years, Dixon clearly took a great deal of pride both in his own youthful determination and in his father's resistance to pressure from authority. The village rector tried to keep the young rebel in school, even promising to provide money for university study out of an endowment fund for able students, and finally urging Fred's father to order his offspring to obey. Characteristically, the elder Dixon chose instead to honour his son's independence; Fred would repeat his father's retort with lasting satisfaction: "You've heard the boy make his decision. Now we'll hear no more about it!"

Having acquired long trousers and a pipe as his badge of manhood, Fred got himself apprenticed to a gardener, served out his term, then went to work tending the grounds on an estate in the south of England, the first of a series of such jobs. The work was poorly paid and uncertain. By 1903, he was unemployed, and there seemed little further prospect in the horticultural trade. London held out some possibility, but he could make no place for himself in its teeming streets. He was now twenty-two years old, over six feet tall, and impressively well-built. A recruiting advertisement for the police force caught his eye, and he sent in, as required, a hand-written application. But his penmanship was virtually illegible — it remained rather craggy, as some of his surviving correspondence shows — and he was turned down. At loose ends, he made the choice taken by more than one young Englishman, and followed his brother George out to Canada, to Winnipeg.

George had gone off on the Canadian adventure against his parents' wishes, and he wrote enthusiastic letters home about the splendid opportunities of this new country. When Fred arrived his brother was indeed the part-owner, with a friend, of the Hotel Coronation, on Main Street north of the city hall, and the young immigrant was hired as night clerk. Then George went bankrupt and lost the hotel, and Fred was out of a job again. Not in the least discouraged, he found something else the next day, working with pick and shovel on a construction site.

Winnipeg was at that time in the throes of a building boom, and there was enough casual employment for a muscular young man who wished to pick up a few dollars. At one point Dixon hired on with the crew of labourers excavating the basement of the new T. Eaton Company store on Portage Avenue. By 1905 George and his friend were once again the proprietors of a hotel, the Metropolitan on Notre Dame Avenue, and when that venture changed hands a year later Fred stayed on as clerk. An old fighter had taught him a few boxing moves, and he toyed briefly with the idea of a career in the ring. Most of all, however, he enjoyed drawing, and a course in drafting and art, from the International Correspondence Schools of Minneapolis, improved his natural skills with pencil and paper. By 1908 he had a full-time position as engraver with the Bemis Bag Company.

Earning a living left Fred with plenty of time and energy to spare. He may have been looking for some manual on graphics when, not long after his arrival in Winnipeg, he climbed the stairs to the Mobius bookshop over the shoe store on Main Street, and encountered the intriguing proprietor and his row upon row of volumes on every conceivable subject. The lively young man caught the professor's attention, and Fred came away with an armload of challenging new reading matter. To begin with, Mobius fed Dixon some of Elbert Hubbard's popular philosophy, and he followed it with Thomas Paine's *The Rights of Man* and with increasingly more complex works on politics and economics, including the theories of Henry George. In short order Fred Dixon joined the reform-minded coterie around Professor Mobius, cementing his definitive friendships with Stubbs, Ivens, Farmer, and others. With Mobius as his mentor he took up the cause that remained at the heart of his lifelong philosophy, the single tax, and his political career was under way.

Henry George and the Single Tax

Henry George was an American whose 1879 book, *Progress and Poverty*, had sold over two million copies in the United States alone and had been translated into a dozen foreign languages. George had run for mayor of New York City, and had lectured in Toronto and Montreal, and a Canadian single tax movement was attracting widespread interest. Contrary to the accepted view of most economists that capital and labour were the twin foundations of modern industrial society, George maintained that land alone was the basis of all wealth, and that monopolistic control of land was at the root of all social evils. Consequently, he argued, there should be a tax on all land that was not in productive use but held for speculation and for personal or corporate gain, and the proceeds of such land should rightfully belong to the community and not to the speculator. By the same token, he maintained, productive industry and the personal income it generated should be relieved of the inhibiting burden of taxation.

Although he was wary of too much government, George advocated the public ownership of utilities. The revenue from the single tax on idle land, he insisted, should be returned to the people in sponsored public works, in schools, libraries, roads, hospitals; and human society would prosper thereby. Properly managed, the resources of the world could support all of its vast population. George's vision of the benefits of the single tax was almost endless: it would result in a more equitable distribution of wealth in the nation and among all nations, it would lead to free trade, and thus to peace the world over.

The Georgeite philosophy must have seemed particularly pertinent at the turn of the century in western Canada, with its vast open spaces inviting development but paradoxically difficult for would-be farmers to obtain. To provide settlement along the ribbon of the Canadian Pacific Railway, the federal government vigorously promoted immigration from Europe, bringing in a flood of people hungry for a decent livelihood and clamouring for land. But much of the available acreage

11

was in the hands of speculators, their greed for profit threatening to destroy the promise of a new world of plenty.

As the much-celebrated gateway to the West, Winnipeg itself was bursting at the seams with immigrants and unable to keep up with the demands for housing and other services. An unsavoury collection of substandard dwellings mushroomed north of the CPR tracks, and new arrivals without means found themselves crammed together in these dirty streets. In all the dislocations of a rapidly changing economy, the evils of the old world seemed to be repeated: poverty, slums, crime, alcoholism, prostitution.

To Fred Dixon, the simplicity of the single tax solution had a direct appeal. Having tended flower gardens back in England that served no other purpose than the pleasure of the rich, he believed passionately that the only proper use for the God-given earth was to feed the world's people and to enrich the lives of all humanity. Give ownership of the land and its resources back to the people, Henry George taught; remove all taxes on the necessities of life for the ordinary man, and on the means by which he earned a living; only by such measures, as the foundation to all other reforms, could the human potential be realized. The strong ethical basis of these arguments and their stress on the worth of the common man sounded a responsive chord in Dixon's own upright self-reliance, and he entered into the movement with characteristic energy. By 1906, a Single Tax League had been established in Winnipeg, with Mobius as its leader and Dixon as secretary-treasurer.

Liberals, Reformers, Labourites, Socialists

The Single Tax League constituted one of a kaleidoscope of political groups competing for popular support in the turbulent Winnipeg of the early twentieth century, and within each faction different ideologies intersected and clashed. Market Square, behind the city hall, served as the open-air theatre for the advocates of every species of political change, and this impromptu citizens' forum became a regular feature of civic life. Crowds of the disaffected or the merely curious gathered to jeer or to cheer, as earnest speakers offered their various and impassioned solutions to the problems of society. There on a Sunday the exotic Professor Mobius could be seen, brilliantly extolling the truths of the single tax from his perch on a folding chair; and, warming to his mission, Dixon also began to match his wits as a Sunday orator against the hecklers in Market Square and on street corners.

At first under Mobius's tutelage and then on his own, Dixon grew into a voracious reader, absorbing an eclectic range of knowledge, from the classics of English literature to current liberal and socialist theories and events in countries around the globe. The young Englishman proved a quick-witted debater and crowd-pleaser, with his imposing height and good looks, and he learned very quickly how to handle an audience, even working consciously to develop his naturally fine speaking voice. His political experience expanded rapidly. Together with S. J. Farmer, now a close friend, he entered into the heated debates of the various political factions, finding some common ground in particular with the reform-minded Manitoba Labor Party.

The Labor Party was assembled in 1906, under the chairmanship of Arthur W. Puttee. Advocating social change by parliamentary means, in the tradition of the British labour movement, it provided a meeting ground for a variety of reformers and socialists, including for a time some of the city's radical Marxists. The party stressed adult education, and in 1909 it organized a series of evening classes in history, economics, and politics, with the increasingly popular Fred Dixon as instructor. Dixon recruited Professor Mobius, and their lectures earnestly expounded the principles of the single tax as the necessary remedy for a society painfully out of order.

Years later, Winnipeg's durable Communist alderman, the remarkable Jacob Penner, recalled his encounter with Dixon in 1906, when Penner, a committed Marxist, belonged to the Winnipeg local of the Socialist Party of Canada (SPC). Having attended one of Mobius's lectures in Market Square, Penner went down to a single tax meeting, heard Dixon and Farmer speak, and invited them in return to visit the Socialists. They did come, said Penner, but "they always harped on the Single Tax theory of Henry George." Penner convinced Dixon that he ought to read Marx. He read *Das Kapital*, Penner remembered years later, "and said he did not agree with a single line."

Rejecting Marxism, Fred Dixon consistently rejected some of the proposals of the more moderate socialists as well, taking issue with some of the very people with whom he was to be allied in the watershed events of 1919. The moderate socialists and the single taxers shared a great deal of common ground, with their similar insistence on the equitable distribution of wealth and on justice for all, and both endorsed public ownership of public utilities, such as the supply of water and energy and of postal and telephone services. Beyond these basics, however, principles diverged sharply. Dixon and his colleagues in the Single Tax League, sturdy believers in individual enterprise, held fast to Henry George's contention that private income should not be taxed, disagreeing endlessly with the proposals of their labourite friends for increased taxation on wealth. More fundamentally still, they disagreed with both radical and moderate socialists on the nature of the society that was to be their goal.

While Henry George had advocated public ownership of utilities, the radicals went further, insisting that not only services but all means of production as well must come under public control. Mere reform of the existing economic system was not the answer for the aggressive leftist faction within the Labor Party's unstable grouping. The Marxists were adamant in their conviction that the profit-based capitalist economy must be eradicated root and branch and a new social order installed under the control of working people. When the British Independent Labour Party voted in 1908 to include in its platform the collective ownership of the means of production, moderate socialists joined the Marxists in demanding the inclusion of this principle in the platform of the Manitoba Labor Party. The single taxers, wholly committed to the principle of individual enterprise, resigned from the Labor Party to pursue a course of their own, and Puttee's fragile coalition began to disintegrate.

The controversy did not remain within the labourites' meeting rooms, as the advocates of the various splinter parties vied for converts, taking their message to Market Square and to street-corner soapboxes. As might be expected, all these noisy agitators and their boisterous following made the civic authorities uneasy, and the police were frequently called in to impose order. In May 1909 Dixon and Mobius were arrested for their part in an open-air controversy. Charged with disturbing public order, they were convicted and fined, to their profound anger and humiliation. This was a violation of the democratic British right of free expression, Dixon protested, in a fury of patriotism and pride, and largely as a direct result of this brush with police suppression the Free Speech Defence League was initiated. The league added one more note to the political clamour and raised enough money to pay the fines of the people charged with the offence; by the following summer the attempts to quell the street oratory seems to have subsided.

Dixon's popularity as a lecturer had spread to the rural areas around Winnipeg, and the proposals for land reform in the single tax movement attracted working farmers to its ranks. In the spring of 1909 rural and urban supporters joined forces to create the Manitoba Single Tax Association, once again with Fred Dixon as secretary-treasurer. At the same time, associating with like-minded men and women concerned with reforming the social order, Dixon grew increasingly aware of the problems of women's suffrage, of the importance of education, and of the temperance struggle.

The problems that beset the growing city of Winnipeg engaged his attention as well, particularly those of the over-crowded North End, where tuberculosis was endemic and outbreaks of typhoid fever and smallpox pushed the death rate to unprecedented levels. In 1907 a group of men and women had organized the Manitoba Health League, with Dixon as vice-president, to demand that steps be taken to provide proper sanitation and clean water and to educate the public, particularly the immigrant population, in such matters as proper hygiene and sound social habits. Earnest believers in self-improvement, the league also went on record as opposed to the notion of public vaccination as a dangerous and unwarranted infringement on personal liberty.

Personal freedom was at the heart of Dixon's credo. To succeed, he contended, a truly democratic government had to ensure the greatest possible measure of social security and economic well-being for the entire community, while guaranteeing freedom of choice for each individual member. True to character, he distrusted bureaucracy of any sort, fearing that in an absolute socialist system the rights of the individual would be subordinated to the supremacy of the state. As for government, he insisted, it acted only by the consent of the people and its powers must be carefully defined.

The direct legislation movement, then gathering force in Europe and the United States, addressed this problem of limiting government control, and a broad range of Manitoba's liberals and reformers were attracted to its ranks. In all his voluminous reading, Dixon had studied direct legislation as it was practiced in Switzerland, and he had been impressed by its results: pure food laws, workmen's insurance laws, government ownership of the railways and the postal service, and other socially desirable innovations. In 1908 he helped found the Manitoba Federation for Direct Legislation, becoming the secretary-treasurer of both that organization and the Single Tax League; and the following year the two groups came together as the Manitoba League for the Taxation of Land Values.

Ordinary people, Dixon argued in his manifesto on direct legislation, "are quite capable of managing their own affairs"; and to give the electorate greater control he outlined a three-part scheme: the "Initiative," the "Referendum," and the "Recall." Elected representatives would continue to conduct most of the business of government, but under the initiative a percentage of the voters — usually eight percent, Dixon said — could propose a law by means of a petition. If the legislature did not pass the law, it then would be submitted within two years to the direct vote of the people. Again by a petition from the electorate, any law passed by the legislature might be challenged, and that law would then be submitted to a referendum for approval or rejection. "The principal advantage of the referendum," Dixon argued, "is that it gives the people the power to prevent the bartering away of public lands and public franchises to private corporations, thus destroying the power of the lobby and tending to purify politics." Finally, as a check on the integrity of politicians, Dixon proposed the recall: twenty-five percent of the electors in any constituency could register their dissatisfaction with their representative by demanding that he stand for reelection. The recall, Dixon added, was "a measure by which the electors may discharge a dishonest or incompetent public servant. . . . No farmer would think of engaging a hired man, no business man would think of engaging a clerk, on any other principle."

Perhaps the most accurate assessment of Dixon's position was made much later by Fred Tipping, a founding member in 1920 of the Independent Labor Party. In a 1967 interview Tipping still persisted in considering Dixon an outsider, still with a trace of the old antagonism:

> I think at that time, what could be said of Fred Dixon was that he was more of a liberal with a small "l" than he could be called a Labor man or a Socialist. . . .He was not in the Labor movement prior to 1920. You have to understand that Dixon's great enthusiasm was for the single tax movement, and he was a reformer rather than a Labor man or a Socialist, but he became very popular throughout Manitoba and the West. . . .

A small-l liberal, a reformer: throughout his political life, Fred Dixon cherished a vision of a society in which the human potential could be fulfilled. All human beings, he held, possessed certain natural rights: the liberty of conscience, the right of free expression, the freedom to pursue happiness, "in so far as it does not interfere with the equal rights of everyone else." In a democratic society, as he understood it, opportunity would be equal, justice would be even-handed, and there would be special privilege for no one. He was a firm believer in the inalienable right of all to an education, and to the unhampered access to the ballot box.

Essentially populist and humanitarian, Dixon's instinct was for the immediate and direct solution rather than for the distant promise of absolute social reorganization. While many of his later pronouncements took on a socialist colouration, stressing the paramount importance of a cooperative rather than a competitive economy, cooperation in essence appears to have meant for him simply the mutually supportive working together of all parts of the body politic, much as Henry George had envisioned. "Communalism," the harmonious life of the entire community, required that workers have "a greater voice in the management of industry," as the *Manitoba Free Press* reported from one of Dixon's addresses, "a greater share of the wealth they produced." No revolutionary, his principles were framed within the established British traditions of personal responsibility.

Electoral Politics, 1910–1916

By 1910 politics and political organizing had grown into a full-time career for Dixon, although he continued to give his official occupation as "engraver." He had established his own office in the Chamber of Commerce, on Princess Street across from the city hall. His letterhead proclaimed that the single tax was "the greatest measure for human liberty ever proposed." Active in the city's interwoven reform groups and much sought after as a speaker, he launched into his first election campaign for a seat in the provincial house, with Farmer as his campaign manager.

At the top of his platform were direct legislation and "The Abolition of Government by Injunction." He listed "The Land Question" and "The Temperance Question" as vital concerns, and he demanded compulsory education and the public ownership of public utilities. Recognizing Dixon's broad popularity, the faltering Manitoba Labor Party agreed to downplay its insistence that the means of production be socialized, and a loose grouping of moderates threw its support behind Dixon as the labour candidate for Winnipeg Centre.

Dixon lost the election to his Conservative opponent, T. W. Taylor, by a mere seventy-three votes, and a recount failed to change the result. The spoiler in the contest, it seemed obvious, was the Marxist W. S. Cummings, the candidate of the Socialist Party of Canada: Cummings trailed far behind, but his ninety-nine votes might well have won the victory for Dixon. In the eyes of Dixon's incensed supporters, the intransigence of the Marxists had acted against the common good.

Partly because of election abuses the Direct Legislation League now reappeared in its own identity, with a membership ranging from some of the city's liberal business men to reformers like Dixon, and even some mild socialists. In January 1911 the league hired Dixon as full-time organizer, at a salary of fifteen hundred dollars per year, to disseminate its literature and promote its principles.

In the next few years Dixon enlarged his political base considerably. His writing now appeared frequently in the press. He contributed a popular column to Arthur W. Puttee's labour weekly, *The Voice*, and he acquired something of a national reputation for his incisive exposition of the single tax philosophy. A number of his letters and articles had already been published in the *Grain Growers' Guide*, and he enjoyed a congenial friendship with its editor, George Chipman. He bought some farm land in Rosser, near Winnipeg; he joined the Manitoba Grain Growers' Association, attending its 1912 convention as delegate and speaker. Through John W. Ward, a friend from the Mobius circle, he had contact with the cooperatives and other farm groups, and he became an indefatigable speaker at farm meetings across Manitoba.

Dixon's name also began to appear with increasing frequency in the minutes of the Political Equality League, moving or seconding various motions and amendments. The leading proponent in Winnipeg of women's suffrage, the league included in its membership Dr. Mary Crawford, Lillian Beynon Thomas, and Nellie McClung, all of them professional women at a time when such self-sufficiency was still uncommon; and the corresponding secretary of the league was another independent young woman, Winona M. Flett, a public stenographer. In April 1914, the minutes noted, Fred Dixon was elected the secretary-treasurer, and Winona Flett the superintendent of literature.

By 1914 there was widespread agreement with the principles advocated by the Direct Legislation League. A letterhead of the association listed an impressive roll of officers. With Dixon as "Organizer," it included, among others: J. H. Ashdown, a former mayor of Winnipeg and the founder of J. H. Ashdown Hardware Company; John Kennedy, vice-president of the Grain Growers' Grain Company and director of the Home Bank; representatives of the Manitoba Grain Growers' Association, the Royal Templars of Temperance, the Manitoba League for the Taxation of Land Values, and the Political Equality League; R. L. Richardson, former MP and editor of the *Winnipeg Tribune*; Arthur Puttee, the editor of *The Voice*, and also a former MP; George Chipman, the editor of the *Grain Growers' Guide*; C. D. McPherson, MLA. and editor of the Portage la Prairie *Graphic*, and many professionals, farmers, and merchants, notably R. M. Mobius and Lewis St. George Stubbs.

The broad range of this membership, across political boundaries, soon proved unacceptable to the Winnipeg Trades and Labor Council. Charging that the Direct Legislation League was only an offshoot of the Liberal Party, and a means for Liberals to attain office, the council withdrew its affiliation in February 1913, although it continued to endorse the league's program for legislative reform. Dixon himself retained the friendships he had formed with some of the Trades and Labor Council socialists, but he had become more convinced than ever that an honest representative of the people must remain free of party domination.

Now well known all over Manitoba, Dixon ran again in the provincial elections of July 1914, this time as an independent, for Seat B in Winnipeg Centre. His platform was much the same as in 1910, with the addition of the vigorous promotion of women's suffrage. "True democracy cannot exist," he declared during the campaign, "while one half of the population is deprived of the franchise." A number of prominent suffragists, including Nellie McClung and Lillian Beynon Thomas, campaigned on his behalf, and both Winona Flett and her sister, Lynn, provided tireless assistance. Dixon had the backing of labour circles, farm groups, and the Direct Legislation League; and, among other well-wishers, Reverend Salem G. Bland sent a cheque and a most fulsome letter of praise for Dixon's "manly and straightforward character" and his "firm grasp of great economic truths."

In a move characteristic of his open, consensual political philosophy, Dixon offered to back the Liberal leader, Tobias Norris, on major progressive issues; and the Liberals, in return, did not enter a candidate in his riding. For the Marxists of the Socialist Party of Canada, and in particular for Bob Russell, now gaining prominence in the railway machinists' union, such a deal was a sacrilege and a betrayal, and they mounted a vigorous campaign to defeat Dixon. Ironically, their candidate was George Armstrong, who, like Russell, was to join Dixon in the prisoners' dock in the fall-out from the 1919 strike.

The election brought Sir Rodmond Roblin's Conservatives back into power, but it also saw the election of the first socialist member of the legislature, Richard Rigg, the candidate of the Social Democratic Party. In Dixon's riding the voters' decision was emphatic. Dixon was elected with 8105 votes, a majority of more than 1500 votes over his Conservative opponent, and Armstrong was as decisively defeated.

Dixon's friend Stubbs was jubilant. From Birtle, Manitoba, where he practiced law, he telegraphed his congratulations, and a few days later sent an exuberant letter, cheering the new member on to battle against Roblin:

> "You done well," and then some. . . . Punch the stuffing out of his rotten old carcass every opportunity you get. Make him realize that the people will no longer tolerate men like him in public life. The people want honesty and decency in public life, and will get it, when they are given a chance.

Congratulations of a different sort arrived a few weeks later, a letter from the Dixon family back in Reading. Fred had sent newspaper clippings of the campaign and of his victory, and his mother was moved to write, laboriously, her own uncertain composition:

> My Dear Son Fred Just a line to Say I am pleased to hear of your Succes in the Election mind what you are at my Dear Son with it from your Dear Old Father Thomas Fletcher Dixon. . . . Martha must Finsh [finnish] come and see Me when you can my Dear Boy . . . Amen . . . . Love

Sister Martha wrote, wistfully, "it Must have been a grate day in your life," and included some neighbourhood news; then she added, "I suppose the next thing we shall hear you have taken unto yourself a wife."

Martha must have had some inside information. On October 14, 1914, Fred Dixon and Winona Flett were married at Central Congregational Church by the Reverend D. S. Hamilton. Dixon's friends and supporters had honoured him at a banquet in the Fort Garry Hotel, and had presented him with a sizable gift of money — "a bank bill large enough to be a rarity among the banks these days," said Arthur Puttee in *The Voice* — and at the church door, "the newly wedded couple were simply blockaded by the crowds anxious to offer congratulations." On behalf of his paper and of labour in general Puttee offered his good wishes, and he reported that Mr. and Mrs. Dixon had left for a two-week honeymoon in Banff, Alberta.

In the Legislature

A four-day session of the Manitoba legislature in September had introduced Dixon to his new career, providing a foretaste of the battles to come. In that session there were only two money matters on the agenda. Proposed changes to the new legislative building then under construction had increased the estimated cost by more than sixty percent, to $4.5 million dollars; the bill authorizing the expenditure passed without much debate — ominously, in view of the furor to come. Secondly, the government proposed to offer a six-month moratorium on mortgage payments as a measure to deal with the prevailing economic depression, and on this issue Dixon sprang immediately to the attack. The measure would do nothing to help the poor, who really needed help, he charged; and in keeping with his single tax convictions, he introduced an amendment limiting the mortgage relief to people who lived on, or cultivated, their own land. The amendment was defeated, and the legislature adjourned until spring.

Dixon's high visibility continued throughout the fall and winter. Concerned with improving the lives of working people and with disseminating political dogma, the various labour and reform groups had made adult education a central activity. By 1914 these sessions had become something of a civic institution, and the Peoples' Forum was incorporated under provincial law, with James Woodsworth as its first president and Dixon assisting with program and planning. Membership was set at a dollar per year, but there was free admission to all events, and every Sunday afternoon, all winter long, working men and women came to listen and learn. There were lectures on political theory and on current events, on history, literature, art, and music. Fred Dixon explained the far-reaching damage land speculators inflicted on society, and Winona Dixon offered an overview of "Women in Industrial and Professional Life." Several branch organizations sprang up in the suburbs, and when Ottawa instituted its own Citizens' Forum, in October 1915, a thousand people filled the meeting hall to hear the inaugural address by Winnipeg's noted Frederick J. Dixon.

When the legislature reconvened in the spring, Dixon wasted no time in following again Stubbs's gleeful instructions to go after the

Roblin party. The Conservatives had held office continuously for fifteen years, and their complacency and corruption were an open scandal. Most flagrant of all and most talked about were the excesses
involved in the construction of the imposing new legislative building
on Broadway Avenue, the wide, well-treed boulevard parallel to the
Assiniboine River. Among other things, gossip pointed out, the elegant
building materials of the public edifice suspiciously reappeared in a private family mansion going up nearby.

Fired as always by an injury to the ordinary citizen, Dixon succeeded
in proving that the contractor for the legislature, Thomas Kelly and
Sons, had cheated the workmen out of ten percent of their wages,
underpaying them while collecting the full contractual amount; and,
moreover, that the government was implicated in the scheme. Some
sixteen thousand dollars in back wages were repaid to the crew, but
aided by Dixon's tireless goading the opposition pushed their accusations further. That building, they charged, had cost the public more
than eight hundred thousand dollars in fraud, and the government had
been a party to these arrangements as well.

The seemingly entrenched Tory administration did not survive the
attack. Under pressure from the opposition, the lieutenant-governor of
the province, Sir Douglas C. Cameron, ordered the appointment of a
royal commission to investigate the matter. Within two weeks, on May
7, the commission issued a report confirming the allegations, and five
days later Premier Rodmond Roblin tendered his resignation.

In the August election that followed, Dixon ran again on much the
same platform as before, and once again the Socialist Party of Canada
nominated George Armstrong to run against him. This time, under
Tobias Norris, the Liberals swept into office, carrying forty-two seats
out of the total of forty-nine, with a platform that incorporated many
of the measures that Dixon was advocating. Dixon himself won by a
large majority, taking all but two of the polls in his constituency, and
the Social Democratic Party's Richard Rigg was reelected as well.
Armstrong was defeated.

Unlike a number of his more doctrinaire compatriots, Dixon had no
objection to working with politicians on the opposite side of the political fence, and in the next year or two he helped enact some decidedly

progressive legislation, including the passage of the province's first Minimum Wage Act, covering, in this first instance, only some public works employees. So close was Dixon's cooperation with the Liberals that the original Workmen's Compensation Bill was introduced by Fred Dixon and seconded for the Liberals by J. W. Breakey.

Even more remarkable was the record of the Norris administration in the area of women's suffrage. A year after his election Norris made good on his campaign promises: in 1916 Manitoba became the first province in Canada to extend the franchise to women; and representatives of the Political Equality League were invited to be present at the session when the legislation was passed. Advances were also made for children and for education. The minimum age for employment was set at fourteen, and children were allowed to work no more than fourteen hours a week. Self-educated himself, having blithely left school too soon, Dixon argued in committee that education was the only way out of poverty for the children of the poor, and he insisted that for its own benefit society must keep children in school until at least the age of fifteen. Slightly less generous, the new School Attendance Act made education compulsory between the ages of five and fourteen.

In his central concern, direct legislation, Dixon achieved less satisfaction. He had resigned as organizer for the Direct Legislation League when he was first elected, in 1914, pleading the pressure of his new responsibilities, but had continued to urge the adoption of the league's proposals, with considerable support. A bill authorizing the referendum was duly passed in the legislature, and a referendum took place at once on the question of prohibition. But the act was challenged in court, and ruled out of order: under British constitutional law, final political authority resided in the Crown, or in its direct representative, the lieutenant-governor, and that authority was violated by the referendum, which in effect shifted ratification of laws to the voters. Thus the court's decision swept the legal ground out from under one of the major tenets of direct legislation, and although Dixon continued to press for its adoption, the movement petered out.

Experienced in the thrust-and-parry of street oratory, Dixon was a formidable opponent on the floor of the legislature, and reporters made much of his sallies. In a debate on compulsory education during

Dixon's first session, the arrogant Premier Roblin had ridiculed the new member for his use of the impolite adjective, "damnable," asking, "Will the honourable member please spell the word?" Dixon's retort had delighted the gallery: "If we had compulsory education, the First Minister could do his own spelling!" Now, as his legislative career matured, he won respect for his thorough study of the subject matter under debate — "the best-informed man in the legislature," Premier Tobias Norris called him; and, as another adversary put it, with admiration and with envy, "Fred Dixon . . . is never dry, even when talking on a dry subject."

The deeply moral foundation of his outlook on life and its roots in the uncomplicated religious faith of his childhood were frequently reflected in his biblical allusions and in the rhythms of his rhetorical style. "Woe unto those who step off the beaten path," he mocked, in a sermon some years later at William Ivens's Labor Church, extolling those exceptional souls who dare to be different and defy authority: "We don't like the men who are trying to lead us out of bondage any more than the Israelites did." He dipped into the storehouse of his broad reading with obvious pleasure, sharing his sense of the unity of all human history; in the Labor Church lecture, he linked "Jesus the Carpenter's son" with all defenders of the truth:

> What should we know of science today but for the defiance of bodily torture by Copernicus, Galileo and Bruno and the social sacrifice of their successors — Darwin, Huxley and others? . . . What political progress would we have made but for men ready to risk all for an ideal — Milton and Cromwell; Mazzini and Garibaldi; Rousseau and Paine; Mackenzie and Papineau? . . . Idealism is the source of all religions, and all religions have good in them. Mahomet, Buddha, and Christ all lit their torches at the divine fire.

Scientists and poets and statesmen: for Dixon, all were brothers, and god-like in the unending struggle for the liberation of humankind. Increasingly his instinct for humane justice began to take shape in the perceptions and the language of the socialists who had become his colleagues and his friends. Invited to deliver the sermon at Central Congregational Church on Labour Day 1915, he shared with his audience his own compassionate distress at the plight of most of the world's people:

> There is something wrong with the world when those who do the work of the world, those who feed, clothe and house the world, are condemned to eat the cheapest kind of food, wear the cheapest clothing and live in the cheapest houses, while many who never did a day's work in their lives roll in luxury.

The Cost of Pacifism

In the anger and stress of the last years of World War I, Dixon's stance deviated sharply from the mainstream. In his all-embracing humanism, he denounced war as immoral, except perhaps in defence of the freedom of the individual, and he insisted on declaring his position openly, defying the fevered patriotism of the general public. Henry George had taught that war was caused by the greed of landowners and monopolists; and Dixon, Farmer, and their friends held fast to their principles. War was barbaric, they argued; it maimed the bodies and destroyed the lives of the common people, and it burdened society with crippling long-term debt; only the wealthy industrialists profited, and with the governments they controlled they used the war hysteria to destroy all movements of social reform. As early as 1912 Dixon had urged the prime minister, Robert Borden, to pursue international cooperation and world trade but to keep Canada out of all foreign military entanglements, and the unfolding horrors of the European conflict reinforced his conviction.

Before 1914 a widespread conviction prevailed among the reform groups in the Canadian West that the developing conflict in Europe was an alien imposition. Once war was actually declared and recruitment for the armed forces began, many voices on the left, including Dixon's, earnestly opposed all moves toward conscription, branding it the ultimate deprivation of human liberty. "No conscription of manpower without conscription of wealth," was their cry, and the press gave their inflammatory protestations full play. As the war dragged on, and the newspapers carried grim reports of desperate losses overseas and of sacrifice on the home front, the objectors were hotly damned as unpatriotic by increasingly bellicose sections of the general public. Returning soldiers bitterly resented the pacifist stance as a slur on the struggle that had cost them so dearly, and their anger often flared into violence.

Many years later, looking back at the tension, Bob Russell recalled Dixon and his involvement in one such incident:

> Fred was fighting a lot of lost causes. . . . A magnetic person . . . an outstanding personality was Dixon, and fearless. He was pacifist all the way through. . . .
>
> He got hit in one of the riots, in that conscription fight we had here. We had a meeting in the old Grand Theatre out in the North End . . . about a block past the subway. We'd had a tremendous meeting there, and the bloody soldiers came in — in uniform, too — and they chased us all. The crowd dispersed. They chased us and we got down into the dressing rooms under the stage and along the damned alleyways and somebody hit Dixon across the head — one of the soldiers. I don't know whether it was a stick or a bottle or what he had. . . . But Dixon was a fearless devil. Wouldn't back up to nobody, physically or any other way.

The climax came in 1917, when the federal government, as a preliminary to conscription for military service, introduced a system of national registration. Dixon declared that he would not sign his registration card — not even, he said, "if I am put in jail, kept on bread and water, and compelled to read nothing but the *Winnipeg Telegram* and the *Manitoba Free Press*." In the legislature both Dixon and his fellow labourite, Dick Rigg, voted against a patriotic resolution introduced by the Liberals in support of conscription, whereupon Premier Norris charged that any man who refused to register should be jailed. When Dixon tried to speak in defence of his views, his fellow legislators shouted "Traitor!" at him, and "Throw him in jail!" Reporting the

speech, the *Free Press* was as hostile as any of the other newspapers, but
it had the grace to record Dixon's insistence on the democratic right to
express his sincere beliefs:

> Mr. Dixon said . . . any tyrant would allow the expression of
> opinion with which he agreed. But freedom demanded the right
> of expression for minorities. The way to meet a weak argument
> was to refute it, not to imprison the upholders of it.

And still he persisted, invoking the illustrious names of his heroes: "I
have sat at the feet of the world's greatest thinkers, Tolstoy, Ruskin,
Carlyle, Sir Thomas More and Jesus Christ, and I cannot forget their
teachings immediately the war drum is sounded." One particularly fiery
address so moved a *Free Press* writer, Vernon Thomas, that he impulsively left the press gallery to shake Dixon's hand, in a public statement
of his own views. The *Free Press* promptly fired him. Disheartened,
Thomas and his wife, Lillian Beynon, left Winnipeg for New York.

The so-called nobility of this war was a myth, Dixon declared, at an
anti-conscription meeting in January 1917 at the Strand Theatre, and
he was not prepared to die for a myth. Outraged at this apparent dismissal of their terrible sacrifice, the Great War Veterans' Association
began a furious campaign to have Dixon removed from office. The
provisions of his direct legislation system were now under judicial
scrutiny, but the veterans challenged Dixon to act according to his own
proposal for the recall and resign from office. Backed by the *Winnipeg
Telegram*, they canvassed his constituency for several months, trying to
obtain enough signatures for the procedure; and although the petition
fell far short of the required number, a *Telegram* editorial nevertheless
sneered that the member for Winnipeg Centre had no alternative but
to resign and submit to a vote:

> Mr. Dixon believes in the recall, or says he does. His theory sure-
> ly cannot be intended to apply exclusively to the other fellow.
> Does he intend to live up to his principles or will he find some
> excuse? He is in a bad fix. If he resigns and runs again, he will be
> beaten. If he doesn't resign, his pose as a reformer and friend of
> the people will become absurd.

In a courteous letter to the paper, Dixon pointed out that the necessary petition had not been presented, but the *Telegram* reported instead that Dixon had declared he would ignore the petition. Dixon wrote again, patiently correcting the misrepresentation. The smear campaign failed, and a move to impeach Dixon was also unsuccessful.

Fred Dixon had been a popular favourite only a short time before, but when in March 1917 he tried to address a public meeting in Market Square, he was manhandled on the platform by a group of veterans and ignominiously forced to run away — and the *Free Press* report was loud in its derision. In the legislature, baiting Dixon became routine; when he rose to speak, both Conservatives and Liberals might begin loud conversations with each other or pointedly turn their backs. At the Grand Theatre riot that Bob Russell remembered, a policeman had to beat off the incensed veterans and haul Dixon into a taxi. Yet Fred Dixon would not compromise his beliefs. "If I have to shed my blood," he declared, "I prefer to shed it here, where I know it will be for freedom."

In the midst of all this vituperation, Dixon's family life held firm, and a resolute body of supporters still remained. On their marriage Winona had given up her job, and a daughter, Doris Muriel, was born in June 1917. The Dixon home attracted a stream of friends and acquaintances. One such visitor left an account of an evening with the family and their friends.

Gertrude Richardson had come from Leicester, England, to live in Roaring River, near Swan River, Manitoba, continuing there to devote herself to women's suffrage and other liberal causes. In a letter to the *Leicester Pioneer* she described a train ride to Winnipeg and her moving encounter with a number of "Ruthenians," as Ukrainian immigrants were called, and other foreigners, who were now despised and harassed as "enemy aliens." By sharp contrast, she captured in a few lines the resolute integrity of the Dixons and their friends, "people whose ideals are those I call the Ideal of the New Humanity":

Mr. Dixon is an Independent — an absolutely fearless opponent of every form of slavery — the modern manifestation of which is conscription. . . . He is, I am very proud to say, an Englishman.

His home life is intensely beautiful. Simplicity marks every detail. His wife is a lovely woman, in form, mind and spirit. She shares his loftiest ideals. When there was talk of imprisonment for all who resisted registration in the beginning of this year Mrs. Dixon made all her arrangements to return to the business world, and earn her living, leaving her baby daughter with her mother.

For deeply distressed idealists like Richardson in this time of barbarous inhumanity, it was as though in some small part of a shattered world certain values remained unshakeable: dignity, decency, and grace.

The Climax of Unrest

The social and economic dislocations of wartime had brought to the surface a deep discontent in Canada's work force, and even before the armistice the difficulties of readjustment to civilian living were already in evidence. Unemployment was high, and thousands of battle-weary soldiers came home to a country badly prepared to absorb them once again. There was talk of granting veterans land as compensation, but the areas being considered were poor, sparsely populated, and undesirable. True to his principles Dixon protested, at an address in the Labor Church in July 1918:

> Justice means . . . that the sacrifice of life which is now being made by the manhood of the nation must in some measure be matched by the sacrifice of wealth. . . . Justice demands that money and mud shall not be more highly regarded than human life. . . . My blood boils when I think that returned soldiers, who have defended all the land in Canada, are offered as their share of it the leavings of the land grabbers. There should be no talk of settling returned soldiers in the backwoods or on the far horizon while millions of acres of fertile land near railways and centres of population are producing nothing but weeds and unearned increment.

Making this plea, Fred Dixon knew at first hand the sacrifice of soldiers: as he was to remind the court at his trial, his own brother, George, would not return from Flanders' fields.

Unrest simmered across the country. In May 1918 a walk-out of Winnipeg's civic workers very nearly escalated into a citywide sympathy strike; in August a one-day general strike brought Vancouver to a standstill; and by the time the armistice was declared in November frequent sporadic strikes were taking place in Winnipeg's shops and factories, and in other Canadian cities. The federal government, under Borden, issued an order-in-council banning all work-stoppages, and on October 4 the police staged raids in Winnipeg's North End, looking for banned literature. The Trades and Labor Council heatedly debated the challenge and voted ninety-two percent in favour of striking against the no-strike order. As Dixon himself would maintain at his trial, the coming explosion was predictable, but authorities on every level only responded with denunciation and repression.

Among Winnipeg's fragmented labour and reform groups, the beginning of some sense of common cause seems to have developed, and March 1918 had seen the formation of the Manitoba branch of the Dominion Labor Party, with Dixon and William Ivens included as members and Farmer as vice-chairman. Dixon was neither a socialist nor a trades unionist, but he was invited to deliver the new party's inaugural address. Named vice-chairman a few months later, he undertook a western tour on behalf of the party in May, and early in 1919 he was elected chairman. In the December 1918 civic elections three DLP candidates were elected from the city's North End wards, joining John Queen and Abe Heaps, of the Social Democratic Party, on the city council. Dixon's victory address urged labour to build on its success and undertake its proper role in the conduct of public affairs, and in the provincial house he pursued, step by legislative step, an increase in the wages of student nurses, the elimination of election deposits, more efficient monitoring of expenditures. To all intents and purposes most moderate and reasonable, the Dominion Labor Party and its leader won approval and a token financial contribution from John W. Dafoe, editor of the *Free Press*.

The federal government's resort to orders-in-council was taken under the War Measures Act, which was kept in effect even after the armistice was declared in November, and under its authority a number of labour organizations had been suppressed, their leaders jailed, and their publications banned. To protest these injustices a meeting was held on December 22 at Winnipeg's enormous Walker Theatre, its three levels filled with angry men and women. Social Democrat John Queen was chairman, and speakers from a wide spectrum of the labour movement addressed the crowd. Fred Dixon appeared on the platform, with his friend from the Mobius circle, William Ivens, and with Bob Russell, who represented a decidedly more extreme position than any of the others.

Seconding the motion for the prisoners' release, Dixon echoed the radical attack on the inordinate power of the wealthy:

> Men who are willing to suffer the tortures of the penitentiary rather than be false to their inner convictions cannot be bad citizens. . . . I think those responsible for the Ross rifle, defective shells, shoddy clothes, paper boots, and the whole black record of profiteering and graft gave ten thousand times more aid and comfort to the enemy than all the socialists and conscientious objectors put together. But the malefactors of great wealth are not in jail. . . . It is only the poor men who had religious or economic objections to war and those who violated one of the numerous Union Government Orders in Council who are in jail.

Dixon's condemnation of wartime wrongdoing and his plea for the right of individual conscience quickly gave way to a far more sweeping protest by other speakers, an escalating attack on the existing government and, it seemed, on the existing social and economic system. The rally, it emerged later, was organized behind the scenes by the radical Socialist Party of Canada. It would be used in the legal action still to come to incriminate its participants.

Dixon did not attend the subsequent meeting, on January 10 in the Majestic Theatre, called by the Socialist Party of Canada to argue the economics of capitalism, nor did he participate in the Calgary convention of union delegates that led to the formation of the militant OBU, the One Big Union, under Bob Russell. He had no direct role in the succession of strike calls that immobilized Winnipeg by May 15, 1919, or in the planning and coordination during the six weeks of the general strike. Still a member of the legislature, he continued to fight within the existing parliamentary structure for human liberties. Once the strike was underway, however, and the business establishment's Citizens' Committee of One Thousand had surfaced to confront the embattled strikers, he responded as always to the workers' cause, quick to defend their inherent right to pursue a better existence.

Dixon was thirty-eight, with a home and a growing family to support, now including a son, James, born in January of the previous year, and he had been working part-time selling life insurance for the Confederation Life Insurance Company. But he offered his services to the strike committee, tirelessly repeating the committee's message of restraint and resolution among large groups and small, to exhort, reassure, and inspire the strikers and their families with the same electrifying eloquence that had first made him a popular leader. The press had never forgiven him for his stand against conscription and continued its barrage of invective, but the tide of public opinion had turned. During the height of the hysteria over conscription, angry mobs had drowned out his arguments and threatened his life; now, in the spring and summer of 1919, he held his audience once again, and even veterans came to listen.

He spoke at the Industrial Bureau, he spoke at Victoria Park, to the Labor Church and to the Soldiers' Parliament. Ten thousand people came to the Labor Church, on a Sunday evening in the fourth week of the strike, to hear him compare the Citizens' Committee of One Thousand with the New Testament "scribes and Pharisees who devoured widows' houses and for a pretence made long prayers." At the legislature, a group of returned soldiers in the visitors' gallery, waiting for an interview with Premier Norris, cheered loudly whenever Dixon's name was mentioned in the debate.

With the city's three newspapers shut down, the printers' unions agreed to work as unpaid volunteers on the special strike edition of the Trades and Labor Council's *Western Labor News*, and the first issue of the *Strike Bulletin* appeared on May 17, under the editorship of William Ivens. Regular publication continued, keeping the strikers informed and united with accounts of day-to-day events and notices of meetings and protests and petitions; and Dixon lent a hand, reporting on the negotiating sessions between the warring sides, explaining developments to the *Strike Bulletin*'s readers. Then, on June 16, at the height of the turmoil, Ivens was arrested and jailed, together with five other strike leaders.

James Woodsworth had arrived in Winnipeg from British Columbia about a week earlier, at Ivens's invitation. Recognizing that it was vital to keep the *Strike Bulletin* going, he went immediately to talk to Dixon at his home, and almost casually the two men undertook a joint responsibility, Woodsworth as editor and Dixon as reporter. Their efforts kept the *Strike Bulletin* in circulation for another week; and, like Ivens, they urged "lawful and orderly methods" in the face of the increasing violence against the strikers by authorities at every level of government.

Their call for restraint was futile. On the following Saturday, June 21, many people under the sponsorship of the pro-strike Soldiers' Committee assembled at the city hall, preparing to stage an "illegal" parade in support of the strike. Police on horseback charged into the crowd, firing at the demonstrators as they fled down nearby streets and alleys. A streetcar operated by a "volunteer" motorman was overturned and set on fire, and on Monday the *Strike Bulletin* carried Dixon's dramatic account of the weekend's horrifying events:

On Saturday about 2:30 p.m., when the parade was scheduled to start, about 50 mounted men swinging baseball bats rode down Main Street. They quickened their pace as they passed the Union bank. The crowd opened and let them through and closed in behind them. They turned and charged through the crowd again, greeted by hisses, boos and some stones. . . .

There were two riderless horses with the squad when it emerged and galloped up Main Street. The men in khaki disappeared at this juncture but the redcoats reined their horses and re-formed opposite the old post office. Then, with revolvers drawn, they galloped down Main Street, turned, and charged right into the crowd on William Avenue, firing as they charged.

One man, standing on the sidewalk, thought the mounties

were firing blank cartridges until a spectator standing beside him dropped with a bullet through his breast. Another standing near-by was shot through the head. . . .

When the mounties rode back to the corner of Portage Avenue and Main Street, after the fray, at least two of them were twirling their reeking tubes high in the air in orthodox Deadeye Dick style. . . .

Dixon headed his report, "Bloody Saturday," and the phrase crystallized the anger of the strikers, finding a permanent place in labour vocabulary.

That same Monday night, as Woodsworth stood talking to Dixon on Main Street near the McLaren Hotel, he was arrested and taken to the Rupert Street jail. The *Strike Bulletin* was raided and banned. The next morning a new publication, the *Western Star*, appeared, with a detailed account of the raid on its predecessor and the imprisonment of the editor, and an impassioned editorial on the shame of "Bloody Saturday." Echoing a biblical prophet's turn of phrase, Dixon charged that the assault on peaceable men and women had been planned ahead, and that it was a copy of the tyranny that the war had supposedly defeated: "What shall the sacrifice profit Canada if she who has helped to destroy Kaiserism in Germany shall allow Kaiserism to be established at home? Whoever ordered the shooting last Saturday is a Kaiser of the deepest dye."

A warrant was issued for Dixon's arrest, and the *Western Star* was banned. The *Enlightener* appeared, still edited by Dixon, still defying the authorities, still rallying Winnipeggers to the cause of justice and freedom. For three days, in hiding from the police, Dixon kept up his clandestine publication.

But on Wednesday, June 25, the *Enlightener* announced the end of the strike, called off for the following day by the strike committee. On Friday evening, at about seven o'clock, Ivens was released on bail, and he returned to his post, to resume the editorship of the *Western Labor News*. Dixon dropped his cover. At midnight he walked into the Rupert Street police station, saying urbanely to the sergeant in charge, "I believe you have a warrant for my arrest." He was placed in a cell, held there for two hours, then transported to the provincial jail at Stony Mountain and held for another two days, and finally, together with Woodsworth, granted bail.

On the day of what Dixon called the strikers' unconditional surrender, he made one more comment in the *Enlightener*, accurately assessing the long-term importance of the strike and predicting the course that the labour movement would now take:

> While impressing the need for collective bargaining and better wages on the community mind, the workers have themselves been taking a university course in politics and economics. They realize now that economic conditions are a reflex of the law of the land, and that if they would secure justice they must get into politics.

On Trial

In the uneasy interval between the end of the strike in June and the beginning of the trials in November, there was a great deal of intense activity on both sides. As normal life was gradually restored and labour organizations regrouped their forces, the judicial authorities struggled to prepare an orderly case out of the tangled record of disputed evidence and irregular procedures. The strike leaders, who had first been jailed and then released on bail, were arrested once again for preliminary hearings beginning in July and then sent back to the penitentiary. At the end of September, an enormous public outcry both in Canada and in Great Britain brought about their release.

Dixon resumed his seat in the legislature and continued to campaign for truth and justice. He spoke at the Industrial Bureau, appealing to his audience to subscribe to a new kind of "Liberty Bond," not the wartime issues of the federal government but the fund for the defence of the accused strike leaders. In July, accompanied by Woodsworth, he had managed to carry out his lecture engagements in the West, and both men undertook a continuous round of appearances to raise money for the defence fund. In August he addressed an assembly at the Columbia Theatre, demanding that the strikers still imprisoned at

Stony Mountain, mostly foreign-born, must be released; public indignation eventually freed these prisoners as well.

The charge against Dixon was originally seditious conspiracy, loosely based, it would seem, on his association with persons deemed to be a threat to His Majesty's realm and on his presence at various "ominous" meetings. As the chief ringleader, Bob Russell was tried first and convicted; Dixon's hearing was set for early in the new year. In the final indictment the charge was altered to the lesser one of seditious libel, and three specific statements of Dixon's were cited: his report on "Bloody Saturday," his attack on "Kaiserism in Canada," and a third comment, "Alas! the poor Alien," intended for the *Strike Bulletin* but intercepted at the print shop. This last was an indignant protest against the summary deportation of some aliens who refused to "scab" (to replace striking workers). Several of the indicted strike leaders had retained the liberal-minded E. J. McMurray as counsel, and Dixon's friend Stubbs also offered to defend him, but with McMurray's approval and advice Dixon chose to appear on his own behalf.

During Christmas that year Dixon spent a few days in Birtle, taking a quick briefing in legal procedures from Stubbs. One evening he joined the Stubbs family in the popular pastime of fortune-telling with a Ouija board. Only half joking, Dixon asked the question that was uppermost on his mind, "Will I be acquitted in January?" The answer was, "Yes," and nobody around the table would admit to having tilted the board.

The case of *Rex v. Dixon* opened on January 29, 1920, before Mr. Justice Galt and a jury of twelve men, with Woodsworth's case still pending, while at the same time in another courtroom the remaining seven accused went on trial. The unprecedented Winnipeg General Strike had made headlines in both Canada and the United States, and now local reporters sat elbow to elbow with correspondents from all the major newspapers on the continent. Spectators vied for seats as the drama unfolded, labour partisans fiercely attentive to all the arguments, solid citizens bristling with outrage at the Crown's allegations. Winona Dixon was there with many of the leaders of the women's movement, whose cause the man on trial had long championed. Dixon proved more than equal to his complex legal task, scrutinizing evidence, deftly cross-examining witnesses, challenging improper procedures — a master performer who delighted his audience with his alert intelligence, his wit, and his eloquence.

It quickly became evident that while the indictment specified libel, the Crown was attempting to involve Dixon in the blanket accusation under which most of the other strike leaders had been charged: conspiracy to undermine the legitimate government of Canada. Despite the conviction of Bob Russell, the chief organizer of the allegedly revolutionary OBU, and considered therefore the most dangerous conspirator, it was by no means clear that the Crown had managed to prove its basic contention that a revolutionary conspiracy had actually been afoot. Nevertheless, Judge Galt was obviously prepared to grant the prosecution every leeway in order to make the charge stick. Over Dixon's very reasonable objection that he was being tried for libel and not for conspiracy, Galt persistently ruled as admissible evidence the Crown's testimony regarding the actions of other alleged conspirators, in a flagrant violation of judicial impartiality.

Argument by argument Dixon proceeded to dissociate himself from any possible collusion with the men who had organized and conducted the strike, and from labour extremists in general, his cool wit meticulously dissecting the illogicalities of the Crown's case: he was not a member of the strike committee or any of its subcommittees; he had not been present at this assembly or that, where the prosecution claimed that revolution had been fomented; he acknowledged that he had read one piece of Marxist literature, the *Communist Manifesto*, but that he had done so in order to debate with the socialists, not to agree with them; there was no evidence that he had distributed subversive material or participated in any plot; and furthermore, ". . . it would be impossible for me to conspire with Armstrong, who ran against me in two elections, or Russell, engaged in knocking hell out of the Labor Party. . . . So far as the Socialist Party of Canada is concerned, they have opposed me in the elections of 1910, 1914, and 1915, and I think it is probable they will oppose me next time." And for that matter, how could he possibly be held responsible for what *Mrs.* Armstrong said or did, as the Crown contended?

In part this defence was clearly the appropriate legal strategy, because the case for the prosecution was untidy, if not decidedly unsound. But the tenor of Dixon's argument, and particularly in his much-acclaimed address to the jury, provided a revealing self-portrait of a man deeply committed to some highly traditional ideals of responsible power, Christian truth, and British justice. He repeated his protest against the deportation without trial of strikers "of foreign birth" who had fought for Canada in the war: "If an alien is brave enough to fight in Flanders for British law and British justice he is entitled to all the privileges of British citizenship." Far from expressing any desire to alter the fundamental structure of society, Dixon assured the jury that "any harsh words I have to say against those who occupy places of power is not to vilify the government but to purify it," but that criticism must be allowed, "if we are to preserve the boasted honour of British institutions. . . . In a British country we have the right to debate and get together and thresh it out and let the truth prevail."

Having repudiated more radical politics than his own, Dixon proceeded to remind the court that union organization was sanctioned by the law of the land, that it was the right of all working people to bargain collectively for their needs. He was not a member of the OBU, he declared, but the OBU was a legal organization and must be heard. He insisted that Russell's metal workers had no choice but to resort to a strike, because all other efforts to remedy their grievances had failed, and that fellow workers in other trades had joined the sympathy strike in the true spirit of brotherhood. This was no revolution, he said, but the orderly pursuit of British freedoms. Having carefully demonstrated that he himself had no part in the conduct of the strike, Dixon repeatedly questioned and corrected the Crown's distorted and even falsified version of the labour action, characteristically in defence of truth and justice.

At times, as Dixon reviewed the speeches and the printed material brought in evidence against him, his rhetoric began to resemble that of the Marxists he disclaimed. "When is an alien not an alien?" he had asked, and answered, "When he is a rich man, a scab herder or a scab." In an address at the Labor Church during the summer of 1918 he had thundered, "Justice decrees that those who do the work of the world should enjoy the wealth they produce and that there should be an end to all the privileges by which the few exploit the many"; he read that speech into the court record, inviting the jury to say if it contained any sedition.

Dixon began his closing address to the jury on the afternoon of February 13, after two arduous weeks of litigation, and continued the following day. He had carefully rehearsed the speech with his mentor, E. J. McMurray, and its style and content mirrored his convictions. The man who presented himself to his peers for judgment was no radical innovator but a moral philosopher and a reformer in the spirit of some of the mighty authorities he cited: Socrates and Euripides, Milton and Galileo, Lincoln and Lord Erskine — and Major G. W. Andrews, the sitting MP for Winnipeg Centre. Above all, Christian teaching rather than political principle lay at the heart of his belief. "The blood of the martyrs is the seed of the church," he repeated, from his own account of Bloody Saturday, and he reminded a taut courtroom of the hymn, "Gates of hell shall never 'gainst the truth prevail." And again, characteristically inspired by the lessons of the past,

> Christians were burned to light the streets of Rome. . . . Many men then thought that might was right and that they could crush Christianity by that method. I say today that Christianity is more powerful than the Roman Empire. . . .

So too, he predicted, "Labor will go on in spite of opposition . . . no bullets or anything else can stop it"; and the grandeur of biblical prophecy informed his vision of the future:

> Those who denounce the sympathetic strike might as well denounce the wheat for ripening, the river for flowing into the sea, or the boy for growing into a man. It is written, "First the blade, then the ear, and then the full corn in the ear," which being translated means, first the craft union, then the federated unions, and then the sympathetic strike. . . .
>
> From a thousand hills a thousand rills gather into a mighty river which sweeps on to the ocean. An attempt to dam the Niagara, in the hope that it would never reach the sea, would be

no more foolish than the attempt to dam labor from its resistless onward sweep toward its natural outlet — co-operative industry.

In the end, after his celebration of the inevitable triumph of labour, Dixon pleaded for intellectual integrity rather than economic need, passionately extolling the liberty of the individual, the inalienable right of the free man to express his thoughts freely. He invited the members of the jury to see their own needs in the aspirations of the man they were to judge:

> I am not seeking martyrdom or running away from it. I have all the natural feelings of a man. I like liberty and I like the sunshine and good food, warm raiment, and a house to live in and inter-course with my friends and my family. . . .
>
> You are the last hope so far as the liberty of the subject is concerned. . . . I want you to look over your history and I want you to consider that — I do not want liberty of speech to be wounded through my body! Whether my body is wounded mat-ters not, but it does matter that liberty of opinion be preserved for yourselves and your children and all the inhabitants of this country. . . .
>
> I want you to think it over in that light, and take it into con-sideration in that light, and having in view your oath, and using your best judgment in giving the decision, give your decision as you would if you knew you were going to be before the throne of your maker tomorrow morning.

Dixon's words, said the *Free Press*, "died slowly away into the tense silence of the court." Visibly irritated, Judge Galt countered with an intimidating barrage of legal precedents, to substantiate his insistence that the strike was illegal from beginning to end, that a revolutionary uprising had been its purpose, and that Dixon by his inflammatory statements had contributed to the intended devastation of his country. Instructing the jury to acquit the accused only if they had any "real" doubt as to his complicity, "a really substantial doubt, not an imaginary one," Galt demanded in effect a verdict of guilty:

The evidence is uncontradicted; there is nothing against it; and it clearly shows, to my mind, the creation of the most infamous conspiracy I have ever heard of in Canada. . . .

It is a lamentable state of affairs that we have a case of a member of our local legislature on trial, but our law calls for no distinction of that kind; we have got to obey the laws of this country, and if we do not we have got to suffer for them, no matter who we are. . . .

You cannot fail to bear in mind the circumstances to which I have drawn your attention, or the horrors imposed upon this city, and from which we were only saved by the pluck and courage and self-denial of the citizens who did not belong to the unions. Now you will retire and consider your verdict.

The jury retired at 4:50 that Saturday afternoon, leaving the learned judge and the Crown attorney to argue about a detail of the instruction, until Dixon intervened politely to resolve the problem. Recalled, the jury listened to some further advice, and then retired once more.

If an immediate and obvious verdict was expected, it did not come. Galt waited until 6:15 p.m., then adjourned until 8:30 that evening. The court reconvened as directed, only to receive a request from the jury for more time, and the judge ordered a resumption on Monday morning at ten o'clock. In the jury room, it emerged later, an uneven battle was taking place. Despite all the tensions that the strike had generated, and Galt's near-explicit directions, Dixon's eloquence had persuaded all but one of the jurors, and it took the next day and part of the night to convince the hold-out and achieve unanimity.

On Monday morning, the familiar courtroom drama was played out. "How say you," intoned the clerk of the Court: "Do you find the prisoner guilty or not guilty?" And to each of the three charges the foreman of the jury solemnly replied, "Not guilty."

There was an uproar in the courtroom, quickly silenced, and then the presiding judge turned to the man in the dock. Unable to overturn the jury's decision, Galt virtually reiterated the accusation of guilt: "I would like to warn you for the future," he said to Dixon, "against engaging in such transactions as you have taken part in — they lend a bad colour to a man's actions, and probably led to this prosecution."

Moreover, he repeated, Dixon had certainly helped foment an absolute-ly illegal and unjustifiable strike. Grudgingly he admitted that "any fair criticism of the government is perfectly allowable in this country," that Dixon had managed to demonstrate his support of constitutional action, and that he had not taken part in that conspiratorial Calgary conference. And then he discharged him, with a final, ungracious warning: "Well, you were not there, and the jury has accordingly acquitted you. I con-gratulate you upon it, and hope that never again will a man of your attainments, education, and power in the community come before a court on such a charge as this."

The community did not share Judge Galt's sour sentiments. Thousands of people turned out to the next meeting of the Dominion Labor Party, overflowing from the Strand Theatre to the Labor Temple, and a prolonged cheer greeted Dixon as he entered the hall. When he was finally allowed to speak, he was repeatedly interrupted by bursts of applause. He thanked his listeners for their support, and reiter-ated his faith in the British institution of trial by jury that had won him his freedom and in all the constitutional processes of true democracy. His profoundly moving address to the jury was rushed into print, to be distributed and sold in aid of the strike leaders' defence fund.

In March, shortly after his acquittal, Dixon was confirmed by accla-mation as chairman of the Dominion Labor Party, with Farmer and Ivens as vice-presidents; and in the *Western Labor News*, he outlined a blueprint for the future:

a new Canada in which manhood shall be more regarded than money, in which liberty will be more regarded than property, in which the laborer shall receive the full product of his toil, in which those who build houses shall inhabit them and those who plant vineyards shall eat the fruits thereof. . . . I am hoping for a Farmer-Labor combination that will sweep the old parties from the hustings and lift the political life of this nation to a higher plane.

Toward Labour Unity:
The Independent Labor Party

Despite Dixon's vision of an enlightened cooperation between all seg-
ments of the body politic and his efforts to enlist the support of the
rural vote for the Dominion Labor Party, factional dissention increasingly thwarted labour's erratic moves toward a coherent political presence. By 1920 an intense struggle for control of the union movement
was under way between the OBU, with its militant industrial strategy,
and the eastern-based, internationally affiliated, more conservative
TLC, the Trades and Labor Congress. Behind the OBU's program of
replacing the prevailing system of separate craft unions with one powerful union of all workers was the Marxist ideology of the Socialist
Party of Canada, informing its spirit if not its actual intention, and
determined that capitalism and the profit system must absolutely give
way to a new world order of working-class rule and production for use.
For the committed socialists, expectations such as Dixon's, that the
capitalist system could be amended and reformed, were folly at best,
and at worst a hindrance and a deterrent to the ultimate workers' triumph.

Provincial elections were called for June 1920. In preparation the
Labor Party adopted a broad platform incorporating proposals ranging
from "the transformation of capitalist property into social property
and production for use instead of profit," to direct legislation, collective bargaining, and a host of specific social benefits. Opposed on principle to "partyism," to what he considered the divisive narrowness of
most party politics, Dixon held that good government was consensual
rather than adversarial, and his party platform reflected this spirit of
cooperation.

Voting in Winnipeg was to take place this time under a new system
of proportional representation that made it advisable for each of the
parties to nominate several candidates. In the meantime the Robson
report on the strike had been published, finding that the action had
indeed exceeded legal limits, but that it had been prompted by intolerable economic difficulties, and that there was no evidence of a revolutionary conspiracy. There was a great deal of public sympathy for the

strikers, and a widespread popular demand for the release of the imprisoned strike leaders. With whatever reluctance, the various factions recognized the strategic advantage of nominating a single slate headed by labour's accused and imprisoned martyrs.

Radicals and moderates continued to squabble throughout the necessary negotiations, with the moderates accusing the Socialist Party of exploiting the labour prisoners for its own ends — as it had manipulated the strike itself, said the members of the Trades and Labor Council. Nevertheless, a unified labour slate of ten candidates, out of a total of forty-one on the Winnipeg ballot, finally appeared: Dixon, Ivens, Tipping, and W. A. James, of the Dominion Labor Party; John Queen, of the Social Democratic Party; W. A. Cartwright, of the Soldiers' and Sailors' Labor Party; and Bill Pritchard, Dick Johns, George Armstrong, and Bob Russell, of the Socialist Party of Canada. In addition, labour sought the farm vote, backing W. A. Bayley in Assiniboia, and a number of other rural candidates. There was one other segment of Manitoba's voting population to be addressed, the newly enfranchised women; and just before election day, Dixon and Tipping appeared at a rally in the Industrial Bureau, with Bayley and with Winona Dixon, who urged the women of the province to vote labour, their true champion.

The result in Winnipeg was an unprecedented triumph for Dixon, who tallied 11,586 first choice votes, almost a quarter of the total, and carried most of the city polls. On his coat-tails, after the laborious process of apportioning second and third choices, three of the jailed strike leaders came in: Ivens, Queen, and Armstrong; Bayley won in Assiniboia, the first schoolteacher elected to the Manitoba legislature; and six other labour candidates were successful in the rural constituencies, for a total of eleven seats. Significantly, three of the four radical Marxists backed by the Socialist Party were defeated: Russell, Pritchard, and Johns.

Dixon was chosen without question as leader of the labour MLAs, but even before the provincial legislature met in the fall, the battle for union power in Winnipeg between the OBU and the Trades and Labor Council erupted into the open, with charges and countercharges that reverberated down the years. Attempting to mediate, Dixon chaired an explosive debate between the two factions, only to hear the TLC representative, W. Hoop, label the strike a Soviet-inspired conspiracy by the OBU, and all those like Fred Dixon and William Ivens who supported its ostensible aim of collective bargaining merely dupes. The Dominion Labor Party itself was split when one of its ward organizations nominated Hoop to run for alderman, and in November both Farmer and Dixon resigned.

A new party now entered the Manitoba political scene, organized by some of the men who had been prominent in the general strike: Dixon, Ivens, Heaps, Farmer, Woodsworth, and others. Officially constituted in November 1920, the Independent Labor Party united under one banner a number of moderate labourites and special interest associations — "a group of nondescripts," the *Free Press* called them. Included were the Direct Legislation League, the Provincial Representation Committee, the Social Democratic Party, and what remained of the Dominion Labor Party. The OBU and the Socialist Party of Canada refused to join. With Dixon as its first leader, the ILP proposed to act on all three levels of government, federal, provincial, and municipal: the labour-left had achieved an effective cohesion, a milestone in the politics of Manitoba and of western Canada.

The new labour party that Dixon helped to create defined itself as "independent" of the organizational warfare that was destroying the unity of working people, and in the Manitoba legislature there was an informal agreement between the various farm representatives and the labour group to cooperate in their mutual interest. Dixon provided the group with powerful leadership — sometimes, however, at the expense of party cohesiveness.

Two years later, in March 1922, Norris's Liberals were defeated in the legislature on a motion of censure. A number of items still were left on the order papers, including a contentious ILP bill in which John Queen was urgently concerned, to permit the Sunday operation of trains to the lakeside resorts. True to his conception of proper government as cooperative and practical, Dixon agreed to let the business remaining continue to its conclusion, on condition that an election be called immediately afterward; and to speed the process, he over-rode party loyalty, agreeing to the elimination of Queen's Sunday Trains Bill

— to the immense fury of his labour colleague. The agenda was completed and an election took place, in July 1922.

Once more Dixon led the city polls, and his surplus helped bring in three other ILP members: Ivens and Queen again, and Farmer, who had also been elected mayor of Winnipeg. Outside the city, Bayley was reelected, but five of labour's seven rural seats were taken by the candidates of the United Farmers of Manitoba. With a total of twenty-seven seats, the United Farmers formed the government, and they extended an invitation to Fred Dixon to become their leader, and therefore the premier of Manitoba. He refused the offer, perhaps because he sought a broader consensus than the single-interest farmers, and perhaps for personal reasons that only became public knowledge some time later. Offered the leadership in Dixon's place, John Bracken was induced to leave his academic post at the Manitoba Agricultural College, and began his long political career.

Even with its depleted number, however, the ILP proved a powerhouse in the Manitoba legislature, an effective voice for reform. Years later Russell himself continued to acknowledge the ability of his rival, Fred Dixon:

> He was a natural leader, a good thinker and a good executive head. He had the personal magnetism and a carrying, penetrating voice that commanded attention and respect, and his oratory was wonderful. Well-read fellow — his quotations were wonderful, and the analogies he made were good and could be understood by the common person. . . . He had the government worried about his speeches. When Dixon got onto a theme he had the knack of keeping at it, just like little drops of water, little drops of sand. And he never stopped — always seeking more, never appeased. We argued with him that [these measures] were only a reform, that they could appease you with those damn things instead of giving you the whole thing, but Dixon was proving in the world of reality the correctness of his theories at the time.

Then, in 1923, with the strength of the ILP and the influence of its leader continuing to grow, Dixon suddenly resigned his position and retired into private life. He would accept no further office, no nomination either for the mayoralty or for a federal seat, and, it was rumoured, he turned down the leadership of Manitoba's Liberals. The ILP continued without him.

Decline

There were cogent personal reasons for Dixon's abrupt and unexplained departure from politics. His two-year-old son, James, had died in November 1920, just as the newly formed ILP demanded the energies of the father. The Dixons' second daughter, Eleanor, was born in March 1922; and, as the province geared up for the election that brought the United Farmers to power, Winona Dixon died of pneumonia, on May 15, ending a seven-year partnership. Mrs. Flett, Winona's mother, took over the care of the children.

Dixon was forced to reconsider his own drastically altered situation. "I must look ahead," he told a friend at the time, "I must look after my dependents." Political achievement had brought him much satisfaction but little practical security — his salary as ILP leader amounted to fifteen hundred dollars a year — and he began selling insurance full time. Concerned always with making it possible for all human beings to develop their own individual abilities to the utmost, Dixon would have regarded the safety net of life insurance as another means to secure the freedom, the dignity, and the independence of ordinary people.

By 1923, his own health problems had become serious and his future ominously uncertain. He had been troubled by a persistent blemish on the side of his head; it was diagnosed as cancerous, and a prolonged and difficult series of surgical treatments began. Repeatedly over the next few years, Dixon entered hospital to have the recurring malignancy excised, and each time he lay immobilized for weeks while the wound was covered by a skin graft from his arm.

As his physical condition began to deteriorate, death struck the family again, twice. In 1924, Dixon lost his nine-year-old first-born, Doris, and within a few weeks Mrs. Flett, his mother-in-law and the mainstay of the household, passed away as well. Lynn Flett gave up her work as a court stenographer to move into the Dixon home as housekeeper —

although there seem to have been some raised eyebrows at the impropriety of this arrangement. Eleanor Dixon survived to maturity, cared for by her aunt.

Among Dixon's friends and associates speculation spread about the source of his malady. Some said that he had been born with a caul over his head, and that the mark it left behind proved his undoing. Others insisted, building a kind of poignant legend around the man, that the cancer originated in that blow on the head he received at the Grand Theatre, fighting the tyranny of conscription.

During the intervals between hospital sessions, Dixon continued as insurance salesman, perhaps even grateful for the increased time he had now to read, and for the solace that reading provided. In 1927 he served on a provincial commission investigating the causes of unemployment, and was appointed to the Workman's Compensation Board. His doctors sent him in the fall of 1929 to Memorial Hospital, New York, for radical treatment. On his return a group of friends presented him with a testimonial and a twenty-five-hundred-dollar purse. The unions had donated a great deal of the money, and the testimonial had been signed, said the *Winnipeg Tribune*, by twelve hundred people, "men and women prominent in every walk of life in Winnipeg and the province, including members of the House of Commons, of the Legislature, the city council, the bench, the civil and civic services." Always restless and eager for self-improvement, Dixon subscribed in his last year to a correspondence course in salesmanship from a school in Chicago, and finished by writing three near-perfect exams.

By February 1931 he could no longer leave his bed. A police guard was assigned to ensure that the area around his home, on Riverwood Avenue in suburban Fort Garry, remained quiet and undisturbed during his last weeks. He died on Wednesday, March 18 , just past his fiftieth birthday.

The funeral was held Saturday, March 21 , at the Fort Rouge Labor Hall on Osborne Street; James Woodsworth made the thirty-six-hour journey by train from Ottawa to conduct the services for his friend. As Dixon's old associates gathered to pay their respects, together with the hundreds who filled the hall and waited outside, a bizarre incident marred the dignity of the proceedings. In the mud of an early

Winnipeg spring, Riverwood Avenue was impassable to motor traffic; the hearse could not get through to the Dixon home. A CPR wagon and a team of horses had to be brought, and eight or nine men sat on the coffin to keep it from falling off on the rough ride to Osborne Street, where the hearse waited.

Woodsworth delivered the eulogy and then, at the crowd's insistence, the casket was brought outside so that all those present could pay their respects. Climbing on a truck, Woodsworth repeated his address. Fred Dixon, he said, "was a man of whom it might truly be said that he made the world better for having lived." The labour paper, the *Weekly News*, headlined the story, "Fred J. Dixon Has Passed On to the Great Majority," and the tributes that poured in, from former adversaries and comrades alike, singled out Dixon's integrity, his courage, and his unfailing championship of common people. "He was placed above party and political differences," wrote John W. Dafoe, in the *Manitoba Free Press*. "The Labor movement," said the president of the Trades and Labor Council, "has room for more men of his character."

For Universal Brotherhood, In God's Name

William Ivens

The Gospel of Social Responsibility

The leading members of McDougall Methodist Church, on Winnipeg's Main Street north of the CPR tracks, had had enough of their controversial pastor, the Reverend William Ivens. Canada was at war, this winter and spring of 1918, and Reverend Ivens persisted in preaching some scandalously unpatriotic ideas. He was a pacifist, and he denounced all warfare as immoral, un-Christian. He said that what he called "the present economic system" breeds war in three ways: economic war, between groups of competitors; class war, between employer and employees, the exploiters and the exploited; and international war, for political and economic advantages. "National individualism," he said, "must breed war," and he maintained that wars would cease if the profit motive were eliminated. "We must find a solution in other means than armaments," he said; and further, "If we keep up the insanc policy of armament when this war is finished, there will be no hope that Christianity can find a solution. The only hope is in building the Parliament of Man, the Federation of the World."

He said that both sides were at fault in this terrible carnage — a suspiciously pro-German pronouncement. At a time when so many of the members' sons were nobly offering their lives to defend king and country, the minister quoted Scripture: "Christ says, 'He that taketh the sword shall perish by it,' " and he refused to support the war effort, as other good clergymen did, by encouraging young men to enlist. The church must provide succour and hope, he said, for those engaged in the war and those suffering at home, but it must not become a recruiting agency for the war. Moreover, to the discomfort of the respectable, middle-class members of the congregation, he constantly inveighed against the ungodly injustices perpetrated on the poor by the affluent and the powerful.

The question of the minister's assertive pacifism dominated the meeting in March that year of the church's Quarterly Board. Speaking on his own behalf, Ivens reiterated his belief in the immorality of armed conflict, although he had already offered not to attack Canada's involvement directly from the pulpit. In return he asked for the right, as a Christian minister, not to support the war and not to turn his pulpit into a recruiting station. The proposed compromise did nothing to allay the complaints of the board members. One speaker insisted angrily that all conscientious objectors should be put in detention camps, and that a man could not stay in the Methodist Church if his sympathies were against the war. Ivens ought to leave the Methodist ministry, another man declared; and still another member was of the opinion that the pastor should "do the manly thing and resign."

There were some voices in the minister's defence. The Methodist Church was committed to relief work among the poor, and a number of speakers pointed out that Ivens had worked tirelessly and most charitably in his duties, and had exerted himself on behalf of the Red Cross. A fervent letter from a woman in the congregation argued that Mr. Ivens was the only minister who had ever paid her a pastoral visit; she had brought a number of friends with her to the church, she said, and if Mr. Ivens were dismissed from McDougall Methodist her entire family would cease to attend. One young man, in a private's uniform, pleaded that "it meant a good deal . . . to be able to attend a church where there was a minister like the Rev. William Ivens, who had a vision of mankind that went beyond the war."

Ivens's pro-labour exhortations had indeed attracted some new people to McDougall Methodist from its predominantly working-class area, but there had been an overall drop in membership during this second year of his ministry. His pacifism was causing so much distress, the meeting was told, that many long-standing members were staying away from services or leaving the church entirely. Concerned about its reputation, the Quarterly Board felt compelled to register a dual resolution, endorsing the war effort and declaring its readiness "to make all necessary sacrifices for the cause of peace." As for the recalcitrant pastor, a motion calling for his resignation was passed by a margin of twelve to seven.

Ivens did not resign, however, nor did he modify his preaching. Defiantly he made his position clear on the Sunday following his censure:

> I am a man first, a pastor second. In this pulpit I will speak only as I understand God. You can have me as your minister or not, but outside the Church I am a man and will not be interfered with in my speech on public questions.

Consequently a special meeting of the board was held on May 15, 1918, and a request was communicated to the Central Methodist Conference "not to send Ivens as pastor." The minister's career was at a crossroads.

William Ivens had first become a member of the McDougall congregation in 1904, when the Reverend A. E. Smith was pastor. Born on June 28, 1878, in the town of Barford, in Warwickshire, England, where his father was a landscape gardener, William had immigrated to

Manitoba in 1896 at the age of eighteen. By the time of World War I, when his principles and pronouncements had become a matter of public debate, two of his brothers were on active duty in the British military, one as a sergeant-major in the Grenadier Guards and another as a lieutenant-colonel in the field artillery.

After arriving in Manitoba in 1896 Ivens worked for several years as a farm labourer, and then moved to Winnipeg. Like Dixon, he discovered Professor Mobius's bookstore on Main Street and talked with some of the reform-minded men who met there. In his memoir A. E. Smith recalls the young man of twenty-six who joined the men's club at McDougall Methodist, took part in the carpet bowling, and spoke of his desire for education. Encouraged by Smith, Ivens enrolled at the Methodists' Wesley College, and as he pursued his studies he managed to support himself on the sixty cents per day he earned working for a market gardener.

At Wesley, Ivens encountered Salem Bland, and the association was to have a shaping influence on his life. Bland, like Smith and James Woodsworth, was an advocate of the Social Gospel, the movement for social and religious reform that had been active in Canada since the 1880s. Mass immigration and the rapid expansion of the Canadian economy in the last decades of the nineteenth century had brought widespread distress and disorder in their wake. The traditional churches were slow to respond, and significant numbers of working people, in their harsh lives, were alienated from conventional religion. Serious thinkers, moved by liberal and progressive ideas and concerned with spiritual values, began to call for a reassessment of the role of religion in society. Specifically, they held, the changing conditions of modern life required a reinterpretation of the truths of Christianity.

Essentially the Social Gospel elevated the concern for human welfare and social justice to a moral imperative, investing labour's drive for political and economic reform with the mantle of divine inspiration. Where traditional Christian teaching valued the spirit above the body, in effect dismissing the woes of the everyday world as transient and unimportant, the Social Gospel shifted the emphasis of religious truth from inner spirituality and the soul's redemption to public service. Human salvation, it taught, cannot be achieved without decent living conditions for all people. "Man's responsibility," Salem Bland told his students, "is for the social as well as the moral and spiritual well-being of his fellow men"; and in the light of Christ's pronouncement about the difficulty of a rich man's entering into the kingdom of heaven, he condemned the domination of society by its business community, and "all the rascalities of high finance, all the abominations of our political system."

Temperance, electoral reform, fair wage legislation, and, particularly as war loomed in Europe, pacifism: these were some of the issues on which the Social Gospellers made common cause with liberals and moderate reformers, such as Manitoba's Fred Dixon and Arthur Puttee, and to a degree their concerns were shared by the Canadian Methodist Church. From before the turn of the century, the church had been active in social causes, and many leading Methodist churchmen continued to be openly troubled about the clash between Christian teaching and the operations of a profit-based economy; in 1918, for example, the General Conference in Hamilton would pass a resolution endorsing "a transference of the whole economic life from a basis of competition and profits to one of co-operation and service." In practice, however, major Methodist churches and schools, generally presided over by successful businessmen, tended to be more conservative. At Wesley College, Salem Bland enjoyed an uneasy prominence, and James Woodsworth, then assistant pastor at Winnipeg's well-to-do Grace Church, struggled with the conflict between his principles and the complacent way of life of his parishioners. Drawn into their orbit, Ivens found his vocation.

He earned the degrees of Bachelor of Divinity and Bachelor of Arts from Wesley College and was ordained into the Methodist ministry, and in 1909 he was granted a Master of Arts degree by the University of Manitoba. For the next half-dozen years he served as pastor in a number of rural communities, developing into an impressive pulpit orator. He returned to Winnipeg in 1916, succeeding A. E. Smith as the minister at McDougall Methodist, and was welcomed back to his home church at the annual picnic in Kildonan Park. He married Louisa Davis; their first son, Milton, was born, and the family moved into a house on Inkster Avenue, a little distance from the church.

At the outset the sandy-haired Englishman impressed his new flock most favourably, with his compelling voice, his intense sincerity, and his splendid, eloquent sermons. An enormously energetic person, he proved to be a very efficient manager as well, succeeding in enhancing McDougall's finances considerably. In 1917 he joined the Winnipeg Ministerial Association and participated actively in its deliberations. As Methodist and as reformer he urged attention to the problems of the city's working women, and he proposed that a petition endorsing prohibition be circulated across Canada. Unequivocally, from his own pulpit, he preached the message of the Social Gospel, that poverty, ignorance, disease, and war were the inevitable by-products of the existing economic system, that such a system violated the teaching of Christ, that the church must devote itself to labour's struggle or it would forfeit its place in the lives of ordinary people.

By 1918 the pastor had become active in the city's labour movement and a member of Fred Dixon's Dominion Labor Party. As the war overseas drew to an end and the complex grievances of Winnipeg's work force erupted into one confrontation after another, Ivens's sermons stressed the justice of the trade union cause. His Sunday services were reported regularly in *The Voice*, and he contributed impressively erudite articles on economic and social subjects to the paper's columns. He appeared frequently at public rallies, where his flamboyant rhetoric provided the city's mainstream newspapers with lively copy; and, to the great indignation of patriotic Methodists, he insisted on attacking the war effort, echoing the pacifism of his labour friends.

In April, after his Quarterly Board had called for his resignation, he visited a number of western points on a speaking tour for labour. The next month, as the long-simmering altercation between the city of Winnipeg and its employees erupted into a work-stoppage and almost into a citywide general strike, Ivens edited the strike information sheet.

In the face of the rebuke by his church board, the pastor's sermons only grew more strident, and he repeated his remarks in *The Voice*. On Sunday, June 14, 1918, he reminded his flock that although Jesus had driven the money-changers out of the temple, the present-day church was dominated by the wealthy middle class. If Christ came among us today, the preacher said, he would likely appear as a common factory worker; and "should we be ready to listen to His message," he asked, "if He delivered it from a soap-box on Market Square? . . . If He appeared today, the great danger is that we should not know Him and so should crucify Him in ignorance."

That month the stationing committee of the Methodist Church met to consider the issue. Letters arrived declaring support for Ivens, and two petitions for his retention were presented with about three hundred signatures, including the names of more than half the McDougall congregation. In addition an appeal signed by some two thousand members of the Labor Temple strongly protested the "great mistake" that the Methodist Church would make if it separated this friend of labour from his post and from the city. The committee offered Ivens another pulpit in Winnipeg, but he declined, saying that his pacifist principles would likely be as unacceptable to a second congregation as to the first. In the end it was decided to remove Ivens from McDougall, leaving him for one year "without station": technically still a Methodist minister, but not assigned to any pulpit.

The Voice reported the decision under the headline, "Ivens fired from McDougall Church," with an interview quoting the pastor's bitter comment:

As I see it, it is clear that since the Methodist Church lays no charge against my character or my religious views, it has come to the place where it puts a man's political convictions on a more important plane than his religious convictions. Further, it seems also to be clearly demonstrated that the Methodist Church no longer stands for a free pulpit and for freedom of conscience.

A Church of Humanity

Ivens's mentors, Salem Bland and James Woodsworth, also parted company from the Methodist Church at this time. Bland was dismissed from the faculty at Wesley College, ostensibly because the college was short of money but quite obviously for his radical views. He continued for a time as a lecturer and a columnist for the *Grain Growers' Guide* before returning to a pulpit in Toronto. Woodsworth had tried to withdraw from the Methodist ministry twice before, but each time had been persuaded to remain.

Under their continuing influence, however, Ivens established a labor church in Winnipeg. The first such congregation had been organized in Manchester, England, in 1891, and several were now in existence in

England and in Canada, incorporating the radical and humanitarian doctrines of the Social Gospel. Winnipeg's assembly, longer-lasting than most, was to play a significant role in the general strike of 1919.

The inaugural meeting of the Winnipeg Labor Church took place in Room 10 of the Labor Temple, the headquarters of Winnipeg's labour movement, on July 8, 1918. In the chair was James Farmer, then one of the leaders of the Dominion Labor Party, and William Ivens preached the sermon. The new denomination declared that "justice, equity, righteousness, a square deal to every man" were "the foundations and essentials of religion," and welcomed "anyone . . . who believes in the need and the possibility of a better day for human society, and who is willing to make some systematic, consistent and constructive contributions of thought, time, influence and means toward that end. . . ." At the meeting's close, two hundred "common toiling people" pledged their membership in a church that promised to "champion their cause, and to provide expression, in a congenial social atmosphere, for their ideals and longings for freedom, justice and truth."

This was a "creedless church," its membership pledge avowed. Ivens's manifesto asserted the "Brotherhood of Man" simultaneously with the "Fatherhood of God." Taking a deliberate stand against the tyranny of fixed, institutionalized dogmas, it proposed that "a person's theological views are a personal affair with which no one has a right to interfere," and that a "genuine practical love for humanity, based on truth and experience, is the proper and sufficient guiding principle of life." In fact as one supporter explained, rather ingenuously, "it is not necessary to believe in God or Christ. . . . Just help others and live a clean life." Arguably a church in name only, and certainly as much political as religious, the Labor Church adopted as its watchword a declaration very much in the spirit of Marxist socialism: "If any man will not work, neither shall he eat. . . . Whoever enjoys the good things of the earth without working for them is stealing the bread of the workers."

Ivens's new church united its adherents in a communal bond. Its teaching validated the discontent of the working class, imbuing it with the sanction of divine truth. To the alienated poor, uncomfortable and even resentful in a self-satisfied middle-class congregation, it offered the reassurance of a structure that resembled the traditional church institution, but one in which they could feel at home. Labor Church services on Sunday were an eclectic blend of labour hymns, ad hoc prayers, and spontaneous discussion, in which the congregation participated vociferously. Here ordinary churchgoers could express their anxieties and their hopes, and learn about the world in which they lived.

Instead of the old hymns, whose familiar pieties now seemed irrelevant, the congregation could join in an anthem of praise for the new and better world that scientific progress must inevitably bring about. "Hymn for the New Day" was one selection that Pastor Ivens composed for his flock:

New learning, science, travel, art,
Each in its sphere hath played its part.
'Tis time for change the wide world o'er,
 As knowledge grows from more to more.

. . .

Thus, Christ, the "Man of Galilee,"
Thus Socrates, to make men free
Voiced Progress, Liberty and Right;
 And Truth had conquered over might.

More alarming still to the outsider were other favourite hymns, often borrowed from the belligerent "Wobblies," the notorious, U.S.-based Industrial Workers of the World. They sang:

Workers of Canada, why crouch ye like cravens,
Why clutch an existence of insult and want?
Why stand to be plucked by an army of ravens,
Or hoodwinked forever by twaddle and cant?

That hymn ended with something very much like a Marxist call to revolution:

Rise in your might, brothers, bear it no longer,
Assemble in masses throughout the whole land:
Show these incapables who are the stronger
When workers and idlers confronted shall stand. . . .

Attendance quickly outgrew the capacity of the Labor Temple hall, and, without a building of its own, this "Church of Humanity" gathered in a succession of meeting halls and theatres across the city. Unionists, suffragists, returned soldiers, all brought their arguments to William Ivens's "open pulpit." On "Women's Sunday," in January 1919, Winona Dixon came with her sister, Lynn Flett, to talk about the women's movement. A spirited debate with members of the audience often ensued, and occasionally the preacher's own views might be challenged. When one veteran denounced a pacifist as "the dirtiest yellow damned cur," Ivens rose grandly to proclaim that he was one of that condemned breed, fighting the capitalist "Hun" at home while the soldiers fought the "Hun" in France, and that "the next great fight would be against the profit system."

Again, during the strike of post office employees and metal workers, in August 1918, a representative of the strikers addressed the congregation, and the assembly backed its support of the union by voting to contribute half of the collection to the strike fund. A precedent was established, repeated several times; William Ivens's remarkable ability to raise funds would serve the strikers well in labour's major battle the following summer.

Of course radicals like Bob Russell and Dick Johns and others made no bones of their disdain for religion of any sort, and on occasion a mischievous visiting atheist could not resist poking fun at his host. Many years later, Alex Shepherd chuckled at one such moment, in the heat of the 1919 strike, when the Labor Church had become the rallying point for the embattled strikers. Shepherd, then treasurer of the machinists' local, and Bill Hoop, of the letter-carriers' union, had joined the crowd at the Columbia Theatre on Main Street for the Sunday evening service:

> Bill Hoop actually was a bit of a God-killer, you know, he'd read up on this Rationalist Press stuff that comes out of London. . . . [He] walked into the . . . Labor Church meeting, when Bill Ivens was on his knees praying, you know, and he says, "I thought I told that man Ivens that there is no God." Boy oh boy oh boy, talk about staggering the whole audience! . . . But Ivens, he had that vibration in his voice when he wanted to put it

60

there . . . he was always trying to show that God was on the side of the strikers, and that the bad men were the ironmasters, and they'd have parables to show [how] Jesus dealt with men of this kind.

There was no income for Ivens himself out of his new house of worship, but his passionate championship of labour had brought him to the attention of the Winnipeg Trades and Labor Council, and a livelihood materialized for him shortly after his dismissal from McDougall Methodist. When Arthur Puttee fell out of favour with the Trades and Labor Council, his moderate labour sympathies overtaken by the growing belligerence of Winnipeg's unions, *The Voice* was silenced, and the council moved to replace it. Several issues of a labour news-sheet appeared sporadically, and then, on August 2, the *Western Labor News* made its debut, with the Reverend William Ivens as editor. The new weekly declared that its policy was to reflect the views of all working-class people and of labour unionism in particular, and Ivens was launched on a new career.

For the charismatic preacher the enhanced prominence was most gratifying. His photograph and his full name, complete with his degrees, accompanied all his articles: while he was editor, he said, that was the way it would be done. "A tremendous egotist," his contemporary and fellow activist, Fred Tipping, commented in a 1970 interview. At the same time, he continued to guide the Labor Church and preached a sermon every Sunday at both its afternoon and its evening sessions.

Ivens's appointment was not received without challenge. By 1918 the restive left-wing element within the Trades and Labor Council was vigorously pursuing its drive to radicalize the movement, and the interest in an alternative, more militant labour organization had begun. Russell and his colleagues in the Socialist Party of Canada charged that the *Western Labor News* was the organ of the ineffectual Dominion Labor Party and of the dubious Labor Church. Ivens, they maintained, was an incompetent editor and his editorials were reactionary, and in December 1918 they succeeded in having a committee appointed to investigate their charges. By that time, however, after only five months in office, Ivens had raised the paper's circulation from sixteen hundred to ten thousand and had paid off the cost of the office equipment. The committee endorsed Ivens's editorship, with only one opposing vote.

In his dual role as preacher and editor Ivens persisted in attacking injustice wherever he saw it, gaining for himself an unhealthy notoriety. The war had ended shortly after he assumed the editorship of the *Western Labor News*, and relations between industry and labour across the country grew even more truculent than before, with Winnipeg increasingly one of the flash points. While at McDougall Methodist, Ivens had visited in the homes of the poor and the destitute, and now article after article dramatised the despair of these unfortunates, excoriating the perpetrators of the inhumanity, the unfeeling "bosses." Stridently the weekly denounced the federal government's policies for postwar reconstruction as callous and inept, and in the escalating series of strikes and threatened strikes that rocked the city Ivens's reports unfailingly urged the justice of the union cause.

In the Radical Limelight

Historians have suggested that the opening salvo leading up to the general strike of May and June 1919 was the boisterous Walker Theatre rally on the previous December 22. A shrill rebelliousness resounded from all the speeches, even those of the so-called "moderates," and was reechoed in the cheers of the angry crowd. Ivens himself introduced the resolution demanding that the federal government liberate all "political prisoners" jailed during the prosecution of the recent war.

Speaking to his motion, he began by labelling the terrible slaughter of the past four years as a European affair rather than a patriotic Canadian sacrifice, but he drew a distinction between the despotic German government and the German people, and insisted that the ordinary Germans like ordinary Austrians, Romanians, Bohemians, and Poles were now Canada's allies in the struggle for freedom, and that therefore all "alien" prisoners should be released. Even more urgently, he pleaded the cause of the prisoners of conscience, the conscientious objectors who were imprisoned only for being true to their highest convictions. He cited that great seventeenth-century advocate of liberty, John Milton, and demanded the freedom to think, to have convictions, and to express those convictions. Was the nation the supreme voice for the individual, he asked, or was there an authority higher than the state? The higher authority, he said, was conscience and the Divine command.

Ivens's motion received clamorous assent, and the condemnation of government policies and practices escalated with each succeeding address. At the end, the *Western Labor News* reported, there were deafening cheers for the Soviet Republic and the working class.

If the Reverend William Ivens had seemed to the alarmed authorities a minor player in the radical agitation up to this point, the incident at the Walker Theatre put him in the spotlight. His Labor Church congregation, now numbering over four hundred, was barred from the Walker Theatre, and one by one the owners of the Rex, the Columbia, the Dominion, and the Majestic theatres also refused to rent him their premises. Forced back to the Labor Temple for his meetings, he was harassed by an order from a city inspector, threatening to close the Temple location because its chairs were not fastened down, as required of a church. A further edict, that discussion from the audience was not allowed, played into the preacher's hands, and the *Western Labor News* shouted its indignation at this offence against freedom of speech.

Ivens was not on the platform at the equally contentious January rally in the Majestic Theatre, but his newspaper gave full play to the proceedings, and his flair for high-flown language continued to issue in Marxist rhetoric as provocative as ever came from the most diehard revolutionary. A February editorial flung the threat of imminent Armageddon at the "capitalist exploiters":

> your system will fall down about your ears with a suddenness and thoroughness that will surprise you. Such was the process in Russia, such is the trend in Germany at this hour, in Germany, Austria, France and Britain, and no man or set of men on earth can stem the tide. Capitalism has gone to seed, its decay is fully due. The time is ripe and rotten ripe for a change. . . .

If there was more than a hint of violence in this partisan eloquence, it was oddly inconsistent with the man's unwavering pacifism.

So notorious did the editor of the *Western Labor News* become that at one point Ottawa made a discreet effort to undermine him, proceeding warily in what must have seemed an extraordinarily precarious situation. An item in the *Western Labor News* for January 31, 1919, attacking the eminent editor of the *Manitoba Free Press*, John W. Dafoe, for his criticism of labour excesses, had caught the eye of the chief press censor for Canada, E. J. Chambers. From Ottawa a few days later Mr. Chambers sent Mr. Dafoe a two-page letter, enclosing a lengthy selection of excerpts from Ivens's other writing, and suggesting a course of action.

Mr. Dafoe would recognize, the communication intimated, that this man Ivens was entirely pro-German, and a dangerous radical. Of course, Chambers hastened to add, the labour movement itself was entirely respectable and its aims proper, but Ivens was leading it down a path it surely did not wish to follow, with his talk about the establishment of justice on earth, and about "a war for . . . right and democracy . . . resounding across the world today." As a result, Chambers continued,

> We have considered whether or not we should suppress the
> *Western Labor News*, because of what it says. But, bearing in mind
> that it is published under the authority of the trade union move-
> ment in Winnipeg, we are reluctant to do so, lest labor would get
> up in arms, and the last state would be worse than the first.

Therefore, the letter hinted, Mr. Dafoe and the *Manitoba Free Press* might endeavour to enlighten loyal citizens about Ivens, but without mention of the communiqué from the press censor. To his credit, Mr. Dafoe made no apparent use of the material Mr. Chambers provided.

Ivens did not attend the Western Labor Conference at Calgary in March, when the One Big Union came into being, but his paper reported the proceedings enthusiastically. Despite the earlier run-in with Russell, he was whole-heartedly in favour of the aggressive union being engineered by the radical group, and several articles in the *Western Labor News* were devoted to the history of the OBU in Australia. One week before the meeting opened, the paper carried Ivens's editorial comment, with particular attention to the broader possibilities of a new social order:

It may . . . be that the day for economic and political action by the workers is at hand. It may be that a definite plan for the formation of soviets will have to be considered in all its phases, but whatever the exact method . . . the one outstanding feature is that this convention must become the torch-bearer of a Dominion-wide plan for labor advance in the very near future.

Caught up in the dream of a righteous society governed by a soviet of workers, the Reverend Ivens may not have been contemplating violent revolution, but his words would return to haunt him. In April, as labour strife in Winnipeg mounted toward an explosion, he preached a sermon at the Labor Church on "Reconstruction," the contentious government plans to bring the economy back to a peace-time footing. Reprinting his argument in the *Western Labor News*, that "if there [is] to be reconstruction, there must first be destruction," he repeated his litany of the horrors — war, poverty, crime, disease — that would be expunged with the destruction of the international profit system.

Meanwhile, fired with enthusiasm by the increasing popularity of his Labor Church, Ivens invited his old friend and mentor, James Woodsworth, now earning an arduous wage on the Vancouver waterfront, to undertake a speaking tour of the West under Labor Church auspices. Woodsworth was only too eager to return to the task he perceived as his calling, disseminating progressive social ideas, and he accepted. The May 9 issue of the *Western Labor News* published his itinerary, with a stop scheduled in Winnipeg on June 8.

"We Will Never Surrender"

By the beginning of May 1919 the city was a tinderbox, and the spark that set it alight was the impasse between Bob Russell's machinists and their "ironmaster" employers. Negotiations broke down absolutely, and on the morning of Thursday, May 15, the domino sequence of walk-outs began, as workers across Winnipeg's entire economy followed their fellow unionists out of the shops and factories.

The city's typographers left their posts on Saturday, May 17, shutting down the three daily newspapers, but the printers offered to serve as unpaid volunteers to produce labour's own *Western Labor News*. The daily *Strike Bulletin* was added, with Ivens as editor, and the first issue appeared on the same Saturday afternoon. A special press subcommittee of the Central Strike Committee — in fact a censorship board — supervised all items published, providing news of strike negotiations, explaining the issues, and identifying what services were available and what city enterprises were permitted to function.

As the information link between the Central Strike Committee and its constituents, the paper and its editor played an indispensable role. Above all, Ivens threw all his persuasive skills into the effort to keep the strikers both steadfast and orderly. Order was vitally important, the committee well understood, because the authorities would use any outbreak of lawlessness as an excuse to impose martial law. "Our fight consists of doing no fighting," the *Strike Bulletin* proclaimed in one of its early issues; and it coaxed its readers to treat this anxious time as a kind of holiday. "The only thing the workers have to do to win this strike," Ivens advised, "is to do nothing. Just eat, sleep, play, love, laugh, and look at the sun." As the tension mounted, however, and real problems arose for the embattled workers, the editor redoubled his efforts to encourage and reassure and help. "No matter how great the provocation," Ivens urged on May 26,

> do not quarrel. Do not say an angry word. Walk away from the fellow who tries to draw you. Take everything to the Central Strike Committee. If you are hungry, go to them. We will share our last crust together. If one starves, we will all starve. We will fight on, and on, and on. We will never surrender.

What could not be surrendered, the *Strike Bulletin* repeated time and time again, what the strike absolutely must achieve, was the right of all working people to a decent standard of living, to collective bargaining and a living wage.

Many of the leading churches took a firm stand against the strike, and, as in virtually every other aspect of the city's life, there was an upheaval among church members. The Methodist Conference in Toronto was told that the striking workers aimed at uncontrolled, unconstitutional power, and in Winnipeg the superintendent decreed that striking workers were to be considered "under ban." At

Westminster Presbyterian, a meeting called to "discuss" the situation turned into a recruiting rally for the special police being organized by the business community's Committee of One Thousand. Dismayed, the minister protested, and a number of strike sympathizers furiously resigned from the congregation.

Now more compelling than ever, the Labor Church provided a source of mutual support to the strikers and their families. As J. S. Woodsworth was to explain later, with unconcealed satisfaction, in his *First History of the Labor Church*, "Ivens's Church had become a 'movement' . . . a revolt against denominationalism and formality and commercialism in the churches":

> Staid old Presbyterian elders refused to darken the doors of the kirk. Wesleyan local preachers could no longer be restrained. Anglican Sunday School teachers resigned their classes. Class lines became clearly drawn, and the "regular" churches stood out as middle class institutions. . . . The new wine could no longer be retained in the old bottles.

On the first Sunday evening after the strike was declared, Ivens rented the large hall of the Industrial Development Bureau, on the corner of Main Street and Water Avenue, and drew a larger congregation than Winnipeg had ever seen before. Bob Russell spoke, commenting wryly on the differences between the old religious institutions he had shunned for years and this new kind of church, where the voice of the common man could be heard. With more than a trace of irreverence, the union leader offered some satirical comments suitable to the place and the occasion, on the "Holy Trinity" of Barrett, Deacon, and Warren, the major machine-shop owners who were the target of labour's wrath. Ivens, at his fiery best, swept his listeners up in a mass prayer, "that the workers may succeed according to the justice of their cause, and fail insofar as their demands are unjust."

No hall was now large enough to accommodate the crowds that flocked to the common man's house of worship. On the second Sunday of the strike, the *Strike Bulletin* headline exulted, a "Vast Assembly" came together in Victoria Park, two blocks from the city hall, to join in a moving reaffirmation of purpose. "Jesus was a carpenter's son," Fred

Dixon reminded his listeners, "not a lawyer, financier or iron-master. . . . He was on the side of the poor;" and He was crucified, Dixon declared, by the high priests, the scribes, and the Pharisees, "the same class of men as comprises the Committee of One Thousand." And Ivens aroused the multitudes to fever pitch by flinging at them the demand of that same despotic establishment power: "The Citizens' Committee says you must call off the sympathetic strikes. What is your answer?" Five thousand voices roared back, "No!"

To help the hardest hit of the strikers, the Women's Labor League, with the fiery Helen Armstrong in charge, took over the task of feeding the neediest, and the collection plate at Ivens's church remained a major source of funds for the emergency kitchen.

Financing the operation was always a touch-and-go affair. "We had some good collections," Ivens remembered many years later, "but there was a trick in it." At one point he challenged his Sunday congregation to be generous, because a visiting union representative from eastern Canada had offered to match the collection plate dollar for dollar, if $300 was raised. "They put up $320," Ivens said, "and so Bob had to dig up $320, and we had $640 Monday morning for the bunch." By the next Sunday, Ivens recalled, they needed to raise $1500, "and I figured if we could arrange $500 ahead of time, I could get $1000 out of the crowd that night.

"So I said to Mrs. Ivens, 'Do you think we can spare $100?' And she said, 'What for?' So I told her. She said, 'Oh, I guess so. . . . You'll get it anyway if you want it." With the hundred dollars out of his own household budget in his pocket, he persuaded the sympathetic owner of one Elmwood factory to put up an equal amount, and then repeated the ploy until he had his seed money. The strike fund met its obligations the next day. In all, Ivens raised about forty-five hundred dollars from the thousands of working people and their friends who flocked to his services during the six weeks of the stand-off.

To the Labor Church in the park came the strike's prominent leaders — Fred Dixon, John Queen, Bob Russell, James Farmer, Roger Bray, George Armstrong — to exhort, to explain, to encourage. On June 8 Canon F. G. Scott, VC, the beloved padre of the Canadian Corps, appeared on the platform, delighting all his "old boys" in the audience. As he told a meeting of the Soldiers' Parliament the next day, he had been invited to attend services at All Saints Church, the fashionable Anglican congregation, but had chosen instead to come to "All Sinners." Scott was followed at the Sunday Labor Church services by James Woodsworth, who had been en route between Prince Rupert and Edmonton when he heard the news of the strike, but had continued his lecture tour, arriving in Winnipeg, as scheduled, on June 8.

In Ivens's own lyrical evocation of that Sunday evening,

> The scene itself was an inspiration. Victoria Park is fringed with trees which constitute the walls of the Labor Church; the greensward is the floor and there are no rented pews; the pulpit is a rough platform in the centre of the park; and the sky, illuminated by the stars, constitutes the roof and dome. Never has a church service in Winnipeg had such a gathering. It will never be forgotten while this generation lives.

Woodsworth spoke for two hours. "Some 10,000 people listened with rapt attention to a masterpiece address on the economic situation," Ivens rejoiced in the *Western Labor News*. The offering that day, he reported further, "amounted to some $1,540.00 and was given to the strike fund to feed the striking girls and the needy families."

On the following Sunday evening, a month after the walk-out began, Woodsworth and Ivens once again took their places side by side before the workers and their friends, gathered in their open-air tabernacle. They were joined by A. E. Smith, a past president of the Manitoba Methodist Conference; and Bill Pritchard, newly arrived from Vancouver, received a noisy welcome. The weather had turned hot and humid, and the Citizens' Committee of One Thousand, the *Strike Bulletin* charged, had blocked the Labor Church from renting the Industrial Bureau for the service, so that the crowd of worshippers had to stand. There was "an excellent band," and the hymns were "rendered with great enthusiasm," said the paper, but several people collapsed from heat and exhaustion.

Woodsworth talked of brotherhood, of the One Big Union and the One Big Church, and he insisted that the old forms of religion were no longer valid. Speaking next, Smith offered an even more radical repudiation of conventional religious institutions. At its General Conference the previous year, he told his audience, the Methodist Church had passed a resolution against the competitive economic system and for a cooperative system, and as a result some rich men had threatened to leave the church. "Let them go," he scoffed, "the Church that thinks more of real estate than of principles has no place in the life of today." The sympathetic strike, he proclaimed, was just as religious a movement as a church revival, as ethical as the fight in Flanders.

Bill Pritchard lived up to his reputation as a brilliant orator with an address on the historical background of the Winnipeg fight for freedom. To "thunderous applause," the *Strike Bulletin* reported, Pritchard pledged the support of the strikers' fellow workers in Vancouver: "If you are whipped we are whipped. If you go down we will go down in the same boat. But if you are to be victorious we must help you. And we will!"

Now, in the midst of his all-consuming involvement in the public cause, Ivens himself suffered a private setback. After a year "without station," he applied to the Manitoba Methodist Conference for an extension of his leave of absence. He was refused and told he must accept a regular pastorate. A "motion of location" was then placed before the Conference, proposing in effect that Ivens was no longer performing his ministerial duties satisfactorily, although the document added that no reflection was thereby intended on his life and character. After much controversy the motion was carried, and William Ivens was removed from the roster of Methodist ministers, his ordination revoked.

Ivens reported the news in a sardonic headline: "Another honor — Wm. Ivens has been locked out of the Methodist Church!" and launched an appeal. In response, a flood of petitions and letters from Methodists to their Conference demanded that Ivens be allowed to continue his ministry to working people. As Reverend John A. Haw pleaded, on trial was the commitment of the Methodist Church to the principles it claimed to hold, "for here is the first case of a minister risking his position to carry the Gospel to a class who, owing to a social position, are disinherited and despoiled."

Nevertheless, the appeal was heard and denied on June 19, a final blow. Two days earlier Ivens had been arrested and imprisoned in the round-up of labour agitators. More than one Methodist felt, as did the

Reverend W. H. Hinks of St. Paul's, that Ivens had been expelled from his church not for any failings as a Christian minister but for his support of the OBU and the strike.

In Defence of Truth and Justice

The police descended on the Ivens home in the early hours of Tuesday, June 17, and hustled the offending preacher and editor off to the central police station, and then, with the other arrested suspects, drove him out to Stony Mountain Penitentiary, leaving behind a devastated household. The accused, said a police report, "protested" against his detention — and Ivens was to protest even more dramatically at his trial. "Would you protest," he would exclaim to the packed courtroom,

> if you were arrested in the middle of the night? If the police came into your wife's bedroom and placed your babies on the hard floor, while they searched under the mattress of the cot to find seditious literature? Would you protest such actions?

Bail was posted for the jailed leaders in the early hours of Thursday, June 19, and a procession of union men made its way through the prairie night to the penitentiary on the outskirts of the city. They forced the reluctant guards to get the warden out of bed in order to complete the necessary formalities, and triumphantly carried away their liberated comrades. To all intents and purposes, however, the strike was effectively broken, and one week later the Strike Committee issued its formal notice of surrender.

Ivens returned to the editor's desk at the *Western Labor News*, technically no longer an ordained minister, but more determined than ever not to be diverted from his chosen spiritual path. Once again from his columns his Old Testament indignation thundered as loudly as before, and the Labor Church summoned its followers to support the ten men martyred in the cause of freedom and justice.

The city banned outdoor meetings, trying to head off further disturbances, but on the Sunday after the strikers' capitulation a crowd of the faithful gathered in a grassy field in Elmwood, just outside the city limits proper. Jesus's Sermon on the Mount was the lesson: "Blessed are ye

71

when men shall revile you, and persecute you, and shall say all manner of evil against you falsely, for my sake." A shabbily dressed man with a soft Scottish burr offered a prayer, that the eyes of the oppressors might be opened, through God's grace, and that working people be granted the courage to stand by their brothers; and Ivens, from the pulpit, pleaded the cause of the imprisoned aliens, "the strangers within our gates." His stirring voice rang out with evangelical zeal, offering the comfort of the Lord to the oppressed. "Seek ye first God's Kingdom," he exhorted the disheartened among his flock, "a kingdom of justice and love!" Jobs and better wages, he assured them, would certainly follow.

More trouble was brewing for the embattled pastor. Although he had fought heart and soul for labour's cause, and his remarkable ability both to sway public opinion and to generate funds remained indispensable, he was caught now between the moderate national Trades and Labor Congress and Bob Russell's militant One Big Union in their struggle for control of the labour movement in Winnipeg. The *Western Labor News* was sponsored by the local Trades and Labor Council, but its editor was greatly drawn to the OBU's vision of a worldwide community of working people. William Ivens was never one to put prudence before conviction, and the newspaper reflected his bias.

The conflict came to a head in August, just as the preliminary hearings for the accused strike leaders began. The OBU attempted to seize control of the Winnipeg Trades and Labor Council and, partly succeeding, set up its own Central Trades Council. There were now two rival labour groups, moderates in one and radicals in the other, their offices located in the same Labor Temple. Maneuvering grimly for mastery, the Trades and Labor Council appointed a press committee to supervise the *Western Labor News*, and decided to let Ivens keep his job as editor, provided he observed the council line. But even as Ivens had apparently made his peace with his sponsors and was involved in his own legal difficulties, the copy that had been prepared for the August 8 issue — presumably at the editor's direction — turned up at the printing office with the announcement that this publication was now sympathetic to the OBU. Ivens was summarily fired.

Meanwhile, as labour men fought each other, legal proceedings against the strike leaders took their course. The accused, Ivens among them, were arraigned, committed for trial at the fall assizes, and bail denied, sent back to prison once again to await their day in court. Ivens's charismatic hold on the emotions of the public proved as strong as ever. A nationwide outcry erupted, to the consternation of the authorities, and in Winnipeg the Labor Church once again provided the rallying-point for protest.

On August 22 five thousand church members and their supporters gathered in the Convention Hall of the Board of Trade building to demand justice and freedom for their absent leader and his friends. An orchestra and a choir led the congregation in the singing of a labour hymn; there was a prayer by James Woodsworth and an address by James Grant of the Soldiers' and Sailors' Labor Party. As the featured speaker Salem Bland hailed his former student as truly in the apostolic succession, martyred in the tradition of Christ's disciples; the Labor Church, he said, insisted on universal brotherhood, as Jesus did, and would soon surpass both Protestantism and Roman Catholicism.

An even more extravagant reception greeted the strike leaders when they were once again set free in September. Ivens was the first to walk out of the Vaughan Street jail, to the cheers of fifteen thousand people, the *Western Labor News* reported, and they carried him on their shoulders around the jailhouse courtyard, chorusing "For He's a Jolly Good Fellow." One by one the remaining leaders emerged, and the crowd roared its satisfaction; then a procession of cars carried the released men down Vaughan Street to Portage Avenue and on to George and Helen Armstrong's home on Edmonton Street. There were more speeches, and an elated William Ivens delighted his supporters with a small, impudent joke: "I've gained eight pounds, and I think I'll go out and rob a bank to get back, they've treated us so well."

On the following days there were still more speeches by all the strike leaders to various labour groups and assemblies, and on Sunday two thousand people came to a rally in Victoria Park. Among others, Ivens spoke, the eighth time he had addressed an audience that day. And in north Winnipeg, where he had been rejected a few years earlier by the McDougall Methodist Church, the West Kildonan branch of the Labor Church offered a resolution of rejoicing, faith, and sound labour conviction:

We the members . . . and citizens of this district here assembled express our great joy at the presence of Mr. Ivens amongst us again, after his outrageous detention in jail, and we hereby affirm our unshaken confidence and trust in him. We also pray God that he may continue to expose and uproot the evils of social oppression and injustice, believing that righteousness exalteth a nation and that the unrest in the country is caused by injustice. We look forward to the near future when industrial warfare shall cease and give place to peace and goodwill and that even the poor worker shall enjoy life, liberty and happiness.

Despite the ban on engaging in further agitation, the ten accused strike leaders fanned out across the country, to plead their cause and raise money for the defence fund wherever they found a sympathetic audience. His persuasive oratory at a premium, Ivens boarded a train for eastern Canada toward the end of September, and everywhere he was preceded by his lurid reputation as a Red, a dangerous rabble-rouser, a traitor. The *Winnipeg Tribune* called him "the chief orator of the strikers," the *Winnipeg Telegram* mocked him as "Ivens the Terrible," and a Montreal paper reported that the Reverend William Ivens had predicted the imminent takeover of all Canadian cities by a Soviet government.

In Sarnia, Ontario, irate citizens mounted a campaign against his visit, with advertisements in newspapers and on posters, and mass rallies to demand that he keep away. Sentinels were stationed at the approaches to the town, Ivens reported in a letter to the *Western Labor News*, but he managed to walk off the ferry and past the watchers undetected, he said, "because I looked like neither a preacher nor a Bolshevik." Cautious and conservative, the Sarnia Trades Council initially would not endorse the Ivens appeal; no assembly hall would rent to Ivens supporters, and an anti-Ivens rally was scheduled in the park. Despite the difficulties, a tumultuous meeting finally took place at the Boilermakers' Union hall, and the celebrated labour orator from Winnipeg more than fulfilled his listeners' expectations, in a dramatic triumph over would-be saboteurs. He reported the event to the *Western Labor News*:

Some put out the lights, others got them on again. Then the wires were cut and the hydro men rushed to reconnect them. Meanwhile, I talked in the pitch darkness, until one fellow brought his automobile headlight in. It was a wonderful meeting. As I left the hall, a big group of the boys formed a body guard and marched me through the surging crowd on the street outside. Policemen cleared the way to let us through, while the crowd cheered.

Convinced, Sarnia workers formed a defence committee and sent their contribution to the trial fund.

Ivens continued on his tight and crowded schedule, visiting London, Brantford, Hamilton, Niagara Falls, and an exhausting number of other locations, often delivering three or four talks a day, encouraging the formation of local support groups, exercising all his oratorical skills to inspire the generosity of his audience. When he reached Toronto he found that a directive had come from Ottawa that he was not to be granted permission to hold public meetings anywhere in the city. His scheduled appearance was cancelled, although the advertisements indicated he would speak on the ostensibly nonpolitical topic of "Temperance." Nevertheless the Toronto Trades Council did organize a defence committee, and canvassed its members to donate "One Day's Pay for Winnipeg."

By the time Ivens reached Winnipeg again on November 4, he had delivered some sixty speeches in six weeks, and his mellifluous speaking voice was harsh and strained. However, when his train pulled into the station, another expectant public several thousand strong was waiting for him at the Board of Trade auditorium, and as the *Western Labor News* reported, he "held the breathless attention of his audience" during the entire course of another inspiring address, and was roundly applauded. Then at last he was allowed to go home.

Ivens was now forty-one. His job at the *Western Labor News* was gone, and while the flourishing Labor Church had expanded to nine district branches, all eager for the involvement of the founder, there was no prospect of income there for the Ivens family. Louisa Ivens had stood by her husband throughout his quarrel with the Methodist Church, his vilification by the mainstream press, his endless, all-consuming preoccupation with the Labor Church, his devotion to the strikers' struggle. Now, it seemed to their friends, the disgrace of his arrest and imprisonment and all the publicity surrounding the case were "almost a death-blow to her." She was not a socialist, and had little interest in the battles that excited her husband, and she pleaded with him to obey the law, to perceive that his obligations to others were sufficiently discharged, to consider his family, now increased by one. At the height of that summer's turmoil, Louisa Ivens had given birth to their second son, Louis William.

At this point William Ivens's career was about to take a further turn. Although the striking unions had gained little or no immediate benefit from their long hold-out, the event had made an enormous impact on public opinion, both for and against, and the political dimension of labour's concerns had become clear. The struggle, it appeared, must now move into the political arena; labour must elect its own representatives to government office. Ivens himself had said so, in a *Western Labor News* article on July 4. Pointing out that the strike leaders had fought in vain against the false charge of fomenting revolution, because of the "terror and obsession of those who face a revolution," he predicted that "our solution lies in the realm of political evolution and not in political revolution."

While Ivens was campaigning in eastern Canada, a nominating committee of labour people from various groupings came together to prepare a slate for the forthcoming civic elections. There were two nominations for mayor: S. J. Farmer and William Ivens, "the man who held labour together." The choice went to Ivens, but when he was notified of the decision, he sent his regrets in a telegram. He was not a property-owner, he explained, since his house was in his wife's name, and therefore he could not be placed on the voter's list; indeed, he said, his role in the strike might prove detrimental to "the cause we all have at heart." He added, however, that he would agree to a nomination for a provincial or a federal seat.

Trial and Sentence

Shortly after Ivens's return to Winnipeg from the East, the fall assizes opened, with Bob Russell's case first on the docket. As was to be expected, the two-year sentence passed by Judge Metcalfe on the OBU leader, in December, provoked furious protests across the country; and Ivens led the chorus of condemnation, choosing to ignore the danger of further incriminating himself.

At the next meeting of the Labor Church, in the Columbia Theatre on the Sunday after Christmas, a newspaper reporter named Merle Manly and a sergeant of the RNWMP named Ronald Smyly were in the audience taking notes. They heard the preacher denounce the verdict against Russell as a "poisoned sentence" given by "a poisoned jury and a poisoned judge." (There was wild cheering, the police operative reported, when Mr. Ivens spoke.) Ivens said that the charge of seditious conspiracy was a farce and a travesty, and to make matters worse for himself he impugned the competence of the presiding magistrate: "If Tommy Metcalfe says a general strike is illegal he says so illegally, and has no law to prove his statement."

Ivens, the report continued, attacked the arbitrary amendment of the Criminal Code to allow the deportation of aliens without trial. "You call that British justice," he mocked, and he referred to Arthur Meighen, the prime minister, as "Artful Meighen." He said that before God Russell was an innocent man, that within Russell's mind there was "a full significance of the life of Christ," and within his breast "a realization of His teachings." If that conviction, said Ivens, amounted to "a bloody revolution or Bolshevism, or seditious conspiracy — very well." (A young man in one of the front rows of the hall, the reporter noted, rose to his feet and exclaimed, "Christ was a martyr, and so is Bob Russell!") Ivens said that he himself had dedicated his life to humanity. "I have done my duty as I saw it," he said, "and if I go to jail, I will come out again to do my duty as I see it." His declaration was duly noted.

In the new year, following Dixon's acquittal, the action against Woodsworth was stayed, and then the Crown proceeded with its case against the other accused strike leaders as a group. The trial, on the charge of seditious conspiracy, began in the Court of King's Bench before Judge Metcalfe on January 20. Ivens, like Heaps, Pritchard, and Queen, chose to appear in his own defense.

When the evidence against the incendiary preacher was presented, Manly and Smyly were summoned to testify as to what had taken place at the Labor Church following the sentencing of Bob Russell. Questioned by the Crown prosecutor, Manly produced a vivid account of Ivens's address, with the striking phrases about a poisoned judge and poisoned jury, but he also included Ivens's firm denial that he was guilty of sedition. "Though I may have said some harsh things about the judiciary and the government here," the pastor had explained to his congregation,

> I have never breathed defiance in the face of the state, or taught or written sedition. . . . I have always stood for parliamentary action, realizing both its weakness and its strength.

Ivens cross-examined the witness at great length, and suggested that the remarks about "Tommy" Metcalfe had been made in a spirit of "jocularity," but the judge rejected the notion. Highly offended by the slight to the dignity of the court, if not to his own person, Metcalfe cited Ivens for contempt. "I think it would be safer if you keep quiet," he told the accused, when Ivens asked to make a statement.

Chief Justice T. G. Mathers heard the contempt-of-court case, with Justices Prendergast and Galt. After a few days' delay, because the accused was appearing before Judge Metcalfe, and, as the chief justice pointed out, "could not be in two places at once," the testimony was scrutinized once more. Ivens was found guilty and bound over to keep the peace for three months. He rejoined his comrades in Metcalfe's court.

For ten weeks in the late winter and early spring of 1920 Winnipeg citizens packed the courtroom, avidly following the give-and-take of legal argument, and reports in the local newspapers were reprinted across the country and even internationally. In the case of the Reverend William Ivens there were few sensational revelations.

When the Mounted Police had searched the Ivens home, they had found, by their own account, nothing of much importance. The books on the shelves included Green's *Short History of the English People* and Edward Bellamy's *Looking Backward*. There were, said the police, newspaper clippings and headings for various speeches and articles, and copies of hymns for the Labor Church. One item, they said, "would appear to advocate revolution," and several might be said to advocate

"Bolshevism and revolution." There was something about the OBU and revolution, and there was a letter from A. E. Smith, enclosing a subscription order to the *Western Labor News*, with a payment of $1.50 and a comment about the subscriber: "This man is a red socialist, and I hope some day you will be as 'red' as he is."

At the office of the *Western Labor News*, in the Chamber of Commerce building, the Mounties had found the usual assortment of routine business communications, subscription orders, and articles for publication. A letter to Ivens from a Mrs. J. B. Parks, dated June 1918, concerned the conscription of her sons; and one from Mrs. Rose Henderson of Montreal, addressed to "Dear Friend Russell" rather than to Ivens, enclosed a copy of a much-discussed diagram of a soviet administration that Lenin was said to have followed, with Mrs. Henderson's painstaking instructions on how to make use of this treasure. "I have had the enclosed tucked away for the past 9 years," she wrote, "awaiting the day which I knew was coming," and she asked to have it returned, "on pain of death," because "Gold cannot buy it." There was also an October 1918 letter from Toronto, advising Ivens of a raid in that city, and about seizures and arrests, and warning him to destroy all incriminating material because a similar assault might occur in Winnipeg.

To this miscellany the RNWMP added an account of Ivens's parentage and the possibly surprising information that the accused's brothers had served their country loyally. There was also the testimony of RNWMP Sergeant Reames that he had been present under cover at many meetings of the Labor Church, and had heard the accused hold forth on the League of Nations, on the OBU, and on the immorality of the profit system, and that Mr. Ivens had said that revolution was coming, but also that he himself was against bloodshed. On the whole, it was the police agent's opinion that Mr. Ivens was genuinely a pacifist and most sincere, and that much of what he said was useful, but — considering the nature of his audience — ill-advised.

William Ivens was, in fact, a rather improbable perpetrator of "sedition," the charge on which all the strike leaders were arrested, although his melodramatic editorials and his flamboyant leadership of the Labor Church had made him the obvious target of establishment suspicion. Utterly devoted to the cause for which his labour friends and colleagues

fought, the expelled Methodist preacher was no Marxist. He had neither the intellectual humanism of Dixon nor the assertive class-consciousness of Russell. Unlike the theological self-searching of
Woodsworth, his faith was basic and direct, and unlike Pritchard, he
seems to have had little interest in socialist theory. In an almost simplis-
tic Christian fashion, his mission was to the poor and downtrodden,
and in that capacity he responded whole-heartedly to the radical
appeal. Defining his politics before the court, he declared himself a
member of the moderate Dominion Labor Party, espousing belief in
political evolution, not revolution, in the British way of gradual, legislated change.

But the Crown hammered home the point that the defendants as a
group had incriminated themselves in word and deed, that violent revolution was what they intended. Crown Prosecutor A. J. Andrews was
especially contemptuous of the Labor Church, calling it "merely a cam-
ouflage for the preaching of sedition and for fanning the flames of
unrest," and sneering that its teaching was designed "to make you forget everything you were ever taught at your mother's knee."

Ivens was the first of the defendants to present his final appeal to the
jury, and his ringing defence fulfilled the expectations of the men and
women who had come to hear the celebrated preacher of brotherhood
and love. (Noting his "very bulky notes," the *Telegram* reporter commented that "It looks like a very long address.") For two-and-a-half
days, including evening sessions as well as morning and afternoon,
Ivens reiterated his protestations, insisting that the evidence against
him was taken out of context, extolling the ideal of pacifism, celebrating the truth of the Labor Church. "It will not be many years," he
prophesied, "before the philosophy of the pacifist seizes the world and
we become a race of idealists"; and Labor Churches, he insisted, would
spread all over the country with the labour movement.

Refuting the charges of the prosecution, pointing a finger at the
injustice and inhumanity with which he and his fellow prisoners had
been treated, he offered his listeners his utter sincerity, his absolute
faith in the divinely sanctioned truth of labour's cause — even as he
obliquely suggested a certain distance between himself and the people
who actually organized the strike. "I was asked to take over the editorship of the *Western Labor News*," he explained, "and I did it to make a

living." He had come to labour's camp, he implied, along a path of spiritual enlightenment, as a moral imperative:

> I am a different Ivens since 1916. Why am I supporting Labor today? I do these things from a sense of duty, a sense of right. As the editor of the Labor Paper, I mixed with the Trades Council and I got my first glimpse of the Labor movement and its terrible struggle. . . . Gentlemen, did I believe the strike was seditious I would have opposed it, but I did not believe it was wrong and I supported it. . . . I never sought to destroy faith in God.

As a pacifist who had dedicated his life to humanity, Ivens said, he was opposed to force of any kind. The lesson of history, he said, was that the problems of industrial unrest could never be solved by violent means, but rather by the ballot, and, according to the *Telegram*, "He said that Labor and capital never would get together until the laborer kept all that he produced and the capitalist kept all that he produced." In his own direct fashion, the pastor affirmed the simple justice of the economic theories debated by his socialist comrades.

By the evening of the second day of his address Ivens was exhausted. His wife and children were ill, the *Telegram* noted, and he had been under extreme pressure, and Judge Metcalfe compassionately permitted the defendant to rest at home the next day. Then he returned to complete his appeal, stressing once again his ethical integrity:

> Once I make up my mind that a thing is right, I will stick by it and will take condemnation from you or anybody else. . . . If you say I am guilty I am prepared to go to the penitentiary. I will ask the people outside to look after my wife and children and I will pay the price, because I will stand for my ideals. . . . My fate is in your hands, [but] my destiny is in the hands of the Almighty and myself.

He asked the jury to speak the first two words he himself had spoken in the courtroom, "Not guilty."

There was a tense, expectant crowd waiting at the Law Courts building on March 27, when the jury indicated it was ready to bring in its verdict. Every seat in the courtroom was taken, and people packed the corridor and spilled out into the street. To quell any possible demonstration, two dozen Mounties were stationed in the building.

As the foreman began to announce the decision, word flashed out into the corridor that all the accused had been declared "not guilty." The crowd broke into jubilant cheers and rushed for the courtroom doors, but was blocked by the bailiffs and the deputy sheriff. In the fracas, said the RNWMP report, one man was hit on the head with a baton by the deputy sheriff and badly cut. "It was said," the report added, "that the man struck the deputy."

Then the actual verdict became clear: only A. A. Heaps was found not guilty, and Roger Bray was guilty only of common nuisance, but all the rest, including the pastor of the Labor Church, were guilty both of common nuisance and of seditious conspiracy. A groan arose from the spectators with each successive pronouncement, and several women began to weep. So hostile did the crowd become, the police report continued, "that the jury men had to be taken from the court house by a private entrance at the back." The police cleared the corridors, but the angry throng continued to mill about outside, and rushed forward again as the prisoners emerged to be taken away. They stopped short at the sight of the police guard, said the report, and "contented themselves by cheering for the prisoners and booing the Police."

Metcalfe pronounced sentence on 6 April, beginning with Ivens. Asked if he had anything to say, Ivens replied that he did not. Said the *Free Press*, he "took his [one-year] sentence calmly and walked out of the court in a most unconcerned manner."

Where Russell was required to serve his two-year sentence in the Stony Mountain penitentiary, the six now convicted were held in the relative freedom of the prison farm. Working outdoors in each other's company, and often under the supervision of sympathetic guards, the men were able to receive frequent visits from family and friends, visits which occasionally began to resemble a holiday outing — at least, to the uninvolved onlooker. On Easter Sunday, services were held in the prison chapel; Ivens led the prayers and offered a short address, and the choir of the Central Labor Church came out to provide the music. "Truly it was a marvellous service," the *Western Labor News* informed its readers: "One has heard the Central Choir sing to packed audiences at the Columbia Theatre and at the Convention Hall to thousands of people, but never have they sung as they did to that handful of men in the confines of the jail."

Nevertheless, much as labour honoured and celebrated its martyrs, their imprisonment placed an enormous burden on their families. For Louisa Ivens, unwell and unable to conceal her humiliation and resentment, an extra measure of anguish was added. A scant two weeks after her husband was sent away, their infant son contracted diphtheria and rapidly became very ill. The father was allowed out of prison for a brief visit, accompanied by a guard, but a day later the baby died.

Private grief now became a public occasion, once again preempting the family's needs, as labour supporters flocked to the funeral on a Sunday afternoon in a spontaneous demonstration of protest against the recent verdict. "Long before the hour of the funeral," said the *Western Labor News*, "without suggestion or prompting, thousands of workers gathered at the corner of Inkster Avenue and Main Street to accompany the mourners." Woodsworth conducted the services at the Ivens home, assuring the parents that they did not stand alone, and offering them the consolation of knowing that they were part of a great movement.

A column of veterans preceded the hearse, leading the funeral procession down Main Street toward city hall, where still more sympathizers waited. Along the route, men and women fell in line or silently paid their respects from the sidewalk, and the line of cars stretched for several blocks. At the graveside, Woodsworth spoke again briefly, the Children's Choir sang, and boys and girls from two Labor Church Sunday schools laid their flowers on the small coffin. Mr. Ivens, said the *Western Labor News*, "stood with bowed head, clasping the hand of his eldest boy, with the ever-present prison guard at his elbow."

The Death of the Labor Church

Ivens's declaration that labour's future lay in political evolution, not revolution, reflected a growing consensus in the several labour factions, that while the strike had failed, the latent labour power it had revealed must now be harnessed to a political vehicle. Provincial elections were called for June 1920, and after considerable wrangling the Dominion

Labor Party, the Socialist Party of Canada, the Social Democratic Party, and the Soldiers' and Sailors' Labor Party arrived at a loose agreement to coordinate their efforts, and in particular to head their unified slate with the names of labour's popular martyrs: Dixon, Ivens, Queen, Pritchard, Johns, Russell, Armstrong — all, except Dixon, now serving their prison sentences.

"Vote for the boys in jail," read election posters all over town, and people did, in unprecedented numbers. In the surplus from Dixon's enormous majority Ivens came in, and the other successful labourites included his friend, A. E. Smith, elected in Brandon. Once again, on July 11, Labor Church members gathered in Victoria Park, two thousand strong, to celebrate simultaneously the second anniversary of its founding and the victory at the polls. Dixon, Smith, and others spoke, Ivens sent an emotional letter from his jail cell, and the stock of the strike leaders soared higher than ever. Dixon's new, more broadly based Independent Labor Party then came into being, and Ivens, still serving his sentence, indicated his support.

Ivens and his colleagues at the prison farm were released on March 1, 1921, and the group was swept up in a jubilant welcome by the Labor Church. The next day, Sunday, there were mass meetings of the church both in the afternoon and in the evening and again on the following Sunday. Dixon was again one of the guest speakers, and Ivens, taking the pulpit, electrified his flock once more. With great fanfare, labour's jailbird champions took their seats in the Manitoba legislature. For William Ivens, this was the beginning of a fifteen-year career in elective office.

The Labor Church, with an ambitious educational program and several faltering local congregations, needed help, but Ivens's new responsibilities in the legislature left him little time for church administrative chores. He invited Woodsworth to return from British Columbia and take the post of secretary, and relieved of the routine church tasks, he continued to preach at its Sunday meetings and to campaign for its support. Woodsworth served as secretary for about half a year, and then, elected to the House of Commons on the Independent Labor Party ticket, went off to Ottawa to begin his long and honoured career on the national political scene.

By the time of Ivens's return to public life, however, the Labor

Church had already lost something of its initial expansive energy. It had been conceived at a moment of high drama in the life of Winnipeg's work force, but in the weary aftermath of the strike, when the comradely struggle had apparently achieved nothing, membership began to dwindle. One by one the branch units disbanded, until only the central church remained.

For all the high-minded integrity of its Christian socialism, there were difficulties for ordinary followers in the teaching that the Labor Church sought to embody. How could the customary church observances celebrating the comforting grandeur of God be accommodated to the cold "scientific" realities of Marxist economics? Woodsworth's *First History of the Labor Church* tells of a small but perplexing dilemma in the home of one Labor Church member: what words could be spoken as grace before meals? If labour economics taught that an unjust distribution of wealth deprived some and rewarded others, what could be said for the bounty on this family's table, and to whom — or to what — should thanks be given? Woodsworth's own solution was to refer to "the efforts of our brothers and sisters the world over," and to acknowledge "our share in the world's work and the world's struggles," but for most people an ideologically correct formula such as this rather lacked emotional sustenance.

Devoted to the task of bringing enlightenment to the deprived working class, the Labor Church provided Sunday schools to instruct the children, and organized adult education courses in history, economics, religion, and public speaking, but an awkward dislocation between the spiritual and the earthly marked each earnest curriculum. Could a Labor Church Sunday-school teacher convey the practical Marxist realities of work and wages through the figure of Jesus the carpenter? Could a most progressive unit on "sex instruction" be followed by a discussion of "Bodies — Temples of the Holy Spirit"?

Under Woodsworth's direction labour members of the legislature had been invited to discuss current affairs at Labor Church services, university professors had lectured on topics ranging from evolution to free trade, and Woodsworth himself had conducted weekly study sessions on "Industrial History and Economics." The church continued for some time to sponsor a variety of activities, including young people's and women's clubs, musical groups and purely social and recreational functions. A "Labor University" in 1923, for example, offered a course in "Current Social and Economic Evolution," including sections on "Surplus Value . . . The Socialist Position . . . International Money . . . Inherent Weakness of Capitalism . . . The Class War. . . ."

Yielding more and more to the secular, the church opened its pulpit to "rationalists" and "free thinkers," such as Winnipeg's resident atheist, Marshall J. Gauvin. The central church continued to operate for a few years, as smaller units disappeared. In what seems to have been the last posted church notice, for the services on Sunday, March 15, 1925, both Christian content and political urgency have apparently all but disappeared from the subjects offered for discussion: "Great Paintings of the World," "The Plays of Shakespeare," "The Real Robbie Burns," and "What the Wheat Pool Can Do."

Ivens himself, in his sermon notes and in his public pronouncements, had insisted again and again that a belief in God was the driving force of socialism, that the emancipation of the masses must begin with the rebirth of truth within the soul of the believer. Indeed the Reverend A .E. Smith, speaking in July 1920, at the first anniversary service of the Labor Church, had asked rhetorically, "Was Christ a Communist?" Without a doubt he was, the former Methodist minister believed.

By and large, however, most of the reformers and the labour activists who found in Ivens's following a ready vehicle for their purposes had no interest in the other-worldly and the transcendental. Sceptical and thoroughly secular, their creed was self-help, not reliance on a remote and unproven divinity.

The Reverend Smith took the next step in his ideological journey and joined the newly created Communist party, and labour politicians of the moderate left, now involved in the stratagems of government on every level, found the Labor Church no longer useful. Ivens himself, his florid rhetoric still effective, now reached a wider audience from the floor of the legislature, and in the gap between Christian belief and left-wing activism, secular and agnostic, the brief life of his church came to an end.

The Voice of the People

Ivens had been re-elected to the provincial legislature in 1922, but he had not been re-appointed to the editorship of the *Western Labor News*, which was losing ground to the competing *OBU Bulletin* and eventually ceased publication. With no other income than the fifteen-hundred-dollar stipend of an MLA, he took a practical step to provide for his family and registered for a correspondence course with the Palmer Chiropractic School in Davenport, Iowa. In 1925 he duly received his diploma as a certified Doctor of Chiropractic and set up an office in the Somerset Building, complete with an impressive letterhead bearing his portrait: "William Ivens, M.A., B.D., D.C. (M.L.A.), Chiropractor, Neuro Vascular Meter Service." Offering treatment for a variety of aches and pains, he indicated that he was available during morning and evening hours — that is, when the legislature was not in session, or when the demands of his party and his constituents permitted. Patients could also be accommodated in the evenings at his home, where Louisa was frequently pressed into service as receptionist, as the patient waited for the doctor to return from some political skirmish.

Modestly successful, he acquired a pleasant summer cottage at Clear Lake, in Manitoba's Riding Mountain National Park, and with unflagging enterprise proceeded to advertise it as a rental property to "particular people only, during July and August. Terms: one week, $25 . . . two months, $175. Cash in advance." He called it "Ukanrest," the "Delightful Summer Home of William and Louisa Ivens," and his copy detailed its attractions: from its "Artistic stone chimney" and "Splendid cookstove," to the wild creatures in the park, and the golf course, the dance hall, and the bakery and butcher shops in the townsite. A solicitous as well as a most exacting landlord, Ivens appealed to his "friends" to keep the place spotlessly clean — "Thus we can all enjoy it equally. You understand!" — and he also worried about his prospective tenants' comfort, advising them, "Take with you: eats; plenty of warm bedding; pillow slips; towels; soap; matches; etc."

More than ever politics now became his central preoccupation. A stalwart of the Independent Labor Party, he remained intensely loyal to his comrades, to the principles which his party espoused, and to the vision of a society transformed in the spirit of true Christianity. He cast his vote in the legislature on issue after issue in favour of what he deemed just and right, and occupied the public eye, an unfailing source of colourful copy for the newspapers, year after year.

When John Bracken became the premier of Manitoba in 1922, he instituted enough progressive legislation, pressured by the labour group, to keep popular support, and in the 1927 election he won a clear majority, with twenty-nine seats. The ILP caucus went down from five seats to three, but a loyal following returned Ivens, Queen, and Farmer. Diminished but still a powerful voice in debate, the ILP group joined battle with their political foes on the issue of allowing private development of the hydroelectric power site at Seven Sisters Falls, and in 1932 on the replacement of the Provincial Savings Bank by the chartered banks — and once again Ivens roared his party's outrage at the usurping of a public institution by the private banking monopoly.

Throughout his party's fluctuating fortunes, the former preacher's legendary ability to mesmerize an audience won the admiration even of his opponents. Douglas Campbell, later the Liberal premier of Manitoba, told of listening to Ivens speak for seven hours, in his "tremendous voice which reverberated all over the chamber." It was said of Ivens that he could hold forth on a given subject for as long as was necessary, without deviating from the point and without putting his listeners to sleep, and the ILP availed itself of his marathon services on more than one occasion.

For all his high-minded seriousness, he was not above enjoying his own prowess at the art of the filibuster. Many years later he told a group of well-wishers of one occasion when the party was determined to forestall a piece of legislation. He had started to speak at midnight, "and my job was to hold the floor until eight o'clock. And I held it, and then some. Then I went home to have a sleep so as to come back for session number two. I often wondered if they cut down on speeches after that. I don't blame them."

In 1933, with the unity of the Independent Labor Party beginning to dissolve and the West now sunk in the deep trough of the Great Depression, the Co-operative Commonwealth Federation came into being, a step toward James Woodsworth's vision of a united community of rural and urban working people. At first the ILP resisted submerging its identity in the untried CCF, although much of the new party's agenda coincided closely with ILP policies, but at a 1936 convention an agreement was reached for a coalition, to be known as the ILP-CCF.

The newly amalgamated party entered the Manitoba elections that year with a fourteen-point platform advocating a number of the humanitarian measures Ivens had championed. Remarkably, Fred Dixon's old crony Lewis St. George Stubbs topped the polls, running this time as an independent. He had been defeated in a 1933 federal election as a labour candidate. Seven ILP-CCF candidates were successful, including Farmer, Queen, and Marcus Hyman, but William Ivens went down to defeat, never to hold elected office again.

A Voice Unheard

The veteran warrior did not lay down his arms. He continued to pour out articles on subjects close to his heart, extolling the spiritual validity of his party's policies or finding support for its principles in the discoveries of modern science. He submitted his work to CCF publications and other journals across Canada, without a great deal of success, but he continued with unabated zeal. His son, Milton, had qualified as a physician and was practicing in the United States. World War II broke out in September 1939, confounding the hopes and dreams of dedicated pacifists like James Woodsworth and William Ivens; and in November of that year, Louisa Ivens died at the age of fifty-eight, a personal sorrow at a time of public devastation.

Unable to make a place for himself again in Manitoba politics, Ivens turned his attention to the neighbouring area of Kenora-Fort Frances-Rainy River, in northern Ontario, where the CCF presence was minimal, and entered, again unsuccessfully, the 1940 federal race. Then, with an eye, perhaps, to the future, he set about organizing CCF supporters in the provincial constituencies of Kenora and Fort Frances. He coaxed "clubs" of party adherents into being, and out of his own pocket — because, as he said, "there was no one to raise a dollar" — he brought in organizational material and party literature. Ontario provincial elections were called in 1943, and Ivens's efforts helped elect the CCF candidate. William Ivens was duly invited to the victory celebration, and as he had every reason to expect, he was named the constituency's candidate in the coming federal elections.

There was little or no money available for a campaign, and almost no response from the national CCF headquarters or from the Ontario or Manitoba offices. Once again Ivens took matters into his own hands. He set up a "literature committee" consisting of himself and two others, and with their agreement had several leaflets of his own composition run off on the mimeograph machine in the Fort Frances constituency office. He wrote newsletters for the Kenora newspaper and tried to find money for reprints to be mailed to voters. He mailed a copy of his own pamphlet, *Canada — Whither Bound?*, to the party's new leader, M. J. Coldwell, and the literature committee agreed to have it distributed, if Ivens agreed to foot the bill. When the Ontario provincial office sent in a few copies of an information sheet on the CCF, he prevailed upon Lloyd Stinson in Winnipeg to reprint enough for a mailing in Kenora.

To Ivens's chagrin, there were complaints about his methods from the constituency to the national office, and demands that his candidacy be revoked; and a polite but emphatic rebuke arrived from the party's national secretary, David Lewis: the election material that Ivens had issued in the CCF name, Lewis wrote, had not been cleared with "some responsible body of the party," violating a cardinal principle of party organization. Moreover, Lewis said, it had been the party experience that leaflets crowded with reading matter were of little value. Ivens answered at length, bitterly protesting his good intentions. When he asked his constituency office what had been done about his material, he was told that a considerable amount was still available, undistributed.

William Ivens did not win a seat in the 1945 federal election. New men had taken their places in the labour ranks, their procedures and their style quite different from the freewheeling exuberance of earlier days, and his brand of expansive political evangelism no longer seemed to command attention.

The Somerset building office had closed in 1940. Ivens had plunged into a campaign to build a chiropractic hospital adjacent to his correspondence college in Davenport, Ohio, and by 1942 he could report that he had raised the sum of forty-nine thousand dollars. A careful letter from the secretary-treasurer of the Chiropractors' Association in Davenport explained that the amount was not nearly enough and it would be difficult to raise more, that locating a hospital near the school was inadvisable, and that "for the time being no action should be taken." Five years later, in 1947, a factory owner in Massachusetts wrote Mr. Ivens to ask how the building was getting on.

Always an indefatigable writer, Ivens offered an article in 1944 to the *Canadian Forum*; the assistant editor, Alan Creighton, returned it, pointing out that the subject had already been covered in the journal's most recent edition. A year later Ivens submitted another piece; Creighton thanked him, but regretted that it was "rather too general in tone for us." Ivens sent party leader Coldwell a manuscript entitled "The Great Crusade"; after some delay, David Lewis answered, saying that it would not make a good pamphlet: it dealt with too many points, none of them adequately, and was too involved and too diffuse to engage the average Canadian elector.

Ivens tried to interest the *Saskatchewan Commonwealth* in forming a Fabian Society in Canada, on the pattern of the renowned British organization; nothing came of the suggestion. He sent the *Commonwealth* a set of six articles on the failure of the CCF to enlist the support of farmers; the assistant editor responded with a tactful rejection, maintaining that the party did indeed have farm support. Ivens wrote to CCF members of parliament, offering ideas for pamphlets and leaflets. A "Dear Bill" letter from the MP for Mackenzie, B.C., thanked him, pointed out the cost of printing, and gently suggested that "probably you have tried to get too much material on each sheet." A letter to his son in 1946, responding to Milton's dismay at the rift between the Allies and their former ally, Russia, developed into a tangled essay on the war, its personalities, its excesses, and the nature of democratic socialism as distinct from totalitarian socialism. In 1952 he sent Coldwell a disapproving analysis of the party's move to replace the Regina Manifesto with a blander declaration, and he addressed the editor of the *Commonwealth* on the same subject. The party proceeded as planned, and the Winnipeg Declaration was passed, in 1956.

On May 31, 1953, a testimonial dinner honouring William Ivens on the occasion of his seventy-fifth birthday was held at the Marlborough Hotel in Winnipeg. The party notables were all there, or sent congratulatory telegrams, and the speeches were mellow with anecdotes of the glory days of labour victories. Various representatives offered congratulations, Alderman John Blumberg presented a gift and told stories about old-time comrades, Stanley Knowles traced the career of the honoured guest item by item, in full, painstaking detail, and there was a program of musical selections. Rising at last to speak, at a quarter past nine, Ivens could only reassure his long-suffering friends that he would not burden them with the two-hour oration he had prepared. He did allow himself to boast a little about his past performance, and to reaffirm once again the sturdy faith he had kept undiminished: "The future is ours, we're on the highway!" The proceedings were recorded, but by some obscure irony the tape ran out before the man being honoured had completed his remarks.

Like several of his comrades-at-arms, Ivens spent his last years in California; and he died in Chula Vista on June 20, 1958, just before his eightieth birthday. Reporting the death of the colourful politician from Manitoba's past, the *Free Press* quoted the words on his testimonial presentation: "an ardent champion of humanity, social justice, and world peace."

To Teach the Alphabet is to Inaugurate a Revolution

William Arthur Pritchard

West Coast Radicalism

Among the nine men who stood trial in the aftermath of the Winnipeg General Strike, William Pritchard had no direct involvement at all in the planning and management of the action. A member of the Vancouver Trades and Labor Council, with a well-deserved reputation as a firebrand orator, he had been thoroughly occupied that spring and early summer with the organization of the One Big Union on the west coast. The OBU adopted its constitution at a meeting in Calgary on June 4, some three weeks after the Winnipeg strike was called, and Pritchard arrived in Winnipeg only on June 10, largely to see what was going on. In the early morning of June 17, when arrest warrants for the alleged strike leaders were being executed, he had already left the city for Vancouver, having attended by invitation a number of Strike Committee sessions, and spoken at several public meetings in Victoria Park.

As an organizer for the aggressive OBU, Pritchard was perceived by alarmed authorities to be something more dangerous than merely an interfering agitator from another province. The OBU movement began in western Canada rather than in the East, out of the significantly more belligerent character of western labour, and nowhere was the spirit more radical than among the tough, militant unionists of the Pacific coast. Given the ultimate OBU goal of uniting the entire labour force into a single instrument of economic power, the appearance in Winnipeg of a known radical from British Columbia may well have been taken as final proof that a Canada-wide insurrection had begun, a violent revolution like the recent and unprecedented annihilation of the traditional rulers of czarist Russia. Such misreading aside, the radicalism of British Columbia throws into sharp relief the ideological tensions in the events of Winnipeg in 1919, and Pritchard's own theoretical absolutism further illuminates the range of dissent within the group of strike activists.

In the last two decades of the nineteenth century a great number of immigrants from Great Britain had arrived on the west coast, among them Pritchard's own father, James. English, Scots, and Welsh, many of them had been members of trade unions and radical political parties, and they had brought with them ideas generated by the British labour movement. A succession of left-wing newspapers published in British Columbia spread socialist thought and promoted unionism, and from Winnipeg Puttee's *The Voice* circulated widely. Unions were established in a number of Pacific area industries, and as early as 1882 there were union-supported candidates for public office.

Immigration of a different sort, from across the Pacific, introduced a disruptive factor into the development of the labour movement and the process of unionization. The feverishly expanding west coast economy demanded cheap labour, and Canadian laws were relaxed to permit the influx of thousands of men from the teeming destitution of Asia, to drive the railway through the mountains, to dredge the rich coal fields of the interior and the Island, to log the towering forests and harvest the ocean's abundance of fish. Incomprehensible and visibly different in appearance and in customs, these strangers seemed to undercut and displace white workers, who saw the brown-skinned interlopers as the enemy, rather than the exploitive employers. An insidious racism persisted for years in the west coast union movement, often defended as simple self-protection, and denied by union members and leaders alike — as, indeed, racial tensions of a different sort marked the labour movement elsewhere in Canada.

Isolated from the rest of Canada by the Rocky Mountains, even after the CPR was completed, the west coast province developed closer ties with the American states to the south, and its workers found a ready affinity with their counterparts across the border. Miners and loggers sought work on either side of the boundary, and a steady stream of left-wing American ideas flowed into British Columbia, carried by itinerant workers, by hard-driving union organizers, and by American books, pamphlets, and papers.

By the late nineteenth century a major rift had become evident among left-wing thinkers concerning the relationship between unions and political activism. In the United States the union movement was dominated by the American Federation of Labor, the AFL, which held to the principle of craft unions, that is, separate unions for each of the various crafts in a given industry. Despite a growing insistence among many labour leaders that unions must cooperate in mutual support and must seek a political platform in order to advance their cause, the AFL maintained that its proper task was to pursue the immediate concerns of its own union members, basically the improvement of wages and working conditions. Essentially conservative in its philosophy, like the Canadian Congress of Labor, the AFL advocated reform rather than revolution. It rejected the Marxist idea of class conflict, urging instead the principle of cooperation between labour and employers, and it insisted that party politics had no place in union activity.

Ranged against the AFL's moderate reformism was the Socialist Labor Party, under the powerful control of a fiery revolutionary

Marxist, Daniel DeLeon. The SLP demanded the elimination of capitalism as such, charging that the AFL's brand of unionism, anti-socialist and non-political, served only to sustain a corrupt and oppressive system, and it mounted a belligerent campaign to replace AFL craft unions with its own politically-oriented locals. A Canadian branch of DeLeon's party, with a corresponding union local, was active in Vancouver at the turn of the century, and clashed hotly with the existing trade unions and the city's Trades and Labor Council.

Perhaps in keeping with the tough, physical nature of their work, British Columbia unionists tended to be a fighting lot. The Western Federation of Miners aggressively opposed the AFL and the capitalist system; and by the turn of the century, when the elder Pritchard arrived to join the labour wars, its organizers were already marshalling the coal miners of Vancouver Island and the British Columbia interior in a grim struggle with the mine owners to humanize their brutal working conditions and gain some job security. Similarly, smelter workers and fishermen engaged in a continuing series of violent labour confrontations, battling against restrictive legislation and "company goons," thugs imported to enforce company orders with fists and guns.

In the west coast logging industry at the turn of the century, conditions were just as bad and produced the same belligerency. "A fellow could go into the woods," Bill Pritchard told an interviewer many years later,

> carrying his own bedding on his back, and it would be a long time before he got any pay, or he might be discharged; and some of them even after they had quit had difficulty collecting their pay. . . . Then there was the rise of the company town, the small town that the company held. Everything belonged to the company. The stores belonged to the company. The workers were paid wages but they had to spend them in the company store. They had to pay rent and the rent was fixed by the company. This would call for a militant response from labor, naturally.

A kaleidoscopic succession of political organizations played out that response in British Columbia, repeating the bitter American competition between revolutionary Marxists and their more moderate, reform-minded fellow-socialists. Could the lot of working people be improved by a gradual process of successive reforms, or must the capitalist system be swept away complete and entire? Are the demands of union members for specific benefits compatible with the larger concerns of revolutionary socialism, or are unions merely reactionary instruments of capitalist competition? Is it valid to work for the relief of immediate inequities, or must socialist energy be devoted absolutely to the absolute restructuring of society? This tug-of-war between the principle of reform and the doctrine of revolution continued to mark the development of Pacific coast socialism, and surfaced as well in the evolution of the labour movement in Winnipeg and the prairie provinces.

In 1902 a convention in Vancouver succeeded finally in achieving a province-wide federation of several factions, calling itself the Socialist Party of British Columbia (SPBC) and endorsing the revolutionary platform just adopted by the Socialist Party of America. At the insistence of reformist members some demands for specific improvements were added to the program. In short order the Nanaimo local of the SPBC grew dissatisfied with the party's concessions to reform and withdrew, led by a brilliant radical theoretician and organizer from California, E. T. Kingsley, to form the Revolutionary Socialist Party of Canada. It was in this pugnacious Island sector that Bill Pritchard's father became active at the turn of the century.

In the provincial election of October 1903, the Socialist Party of British Columbia made significant gains, seeming to validate radical doctrine: eliminating capitalism was the undeniable way to solve society's ills. Late in 1904 the ultra-radical splinter group on Vancouver Island rejoined the now dominant SPBC. Renamed the Socialist Party of Canada (SPC), the Marxist left in British Columbia extended its leadership of radical politics Dominion-wide, with an executive committee located in Vancouver, and including Kingsley and Wallis Lefeaux, a lawyer and one of the party's leading advisors, and, among others, James Pritchard.

By and large, it was SPC policy to pursue its ultimate goal by political means, through the ballot, even as its unions resorted to the strike as a direct confrontation with entrenched employers. To some opponents, however, the party's philosophy ominously resembled the revolutionary doctrine of syndicalism, the idea that the world's workers should — and would — seize control of the economy, by whatever means necessary, and replace capitalism with a system of "syndics," control by the workers themselves. Reflecting on those early years, Bill Pritchard vehemently repudiated the alleged syndicalist connection, insisting that the Socialist Party did not advocate the violent destruction of legitimate government; nevertheless, its rhetoric often seemed dangerously inflammatory.

Even more threatening to established authority was the movement founded in 1906 by Daniel De Leon, the Industrial Workers of the World. The IWW, or "Wobblies," as they came to be known, gained a larger foothold in British Columbia and to an extent in Alberta than elsewhere in Canada. In the United States the aim of the IWW, as formulated by one of its most outspoken leaders, "Big Bill" Haywood, was "the emancipation of the working class from the slave bondage of capitalism." Its reputation for violence owed something to the implicit threat of a worldwide alliance of the working class, not unlike the syndicalist model, as well as to the physical belligerence of its tactics in labour disputes — "hitting a ballot box with an axe," was Pritchard's derisive description.

While the west coast SPC unions worked to organize the relatively stable portion of the work force among the longshoremen and the metal workers and in the resource industries, the IWW found its constituency among the itinerant, seasonal workers. These were the unskilled, often foreign-born "bindle-stiffs," who carried their blankets and other meagre possessions from one location to another, and who were generally ignored by organized labour. Moving among them, with Karl Marx in their kit-bags, the emissaries of the IWW brought their message of radical dissent to mining bunkhouses and forest encampments, usually with company police at their heels. On the whole, however, despite its stormy history, the IWW tended to make common cause with socialist groups.

Debut of a Socialist

Bill Pritchard had been twelve years old in 1900 when his father left for Canada, and he had learned something of British Columbia politics from James's letters home. He had also developed the reading habit early; and when he was exposed to his father's books, he remembered, he "jumped into the socialist classics head-first — the works of Trotsky, Marx. . . . And when I grabbed Marx . . . [and] came to his opening statement in *Kapital*, [I thought], this is the moral thinking I've been conditioned to in my own schooling, while I was looking for a blue-print of a new Jerusalem."

Young Bill's basic education in the local schools in Swinton, near Manchester, had ended shortly before his thirteenth birthday. He was apprenticed to a large firm of Lancashire building contractors, to help support his family while he learned the rudiments of the building trade, as his younger brother would do in his turn. Nevertheless, Bill pushed on to attend night classes for seven years at the Royal Institute of Technology and at the Manchester School of Technology, acquiring both background and technical experience in management. Small for his age but wiry, he developed a reputation as a weight lifter and a pugnacious amateur soccer player. There was, however, little prospect of economic security at home, and when James returned to Manchester, in 1911, emigration seemed to be the best course for his son. In May of that year Bill accompanied his father back to Canada. They stopped briefly in Montreal, where James had lived for about a year, working in the rail yards, and then they boarded the train for the long ride across the country to Vancouver.

Bill's memoir picks up the story of his instant introduction to political activism in his new territory:

Friday, May 19, around noon, we arrived in Vancouver, and went immediately to the shop where the *Western Clarion* was printed, and where E. T. Kingsley had a desk. Next, in the afternoon, after visiting the local headquarters, met with D. G. McKenzie, the then editor. . . . Met several other party members as we strolled the streets that same day. . . .

On Sunday evening, May 21, went to my first socialist meeting, held in the Empress Theatre. Speaker, the late Wallis W. Lefeaux; the chairman, his brother Frank. To the meeting of the local, in Mount Pleasant, the following Tuesday evening, where I signed an application form, being admitted the following Tuesday, May 30, 1911.

What Bill Pritchard found in Vancouver Local No. 1 of the Socialist Party of Canada was a unit totally dedicated to teaching the principles of Marxist socialism. Prospective members might be recommended for immediate admission, as young Bill obviously was by his father, but more often candidates were carefully screened for their understanding of the party's platform. If there seemed to be insufficient knowledge or if, as Pritchard recalled, the candidate seemed overly impressed by prominent leaders, the selection committee might suggest a period of further study, after which the application would be reviewed. "We discounted leadership," Pritchard insisted, in a lengthy interview half a century later; "either the policy comes from a consensus of the body or it's of no use. . . . Chances were that if someone bobbed up who looked like a leader, his head would come off." It was the rank-and-file that mattered, the party's "Jimmy Higginses," as Pritchard called them. Jimmy Higgins was the character created by novelist Upton Sinclair who became something of a byword in left-wing circles; he arranged the chairs for meetings and distributed party literature at the door and cleaned up afterward — the unassuming volunteer at the party's core.

From the outset, Pritchard explained, the party understood that "revolution can't take place until it has taken place in the thought processes of an adequate majority," and its program was organized accordingly:

The local possessed a good library, with all the socialist classics extant at that time, and a great number of scientific works on various subjects on the tables in the reading room, or in areas set aside for that purpose, displaying current magazines and journals. In the winter months an economics class was held on Sunday afternoons, moderated by George Morgan; Tuesday, the local business meeting; Thursday, a history class run by the late J. D. Harrington; and for a little time, on Friday night a class for those interested in becoming party speakers, conducted by that irrepressible red-headed orator, H. M. Fitzgerald. During these days, 1911–16, street corner meetings were held by Fitzgerald on the corner of Hastings and Columbia. It was on this soap-box that I made my debut as a socialist speaker.

There were about 120 members of the local when Bill Pritchard joined, a few from time to time on the payroll, but most volunteering their services to the party after a normal working day. Several in the local had an academic background in history and economics, some spoke and wrote French or German, and there were scores of well-versed socialists, Pritchard said. The members kept them all on their toes: "If you made a slip even in terminology in the articles in the *Clarion*, particularly in the editorials, you'd hear from some local with a blast."

It was in this company of equals that Bill Pritchard found his niche. What his memoir conveys most of all is the camaraderie and the high-spirited vitality of the group's activities in those years. There were open-air meetings in what is now historic Gastown, and meetings every Sunday evening in the Empress Theatre, usually filling its two thousand seats to capacity. At times, particularly toward the end of World War I, interest ran so high that three theatres had to be engaged at once: three speakers in rotation, each allotted about twenty-five minutes, and then on to the next theatre, with a chairman in each place to keep the crowd going while the changeover was made.

At no other time in his hectic career, Pritchard said, did he encounter so complete a rapport between speaker and audience. There was little resort to red flag symbolism — "steam and hysteria" he called it — but always an emphasis on knowledge and information, on informed analysis. He recalled one set of his own lectures in particular, delivered over three successive Sundays, on the significance of the Paris commune uprising in the French Revolution, which, like the Peterloo massacre of protesting English working people in Manchester, demonstrated what workers could do under duress.

Out of its limited resources, informally, the Vancouver local tried to look after its members. If someone was particularly hard up, the others might pass the hat or share food and clothing. Over the course of its history the local occupied offices in different premises in the downtown area, and these doubled as club rooms, where many members spent their free time. There were "smokers," parties for the men, and in the summertime family picnics on the beach at Kitsilano or Jericho or Spanish Banks. Entertainment was homegrown: one member never tired of performing his favourite song from Robin Hood, "Brown October Ale"; another, an accomplished elocutionist, was called on so frequently to recite the stirring tale of the gladiator Spartacus that his audience would join ritually in the climax: "Fail? Fail? In the bright lexicon of youth there is no such word as fail!" On Saturday nights there was a "business social" and a dance in the clubrooms, and quite frequently some out-of-work member might bed down there, having been given the job of janitor so that he would have a place to stay.

The building trades were on strike when Bill Pritchard first arrived in Vancouver, and he worked with pick and shovel for a month, clearing school grounds. Then he found a position as accountant for a plumbing, heating, and electrical firm on Pender Street, and in June 1913 he married. But times were bad, and just when he needed a job most the company went out of business. The party stepped into the breach, sending him on a lecture tour for a few days in the north Okanagan valley. Here, several miles from Enderby, he had his first glimpse of a logging camp, and he recorded his impressions of the attentive bunkhouse boys, "shrouded in a steaming fog produced from the wet clothing of the loggers, hanging from a line which ran the length of the bunkhouse."

Soon afterward, sent to Cumberland on Vancouver Island to address a coal-miners' local in the throes of a bitter strike, he was "surprised by the quality of the inquiries" at his meetings, and pleased to find a man from a village not two miles from his own home town, and the man's wife, "a Lancashire lass [and] a fighting member of the women's auxiliary of the strike committee." Some six years later an advertisement in the *Western Clarion* still testified to the local's continuing spirit:

> Local Cumberland B.C. No. 70. Business meetings every first and third Sunday in the month at 10:30 am. Economic classes every Monday and Friday at 7:00 pm. in the Socialist Hall, opposite the Post Office. Regular propaganda meetings at every opportunity.

In the fall of 1914, shortly after war broke out, Pritchard was appointed editor of the *Western Clarion*, a position he kept until 1917. The pay was meagre, when the party could afford to pay at all, but he found the experience fascinating. He wrote articles and book reviews for the paper and most of its editorials; he could reprint material from socialist-oriented papers in Great Britain and the United States, and there were excellent contributions by party members from the Maritimes to Vancouver Island. Routinely, he supervised the layout and attended to the distribution. The paper came off the press at 4:30 on Friday afternoon, and with Pritchard cranking the manually-operated addressing machine a staff of faithful volunteers had the *Clarion* in the mail by seven that evening.

SPC locals across the country, as far east as the Maritimes and in the United States, were among the subscribers; copies were also sent, by request, to university libraries; and there was an exchange with a number of American and British labour periodicals. The local's executive also supervised the publication of a steady stream of pamphlets, both reprints and by local party members, and distributed imported material, chiefly from the socialist-oriented Charles H. Kerr Company of Chicago.

Once a month Pritchard took his turn as speaker at the Sunday evening meetings in the Empress Theatre. He engaged in one debate on "The Revolutionary Position of the Socialist Party of Canada versus the Reformist Position of the Social Democratic Party," and in another, with an elderly professor from Seattle who "claimed to have sat at the feet of Henry George," on "Socialism versus the Single Tax." Then, at the end of 1915, the Alberta SPC asked him to undertake a three-month propaganda tour, in its campaign to persuade farmers of their common cause with wage workers. Pritchard was then twenty-seven years old, with a growing family. "I talked it over with my wife," he recalled afterward, "since it meant leaving her with two small boys, the youngest only three months old." Her response, as he remembered it, seems to suggest a commitment as intense as his own: "If the party thinks you should go, Will, I think you should."

Prairie People: Hardship and Strength

The winter of 1915 was one of the coldest Alberta had ever experienced, and especially so for someone from the mild Pacific coast. At Calgary, where Pritchard boarded a train on the newly completed CNR line to Hanna, Alberta, the outside temperature was an appalling forty degrees below zero, and there was no heat in the train. For miles he sat there, he told an interviewer many years later, huddled in his seat and shivering, an indication of what was yet to come, day after day, from the railway stop to his actual destination, always in "a different sleigh behind horseflesh . . . for some fifty miles over the frozen terrain." In Drumheller the engagement had to be cancelled, when the temperature, as Pritchard recalled it, went down to fifty-eight degrees below zero. His hosts at each stop might be a farm family somewhere in the area, and he was always short of cash, since the trip was financed out of the collection plate at the various meetings. If the schedule was disrupted there was no money for a hotel. It was, he commented some fifty years later, a task only a young man would undertake.

Moreover, if Pritchard was unprepared for the savage weather he encountered, his hosts were perhaps even more surprised when the fire-eating revolutionary they had expected actually appeared: a rather slight, gregarious young man, with a lively sense of humour. At one stop the only person left on the platform when the other passengers and their friends had dispersed was a burly man in a fur coat, who glanced at Pritchard and was about to move on. Pritchard stopped him:

> "Looking for someone?" I asked. In a deep basso profundo that seemed to come from his boots he said, "I'm looking for a man named Pritchard." "My name is Pritchard, " said I. "From Vancouver?" rumbled the query. "Yes," I answered. "Are you the fellow who writes those editorials in the *Clarion*?" "Yes, most of them." He looked me up and down, all of my five feet seven — he was a good six-footer — and then uttered one of the most eloquent expletives I ever heard: "Good God!"

About one small town on the Saskatchewan border, Pritchard said, he remembered everything but the name, and the name of the man that was to meet him. He arrived at the depot from Hanna in a howling blizzard, and no one was in sight. A Mountie told him that the fellow he was looking for lived about eighteen miles northwest of the station, and that it would be suicidal, in the storm, to try to get there. The next train, he found out, was two hours late, so that all he could do was take shelter in the lobby of the town's one hotel, and wait. "Thus for that day and night, and the following day and night, I sat beside the sizzling radiator, turning myself round occasionally, like a chicken on a spit, to try to keep warm on both sides." He was to decide that trains were always "two hours late" in this "British Siberia."

When the train finally appeared, Pritchard travelled back to Hanna, now having missed the scheduled engagement there as well, and was told that he must leave at once, to avoid another cancellation. "Well, I was given a quick meal," his story continues, "[and] without bed or sleep I was bundled off again into the fine, clear, Albertan champagne atmosphere for a ride of some forty-odd miles, only to find on arrival that the meeting had been scheduled for the previous evening." All was not lost, however. A summons on the rural party line brought all the neighbours together for a well-attended meeting that afternoon. "After which," Pritchard concluded, "I was put to bed, had a good sleep for the first time in three nights, and next morning was off again for my next appointment."

Then there was the frosty evening when all the members of his large host family piled into a sleigh for the ride to the meeting, about three miles down the road. The parents and one or two of the younger children rode up front, and the rest squeezed in where they could among the refreshments and other gear, with the baby on top, bundled into a warm little cocoon, and Pritchard himself riding the back runners as he clung to the rail. Suddenly, at a drift in the road, the horses reared and plunged, and the sleigh pitched from side to side; then the farmer regained control, and the sleigh moved on. Only the rider on the back runners noticed a bundle fly up over his head and into the snow. As the sleigh bells jingled away merrily, farther and farther, Pritchard dropped off into the darkness, found the baby in her nest of blankets, "warm, serene, and still asleep," and, half-frozen, struggled on with her, toward the distant lights of the schoolhouse. His welcome on that occasion was even more enthusiastic than usual.

Most impressive of all was the remarkable attendance at these meetings, with people coming from miles around. The lecture was usually preceded by a social, with refreshments, and followed by a dance for the young people. Pritchard would stay on to talk and answer questions, to distribute the socialist literature he had brought and to sell subscriptions to the *Western Clarion*. In Castor the local organizers had rented the movie palace for the meeting, to begin at eleven o'clock in the evening, after the regular bill. At eleven, however, such a crowd of people had assembled, eager to get in out of the cold, that the theatre owner, with a shrewd eye to business, ran the picture again, and the lecturer was able to catch a few hours' sleep before the meeting began, at one in the morning.

Despite the weather, or perhaps because of it, the tour provided the visitor with an extraordinary portrait of rural life on the prairies, of its harsh loneliness and mutual support, and of the unexpected reservoirs of spiritual strength among its hardy people. In isolated farm homes he was constantly amazed by the number and quality of well-thumbed books on the shelves, including scientific works and the socialist classics. In a crowded schoolroom one bitterly cold night, he gave a talk on "The Materialist Conception of History"; and afterward a very serious young man identified himself as a travelling lay preacher on horseback, and engaged the visitor in an earnest discussion, "his theological conceptions as opposed to my materialist ones," until dawn broke. In another schoolroom, after the lecture had ended and while a fiddle rasped out its tunes for the dancing couples, he sat beside the Catholic lady teacher, on the little schoolhouse seats, talking about what she called "social problems"; until, exhausted as usual by a non-stop schedule, he fell asleep on her shoulder. He was teased, of course, and some fifty years later would repeat his cheeky retort: "So, what softer pillow around here could a fellow find?"

A born observer, with an eye for detail, Pritchard captured the look of little towns like Leduc, as it was before the discovery of oil, "its three grain elevators standing out against the one-story architecture." Perhaps most poignant of all is his sketch of the woman he encountered in a farmhouse outside Leduc, coming back from a meeting with his host for the night:

> I judged her to be in her thirties. . . . She had come to Leduc from London, England, to become a farm wife. She admitted to a degree of loneliness, but did so in a charming manner, saying that her duties kept her occupied in the daytime, and she had the company of her husband in the evenings, which were spent in reading and discussions.

At this she indicated a well-stocked and fairly large bookcase. Apart from scientific works on a variety of subjects, I was astonished to see in this isolated spot — the road ended at the farm gate — one of the best socialist libraries I had ever seen in a home. Thus, she said, she conquered her loneliness. In the seventeen years since she passed through Leduc, on her way from London, she had been back to that little evidence of civilization only once. Edmonton, which lay some twenty miles to the northeast, she had never visited, though often at nights she would gaze out of the window to view the reflection of that city's lights on the sky.

There were many encounters, during that cold winter's journey, and Pritchard remembered always the "comradely discussions" he had, in this small town or that, with party organizers or party members, all of them finding a meaning to their bleak existence in the convictions they shared with others, messengers like this from the outside world.

As for Pritchard himself, his arduous tour of duty in the common cause ended at the beginning of April 1916 in a personal tragedy, the death of his infant son on the very night of his return. Describing his homecoming rather diffidently, as if such matters ought to be subordinated to the larger political concerns, he commented stoically in his memoir, "I have always thought that one's personal griefs are private matters." After the funeral and a few days' rest he returned to work.

Politics and Militant Pacifism

Shortly after the Alberta tour Pritchard was asked by the Cumberland local of the SPC to run for the Comox seat in a federal election. The constituency was enormous, extending from Nanaimo to the northern tip of Vancouver Island, and including the offshore islands in the Strait of Georgia and Powell River on the mainland.

A new set of adventures now presented itself, as he campaigned in the remote coastal forests. On a visit to a logging camp he first saw a giant tree being "falled": "The clash of the falling timber," he said, "is like a clang from the hammer of God." At Rock Bay he saw a huge school of playful whales, their noise "like the trumpeting of elephants";

and navigating Johnston Strait in a small boat, with the tide running, showed him the awesome power of that wall of water. To get to Lund, north of Powell River, he tramped for seven hours on a road that petered out into a forest trail, and then he crossed precariously over a ravine, on a makeshift, wobbly bridge of timber stringers. Once over, he came upon an Indian settlement, with "an old Indian adzing out a dugout canoe, the women occupied with their chores, and the children and dogs playing, as children and dogs everywhere are wont to do." For a townsman from England, these remained indelible impressions of a primeval wilderness.

Pritchard's stories frequently call attention, with some amusement, to the incongruous figure he must have cut in that rough-hewn territory. To improve his credibility as a candidate, some friends and supporters had outfitted him in a new suit, and he was concerned with keeping it presentable. From the Indian settlement, on the final leg of his journey to Lund, the only way he could travel was up the white-water Skookumchuk River, in a dugout canoe paddled by the taciturn old boatman, and he had to sit in the bottom of the craft, in an inch of water. He arrived, he said, "rather damp about the buttocks," and before that campaign was over, his clothes were considerably the worse for wear. It was about this time also that he first encountered and talked with James Woodsworth, at a meeting in Gibson's Landing (now called Gibsons), where the Woodsworths were then living. Pritchard had walked the five miles from Roberts Creek to Gibson's Landing in a pouring rain, and he came, he said, "steaming like a clam in a stew."

Despite the warm support Pritchard seemed to find at every stop on his campaign, he made only a modest showing in the 1916 by-election, and he returned to regular party work, striving to harness the nationwide discontent to socialist purposes. Marxist opposition to the war was not popular, in the fervent patriotism of World War I, despite the protest of the left that the European conflagration was, in Pritchard's words, "a last political resort of rival capitalist powers to grab a greater portion of the surplus values wrung from the workers." In the general election of 1917 the party nominated Pritchard for Vancouver West — "as usual," he said, "they were out for propaganda, not to get elected" — and he was defeated again. To his great satisfaction, however, he won a majority in the soldiers' vote, the ballots of the men in the trenches.

In 1917 Pritchard gave up the editorship of the *Western Clarion*, unable to support his family on its inadequate salary. Working a twelve-hour shift as a longshoreman, spending his evenings in heated debate at political meetings, returning to the waterfront again at six the next morning, he ran the danger of being blacklisted because of his union activity.

Then, in 1918, he found himself reclassified to the top category for conscription. He was thirty years old, with a wife and three small children: the oldest, James Arthur, now four, one-year-old Eleanor, and the baby, Gilbert. Like a number of his peers, he made a considered decision: if called, he would not go.

He was not alone in his stand. In British Columbia many men slipped across the border to the United States, and many more disappeared into the remote forests on the Island and the mainland, setting up rough-and-ready wilderness communities. One of these ragtag outlaws camping in the almost inaccessible hinterland was Albert "Ginger" Goodwin, whose death in August of 1918 at the hands of the RNWMP touched off a most alarming furor on the west coast, in what must have seemed to the authorities a growing wave of insurrection.

An ardent socialist, Goodwin had organized the hard-rock coal miners around Trail for the United Mine Workers, earning the enmity of the employer as a troublemaker. He had initially been classified as unfit for army service, but then was reclassified to the top category for conscription, almost certainly because Consolidated Mines wanted to remove him from the scene. As a result, he had taken to the mountains around Comox Lake, near Cumberland.

"Goodwin didn't show too much judgment," Pritchard conceded, years later. "He was very popular with the girls and he'd come down into Cumberland on Saturday nights to the dance, with the Dominion Police searching for him all over the place, even though the local chief of police, a returned soldier, told him to keep out of their sight." On this particular occasion, he had apparently been hunting for game to replenish the camp's food supply when he was ambushed and shot without warning as he came down a forest trail, and his death inflamed an already explosive situation.

At the insistence of the party, Pritchard went to Cumberland to attend the funeral, and found the Italian miners there, he said, so "steamed up" that he had to convince them "not to start anything," not to give the authorities a pretext for reprisals. The sympathetic police chief warned the federal agents to stay out of town until the funeral was over, and then led the mile-long procession to the cemetery in Happy Valley. Goodwin was buried without incident, but his killing touched off violent strikes in the mining camps and an even more menacing protest in Vancouver.

In Vancouver, Pritchard found out later, there was near chaos. The Trades and Labor Council called a twenty-four-hour strike, shutting down the docks, the street-railway system, and other industries. Pritchard's younger brother was in the city's Shaughnessy Hospital at the time, recuperating from injuries he had received in France, and he reported that a group of "the better ladies" had come to the wards with a generous supply of "booze" for the convalescent veterans, to try to persuade them to operate the steetcars. They did not succeed, but at the instigation of "business interests," Pritchard said, some returned soldiers attacked the Labor Temple and roughed up the secretary, Victor Midgley.

Even worse, "certain elements," in Pritchard's words, "made threats," drawing up a list of seven men including himself and Midgley who were ordered to get out of town with their families within the week, or be driven out. It was the mayor of Vancouver himself, Harry Gale, who communicated the ultimatum to the pugnacious boilermakers' union, and the boilermakers together with the longshoremen who defeated the move. Informed that the veterans were planning an attack on the longshoremen's hall, the men rigged up a battering ram aimed at the stairway that was the only approach to their door, and invited the mayor to inspect the mechanism, pointing out that he had better cool off the situation if he wanted to avoid serious trouble. Then a spontaneously assembled delegation of unionists presented Gale with a counter-threat: they had their own secret list of targets, they said, and "anything that happens to any one of our men will be visited on his counterpart on our list — and you are number one!"

No attack took place. By the time Pritchard's boat docked in Vancouver, all was quiet on the waterfront, and the only person waiting to meet him was his father, peaceably smoking his pipe. Labour had shown its strength by the control it exercised in a dangerously volatile situation, and Bill would later repeat with some satisfaction that he out-lasted his adversary, remaining in Vancouver long after Mayor Gale had left.

Inception of the OBU

With the wartime expansion of industry in Canada's western provinces, western labour had grown more self-assertive and more restive under the domination of the Canadian Labour Congress from its headquarters in Ontario. When the Congress met in Quebec City, in September 1918, an open split between East and West emerged over the Congress policy of wartime cooperation with the Conservative government. There were over four hundred delegates from eastern unions and only forty-five from the West, and an uneven struggle took place, as one after another the contentious, western-sponsored resolutions were rejected.

At this failure to gain recognition the western group met in caucus and scheduled a separate conference of western unionists, to be held in Calgary before the next Congress convention. The organizers asked the British Columbia Federation of Labor, the strongest and most militant of the western labour groups, to move its annual meeting from Victoria to Calgary, and the Western Labor Conference, rescheduled because of the deadly flu epidemic that swept the country that winter, assembled on March 11, 1919.

Before the conference began, the British Columbia group, including Victor Midgley, Jack Kavanagh, and others, and led by Bill Pritchard, met in closed session, to plan their strategy. Initially, Pritchard's account maintains, they intended simply to reorganize the B. C. Federation into a solid institution within the Trades and Labor Congress, one that would speak for specifically western needs. As the discussion continued, however, interest seemed to develop spontaneously in a strong, new, all-industrial union, rivalling the Congress.

The Trades and Labor Congress, like the American Federation of Labor, was immovably committed to craft unionism; what these western socialists wanted was the bringing together of the separated crafts into a new body, including unskilled labourers as well as skilled tradesmen, and thus more capable of enforcing its demands by direct action, such as a general strike. Behind the developing proposal, however, for at least some of the Marxist delegates, lay the ultimate Marxist expectation that the working class would come to power, in a fundamental upheaval in the entire social order. For want of a better title for the proposed new entity, the strategists began using a name by which the IWW was sometimes called, the One Big Union.

For the three days of the conference Pritchard and Kavanagh took charge, along with Manitoba's Bob Russell and Dick Johns and other members of the Socialist Party of Canada. Carrying with them other radically inclined delegates who were not actually in the party, they marshalled the countless dissatisfactions of the crowd behind their own ideological certainties, and a passionate militancy arose in the assembly. Red flags sprouted on the convention floor and revolutionary rhetoric inflamed the proposals and the responses.

The session gave uproarious approval to a series of resolutions demanding the withdrawal of Allied troops from Russia, urging a general strike of Canadian labour to back that demand, and sending fraternal greetings to the new Soviet state. The aroused delegates charged the Canadian government to restore the civil liberties it had revoked, and then entered on record as the ultimate goal of this new form of worker organization the replacement of the parliamentary system itself. As reported in the *Western Labor News*, the resolution's wording, its syntax rather muddled, unmistakably reflected Marxist revolutionary principles:

> Whereas, holding the belief in the ultimate supremacy of the Working Class in matters economic and political, and that the light of modern developments have proved that the legitimate aspirations of the Labor movement are repeatedly obstructed by the existing political forms, clearly show the capitalistic nature of the parliamentary machinery, this Convention expresses its open conviction that the system of Industrial Soviet Control by selection of representatives from industries is more efficient and of greater political value than the present form of Government.

Unequivocally they spelled out where their loyalties lay:

> this Convention declares its full acceptance of the principle of

"Proletariat Dictatorship" as being absolute and efficient for the transformation of capitalistic private property to communal wealth;

and again, protesting the harsh measures taken against non-British immigrants, they declared

that the interests of all members of the working class being identical, that this body of workers recognize no alien but the capitalist. . . .

This utopian vision of a universal family of working people lost some of its authenticity, perhaps, when the self-same motion addressed a contradictory, more immediate and self-serving problem, the perception that unspecified "aliens" were depriving true Canadians of their jobs:

also that we are opposed to any wholesale immigration of workers from various parts of the world and who would be brought here at the request of the ruling class.

Then, repudiating the Congress as the ineffective tool of a capitalist government, they demanded secession and the formation of a new "industrial Union," and designated Dick Johns as the head of a policy committee, with instructions to draw up a set of recommendations for change.

A sensational incident punctuated the subsequent debate. According to the *Western Labor News*, Congress vice-president David Rees rose on a point of privilege, pointed dramatically to a man in the balcony, and identified him as William Gosden, alias Smith, alias Brown, well-known in Calgary as an agent provocateur. Under a false name he had wormed his way into a B. C. miners' union, declared Rees, and when he was arrested along with some of the others, the unsuspecting miners had even stoned the policeman. The convention did not take the informer's presence seriously, or Rees's warning that there might be police spotters in their midst, but rocked with laughter when someone suggested that Gosden should be introduced for all to see.

Like some other delegates, however, Rees was becoming distinctly uneasy about industrial unions and union militancy. General strikes, he argued, were irresponsible at a time of widespread unemployment; wage negotiations and the cost of living were the prime union realities, and not the grandiose political dreams of the radicals. He had chaired the official opening of the Western Labor Conference, but before the proceedings were over, when it became clear that the radical position would prevail, he left angrily, to attend a meeting of his United Mine Workers in Minneapolis.

The resolutions introduced by the Johns committee confirmed the secessionist fervour of the meeting, and proposed a course of action. A central committee was to be set up, with sections from the four western provinces, to disseminate information about the OBU and to prepare a referendum among all members of existing unions on their willingness to join the new workers' organization. To provide interim funds for the new organization, the central committee requested a two-cent levy on each union member across the country.

Then the Western Labor Conference closed, postponing to a later date the actual drafting of a structure and a program for the breakaway union.

Pritchard, assessing the event in retrospect, insisted that he was concerned only with effective union organization, to combat capitalism on economic grounds, and that he rejected in principle the syndicalist belief endorsed by the IWW that unions would take control of the world's governments. Rather, he said, he was convinced that the world's workers would inevitably become more politicized, bringing about the destined change in the world economic order, and that overthrowing existing political systems by any means, violent or otherwise, was not part of a union's agenda. As he was to protest at his trial in Winnipeg, "Only fools try to make revolutions. Wise men conform to them."

Meanwhile, having decided that the constitution of the OBU would be developed at the founding conference still to come, the organizers canvassed for its support. In logging outposts and mining camps as well as in the urban shops, they devoted endless hours to its cause: Pritchard, Midgley, and Kavanagh in British Columbia, Joe and Sarah Knight and Carl Berg in Alberta, R. Hazeltine in Saskatchewan, Russell and Johns in Manitoba; and east of the Manitoba border, OBU interest was generated in northern Ontario and Nova Scotia, and in Toronto and Montreal. Nevertheless, for all the excitement that had prevailed at

the Calgary conference and the satisfaction of asserting a western identity in defiance of eastern domination, many unionists shared Rees's
reluctance to splinter the labour movement by undermining the Trades
and Labor Congress.

From the outset Pritchard and others, notably Midgley and
Kavanagh, had regarded their design for labour amalgamation as more
than a localized, merely western-Canadian phenomenon. Believing
intensely that international cooperation was required and even
inevitable, they took their campaign across the border to the northern
United States, generating some interest. At first the IWW welcomed
the Canadian development as an affirmation of their own philosophy of
uniting all working people. But when it became clear that the proponents of the Canadian OBU were not wholly committed to the dream
of taking over the world's governments, and had no use at all for the
Wobblies' much-publicized inclination toward two-fisted violence, the
IWW began a campaign of open vilification.

More effective in limiting the OBU's success was the firm hold that
the AFL exercised on its member unions. An effort was indeed gaining
some prominence within the AFL's ranks to centralize union control,
not unlike the scheme of the Canadian OBU, but the proposals
amounted to little more than a shift of emphasis in the existing structure, and the AFL had little difficulty in suppressing the dissident
movement. In the end, for all the apparent success of Pritchard and the
others in their initial foray among their American comrades, the OBU
would fail to take hold across the border.

In Canada there was trouble among the hard-rock miners in the
Kootenays, where mine owners aided by the police forcibly drove away
the radical trouble-makers. In Calgary, opponents charged that the
OBU would never be more than "a dinky little union," breaking up
labour solidarity by operating outside the AFL; but the Trades and
Labor Council there eventually voted to secede, and to tax its members
in order to raise funds for the OBU. Elsewhere, many of the incumbent
union officials were committed to the AFL-allied Trades and Labor
Congress, and refused to allow the allocation of any funds to the rebels.
In more than one instance, control of the union treasury became a matter for court challenge, when OBU adherents tried surreptitiously to
take over a local's bank account.

Winnipeg proved a stronghold of OBU interest; Edmonton absolutely rejected supporting the upstart organization. In April, Carl Berg wired a plea to Bob Russell in Winnipeg to help his Edmonton colleagues by addressing a mass meeting; but Russell was unable to come, completely taken up with OBU problems in his own territory. And it was at this same exhausting time that Russell himself appealed to Midgley in Vancouver to send him either Pritchard or Kavanagh for an OBU meeting in Winnipeg, and Midgley telegraphed his response: "We cannot spare either P. or K. They have more than they can attend to here for the next month."

Across the country, union members were sending in their ballots either for or against secession from the TLC, and by the middle of May the results seemed likely, though not certain, to favour the OBU. On May 16, one day after the general strike erupted in Winnipeg, the OBU Central Committee called a founding conference for June 4, once again in Calgary. The proceedings actually got underway three days late, and with Russell and Johns unable to attend, and some ideological disagreement beginning to erode enthusiasm for the OBU, only about twenty-five delegates were present. Under these strained circumstances, the discussions were held in secret, and only official communiques were released.

The OBU constitution drafted in Calgary reaffirmed the principles of class struggle, the elimination of capitalism, and the replacement of "production for profit" by "production for use," but provided only a general outline for the union's operation. The conference disbanded with a working committee in place, charged with disseminating information to union locals, but leaving a great many details unresolved.

Observer in Jeopardy

It was only at the conclusion of these deliberations that the western delegates turned their attention to what was happening in Winnipeg. Until then, Pritchard later remarked, they had only known what they had read in the papers; he did remember, he said, standing with his brother in front of the *Vancouver Province*, reading a report on the bulletin board. Now the committee told him, "Bill, you'd better go down there and see. You may be able to settle that thing, and if you do, you'll be the biggest man in Canada." Expecting to be with the strikers no more than a day or two, Pritchard complied. On the train east, James Farmer came aboard at Brandon, sent by the Strike Committee to brief him on what was happening, and they pulled into Winnipeg late on the night of June 10.

To Pritchard's surprise, because only a few people, as far as he knew, had been aware of the Winnipeg trip, information about his impending arrival had reached civic authorities, and he was front-page news that day in the local papers. Editorials proclaimed that he ought to be shipped back at once — run out of town on a rail. The next day thousands of people crowded into Victoria Park to hear Pritchard deliver what William Ivens called "an electrifying speech" of encouragement. At the Strike Committee's request, he joined a small sub-committee at a meeting in the Royal Alexandra Hotel, where Canon F. G. Scott was trying to bring about a reconciliation between the strikers and the soldiers who opposed them; but the talk seemed to be going nowhere, and Pritchard paid little attention.

On the following day he took the platform along with Woodsworth and A. E. Smith, and once again, the *Strike Bulletin* reported, the visitor from Vancouver received thunderous applause for his stirring call to action against social injustice: "In Britain," he exclaimed, "there are those who produce all and possess nothing, and those who produce nothing and possess all; in Canada, there are those who live and do not work, and those who work and do not live!" He met and talked with strikers and their leaders, argued with some and agreed with others, and then, his assigned task of observing the situation done, he boarded the train again to go home.

Accustomed to the truculence of B. C. labour action, Pritchard found the control of the Strike Committee remarkable. Winnipeg, he said, was the most peaceful city he had ever seen. Organized meetings kept the people off the streets, regular bulletins kept them informed. Long after the event, he summed up his impressions for an interviewer: "It taught me enough faith in the working class, that despite its idiocy and ignorance, when it is faced with a definite set of circumstances, it will set up the necessary machinery and organization to deal with the problem. Because that is the class that does everything today to maintain society — it even fights the wars on behalf of property." The curious trace of derision here for the "idiocy" of the working class, even as in retrospect he praised its achievements in the strike, anticipates Pritchard's eventual disenchantment with the role of agitator for reform.

Meanwhile, he continued the battle energetically. On his way back to Vancouver, he stopped in Brandon on Monday, June 16; he attended one meeting there, was slated for another the next day, and was then to continue his journey. That night the Mounted Police in Winnipeg arrested six of the strike leaders, and herded them off to the penitentiary. They had a warrant for Pritchard as well, and came looking for him at the scheduled Brandon meeting, but their quarry had been warned and stayed away. A cat-and-mouse game followed as Pritchard, shrewdly aware of how valuable publicity was to the workers' cause, determined to make it as hard as possible for the authorities to find him. He would give himself up at a time of his own choosing, in his home town of Vancouver.

A friend bought two tickets on the CNR to Moose Jaw. Avoiding the railway depot, they caught the train in the yards as it was moving out. In Moose Jaw they spent the night in a hotel, listening to the newsboys in the street shouting, "Pritchard still at large!" From Moose Jaw they switched to the CPR for Vancouver, intending to by-pass Calgary by some means. As they approached Calgary early on the morning of June 19 there seemed to be no trouble — and then Pritchard was apprehended on the train by Staff Sergeant Hall of the RNWMP. Protesting peaceably that restraints were unnecessary, Pritchard was taken off the train in handcuffs and removed to the city jail, but not before he had discovered a common bond with his captor, both having been born in Manchester.

The Calgary jail was then so filthy, Pritchard recalled, that he stood up all that first night, and when he was interviewed by a RNWMP commissioner the next day his one request was for a bath. "And by jingo," he said,

> two stalwarts came down in a car, and they took me to Mounted Police Headquarters, where the guardians of the law were sitting around a table, playing cards. They handed me my grip, with the hollow-ground razor I wasn't allowed to have at the jail, in case I

decided to cut my throat, and showed me where the bathroom was: one flight up — I could easily have jumped through the window. I had a darned good bath and went back. "All right, boys," I said, "I'm ready." "Oh, take your time," they said. So I sat down for a while, then remarked, "I should get back, you know." "Would you like a ride around the city?" they asked. And they took me in a car all around Calgary before they put me back in jail.

Eight days later he was escorted to Winnipeg by a lone Mountie, an amiable Irish boy, who gave him the lower bunk, let him use the men's room unsupervised, and invited him to order anything he wanted in the dining car, beyond the dollar per meal the government provided. "A funny thing is happening in our outfit," his Mountie escort told him; "we're getting all kinds of guys who know nothing about a horse." Spies, Pritchard understood, recruited by the RNWMP specifically to infiltrate suspect organizations.

In Winnipeg Pritchard was taken directly to Stony Mountain, where he was received by a rather reluctant Warden Graham. The other arrested strike leaders had just been released from the penitentiary, although the foreign-born prisoners still remained, and the entire proceedings struck the warden, Pritchard maintained, as irregular. After eight days, bail was arranged for Pritchard, at $20,000, and the embattled group, including Russell and others, met for a memorable social evening at someone's home in Weston. Pritchard was bound over to keep the peace and to return for his trial, and then permitted at last to go home.

A few weeks later, in July, Pritchard was recalled for preliminary hearings and jailed with the others, bail denied, for another month, until the national outcry brought about their release. Home again, and with his ability to promote the OBU now restricted, Pritchard spent the months leading up to his trial preparing for it, in writing a number of articles for the *Western Clarion*, and in delivering a series of lectures to the Prince Rupert SPC local.

The Meaning of Revolution

At the end of January, with Russell in prison, Dixon acquitted, and the case against Woodsworth dropped, the remaining seven came to trial before Metcalfe, all indicted together on six counts of seditious conspiracy and one of common nuisance. ("When they got to the sixth count they must have run short," Pritchard told the jury.) Conducting his own defence, Pritchard was aided by his old friend from the Socialist Party of Canada, Wallis Lefeaux.

Pritchard's wife insisted on coming from Vancouver, bringing the two boys but leaving their daughter Eleanor with friends. They rented a two-room apartment, and each day Pritchard travelled to and from the law courts by public transit, two streetcars each way, he said, and a walk for the better part of a mile.

From its opening until sentence was passed on April 6, the trial lasted ten difficult weeks. At the outset the defence asked for a change of venue, citing the high level of emotion in Winnipeg, and then attempted to have the presiding judge disqualify himself on the grounds that he had already tried Russell. Both motions were denied. Then the entire panel of potential jurors was challenged, on information that they had been canvassed by police agents. Twelve men were finally selected, "all farmers," Pritchard described them, "good men and true, but called upon to decide a great number of intricate legal questions relating to an industrial dispute."

In view of the extraordinary circumstances, the accused were allowed to sit at the counsel table rather than in the prisoners' box, and the legalistic exchanges ground on, day after day, with the prosecution attempting to tie all the accused together in a common, conspiratorial guilt, and the defence arguing each case on its own merits, even as all the accused denounced the actions of the authorities. The Crown made much of the testimony of one Zaneth, or Zanetti, an Austrian or an Italian, a police informer, who had actually infiltrated the Socialist Party so deeply as to become the literature agent of the Calgary local. Pritchard heaped contempt on this shadowy figure, demolishing the Crown's sensational allegations, at least to his own satisfaction.

It had been clear from the outset that by the charge of seditious conspiracy the authorities were alleging a far broader intent than the organization of the strike itself. Pritchard pointed out that the strike was authorized by the Trades and Labor Council, but only one of its officials was arrested: Russell, a member of the Socialist Party of Canada; and that of the eight men indicted for seditious conspiracy, four were SPC members. Behind the show of specific strike-related indictments, Pritchard remained convinced, was the authorities' determination to prevent that inevitable access by working people to the control of their lives which was the central tenet of the SPC's doctrine. To that end, he charged in his opening remarks to the jury, a "bogey" had been "conjured forth," an impression that law and order were endangered. From "every cobwebbed corner of every shack of every working man whom they considered suspect," and "every ash-barrel that exists in the Dominion of Canada," he declared,

> from speeches given by people we don't know, in places we have never been, and circumstances of which we have no knowledge . . . they have carved out terms, "red," "bolshevik," "socialism," "evolution," "revolution," "proletarian," "bourgeoisie," etc.

Seen in the perspective of history, a wildly exaggerated "Red Scare" was rampant in Canada as in the United States, in the turmoil following World War I. On both sides of the Atlantic many ideologues of the left hailed the Russian Revolution of 1917 as the opening event of the people's movement to power that they confidently predicted. But the destruction of imperial authority had invested the terms that Pritchard strung together for the jury with a peculiar and perhaps permanent aura of menace in the public mind, and liberal thinkers of almost any description might be tarred with the label of "Bolshevik," as atheists and "free thinkers." They denied God, people said; they advocated "free love," and were bent on destroying the family.

At his trial Pritchard hotly denied the charge of immorality, and he read from the *Communist Manifesto* to demonstrate that Marxists wanted to put an end to the "bourgeois exploitation of children," and to the use of women as "mere instruments of production." Nor did the Socialist Party of Canada foment insurrection. Pritchard read from the class-conscious language of its manifesto a specific rejection of violence as a political instrument:

The fists of the working class, weakened by hunger, are too insignificant against the Gatling guns in the hands of the capitalists. An armed revolution therefore is out of the question so long as the ruling power is in the hands of the capitalist class. The field for the class struggle is therefore in Parliament.

As for his own notorious atheism, he offered the logical argument that his views on that subject had no bearing on the issue at hand.

The Crown concluded its case on March 4, and Pritchard's turn to address the jury came on the morning of March 23. (Reporting the event, the *Toronto Telegram* noted that the speaker had a large glass of buttermilk before him rather than the customary water.) In this moment at the centre of attention, Pritchard did not, for the most part, resort to the emotional impact of a personal appeal, true to his lifelong principle that the individual must be subordinate to the cause for which he stands. Rather he chose to expound the philosophy of the radical left, and especially his own brand of socialism.

Pritchard described capitalism as bankrupt, made obsolete by the very advances it had produced: ". . . more deadly to your modern system of international credit than any One Big Union or Socialist Party is the fact that last year we crossed the Atlantic without touching water" — a reference to the amazing new airplane technology. He defined modern business as "sabotage — the destroying of one fellow's property by the operation of another fellow's property"; and he hit a responsive chord among the spectators in the courtroom by citing the flagrant profiteering of big business in the recent war, and the domination of the Canadian economy by Wall Street financiers.

Passionately he told of the ruthless exploitation of copper miners in British Columbia, and he dramatized the ordinary man's plight. Does the corporation lawyer know what it is, he asked, to work in a coal mine, "to bend his back before the face of the rock, or push wagons from the drive to the bottom of the shaft . . . for seventeen hours at a stretch?" To this graphic portrait of the labouring life that he knew on the west coast he added the struggle of "the little fellow who tries to run a grocery store on the corner," or the worker at the factory gate who must try to get himself hired ahead of the others, or the farmer on a quarter acre of land who must get to the elevator first in order to sell his wheat; and he pleaded their cause: "You realize that kind of thing cannot go on eternally. What is the use of each of us trying to get ahead of the other fellow when there will always be some fellow who will lose out after all?"

Man, he argued, is a social being, and must reject any anarchist attempt to bring "disruption and disorder in the machinery the world must use for the maintenance of humanity. . . . We are all inter-dependent," he said, and inviting his listeners to look beyond the immediate confines of the courtroom, he taught that all labour is interrelated, worldwide:

> The wheat that you produce on your land ties you up to every other country in the world. The ships that I load and unload connect me, may be, with the labours of the Chinese coolies of Shanghai, Hong Kong, and other oriental ports; and brother Johns, as he works with the micrometer and the lathe in the machine shops, his labor is connected with the slaves of the American rolling mills.

That dreaded word, "revolution," Pritchard maintained, "has been used by historians all along the line to indicate certain great political changes or certain great industrial changes." Quoting Robert Ingersoll, he reminded his listeners that

> to teach the alphabet is to inaugurate a revolution. Every library is an arsenal filled with the weapons and ammunition of progress;

and that the "revolution" he and his alleged co-conspirators were accused of inciting was no more than the "evolution," by a legislative process, of the inevitable course of human affairs, to which wise men conform.

As for the astonishing Russian Revolution, Pritchard later maintained, perhaps with the wisdom of hindsight, that he understood from the beginning that the Soviet phenomenon was an aberration. "The establishment of a Socialist organization on a feudal dunghill is impossible," he declared in a 1969 interview, long before the disintegration in the 1980s of the USSR. "In any advanced country today," he insisted, "power is in Parliament — Parliament or Congress."

Pritchard's summing up before the jury occupied two entire days, from ten in the morning to ten in the evening. It was printed and circulated by his admirers in the movement, and he won the praise of the *Toronto Telegram*, among others, for "his clear, cool, and concise manner of dealing with his subject." He said later that he would have documented his case even further, but he knew it was seed-time on the prairies, and the jury of farmers could not be detained any longer. Striking a note of pathos, the *Winnipeg Tribune* reported that he had "bared his soul to the light of British justice," but William Pritchard made no such weak entreaty. The close of his marathon address was an unrepentant challenge: "I have done nothing of which I am ashamed; I have said nothing for which I need apologize." Proudly, he reiterated the creed of his socialist comrades-at-arms, that change was inevitable:

> A new order of things is born, the powers of evil die poisoned by their crime. The greedy and the cruel, the devourers of people, are bursting with an indigestion of blood. However sorely stricken by the sins of their blind or corrupt masters, mutilated, decimated, the proletarians remain erect; they will unite to form one universal proletariat and we shall see fulfilled the great Socialist prophecy, "The union of the workers will be the peace of the world."

Pritchard probably knew that the verdict would go against him. Judge Metcalfe directed the jury's attention to the salient points in the case: Pritchard was on the central committee at the infamous Calgary convention, and a propagandist for the OBU; he was in correspondence with Russell, and one of the agitators purposefully sent to Winnipeg; if these activities contributed to the carrying out of unlawful acts, as cited in the seven counts, then Pritchard, like the other accused, was guilty as charged.

The jury returned the expected verdict of guilty, and Judge Metcalfe handed down the one-year sentence on the morning of 6 April, in a courtroom so crowded that the wives and families of some of the accused had to be seated in the jury box. Called in his turn to respond, the press reported, Pritchard said that "if a man be true to himself, he would be true to all men." Then he thanked the judge, and walked firmly from the court.

In 1933, at a political meeting in Vancouver, Pritchard was to encounter the jury foreman again, Mr. Bruce, a richly moustached Scot with a rolling brogue. "We had a jolly time together," Pritchard said. But when Bruce offered to describe what had taken place among the jurors, Pritchard refused: "The secrets of the jury room are not revealed in British procedures."

Decline of the Socialist Party of Canada

The months that Pritchard spent at the provincial prison farm apparently left him with little resentment. If there was any bitterness, he said, it was against the system that had produced the problems. On being admitted to jail, when the particulars of his parentage were being recorded, he managed to amuse himself, and perhaps get his own back a little, by playing a very small joke on the rather dull-witted prison guard in charge: asked several times to give his mother's maiden name, her name before marriage, the prisoner repeated, straight-faced, "Priscilla Pritchard," mischievously omitting the explanation, that his parents were cousins, until the bedeviled guard lost his temper.

About the details of his existence behind bars Pritchard said little in his reminiscences, choosing to recall only the classes he conducted for some of the foreign-born inmates and the occasional amusing or instructive incident with his friends or with guards. He allowed his name to stand on the unified slate of labour candidates in the provincial elections of 1920, and lost, as did most of the Socialist Party representatives. Asked if he considered himself a martyr, he replied, "Certainly not! The working class needs neither leaders nor martyrs. Leaders can lead one up, and then down again; and martyrs go to their martyrdom like sleepy men to their beds." He had simply done what had to be done.

The strike and the subsequent imprisonment of its leaders had dealt a severe blow to the radical left, stalling the organization of the OBU before it was well begun, and depriving the Socialist Party of its most compelling speakers. Desperately, the SPC wrote to comrades in the United States for help, and in response Adolph Kohn, then visiting Detroit from England, agreed to come to Winnipeg for a year. An enthusiastic, forceful speaker, Kohn packed the Strand Theatre every Sunday afternoon that fall and winter.

Argument was the SPC's lifeblood. In February, anticipating Pritchard's release, the party arranged a debate on the subject of the newly instituted League of Nations: was it in the best interests of the working class? The affirmative was to be taken by W. F. Osborne, professor of history and French at the University of Manitoba. Pritchard had been seriously ill at the end of his sentence, unconscious for two weeks in the prison hospital, and he told his eager supporters that he had spent the last several months "where very little news of the outside world penetrated." Nevertheless he undertook to uphold the negative, asking only for a copy of the league's covenant. The party's lively young student members provided the document — Pritchard claimed that they gleefully lifted the professor's own copy — and interest in the event began to mount.

Early on the morning of February 28, 1921, the labour prisoners were released, and the next evening a celebratory reception took place at the huge, barnlike Industrial Bureau. Still very weak, Pritchard spoke briefly. A few days later, the much-publicized debate brought a crowd of thousands to the same hall, and several hundred more had to be turned away.

Osborne proved to be a smooth, polished, logical debater, his opponent said generously — considering his point of view, that is; but clinging to the back of a chair for support, Pritchard was certain that he had won, especially when the professor had to abandon his prepared notes to take on the arguments flung at him from the noisy, partisan audience. A successful event, for the party's purposes: the pass-the-hat collection brought in $411, a quarter of which went to a charity of Professor Osborne's choice, $100 for the rent of the hall, and the rest, after expenses, to SPC coffers. Delighted, the party members arranged another debate for their star, with another academic, on the subject of free trade.

Pushed beyond his limit, Pritchard collapsed, unable to go on, an hour before he was due to speak. Adolph Kohn replaced him in the debate, and party members pitched in to help the family. The return to Vancouver, more than two weeks later, was tumultuous, with more parades and more public appearances, and Bill's proud father encouraging his son to accept these honours on behalf of socialism and the party. The entire family was strained to exhaustion, but only afterwards was there time for a month's rest.

The activist's ruthless dedication to his cause allowed little consideration for the troubles of his wife and children. Pritchard went back to the waterfront again, and back to more work for the party. He ran, unsuccessfully, as SPC candidate for Nanaimo in the federal election of 1921, the year in which James Woodsworth won a seat in Winnipeg and William Irvine in Alberta. He wrote for the *Western Clarion* and took his turn on the Empress Theatre platform.

That summer of 1921 a major conflict broke open the ranks of the Socialist Party, setting in motion an inexorable process of decay. The Third Communist International, organized by Trotsky and Lenin in 1919, issued its Twenty-One Points, calling on all working-class parties to follow what Pritchard called contemptuously its "imperatives," its blueprint for revolutionary Marxism the world over; and across Canada some SPC members insisted that their party conform. They were "entranced by the Russian Revolution," Pritchard said; they did not understand the true nature of the Soviet system, that it was not truly Marxist but anarchic, and unworkable because of the backward state of Russia's economy and the ignorance of its people.

At a "hot and steamy meeting" of the SPC he declared his intense opposition on many grounds, but chiefly because "as a socialist I object to dictatorship, whether it comes from Jerusalem or Moscow." A significant number of dissidents broke away, however, including the Knights in Alberta and Kavanagh in British Columbia, to form the Workers' Party, and later the Communist Party. The SPC survived the crisis, but attendance at its meetings diminished.

Acquiescence with the dictates of a governing hierarchy was not for Bill Pritchard, with his tough-minded pursuit of principle, his insistence on the importance of a knowledgeable proletariat, and his distrust of unchecked "leadership." With enduring anger he continued to heap scorn on the "Gilbert-and-Sullivan antics" of the Communists, on the character assassination that was their stock-in-trade, on their dishonest appropriation of such "working-class martyrs" as Ginger Goodwin, and above all on their blind obedience to central authority. When he was interviewed years later, in 1971, he was still virulently anti-Communist, and confirmed in his opposition by all that had happened during the past half-century in China and the Soviet Union. "If this is socialism," he said, "I've wasted my life. I don't want any part of it."

In 1922 he again was president and business agent of the longshore-men's union, for the six months permitted by union rules, and then returned to the docks. A year later a disastrous two-month strike against the shipping interests erupted on the Vancouver waterfront. Pritchard edited the strikers' newspaper and addressed countless meetings, but the action was doomed from the start, he said in retrospect, because there was very little room for negotiation. Striving for labour unity, he made a desperate attempt to marshall the workers along the Seattle waterfront, but the shipping companies had broken every other longshoremen's organization on the coast, down as far as San Diego, California. The strikers had little taste for further struggle and capitulated. For his part in the action Pritchard himself was blacklisted, thereby forfeiting, he said, the pension he would have enjoyed had he toed the line.

As well, the attempt to organize the OBU was not going well on the Pacific coast, although for a short time its influence extended as far as Butte, Montana. The Canadian longshoremen could not be persuaded to affiliate with the new union, and while the Vancouver street-railway-men joined, their effectiveness was limited. The OBU, Pritchard maintained, was broken by a combination of the capitalists, the government, and the international unions — most ruthless of all the AFL, cutting down OBU members with the threat of starvation. In the coal mines and in the shipyards, men who were hired for work had to tear up their OBU cards and join the company-approved AFL union. "There was nowhere else to go," Pritchard commented bitterly. "I was the first president, but I never functioned."

The moment had also passed for the SPC, with some of its members drawn into the Communist camp, and others shifting toward more pragmatic, reformist policies. By 1922 Pritchard was already at odds with the party, according to Alex Shepherd, who was then the secretary of the Winnipeg branch, and by the next year the SPC's existence was little more than nominal. Nevertheless Pritchard remained convinced of the validity of true Marxism, as he understood it; and in telling the story of the west coast labour movement, as he was frequently called on to do in his later years, he drew attention, with obvious pride, to the very early emergence of the Socialist Party of Canada among its companion parties in world socialism.

The Socialist as Reeve

For all his disaffection from union and party activity, Pritchard could not remain away from politics for long. Living in Burnaby, he quickly became involved in municipal affairs. He was elected to the local council in 1928 and reelected the following year. In 1930 a substantial majority voted him in as reeve, and an even larger majority returned him a year later. He was elected president of the Union of British Columbia Municipalities, and then became chairman of the unemployment committee of the national Union of Canadian Municipalities.

A cheery newspaper profile of Reeve Pritchard in 1932 offered a dimension of his personality that the serious-minded socialist rarely revealed to the inquiring historians of a later generation. A "silvery-toned tenor," the reporter called him, and a fine musician, as befits a man of Welsh descent, he was said to delight in performing, either as soloist or in chorus. He organized young people's orchestras and male voice choirs; he conducted operatic concerts, and was even invited to sing on a radio program. A swimmer, a soccer fan, an eager gardener, and a hard-working member of the Greater Vancouver Water and Sewage boards, "at night," the profile concluded, "he sings."

There was not a great deal to sing about in the Burnaby of the thirties, the years of the Great Depression, and for the Pritchards themselves life was as difficult as ever. Once again, whether travelling back and forth to fulfil his various new responsibilities or struggling with the accumulated problems of the municipality, Bill's time was at the command of the public, and there was no privacy for the family. He campaigned among the people, "at such places as barber shops and gas stations, wherever people lingered to talk," one account says, and he was constantly on call: "Even on Sundays I'd have a delegation in the house, and one coming to the back door, and at the same time I could see another coming up the street."

As for the town of Burnaby, years of unplanned development and unpaid taxes had left the municipality unable to cope with the massive difficulties brought on by the depression. Sixteen thousand people were on relief by the fall of 1931, out of a total population of twenty-five thousand. Assistance could be provided only to those in desperate need, and payments were so low that many people found themselves without the bare necessities of existence, but even so there was not enough money in the relief budget to meet the demand. At Pritchard's urging some welfare recipients were hired to do municipal work, with the costs to be shared by the provincial and federal governments, and these men immediately began grading lanes, clearing parks, and several other projects.

As agreed, Burnaby submitted progress reports to the provincial office in Victoria, but the promised reimbursement did not materialize. Pritchard wrote to Victoria, then made the trip there, trying to break the bottleneck, to no avail. The municipality did have some funds in one account, but from a bond issue designated for such expenditures as road repair and water supply, and therefore technically unavailable to the relief program. Pritchard was furious: "The money to pay the wages of our workers on water was there, but there was no money to pay the poor sons of guns who were working on the lanes, who had been out of work for months. What do you do? Do you obey the law? Not with me . . . I had neighbours and I could see their children's faces day by day becoming more drawn."

With the consent of his treasurer and his chairman of finance, Pritchard paid the relief workers' wages out of the bond money, and was promptly charged by his political opponents with misuse of funds. His supporters rallied to his defence with a door-to-door collection to cover his legal fees, and the judge who heard the case vindicated Reeve Pritchard's action, recommending that it be ratified. "I would do the same thing again," Pritchard declared. By December 1932, however, Burnaby's finances had become so unmanageable that storekeepers, who could not be paid, refused to fill further relief orders, and fourteen families went hungry. Once again, out of the same compassion for the problems of ordinary working people, Pritchard took steps, insisting that the administration of the municipality be taken over by a provincial commissioner, so that relief payments could be met more adequately.

The depression years were only slightly less precarious for the Pritchard family. "It was everlasting belt-tightening for myself and the family," he told an interviewer, in a rare moment of regret; "I sometimes look back and wonder why I inflicted that upon the kids . . . my own kids." One year he was unable to cover the taxes on their modest house, and he remembered always the help he received from Gilbert, his younger son, who was working in the woods as a blacksmith's helper: ". . . and that boy, when the camps were closing down, instead of coming to town with his pay, and having a little time — and he wanted to see his sister; he always used to take her out when he came in — he stayed in camp, lived there and sent me the money to pay the taxes. So I appreciate those kids — I've got that much sentiment."

In politics, too, Pritchard met with further problems. After the formation of the CCF as a national party, a British Columbia wing came together, out of the remains of the SPC and other labour groups, with Pritchard as leader, and under this banner he ran in 1933 for the provincial seat of Vancouver-Point Grey. He had, however, spent his adult life, as Alex Shepherd commented, hammering away at newspaper editors and reporters as "capitalist hacks and lickspittles," and in this campaign a hostile press zealously resurrected all his former misdeeds.

Discussing the oppressive wage system, at the Western Labor Conference in Calgary, he had proclaimed dramatically, "the worst enemy of the working man today is the late lamented Mr. Christ," loudly applauded by most of the audience. The incautious phrase returned to plague him again and again. Like a great many socialists of his time, Pritchard had no use for religion, believing fervently that the teaching of Christian humility helped keep the downtrodden masses in their place, and occasionally his irrepressible wit overcame his discretion and scandalized listeners. He sneered at religionists for battening on the bones of the dead Christ; he appeared at a strike meeting in Winnipeg, flanked by Woodsworth on one side and A. E. Smith on the other, and referred slyly to himself in that situation as "like that other person ensconced between two characters." Then, fortunately, only Woodsworth had caught the allusion to Christ crucified between two thieves.

Now his opponents raised the "Mr. Christ" issue again, an outraged clergyman thundered at him from the pulpit, and a flurry of letters to the editor titillated the readers of the *Vancouver Province*, including one from his mother, protesting that her son "engaged in Christian work," that "he never gave me cause for a moment's unhappiness," and that she alone knew "what he and his brother have suffered in the interests of the working class." Rather lamely, Pritchard replied to his critics that as he "looked back upon his youth," he regretted the "chance remark" that may have offended certain people, adding, with perhaps more credibility, that he had "the highest respect for the Sermon on the Mount, as representing the highest ideals of humanity."

It was not an auspicious moment, and the voters rejected Pritchard's candidacy. As the CCF increasingly took the lead in the British Columbia left-wing movement, he quit the party and made one more bid for public office, on a ticket of his own devising. In the 1937 general election he ran as a "B.C. Constructive" candidate in Vancouver East, and lost.

There was little left now of Pritchard's trust in the working class and in its ability to generate a political party that would change the world. The voters were featherheaded, he said, and as for union members, they wanted a bigger pay packet, but they cast their ballots another way when it came to elections. Besides, there were problems at home, terrible problems, his friend Shepherd hinted long afterward, discreetly adding only that Pritchard's family unhappiness probably contributed to much of the political turmoil. With his usual reserve about personal affairs, Pritchard never discussed these matters in public, then or later.

Then occurred a devastating and final blow. A terse newspaper notice on January 24, 1938, indicated that Mildred Eleanor Pritchard, daughter of Mr. and Mrs. William A. Pritchard, had died at the age of twenty-one, and would be buried in Forest Lawn Cemetery. Friends of the family knew that she had taken her own life.

Bill Pritchard left British Columbia, and to all intents and purposes dropped out of sight.

Reprise

By the sixties and seventies, when left-of-centre thought was moving into a position of some political power in Canada, though perhaps not quite as its early apostles had expected, interest in that older generation had revived. Academics and trade unionists of a new day had rediscovered Bill Pritchard. He was living in Los Angeles, still a socialist, now a member of the tiny Socialist Party of America, and still a trenchant observer of politics and people. In 1969, to celebrate the fiftieth anniversary of the Winnipeg General Strike, the United Steelworkers' magazine published a recollection of that watershed event by William A. Pritchard, then eighty-one years old. The strike was "a magnificent example of working class solidarity and courage," the old warrior concluded, reiterating his fundamental belief in the strength of ordinary people.

A number of academics sought out Pritchard, to record on tape a piece of living history, and on one of his visits to Vancouver and Victoria he spoke at several meetings, was interviewed by the press, and appeared on a radio talk show. A talk prepared in 1971 for delivery to the students of the University of Winnipeg was published and distributed by his son James, and "the eager students of the academies," as Bill called them, continued to call on him and to delight him with their understanding of Marxist teaching.

To these new friends Pritchard had as little to say as ever about the circumstances of his life or his activities after he left Vancouver, except for one odd, rather unexpected reference to having been at one time in charge of a poolroom. In the interval, old friends had heard from him only rarely, but in 1961, when Bob Russell was honoured by the Vancouver trade unions, Pritchard sent his old comrade "Rabbie" a warm and nostalgic greeting. There were very few left now, he said, with whom he could "associate on working class matters," but in the past ten years he had moved in a rather close musical circle: "I have managed the composition of several choruses and other things, including an opera based on the story of the martyrs of Tolpuddle, really the beginning of trades unions in Britain." As for the firebrand oratory that had marked his labour career, he wrote his friend Alex Shepherd a few years later that most of his speaking was now confined to the funeral parlour, carrying out a last service for several old friends.

In 1975, when Bill Pritchard was eighty-seven, Burnaby honoured its former reeve by making him a freeman of the city, and presenting him with the traditional gold key. In response to continuing requests and inquiries, he recorded on tape what he called his "rambling reminiscences," leading up to a kind of final credo:

I speak for no party, and, by the same token, do not speak against any. I have gotten a long way from telling any inquirer what he must do and where he should go. If he is really interested, he can

133

be allowed to make his own judgments. . . . My only desire is to convey to these inquiring youngsters my conception of socialism as a philosophy and a visualization of a possible future society; and I hope that this is offered only as a point of view to be seriously examined and subjected to thorough criticism. If I am remembered I hope it will not be for what I have done but for what I tried to do.

Not long after, Bill Pritchard died in his California home.

The Union Makes Us Strong

Robert Boyd Russell

Roots of a Rebel

On Labour Day 1964 a delegation from the Conservative government of Manitoba waited on an ailing Bob Russell at his home on Winnipeg's well-kept Kingston Row, to present him with an "Address of Appreciation," bearing the official seal of the province and signed by Premier Duff Roblin and Labour Minister Obie Baisley. History had vindicated the veteran trade unionist during his own lifetime. Branded as a "Bolshevik" during the work stoppage of 1919 and jailed for conspiring to undermine the legitimate government of his country, Robert

Boyd Russell was now honoured as the "Grand Old Man of Labour"; and the strikers' battle, which had apparently been lost four decades earlier, had now become part of the city's progressive tradition.

Russell's roots were in British socialism, and particularly in the feisty class-consciousness of the Scottish working poor. Born in 1888, he grew up in Springburn, the working-class district of Glasgow, where political activism was a staple of existence. His father, a worker in a brass foundry, had joined Scotland's Independent Labour Party, and vehemently supported its policy of fundamental social change. "Two of my father's brothers were ministers of the gospel," Russell remembered, "and they used to land in the house every night. My father was a socialist — he was always arguing with them, and I suppose I absorbed all that. He was a rebel by nature — he even sided with the Boers against the British."

A youngster in Springburn received an early introduction to the working world; he was expected to contribute whatever he could earn to his family's meagre income. Young Russell became a baker's boy when he was still at school, making his rounds every morning before class, with his tray balanced on his head. His formal schooling ended when he was twelve and he was apprenticed in the John Brown shipyards on the Clyde. In due time he qualified as a master mechanic and joined the mechanics' union, the Amalgamated Society of Engineers of Great Britain. He was employed for a period in a locomotive works.

As he was to tell an interviewer many years later, there was no clear beginning to his life in politics. He had always been in the labour movement, always among people deeply concerned with social problems, and he followed his father into the Independent Labour Party at an early age. Most weekends, Russell remembered, "I used to be down around Glasgow Square, listening to the haranguers." Sunday evenings meant attendance at a labour forum.

By the early 1900s hard times in Scotland were sending away many of its young people, and at twenty-three Russell too made ready to emigrate. His first choice was the exotic African Gold Coast, he said, but "people were dying there, of malaria and such things, and my father wouldn't hear of it. He told me to go to America." Two of the Hampton boys across the street, John and James, were already in

Canada, and their brother Bert was about to follow. The decision was made: Bob Russell and Bert Hampton would go together, and Bert's sister, Margaret (Peggy), made up her mind to join them.

Peggy Hampton had been born on the same street as Bob, and they had been schoolchildren together. He would often persuade her to come with him to his socialist meetings, although the Hamptons were a church-going family, and she did not like to miss Sunday evening services. A tiny young woman, only four feet nine inches tall to Bob's five feet ten, she had no qualms about venturing into the unknown. "Like a little bulldog," her daughter would describe her; "she could get very angry about things. When she got into something, she really hung on."

In April 1911 the three young people embarked for the New World. They landed in Halifax, took the train to Montreal, stopped there a day or two, and then headed west, to Winnipeg. Peggy stayed with friends in Weston, near the CPR shops, while Bob and her brother shared a room in a downtown rooming house. Within a few days Russell was hired by the CPR as a machinist, and a month later, in May, Bob and Peggy were married in Westminster Church on Maryland Street. They moved into an apartment on Elgin Avenue, with a table and chairs, a bed, and not much else. A piano was added later, and became the musical heart of the household. It was there, in 1912, that their daughter, also named Margaret, was born.

"Nothing But Sober, White Machinists"

The young Scotsman quickly took the measure of his new location. The largest employers in town were the railways; almost four thousand men worked for the CPR alone. In addition a sizable number of metal workers were employed in three large, independent "contract shops": Vulcan Iron Works, Dominion Bridge Company, Manitoba Bridge and Iron Works. The "ironmasters," as they were called, dominated the labour scene in Winnipeg, setting the pattern for other employers. Like Russell, many of the skilled mechanics came from the British Isles, but there was also a constantly renewed labour pool of new Canadians from many backgrounds, eager to work but unsure of themselves in an unfamiliar situation, and just beginning to find a common language and a mutual understanding.

Local union organization was generally fragmented and ineffective. On the railways, the freight-handlers, brakemen, switchmen, and other "running trades" had been organized since 1902 as a single union, the United Brotherhood of Railway Employees, and they negotiated terms from that position of consolidated strength. Among the shop workers, by contrast, a number of separate craft unions struggled for a foothold, each essentially an exclusive society of highly qualified tradesmen, not open to semiskilled workmen or labourers, and each attempting to deal separately with the employer on behalf of its own members. The railways were consequently in a position to dictate wages and working conditions. They might consent to discuss terms with the various crafts in their shops, but all agreements, they insisted, were signed with informal "committees of employees" only, and they refused to grant the unions official recognition.

Following the lead of the railways, the majority of the contract shops pursued an even more adamant anti-union policy. Attempts to organize the workers were ruthlessly suppressed, so that an employee might be fired for suspected union membership. Barrett, the Vulcan Iron Works boss, was reputed to have declared, "God gave me this plant, and by God I'll run it the way I want to!"

In the Winnipeg railway shops, when Russell came to work there, a machinists' craft union was in place, the International Association of Machinists (IAM), an affiliate of the American Federation of Labor (AFL). Several years earlier, he found out, the machinists had tried to interest his old union, Britain's Amalgamated Society of Engineers, in coming into the Canadian shops, but without success: "They said this was the frozen north, so they told us to get in touch with the Machinists' Union down in Washington, D.C.," Russell told a later interviewer. "Well, the Americans weren't very much interested insofar as spending money was concerned, but they were prepared to give us the paraphernalia and the dues books, and they told us to get organized." Organize the men did, to form Lodge 122, with members recruited and an executive elected from employees of both the CPR and the CNR, but still not recognized by the employers.

In those years, Russell explained, there were "tremendous jealousies" in the various crafts, with the skilled craftsmen intensely proud of their own mastery, identifying their union local as an exclusive "lodge" and determined to keep the unskilled labourers out:

> At that time, you see, they wouldn't take negroes into the organization — the machinists wouldn't, and most of the other crafts were the same. As for the labourer, he was just put in the same category as what the negro was, you see. You couldn't even organize your helpers in the machinists' union — they had to be in separate lodges, in case they contaminated the other fellow. . . . The helper couldn't tighten up a nut, couldn't do nothing. . . . You'd be working on a locomotive, tightening up the cylinders on the right-hand side, and your helper could very easily have tightened up the nuts on the other side. But no: it was sacrilege, if you ever allowed a helper to raise a spanner. All he was to do was the heavy stuff, the lifting.

When Russell presented himself for membership, together with several others including Dick Johns, he took immediate exception to the restrictive practice. His very admission to the local was a declaration of independence, a refusal to play by rules he did not endorse:

> So they took us in front of the president, the assembly all stood up, and they asked us to cross our left hand over our heart and raise our right hand to God and take this oath. But when they come to the part that said, "I shall never nominate for membership in the International Association of Machinists anything but a sober and industrious white machinist" — well, we refused. We were not taking that kind of oath, nothing but "sober, white machinists."

The presiding officers were thrown into confusion, the rebels were sent home, and a hasty consultation took place. The next day the president offered to omit the disputed phrase, and the new recruits were sworn in — privately, not in the presence of the whole membership. They promised only to be honourable and true to the Machinists' Union.

In Russell's retelling of the story, a faint mockery of the lodge's ritu-
alistic mumbo jumbo is evident, and an objection as well to the discrimination against blacks. But the formula of the membership oath
was dictated by the American parent organization, and colour was not a
major factor in the demography of early twentieth-century Winnipeg.
Russell's opposition, from the outset, was directed at the exclusion of
the semiskilled and the unskilled "helpers" from the protection of the
mechanics' union, an equally invidious discrimination, he understood,
by one class of workers against another. In retrospect what he himself
identified here was the beginning of his battle to replace the narrowly
defined craft union with an all-encompassing industrial union, and possibly also the beginning of a determination to politicize the entire
working class.

Under the umbrella of the AFL, the American union movement
avoided direct involvement in politics, defining its mandate as the pursuit of its members' specific interests; but in the British labour movement politics and union activism went hand in hand. Russell had studied Karl Marx in Scotland and had developed a firm conviction that the
interests of all working people were the same, and in conflict with the
designs of capital. Self-taught, versed in the writings of labour polemi-
cists, his contributions to labour publications became forceful and
direct, but he identified absolutely with ordinary people, and his speech
retained the common man's rough-hewn idiom, along with his own
indelible Scottish burr.

The Politics of Union Organization

Aggressive and energetic, Bob Russell quickly attracted attention
among his mates in the shops. He became the treasurer of Lodge 122,
and within a year or two began contributing a regular column to the
Machinists' Bulletin, the newspaper of the IAM in Canada. Still a working man on the shop floor, and proud of it, he served on union committees, appeared at public meetings, participated in labour negotiations,
and carried the battle for stronger and larger unions wherever he could.

His insistent theme was the need to go beyond restrictive union
practices. "The days of the craft unions are over," he wrote in 1913:

The call of the working class for industrial union has gone out in order to meet the great change in industrial expansion and construction of new machinery. . . . The hands of the working class must be more powerful than all the new machinery which the capitalist class will use to make you slaves.

Bringing the conflict home to an immediate issue, he took up the cause of the unorganized and underpaid apprentices, arguing, "These boys are our brothers, our responsibility," and he demanded again and again that the machinists acknowledge their brotherhood with the labourers who worked beside them.

Russell rose quickly in the Machinists' hierarchy. In 1915 he was elected to the executive of Section 1, the CPR division of the Canadian IAM, and the following year he was named chairman, with a seat as well on the union's national executive. At the same time, as the demands on his time and energy grew, his family responsibilities were also expanding. A second child, David, was born in 1916, and the Russells moved from their small apartment to a house on Ross Avenue, also in Weston, across the street from the home of John Queen and his family.

Coming from a Labour Party background in Glasgow, Bob Russell was inevitably drawn into Winnipeg's political scene. The Socialist Party of Canada had been active in the city since before the turn of the century, disciples of Karl Marx strenuously insisting on the inevitability of a social and economic revolution. To that end, as Bill Pritchard maintained, describing the SPC's endeavours in British Columbia, the education of workers was a prime objective. Unions served some purpose, the SPC granted, by making their members aware of the oppression of the working class by the bosses, but the most absolute of the SPC theorists decreed that the limited concessions exacted by union action served only to delay the coming revolt of the masses. In practice, however, the SPC found union organization a ready instrument for disseminating its ideas, and when it was convenient the party made common cause with the union movement and with moderates on the left. Russell became a member of the Socialist Party of Canada, finding no conflict between his union role and his political convictions.

Russell's neighbour, John Queen, was a member of the rival, reformist Social Democratic Party, and the two crossed swords in endless political argument. The Social Democrats, Russell contended, believed in "the emancipation of the working class almost one at a time . . . progressing by evolution," but the Socialist Party understood better:

> Old Daniel DeLeon . . . used to point out that you can take a poodle dog and you can cut its hair and you can tie a ribbon around its neck; you can make it look like a lion, all shaved and the tail put up in a tassel at the end, but a poodle dog it was and a poodle dog it remains. . . . You had to cross it with some other thing, and the offspring of that was no longer a poodle dog. . . . If you're going to build a new building, you've got to tear down the old.

When World War I was declared Russell responded with a tirade in the *Machinists' Bulletin* against the established economic order its "insane commercial and capitalist rivalry. . . . This is a capitalists' war, so why should we let ourselves be gulled to fight their battles?" The column provoked a heated retort in the *Bulletin* and, it would seem, considerable pressure from the IAM head office to refrain from unpatriotic controversy, but Russell was undaunted and continued to take issue with the union's official policies.

The labour cause, as Bob Russell saw it from the beginning of his career, was indivisible, and he called repeatedly for the working class to become aware of what must be done. When workers vote, he stormed in the *Machinists' Bulletin* , they "never give a thought to the things that concern us most, our daily bread"; and when the gentlemanly reformer, Fred Dixon, was elected to the provincial legislature in 1914, Russell commented sardonically that "as usual the working class let themselves be gulled for another four years. . . . They preferred," he said, "to vote for the dopey stuff called 'direct legislation'."

In his later years Russell acknowledged, with a kind of reluctant generosity, the effectiveness of his old adversaries, even as he reiterated a commitment to Marxist absolutism. Fred Dixon, he told an interviewer, was a natural leader and a good thinker, even though Queen and people like him became "contaminated" with ideas on the single tax and direct legislation and other "dopey stuff." In hindsight Russell was apt to declare that he had never objected to the minor reforms that brought some small pleasure into the lives of working people, such as John Queen's battle for Sunday trains to the summer resorts; but he still insisted that in principle the SPC was right:

> Sure, they were only palliators all right, but they were accomplishments that a hell of a lot of people enjoyed. . . . But why not go for the whole damn works, and then the other fellow will be compelled to hand these things out anyway?

As World War I raged in the bloody fields of Europe, battles over principles and tactics were fought out in the crowded meetings of Winnipeg's Trades and Labor Council, and the entire Labor Temple crackled with nonconformist electricity. Half a century later Russell remembered these encounters warmly, but the various antagonists were in a determined competition for ascendancy, and the Socialist Party members made full use of the opportunity to hone their strategy. Rather than compete for union office, Russell explained, they tried to manage the discussion on the floor, to manipulate the meeting by presenting their radical proposals as if these ideas came spontaneously from the membership at large. "I think," Russell commented, looking back, still apparently pleased with his old party's cunning, "that's where some of our Communist friends learned the tactic of splitting themselves here and there among the audience." An adversarial and even subversive stance of this sort was to characterize SPC policy, as the left moved uncertainly toward a common political goal.

Was the plight of "the working class" to be ameliorated by piecemeal improvements, as urged by Dixon and many other reformers, or was an absolute change in society the overriding goal? Russell was battling simultaneously for enhanced union power and for a radically different world, with working people in control. Both aims are discernible, undifferentiated, in his early assertions. Increasingly, his impatience with stop-gap measures would pit him against some of his colleagues in the labour movement, and ultimately a choice would be forced upon him between the survival of the union he created and the advancement of world revolution.

The War Years in the Shops

By 1913 the building boom in Winnipeg had collapsed. The CPR cut back its operation, dismissing many of its fifteen hundred unskilled labourers and putting nearly two thousand skilled workers on part-time hours; and toward the end of 1914, with industry still stagnant, the railway began closing its repair shops for prolonged periods. The shop unions were hit hard; unemployed members could not pay their dues, membership declined, organizing became difficult.

Then, by early 1916, work began to trickle back into the railway shops, chiefly for the production of munitions. As more men enlisted in the armed forces, a manpower shortage developed, and with it an opportunity for the union movement to gain ground. Yet even with the increasing demand for competent craftsmen, particularly machinists, working conditions were very bad, Russell remembered. Wages were low and hours long. In the railway shops the most skilled trades were getting forty-two cents per hour, working ten hours a day and six days a week, including Saturday, and efforts to wring concessions from a reluctant employer were almost invariably branded as treasonous in a time of national emergency. The War Measures Act further constrained workers' options. "If you were found without a job," Russell said, "you were a vagrant and you were jailed." All in all, he reflected, looking back at this troubled time, "We certainly needed a union."

Many of the machinists had been drawn to western Canada by the promise of land grants. To fulfil the grant conditions, Russell said, they would work in the shops during the winter, and then go back to improve their homesteads during the growing season. These arrangements suited the railways very well: they were only too glad to get rid of employees during the slack summer months. "Easily half the union members," Russell recalled, were central Europeans, "good boys, active — very active — rebels where they came from. . . . And of course when they got here and found the conditions were pretty raw, they jumped in and participated in the fight." On the other hand, he pointed out, with a touch of unconscious superiority, most of the leaders were "old country English and Scottish," and they took charge because of their greater experience and self-confidence:

> Well, you come from Britain where you quit at twelve o'clock on a Saturday and go to football games . . . we couldn't understand this working all those long hours, seven o'clock in the morning till five o'clock in the evening, working on a Saturday. So we decided we were going to remedy that situation, and get the shorter work week, and have some fun. We approached the management, and they said no.
>
> So all of the Old Country fellows refused to work on a Saturday afternoon. . . . We blew the whistle for a stop and we stopped — refused to go back again. . . . The CPR didn't retaliate. Some of the men who wanted to work would work — just a handful — but they soon got wise to it. So they closed the shops on Saturday afternoon, and that's how we established the half-day Saturday in western Canada.

"We were the first," Russell boasted proudly, ahead of their eastern union brothers in obtaining both the shorter work week and higher wages.

World-wide, during these years, a groundswell had begun in the labour movement to broaden union membership. There was the Spartacus movement in Germany, the Industrial Workers of the World in the United States, and the radical agitation on the Canadian west coast; and within the IAM itself the local in St. Louis, Missouri, was stirring up a controversy by its campaign to amalgamate all the metal workers into a single union. Urged on by activists like Russell, the Canadian machinists intensified recruiting in the railway and contract shops, spreading east through Fort William to Toronto and Mimico, and then, with some difficulty because of the language barrier, to the French-speaking locals in the various shops in Quebec. "It wasn't like a big, high-falutin', high-paid officer that was coming," Russell said; "it was the guys from the shops that was coming, talking turkey to them. . . ."

As a means to an end they supported the growth of the different craft unions in the shops and the assembly of the locals into federations. The battle was long and arduous, with the railways adamantly refusing to recognize either the combined or the separate associations, and ruthless in suppressing strike action. One shop, Russell said, the Grand Trunk Pacific, was an unorganized territory and always "a thorn in our side, because when we went into negotiations with the CPR or the CNR it was always the Grand Trunk Pacific that was held up to you: how can we pay this when the other railroad is working for that?... So we organized it and we struck it."

The company retaliated by bringing new emigrants from England and Scotland directly on the colonist trains into the roundhouses at Rivers, Manitoba, and housing them there, but the embattled machinists held their ground and won their point. When the strike was settled they closed ranks to take a covert revenge on the company and its strikebreakers. "Those were pretty rough days," Russell reflected:

> When those fellows who had been doing scabs went out to get jobs elsewhere, in the CP or in the CNR, you never saw a bunch of men got rid of as quick in your life. A fellow would be working up at the top of a locomotive; he'd lay down a long iron spanner, and it would fall down. Nobody had kicked it, of course. Things would fall off the running board; cross rods would fall; a bolt would be loose and everything would fall. It was sabotage of the worst kind, instinctive sabotage. A terrible time, just like the woolly west you read about down in the United States.

For their part the railways had their own methods of managing their employees, methods which Russell recalled with abiding contempt:

> [The CPR] provided recreation activities — social clubs, baseball teams, football teams. There were dances at the Royal Alexandra Hotel on Saturday nights, and the common stuff from the shops would go down there and dance with the foreman or the foreman's wife. . . . Well of course, the rebels that were out from Europe, they were having none of this kind of stuff . . . but you always had a bunch that were willing to hobnob with the boss. . . .

The belligerent union campaign put the western machinists decidedly out of step with their parent union, the American IAM, which offered no help to the Winnipeg local. Russell was still indignant some fifty years later:

> You had to get permission from the International before you struck. Well, they wouldn't give permission to strike and we'd strike anyway. We'd win the fight and then they'd come out in their magazine, telling all the glories that the locals in Canada had won, and yet we never once collected strike pay in any of those strikes. And when it come to organization . . . there was only a small mite that they would throw into the kitty.

The locals became more self-reliant, Russell conceded, but if "the employer" was his sworn enemy, he remained almost equally hostile to "the International," the domineering, indifferent IAM.

The unions slowly gained ground, making the most of the opportunities that wartime shortages of manpower presented, but always impeded by the competition between the crafts themselves. Russell remembered one confrontation, in about 1915 or 1916, when Grant Hall, the western vice president of the railway, offered all the shop crafts together a lump-sum increase, to be divided as they chose. A squabble immediately broke out, with the machinists demanding the lion's share of the gain, and then the boiler makers and the other trades in turn, said Russell, "taking their whack at the kitty," until nothing at all was left for the car repairers and the coach builders, the trades with the largest number of men.

"That's no dice," the men decided, "that's no good," and they demanded and obtained a uniform increase across the board. But they also heard an ominous reminder from the canny Grant Hall: "Remember, he says, apples will grow again, and when they do, we'll be in the vineyard doing the picking. . . ."

Still, in the perspective of years, Russell would remember his old opponent rather fondly. Hall, he said, was "a damned good Marxian student himself," and he recalled with particular amusement one entire afternoon they had spent discussing economic theory when they should have been negotiating a wage increase. Tough and shrewd as the labour men had to be, they recognized a skilled adversary across the bargaining table.

In the end, wartime pressures helped break down the distinction between the machinists and their excluded helpers. By 1918 there was a shortage of skilled machinists, and the men who had learned their trade by observation and experience were allowed to apply for promotion to machinists and for membership in the strong machinists' lodges. Further, the machinists now proceeded to recruit the shop labourers, persuading them to leave their own ineffective locals.

The achievement was not without its problems, as Russell found to his chagrin. One small labourers' union, for example, had been collecting its modest dues from its members out of their very limited wages, without providing much in return, and now the officers seemed to be urging their members to transfer to the machinists, while they themselves remained behind. "And then we found out," Russell said, "that three of the king-pins, the president, vice-president, and secretary-treasurer, had taken the union funds . . . and they had invested it in CPR stock. They had thousands of dollars at work, and the damn CPR stock had been split about four times . . . and with nobody else left in the local they divided the spoils amongst themselves!"

Campaigning tirelessly for union effectiveness, Bob Russell became the IAM's business agent in 1917, his first paid union job, and early in 1918 he left the shop floor, perhaps with some regret, to take the full-time position of secretary-treasurer of the IAM in Canada, representing all the machinists in the railway shops across the country.

With unity achieved within the different trades, the next step toward Russell's vision of a united labour force was not long in coming. Three regional divisions of railway workers already operated within the AFL in the United States; and at a convention in Winnipeg, in February 1918, Division 4 was established, bringing together all the railway crafts across Canada, with Winnipeg designated the division's headquarters. A year earlier the Canadian Railway War Board had been formed, to coordinate rail transportation in Canada; and beginning in April 1918, in Montreal, the combined employers faced the combined employees across the bargaining table, thereby giving de facto recognition to one unified organization for all the shop crafts.

"The war was still on," Russell continued, and the Minister notified this new federation that if we dared to strike we'd all be put in khaki and set back to work at $1.10 a day, the same as what the soldiers was getting. But we wouldn't buckle under. We said to them, All right, you put us in khaki at $1.10 a day and see how many locomotives and how many coaches and how many street cars you get out of these shops.

There was an impasse, but just at this time, faced with similar demands from its own railway shop workers, the United States Railroad Administration, under Colonel William McAdoo, granted a uniform wage increase to all the shop crafts across the country; and the Canadian Railway War Board, presumably with government approval, offered the same terms. As a slightly derisive acknowledgement, the machinists took to calling their newly promoted helpers "McAdoo mechanics."

The offer came, however, with the stipulation that the unions were to give up their right to strike, and this loss of their one effective weapon was particularly unacceptable to the western unionists. There was pressure from both the Trades and Labor Congress and the American Federation of Labor to comply, and the eastern union delegates at the negotiating table, generally less combative than their western colleagues, agreed to endorse the Railway War Board's offer, and urged their locals to accept. The western delegates angrily declared their categorical opposition and left for home.

Put to the vote, the deal was approved by almost all the eastern locals, by far the majority in Division 4, and the settlement was passed into law by order-in-council, in July 1918. In Winnipeg, on the other hand, the union rank-and-file would not be swayed, even by the IAM threat to revoke their charters. They voted to support a national strike to enforce their stand, and retaliated against their American executives by withholding dues from the central office for several months.

The Metal Trades Council

Russell, in the meantime, was driving hard to force Winnipeg's independent contract shops into recognizing the union. The tight-fisted "ironmasters," as determined as ever not to countenance the organization of their workers, had granted some concessions in their munitions divisions, but wages in the shops as a whole, the union maintained, were below the overall scale in the industry. In May 1917 Lodge 457 had taken its members out on strike, demanding a wage increase, but the major metal-shop owners had fought back with strikebreakers, with anti-picketing injunctions, and with damage suits against individual strike leaders. The Winnipeg Trades and Labor Council had called on union members across Canada to mount a sympathetic strike in support of the local, but after several tense weeks the effort had collapsed under the threat of further legal action.

Now, during the spring of 1918, while the negotiations were under way in Montreal with the Railway War Board, Russell was determined to achieve for the contract machinists what they had been denied the year before. His chief colleague in the campaign was Dick Johns, like himself a machinist at the CPR and a member of the Socialist Party of Canada. Day after day Bob Russell was to be found at the gates of the city's metalcraft factories, talking to the men coming on shift or leaving, tirelessly urging them to put their faith in the power of united action, to join the union in defiance of company orders. An enormously persuasive man, his salty informality perhaps even more convincing in the give-and-take of a small cluster of people than as a speaker on a platform, he succeeded in recruiting enough new union members to become the target of the ironmasters' lasting hostility.

As a final tactic Russell and Johns brought together all six of the city's metalcraft unions, both railway and contract-shop employees, into the Metal Trades Council, with J. R. Adair as chairman and Russell as secretary. Once again, in June 1918, the contract-shop unions scheduled a strike against forty-five city establishments, demanding recognition of their unions and of the MTC, and wage parity with the railway shops. The federal government, acutely aware of the belligerence of western labour, called a temporary halt to the threatened walkout, and appointed a commission of three to investigate, with Fred J. Tipping, the president of the Winnipeg Trades and Labor Council, as the labour representative.

Russell appeared before the commission to argue that the ironmasters' refusal to engage in collective bargaining was out of line with practices elsewhere, and that their wage scale was below the norm. Unfortunately for the union cause, however, Russell's own evidence indicated beyond a doubt that Winnipeg metal shops paid their workers much the same as other shops in both Canada and the United States. The ironmasters hardened their opposition, and absolutely refused to grant official status to the Metal Trades Council.

Without waiting for the commission's report, the metal workers demanded that the employers enter into immediate negotiations or face a work stoppage beginning on Monday, July 22. Russell now seemed to weaken, undermined, perhaps, by his own miscalculation. He agreed on July 20 to keep his members on the job until after the commission had issued its findings; but a day later he warned that the shopmen could be held back no longer. There was no movement of the employers, and on July 22 the contract shop workers walked out. Russell appeared to have lost control of his people, and the ugly mood in the city became so extreme that the relatively moderate Trades and Labor Council once again moved to poll its member unions on the question of a general sympathy strike.

The commission's findings, after almost three weeks more of mounting tension, caused further trouble. Reaching for a workable compromise, it proposed a limited degree of collective bargaining, that each employer agree to negotiate a contract with the organized workers in his own shop, but not with the Metal Trades Council. The men were in no mood for partial measures, however, and to add to their fury the commission's unacceptable directive was endorsed by Fred Tipping, supposedly labour's advocate.

Russell exhorted a noisy mass meeting of the strikers and their supporters to stand fast, assuring them that the railway workers would come out across the country in a sympathy strike. A week later, after some debate, the Trades and Labor Council passed its second motion that summer in favour of a general sympathy strike, and shortly afterward Tipping was suspended for a year from his position as president. The ironmasters followed their customary practice and took legal action, and the prolonged impasse gradually eroded the strikers' resolution. One by one they drifted back to work, bowing to their employers' conditions, leaving behind a residue of intense resentment. Russell and Tipping traded accusations, each charging the other with incompetence and betrayal.

Russell's defeat rankled and he attributed it to insufficient unity in the labour ranks and a failure to carry out the threatened general strike. Within the Trades and Labor Council there was a sizable representation of Socialist Party members, now determined to assert themselves. In the council elections held in December of that year they mounted a full-scale campaign to gain control, but lost to the moderates. Bob Russell was defeated for the presidency, but commented that they had "pretty near got control. . . . When we get it we will use it to our advantage."

Meanwhile, across the Atlantic the Russian Revolution of 1917 seemingly played out the enthralling drama of proletarian triumph that Marxist socialism taught was inevitable, and strikes and uprisings elsewhere in Europe and the United States erupted in its wake — proof, if proof were needed, that the climactic moment was near.

One Big Union: Run-Up to the General Strike

At the Trades and Labor Congress meeting in Quebec City in September 1918, Russell and Johns were still smarting over the failure of the metal trades strike, and when the western contingent could not make its voice heard, the two Winnipeggers were among the most insistent on a separate conference of western labour. As plans for the proposed assembly began to take shape, its purpose came immediately under question: was it to create a more effective representation of the West within the Trades and Labor Congress, or to bring about secession and a separate organization? The issue was complicated further by the dominant presence of members of the Socialist Party of Canada. As avowed Marxists, Russell and Johns and British Columbia's Bill Pritchard and a number of others in all the provincial delegations subscribed to the doctrine that the working class was destined to rule the world; but how and when that was to take place, and what role the union movement was to play, was not clear.

In October 1918, although the war was coming to an end, an order-in-council outlawed all strikes in wartime, and even the compliant Trades and Labor Congress challenged Ottawa to justify this restriction of union rights. When the authorities attempted to use the edict to quell a strike of CPR freight-handlers in Calgary, arresting several strike leaders, there was fierce resistance. Calgary unions threatened a general strike, and support came from other cities. The Winnipeg Trades and Labor Council approved a vote on a general strike in sympathy with its Alberta brothers, as it had done, inconclusively, in the case of its own metal trades strikers. The government backed down, and the arrested men were released without penalty. Even as a threat, "direct action," labour's term for the strike as a frontal assault on authority, appeared to be proving its effectiveness.

More fuel was added to the radical fire: the increased use of orders-in-council to put down radical dissent, the banning of labour-oriented foreign-language publications and ethnic organizations deemed "alien" or "Bolshevik." Western labour, with its large component of immigrants from eastern Europe, recognized the move as directed specifically against its various ethnic locals, and was incited to further denunciation of an unacceptable government and an unacceptable system.

At the protest meeting in the Walker Theatre on that Sunday afternoon before Christmas 1918, Bob Russell, the last speaker, denounced the sending of troops to Russia "to protect the investments of capitalists in Allied countries," and he prophesied that "capitalism must eventually disappear, just as the feudal system had disappeared to give place to capitalism." At the subsequent Majestic Theatre rally, now openly a Socialist Party event, he seized the occasion to heap scorn on the mildly reformist Winnipeg Labor Party: its programme, he said, tried to cover "every possible freak thought that ever existed;" and the Dominion Labor Party, he charged, merely attempted to reconstruct the capitalist system and was therefore doomed to failure. In the end, of course, the punitive arm of the law would make no distinction between the "true" socialists and the reformers Russell scorned.

All of these conflicts and concerns erupted at the Western Labor Conference in March 1919, as Socialist Party members took the lead in the deliberations. Russell arrived in Calgary with Johns and their contingent from Manitoba, primarily to push for the industrial union he had long advocated, in defiance of the traditional craft unionism of the Trades and Labor Congress. Within the dominant group, however, in keeping with the Marxist philosophy of the Socialist Party, British Columbia's Kavanagh and and Alberta's husband-and-wife team, Joseph and Sarah Knight, were excited by what they saw as an opportunity to further the class struggle, and in this sense their aim was avowedly revolutionary.

In their later years Pritchard and Russell emphatically maintained that the One Big Union they helped create in Calgary was designed only to further union interests. It was not a political party and not intended to initiate something like a syndicalist takeover of the country's government. Still, when Russell was asked to clarify, in retrospect, the union movement's role in politics, he protested that, as he had understood from the beginning, the two are inseparable. "What you gain in the economic field you could lose by political action," he said, and he insisted that he had realized very early the necessity of directing union strategy in the light of socialist principles. If the agenda for the Calgary conference was to join together all Canadian unions into one effective structure embracing all industries, the ultimate goal must surely have seemed in sight, the coming together of all the working people of the world into one great instrument of working-class power.

Out of this tangle of intentions and expectations, the One Big Union emerged, and the recruiting of unions and unionists to the new organization began. Back home again, in a Winnipeg being ripped apart by labour strife, Russell and Johns set about enlisting members and raising money. By the end of March the *OBU Bulletin* appeared out of Edmonton, and Russell added writing for that publication to his work load. As the secretary-treasurer of IAM Division 4, he had immediate access to the railway shopmen, and he used these channels to promote the OBU at every opportunity. The struggle for control of the Trades and Labor Council continued, and the balance remained in the hands of moderates, but the council was being pushed farther and farther toward the Socialist Party left. It voted to contribute to the OBU fund, and to permit "educational" meetings for the OBU under its auspices.

Delighted by the success of their fellow proletarians in Europe against the Russian czar, some labour men had taken to addressing each other as "comrade" rather than the customary "brother." As the mainstream press trumpeted the horror of Red subversives among unwary Canadians, labour radicals adopted the revolutionary vocabulary, part tongue-in-cheek, mocking their detractors, and part in earnest.

"Dear Comrade," Bob Russell wrote to Tom Cassidy in North Bay, "I am pleased to note your little reminder of Reds keeping in touch at these times . . . and that you have sent to Vancouver for one hundred Bolsheviki and Soviets." Presumably he was referring to the OBU literature Cassidy had ordered: the Winnipeg office had ten thousand pieces for distribution across the East. Charles Dickie, the secretary-treasurer of Division 4, sent his compliments to his friend: "Well Bob I see by the press reports that you are Chairman of the SOVIET in Winnipeg, more power to you." From Edmonton Carl Berg reported to Russell, "I just got in a shipment of Bolsheviki funds" — meaning the $250 he had received from a miners' local. In the eyes of a hostile police force, here was proof positive that foreign interests had infiltrated the country, instigating all the labour unrest.

Indeed, the "Reds" did keep in touch, eagerly exchanging information and laying plans for the coming takeover, although whether their target was the union movement or the entire country was never quite clear. The diagram of a soviet administration that was found in Ivens's papers circulated among them and was reprinted in the *Western Labor News*. "Yours for the OBU," Russell signed his letter, offering Victor Midgley the printing plate of the diagram for use in the *B.C. Federationist*. And again, as far back as November 1918, in the run-up to the ominous Calgary Conference, Russell had intimated to Joe Knight, "As you can readily realize we could pack it with Reds and no doubt start something"; and he had signed this piece of self-incrimination, "Yours in revolt."

All of this correspondence seemed prove to all levels of government that in Winnipeg lawful institutions were on the verge of collapse, and even worse, that Bolshevik subversion had penetrated this prairie out-post, aided and abetted by the very visible "foreigners" among its popu-lation. Covert agents of the Mounted Police had taken note of the pro-ceedings at the Walker and the Majestic theatres; they had made their way into union halls and labour rallies, and into the excited delibera-tions of the Calgary Conference. The reports of these operatives were often a trifle lurid: "The Bolsheviks have, or are using, violet rays [sic] to cause blindness," one early item read; but rumours about firearms smuggled into the country were seriously investigated, sensational fare for the subsequent legal proceedings.

In the weeks after Calgary it became evident that the creation of the OBU would be difficult, despite the early enthusiasm of its originators. Aided by the formidable strength of the AFL, the TLC fought back, sending organizers to counter the radical inroads on union member-ship. If the majority in a local voted to join the new union, then there were legal obstacles, and a number of locals opting to secede were expelled from their international unions and had their assets frozen by the courts. In Winnipeg, the money promised by the Trades and Labor Council and desperately needed to finance publications and lectures was held up for weeks.

By early summer Russell was thoroughly embroiled in the simulta-neous worries of a struggling OBU and his own striking machinists. When the constitutional conference of the OBU met on June 4, he was locked into the confrontation with Winnipeg employers and authori-ties, and could not attend.

A City in Conflict

In April 1919 Russell's Metal Trades Council had once again submitted its demands to the contract shops: union recognition, a higher wage scale, a forty-four-hour week. The three leaders in the city's metals industry had refused once again to deal with the MTC, and a letter from Vulcan Iron Works to all its employees spelled out its position: this was an "open shop;" there could be discussion with individual employees or groups of employees, but no dealing with committees that included persons employed by other firms — that is, with representatives of a union or the Metal Trades Council. The case was then put before the members of all the constituent unions of the MTC at a meeting in the Labor Temple on the last night of April. They voted unanimously to strike at once, agreeing only at the urging of the executive to wait one day longer for a response from the ironmasters. There was no response, and on the morning of Friday, May 2, the metal workers in all the contract shops across the city walked out on strike.

Unresolved disputes remained as well in the city's construction industry, among the retail clerks, and in the various civic departments, so that virtually the entire labour force was in a fractious mood. The unions were ready for the bold measure, never actually undertaken before, of a general walk-out in sympathy with their striking comrades. Bob Russell electrified an emergency meeting of the Trades and Labor Council with a call to action, absolute and immediate, for the sake of labour everywhere, and a referendum on a general strike was ordered among all affiliated unions. In the meantime, preparations for a city-wide work stoppage were set in motion.

At the Trades and Labor Council meeting on Tuesday, May 13, with hundreds of keyed-up unionists packed into the assembly room and spilling out into the corridor, the chairman reported that the ironmasters had once again refused to deal with the Metal Trades Council, and that Premier Norris had now announced the appointment of an arbitration committee, to consist of Bob Russell, the MTC lawyer T. J. Murray, and two representatives of the contract shops. This last-minute intervention was brushed aside by the council: union recognition must come first. Then the members cheered the results of the referendum, a huge majority for the sympathy strike, and they cheered again when the chairman announced the time for the action to begin: Thursday morning, May 15, at eleven o'clock. By Thursday evening, virtually all business in the city had come to a halt.

As the acrimonious negotiations with the ironmasters lurched on, with Russell unremitting in his demands, the Central Strike Committee to an extent controlled the pulse of the city's activities, becoming a kind of temporary government; and Russell, for one, could only reflect wryly on the efficiency of the strikers' unaccustomed exercise of power. "It is a fine spectacle," he wrote to Midgley, "to see

employers coming to the Labor Temple, asking for permission to operate their various industries." For Winnipeg's apprehensive elite, however, the strikers' very competence was further evidence that a revolutionary conspiracy was under way.

The impression was not limited to the city's "better" citizens alone
that something more was intended by this labour action than the
recognition of collective bargaining. At the trial that followed, one of
the RNWMP officers testified that he had heard a striker declare, "The
government of the city has been shifted from the City Hall to the
Labor Temple, and we mean to keep it there." Russell himself told the
story, perhaps apocryphal, of encountering a pair of North End women
on a Winnipeg street, "pulling each other's hair, screaming and kick-
ing": in anticipation of the great victory of the working class, they had
gone down to affluent Wellington Crescent to select houses for themselves, in the redistribution they were sure would follow, and both fan-
cied the same mansion.

Such incidents aside, the mood in Winnipeg was tense and anxious
for the six long weeks of the strike. In the continuous round of negotiations, Russell was constantly at the helm, pressing his demands with the
metal-works owners, while George Armstrong wrangled with the
building contractors and Abe Heaps and John Queen fought the battle
on city council. Alex Shepherd, then the secretary-treasurer of IAM
Local 457, remained deeply impressed with the machinist leader's performance. "Russell had great capabilities," he wrote to a later historian:

> If there was a jam-up going on in the General Strike Committee
> (as there frequently was) and it was an important issue, Russell
> had the ability to review all angles of the debate, showing the
> strength or weakness of each position and finally suggesting the
> solution that should be adopted. It invariably was. . . . Russell
> was the real brains in the conduct of the strike. . . . He had his
> fingers on all decisions made, and when taken, stood behind the
> consequences.

Thus, Russell's role was only too visible, and his much-publicized promotion of the One Big Union could now more than ever be seen as a

dangerous step toward the domination of Canadian society by the working class. Moreover, Winnipeg had become the hub of the country-wide railway system, and the closing of the repair shops was seriously hampering national operations. Now the running trades themselves talked of going out in sympathy, and on the evening of June 15 the Canadian Pacific switchmen and trainmen struck.

By this time Winnipeg's strikers would accept nothing short of full union recognition. On June 16, the machine-shop owners published an apparently conciliatory offer in the papers, without submitting it first to the negotiating committee, ostensibly declaring their willingness to recognize a union of contract shop workers, but ignoring the Metal Trades Council and the Trades and Labor Council. In the circumstances the Strike Committee did not respond. When the authorities finally moved against the strikers, in the early hours of Tuesday, June 17, after almost five weeks of frustration, Russell's name headed the list of ringleaders for whom arrest warrants were issued.

Bob and Peggy's daughter Margaret was then five years old, and she retained an indelible memory of that moment at the family home in Weston:

> The night the Mounties came, it was after midnight, maybe around two in the morning, and we were all sleeping out on the back verandah. They were all around in the yard, and then they came bursting into the house — my dad let them in. They went through all the drawers, threw everything out on the floor. My mother was very upset, but my dad just said, "It's happened, and that's it. Nothing you can do about it."

Union men, shocked and thrown off balance, said that the chief of police himself, Chris Newton, served the warrant, with an apology: "We've come to take you, Bob. Sorry it had to be you." He had known Bob Russell for many years, they said, and now had the task of enforcing the law.

Russell joined the others who were caught in the police net that night and driven out to the federal penitentiary in a flotilla of private cars. Police raided the offices of the Labor Temple, the Ukrainian

Labor Temple, and the Jewish Liberty Temple, looking for incriminating evidence. At the Labor Temple, the *Strike Bulletin* told its readers that day, a squad of Mounties smashed a plate glass window, entered and searched every room, opened every desk; and on the second floor, where Brother Russell had his office, the paper reported, the police allegedly found copies of the *Red Flag*, published in Vancouver, and a quantity of literature "endorsing the Soviet Government as the one body approaching perfection."

By the following Thursday, arrangements had been made for the release on bail of the first leaders arrested, and Bob Russell returned home to await trial. The sensational drama in the small Canadian city had been reported in newspapers thousands of miles away, and from Russell's mother in Scotland to her son came a two-word cable: "Have courage."

Union Disunity: OBU Against TLC

While strikers and employers battled in Winnipeg, the constitution for the OBU had been drawn up in Calgary, with a preamble rich in the language of class conflict:

> Modern industrial society is divided into two classes, those who possess and do not produce, and those who produce and do not possess. . . . Between these two classes a continual struggle takes place. . . . In the struggle over the purchase and sale of labor power the buyers are always masters — the sellers always workers. From this fact arises the inevitable class struggle. . . .

Accordingly the new union was to be based on "class and class needs . . . irrespective of nationality, sex, or craft," and its purpose would be to educate the working class for its forthcoming role. In keeping also with its democratic principles, all OBU officers, elected or salaried, were to be subject to provisions for a "recall," and no officer, organizer, or secretary was to be paid more than forty dollars per week because, as Russell explained, that was the average wage paid to a mechanic in the shops at the time.

Now officially constituted, the OBU declared itself an industrial union, offering working people a new and better way to negotiate with management. This was the message that organizers had already been taking to locals across the country, in a vigorous recruiting campaign. At the nerve centre of the OBU design would be its Central Labor Council, bringing together the workers in all the crafts and all the industries of a given area into a single body — in effect, a step forward in Russell's long drive toward the unification of all working people.

Still, the precise nature of the OBU's participation in politics remained unresolved. Should this new labour body support labour candidates in parliamentary elections, or should it shun all such "palliators" as manifestations of capitalist control? This question the newly proclaimed constitution did not address. Moreover, behind the question lay a larger and even more troublesome dilemma: was the new union to operate within the existing social structure or was it to defeat and destroy that structure? The difficulty was already causing dissension among OBU activists, and would surface only a year or two later at a crucial moment in Russell's career.

In Winnipeg by the middle of July a battle erupted into the open between the Trades and Labor Council and the OBU. Although the members of the TLC voted 8,841 to 705 in favour of adopting the OBU constitution, the moderates under R. A. Rigg succeeded in blocking the move. Ousted from the Trades and Labor Council, the OBU adherents formed their own Central Labor Council on August 5, with Bob Russell as secretary-treasurer, and the *OBU Bulletin* was moved from Edmonton to Winnipeg, to compete with the *Western Labor News*. Winnipeg had now become the driving centre of OBU activity. When speakers were sent out across Canada to raise money for the strikers' defence fund, Russell remained behind, determined to weld together the all-labour alliance he had long advocated.

In Vancouver, the Trades and Labor Council severed its connections with the Trades and Labor Congress of Canada and the AFL, and identified with the OBU. At a meeting in Nelson, British Columbia's hard-rock miners broke away from the International Union of Mine, Mill, and Smelter Workers to form District No. 1 of the Metalliferous Miners of the OBU. The miners of Alberta and eastern British

Columbia left the United Mine Workers of America and joined the new union, and teamsters, fishpackers, and lumberworkers followed suit. Reaching across the American border, Bob Russell spent a few days in Chicago, helping to organize a small OBU unit among railway shop workers.

By November, when the trials of the strike leaders began, the membership had reached more than nine thousand and was still growing. Russell and Johns brought the railway machine shops on board, as well as the contract-shop metal-workers. The carpenters and other building trades joined, followed by some of the city's smaller craft unions, the bakers and the confectioners, the tailors and the teamsters. A sizable number of workers in the city's large garment industry signed with the OBU. Classes in economics were established, as if to make ready for the coming class struggle.

In Calgary, however, there was effective opposition from members of the Trades and Labor Council loyal to the TLC–AFL. Both the employers and the international unions affiliated with the American Federation of Labor fought a determined battle against the gains of the rival OBU. The AFL sent in organizers to convince wavering locals to reject the upstart union, and employers, now obliged to accept the principle of collective bargaining, insisted on negotiating only with representatives of the internationals. The railways would talk only with Division 4. Some employers barred OBU organizers and their literature from the workplace, or demanded that their employees sign agreements not to support a general strike, the OBU's chief weapon.

Nevertheless, by the end of 1919, when Bob Russell's trial claimed the headlines in Winnipeg newspapers and elsewhere, the pugnacious new union had enlisted a Canadian membership of 41,150, with 101 local units, eight Central Labor Committees, and two district boards, and the circulation of the OBU *Bulletin* topped 8,500 subscribers.

A "Red" on Trial

Of the fifteen men on the Central Strike Committee who jointly directed the action, only one, Russell, was charged, and the Crown opted to try him first, separately from the rest. Bob Russell was the most effective labour leader in the city, Russell was a leading member of the Socialist Party of Canada, and it was Russell's OBU that proclaimed as its agenda the takeover by labour of the country's government. Whether a revolution by violence was intended became the central issue in the trials that followed. By early winter the government was ready to proceed, with Judge Metcalfe presiding. The crown prosecutor was A. J. Andrews, who had condemned himself in labour's eyes during the previous summer's conflict by his relentless campaign against the strikers. Acting for Russell was a team of attorneys headed by W. R. Cassidy, KC, of Vancouver, and including E. J. McMurray, J. Edward Bird, and Bill Pritchard's mentor, Wallis Lefeaux.

Russell's case, beginning November 24, was noteworthy in the first instance for the staggering quantity of evidence produced by the prosecution, and then for the repeated clashes between the prosecution and the defence over the admissibility and validity of the evidence. Only specific charges against the accused ought to be considered, Cassidy protested, rather than "to throw a body of men of men together and try to convict A on what B or C said, and all that sort of rubbish. It should not be tolerated!" Metcalfe ruled against the argument.

At one point, as the records show, Cassidy defied the judge's instructions, and Metcalfe ordered a bailiff to eject him from the courtroom; then the judge relented and let Cassidy off with a reprimand. So tedious and exhausting did the process become, Russell maintained afterward, that the learned jurist fell asleep from time to time on the bench; and when the trial finally drew to an end, Metcalfe himself commented on the twenty-three long days they had been sitting, and on the 703 exhibits, and on his own state, "almost physically unfit to complete my part of this trial."

The Crown set out to prove that Russell had conspired with the others to destroy the legitimate government of the country, harking back to the "Red Scare," the still pervasive fear that the same calamity that had shattered the Russian regime in 1917 was in store for the unwary nations of the western world. The defence argued that no conspiracy existed or could exist between men of such diverse beliefs as those held by the several men now indicted. "The accused have different labour affiliations," Cassidy protested: "four of them are Socialists, four are not; and they have been shown by evidence to have been continually fighting among themselves" — as indeed they had. Time and again Cassidy argued that Russell had done only what he was required to do as a trade unionist, what was permissible under the law, and that the views he held were those of the Socialist Party of Canada, a legal association under the Canadian constitution.

At the core of the issue, the opposing sides hotly contended the meaning of the charge itself, "seditious conspiracy." Conspiracy, Judge Metcalfe explained to the jury, requires that the evidence show collaboration among a number of people, "that the parties . . . have pursued a line of conduct arising in the estimation of the jury from a common intention." Russell and his colleagues had together planned and carried out a general sympathy strike in order to force agreement to certain demands: of that common intention there was ample evidence. The defence team maintained that all of these activities were within the boundaries allowed by law to labour unions; the prosecution insisted that these limits had been exceeded, and the judge concurred: "It is a serious offence to conspire, combine, or agree unlawfully to unduly limit facilities for transporting, supplying and storing commodities, or to restrain trade." Most of Metcalfe's marathon summing-up underlined the statutory violations of a general strike, not only in Russell's activities but also in those of the men he was deemed to have led.

But there was the subtext in the charge, far less readily addressed. In all the exhibits and the testimony of police witnesses and the undeniably revolutionary utterances of the accused, no valid evidence existed of a common intention to carry out an actual Bolshevik revolution. No battle plans were found, no weapons. Nevertheless, Metcalfe cited as "millstones" in his mind the alarming phrases in Russell's correspondence, "such nice, short, crispy, well-expressed sentences," he called them, as "Reds getting control," and all the similar statements amassed by the police. The defence argued that while the accused had predicted a coming revolution, the mere prediction did not imply an intention to bring about a change by violence, by armed revolt.

Rather, the defence attorneys maintained, labour people regularly used the term "revolution" for the comprehensive changes in society that the future would inevitably bring. Pritchard at his own trial, and

Dixon at his, insisted that "revolution" meant only the normal course of social evolution; the very moderate Fred Tipping, commenting on Russell's trial to a later scholar, made the same observation: "It's a term, a common term. A wheel has so many revolutions a minute; it's simply a turning around. . . ."

Yet Russell had indeed declared, at the Walker Theatre, "The red flag is flying in every civilized country in the world, and it will fly here," and the shining image of a populist revolt had been held up over and over again as a beacon to unhappy people in troubled times. Metcalfe found a telling metaphor to characterize the "sedition" that the authorities alleged:

A torch applied to a green field may not be likely to cause a fire, yet when the grass is ripe and dry a spark may cause a conflagration. Just so, words spoken in privacy, or during a quarrel, or in the heat of the moment, or in normal times, may be unlikely to have a seditious effect, and may be overlooked; yet when spoken in times of stress and in more public places may be likely to cause such discontent, hostility, and disturbances as to be seditious.

Moreover, he added, "If the words spoken or published are seditious, it is no defence that they are true."

The learned judge appears to have implied that labour's words may indeed have been true, in demanding drastic correction for the injustices of existing society. Against this seemingly inadvertent admission, much of Metcalfe's address appealed to patriotic sentiments, exhorting the jurors to remember the blessings that their country provided.

The jury found Russell guilty on all counts, and according to custom he was invited to address the court. His response, as reported in the *Western Labor News*, placed conviction and service ahead of self:

I have been unduly honoured in being named leader in a movement where there are no leaders but only mouthpieces. I carried out my instructions from the rank and file as a paid servant to the best of my ability. . . .

165

He maintained that he had not been allowed to demonstrate that his real intentions during the strike were free of anything criminal; and he added, said the sympathetic labour paper, "I am a married man and a father. I do not understand the law and still less the procedure of this court."

On the day before Christmas 1919, Judge Metcalfe sentenced Russell to two years in prison. Then, in a curiously revealing gesture, he sent the convicted Bolshevik home, without bond, to spend Christmas day with his family; and the sharp irony of that small gift served to enhance Russell's status as a martyr in labour's cause. The memory of that day stayed with Peggy Russell. Years later she told Mary Jordan, the OBU's long-time secretary, that Bob had promised that while he lived he would always be with her at Christmas, because he had taken her away from her family in Scotland. On the following morning, the police arrived at the house in Weston, handcuffed the prisoner, and drove him off to Stony Mountain.

There is also an epilogue to the tale of the trial. Metcalfe presided over the remaining conspiracy trials, but his health was broken. Before he died, he sent for Russell, wanting to speak to him. Russell refused to go, saying bitterly, "Let him die with his guilty conscience." In time, Mary Jordan said of her employer and friend, Russell came to regret his failure of humanity.

He served his sentence at the penitentiary rather than at the prison farm to which the others, with lesser terms, were confined, but he laid no particular stress on his experiences behind bars. While the labour press dwelt on the "grim forbidding walls" that incarcerated their comrade, in a "living tomb . . . where the laughing voices and the rippling laughter of children is never heard, where the angelic presence, the sunny smile, and the gentle touch of a woman's hand is unknown," the prisoner refused to complain, but salvaged a victory out of defeat, in the conviction of the truth of his cause. After he had served one month of his sentence, Russell reported, he was told that if he admitted he had done wrong, he would be released. "I told them," he said, "to go jump in the lake."

It was not an easy time for the Russell family, Bob's daughter, now Margaret Sykes, remembered long afterward. Bob insisted that they must hold their heads up high, that they must not feel any disgrace or embarrassment, that the children must go to school in Weston, among the children of the working people whose cause their father championed. "I was proud of my dad for what he did, and I still am," Mrs. Sykes told an interviewer, "because he did it for the working class, for the people."

The Defence Committee retained W. H. Trueman to appeal the Russell case, pursuing the available legal channels. A presentation to the Canadian Court of Appeals was rejected, and Trueman took the case to the Privy Council in Britain. The Council ruled that proper procedures had been followed, and there was no further recourse. The first and second regular conventions of the OBU, in January and October 1920, were held without Bob Russell.

In the dispirited aftermath of the failed strike, the battle between the Trades and Labour Congress and the OBU continued. The TLC publicly repudiated the policies for which Russell had been convicted; it opposed the appeal to the Privy Council, and charged that OBU organizers were content to let Russell stay in jail, for propaganda purposes. Not so, OBU supporters retorted angrily, it was "the International officers and their satellites" that prevented Russell's release, seeming to agree that he was indeed guilty of sedition.

As scornful as ever of mere "reformers" advocating "palliators," Russell agreed to run with the other "jailbirds" on the unified labour slate in the 1920 provincial election, but only after a month of persuasion. When the returns were in, Russell and his outspoken radical comrades, Pritchard and Johns, went down to defeat. Most voters, it would seem, rejected extreme radicalism and its Marxist rhetoric, and the OBU was perceived by many labourites as the cause of labour's undoing.

On December 11, 1920, Russell was freed, having served less than half his sentence. A Trades and Labor Council mission had gone to Ottawa on his behalf, and there was also a persistent rumour that Winnipeg's business interests had engineered his parole, convinced that whatever Russell's misdeeds, his services were required to manage labour relations. E. J. McMurray suggested that he study for a degree in law and offered to take him into his own office, but Bob Russell remained with his chosen course as a union man.

OBU Lottery, OBU Summer Camp

Russell came back to a labour movement suffering severely from the after-effects of the general strike. Thousands of workers, blackballed by vengeful former employers, left Winnipeg to look for work elsewhere. Alex Shepherd's family and George Armstrong's went to Chicago for a time; the SPC in Winnipeg lost fully one-third of its members to the United States. Postal employees and telephone workers who had refused orders to return to work during the strike were summarily dismissed. Fifty-three firemen were not reinstated, and activists in the civil service lost their jobs. If a man held an OBU card, many firms would not hire him. Virtually the entire Winnipeg police force had been dismissed because of their offer to support the strikers, and many had not been rehired. These experienced law officers sought employment wherever they could; some even turned up, Russell said, as luggage men at the Royal York Hotel in Toronto, and one, to his great surprise, as the chief of police in Dauphin, Manitoba.

As for the OBU, its growth had been irreparably stunted. The once promising west-coast territory was beginning to crumble, OBU membership in Vancouver had declined to the point that not a single delegate from that city had attended the October convention, and OBU headquarters had been moved to Winnipeg. By the end of 1921 the loggers had turned their backs on the OBU, and the internationals had once again solidified the affiliation of the B.C. hard-rock miners and the coal miners of both British Columbia and Alberta. There was only scattered support in the rest of Alberta and in Saskatchewan, and the campaign in the East was faltering.

In Winnipeg, for a time, some limited gains continued to be made. While Russell was still in jail, in August 1920 the Winnipeg Central Labor Council had achieved its most enduring success when the nine hundred members of the street-railway union had signed with the OBU. The garment industry remained an OBU stronghold for a few years, and some support continued in the building trades. In the railway shops, where Johns and Russell began, most of the workers had taken out OBU membership, but the railways would negotiate only with Division 4 of the AFL, and the postwar depression made the workers' jobs uncertain. By 1921 membership dues were in arrears, the *OBU Bulletin* could not pay its way, and the treasury was nearly empty.

At this crisis point the OBU was desperate for a strategy that would keep the paper going. The British-born among the leaders avidly followed the Old Country football leagues, and someone suggested that publishing the scores would attract readers. An even more inspired proposal followed, to have the *OBU Bulletin* run a weekly lottery on the scores. Gambling, then as now, had an irresistible appeal — Bob himself, his daughter recalled fondly, loved to go out to the racetrack now and then, to have a flutter on the ponies. A contest was worked out, requiring a coupon printed in the *OBU Bulletin* and offering a small cash prize to the winner; and the first coupon went out on December 8, 1921.

The scheme succeeded far beyond expectation. Thousands of papers were purchased, by die-hard unionists and their bosses alike, and money poured into OBU coffers. Its legality constantly challenged, the contest's rules were changed several times without affecting its popularity, and a large staff had to be hired to handle the details. At its height, the lottery sold half a million copies of the *OBU Bulletin* a week and distributed hundreds of thousands of dollars in prize money. The bonanza did not peter out until 1928.

Technically prohibited from using lottery profits for union purposes, the OBU nevertheless managed to finance an attractive social and recreational program, to take over the mortgage on the building that housed its offices, and to consider other investments. There were toboggan parties and billiard tournaments, there were a band and an athletic program, there were even socialist playing cards to buy. True to its mandate, the OBU held classes for its members, offering both education in economics and technical training to help workers upgrade their skills.

Closest to Russell's heart was the summer camp for the children of workers, at Gimli on Lake Winnipeg, lovingly built by OBU tradesmen. Bob would take his own family down on a weekend, to join in a rousing game of baseball, or to attend to a prize-giving, or just to visit with the campers. Years later, he said, he walked into a candy store on Portage Avenue, and the young woman behind the counter recognized him, and talked about what the OBU camp had meant to her. Offering a small amenity to a part of society for whom few resources were available, the camp was one of the "palliators" that in theory Russell scorned.

Boring from Within: The Communist Verdict on the OBU

Russell was about to face a major confrontation with a political party whose agenda for achieving the final class struggle called for the abandonment of the OBU. Inevitably the challenge was initiated by the Soviet Union, the source of inspiration and example to many labour people around the world. The Third Communist International, or Comintern, had been founded in Moscow in 1919, to centralize under Soviet control the Marxist parties active in other countries. Two years later, at the Comintern's second congress, an official summons went out to all radical groups to join and to subscribe to an agenda of twenty-one principles. The required structure and strategy for such groups were defined, and all decisions were to be submitted for approval by the central body.

In the Socialist Party of Canada, the Soviet alignment was the subject of passionate debate. Avowed Marxists like Bill Pritchard of Vancouver, refusing to surrender their right of independent criticism, rejected the domination of Moscow, and were denounced by equally dedicated Marxists like Vancouver's Jack Kavanagh and Edmonton's Joe and Sarah Knight, who saw the future in the Comintern's glass. Kavanagh and the Knights were among the OBU's strongest organizers, and the clash struck at the heart of Russell's union. When the Comintern called a meeting for July 1921 to inaugurate its trade union arm, the International Congress of Revolutionary Trade and Industrial Unions, or Profintern, a representative of the American Communist Party, Ella Reeve Bloor, was sent to persuade Bob Russell to come to Moscow for the deliberations. Russell declined, whether for personal reasons or out of political reservations, and Joe Knight attended as the official delegate.

Knight's report was delivered to the third OBU convention in

170

September 1921, after a summer of incomplete information, confusion, and dissension. By the decision of the Comintern, he said, radicals throughout the world were to infiltrate unions and achieve control by "boring from within," in order to create a ready instrument for a Communist takeover. For these purposes large established unions like the AFL were useful and must not be destroyed by dissident, break-away factions. Nevertheless, Knight assured the delegates, the OBU was still considered valid because of its local strength, and he proposed immediate affiliation with the Profintern. Russell went on record in the debate as approving the proposal, but the conference asked for more particulars. The official account of the Comintern design finally came from the American Communists — the Canadian delegates to Moscow were strangely uncommunicative — and there was obviously no special dispensation for the OBU. Like all unions, Russell's fledgling rival to the AFL was expendable, equally subject to "boring from within."

Under the all-powerful centralizing demand from Moscow, the kaleidoscope of parties on the Canadian left took still another turn. In the federal election of December 1921, the Liberal candidate for Winnipeg North was E. J. McMurray, the same pro-labour attorney who had acted for the defence in the strike trials. The newly formed Independent Labor Party chose tacitly not to oppose McMurray, but Jacob Penner ran as a "Labor Party" candidate, calling specifically for a Soviet alignment. Russell entered his own independent candidacy against both Penner and McMurray, and was once again defeated. The labour vote split in a rancorous campaign, and McMurray was elected. Arguably, Russell had by this time moved some distance from the Soviet supporters among his comrades.

Meanwhile, in the early summer of 1921 a Canadian Communist party had been founded, in secret, at a meeting in Guelph, Ontario. Dedicated to obliterating the existing social order, it declared itself an underground, illegal organization, and proceeded to create a public identity, a party for official purposes. In February 1922 Canadian radicals were invited to the founding meeting in Toronto of the Workers' Party, and Russell attended, to learn for himself what Moscow wanted. In the interests of the grand design, he was told, the OBU must yield. It would be phased out, replaced once again by the craft unions of the

larger, richer, more expedient Trades and Labor Congress. The industrial union to which Russell had devoted his life would, of course, go by
the board. To ram home the point, all those who resisted the Red
embrace, and most particularly Bob Russell, were labelled reactionaries,
traitors to the workers' cause, the last defendants of an obsolete creed.

The fragile alliance within the OBU exploded. Communist members called Russell a liar when he reported to the Winnipeg Central
Labor Council on the proposed fate of their union, and they continued
to vilify him even after the official publication of the Workers' Party
confirmed his account. Jack Kavanagh became the editor of the
Communist *Worker*, the Knights and others vociferously demanded
that the OBU throw its lot in with the international revolutionary
movement, and all through western Canada and in the East Profintern
supporters within OBU units began urging the members to return to
their craft unions, in the best technique of "boring from within."

The OBU membership desperately fought out the issue in a series
of meetings in the spring of 1922, and on May 12 they reached a decision: a resolution was passed rejecting the Communist policy and calling it "against the best interests of the working class." Several months
of turmoil later, in November, Russell and his supporters on the
Central Labor Council pushed the Communists out of all the executive
positions in the OBU. Years later, still angry, Russell sneered that they
went back to the Trades and Labor Congress and the AFL "just like a
dog going back to his vomit."

It was a pyrrhic victory. Even labour supporters had tended to see
the OBU from its beginning as resembling the disreputable, violence-
prone Industrial Workers of the World — "I Won't Work," some
detractors called the brawling dissidents. Again, as the Canadian
Communists increasingly played their subversive role, hostile to all
other left-wing groups, the connection between the OBU and the
Marxists gave Russell's union a dubious aura, one that the gambling
feature in its *OBU Bulletin* did nothing to dispel; and coming in the
wake of the still potent "Red Scare," the union's very public fight with
its own Communist members only tarnished its image further.

Ordered by Moscow to endorse the revolutionary chimera of a
utopia achieved by force, Russell had chosen his union instead, and the

tangible benefits it would bring. The OBU, sheared of its visionary excitement, fought for its existence on its claim to be a more effective mode of union organization, able to serve its members better than the craft-based TLC-AFL. The principle of the industrial union would later be vindicated, with the emergence of the Congress of Industrial Organizations (CIO), but in the short term the OBU was stopped in its tracks. Industrial unionism was still ahead of its time, and revolutionary change as trumpeted by the disruptive Communists had lost its appeal for the vast majority of working people.

Decline of the OBU

By the end of 1922 the recruiting drive for OBU membership had slowed to a crawl. Despite the remarkable sums of lottery cash that poured into the *OBU Bulletin*, the union had little money for organizers, since lottery funds could not be used to meet operating expenses, and the police kept a suspicious eye on the OBU's financial records. One full-time organizer, Tom Cassidy, struggled to cover the prairies, arranging rallies wherever there was a show of interest, and paying his way out of the proceeds of the collection plate.

Trying to offset the inroads of the international unions into the railway repair shops, Russell campaigned for the OBU in the railroad towns of northwestern Ontario, with only minor results, and in May 1923 he undertook a swing through the West. But for all his prestige among the shop-workers, the trip proved a dreary disappointment. Calgary and Edmonton, he was forced to admit, had virtually to be written off.

In the midst of these difficulties, Peggy Russell gave birth to their third child, a girl, and Russell rushed home to be with his wife, as he had promised, but he could only stay a day or so before returning to his unrewarding task. The baby died shortly after, leaving Peggy distraught and resentful of the demands made on her husband.

That August, the annual OBU convention reported a catastrophic drop in paid membership to only thirty-one hundred. The office staff was cut, and there was barely enough money to pay a living wage to Russell himself as secretary of the Central Labor Council.

Political ambition continued to stir within the struggling unionist.

In the by-election for Winnipeg North in autumn 1923 the ILP proposed to run the popular North End city councillor A. A. Heaps as labour candidate against E. J. McMurray. Bob Russell defiantly declared his own candidacy, as an independent. At the ILP nomination meeting the OBU leader was roundly denounced for a move that would have divided the labour vote, and his motives were questioned. Russell withdrew, unwillingly.

At this point a sex scandal rocked the OBU. Tom Cassidy was a fiery and generally effective OBU organizer, but he also insisted on expressing in public his very "advanced" views on the relationship between men and women, on abortion and on birth control. "Free love," the whispers said, was what Tom Cassidy practiced, just like all those revolutionaries. In September the organizer was surprised in a Brandon hotel room with a young woman from the OBU office, and although the union's embarrassed executives tried to deal with the matter discreetly the uproar only subsided with Cassidy's death, of tuberculosis, the following February.

The toehold that the OBU had established in the Winnipeg railway shops could not be sustained. Back in the years of wartime shortages, when the machinists had been able to exact concessions from the employer, Grant Hall had warned that "apples will grow again." In the difficult postwar years the workers were ripe for picking. "We were working five days a month sometimes," said Russell, "it was cut-down time, cut-down time, cut-down time, until they near half-starved us into submission."

Early in 1924 Division 4 agreed to cooperate with the Canadian National Railways on a scheme to reward — or dismiss — workers according to their productivity and output, overriding the union principle of seniority. A "slave scheme," Russell stormed, recognizing the attack on his union by both the AFL and management. When the CNR fired some of the OBU's key men in the Transcona shops for campaigning against the plan, Russell called a series of one-hour strikes to force the company to reinstate them. The effort failed, the plan went ahead, and OBU membership in the shops dwindled away.

That year also saw a flurry of hopeful activity in the Nova Scotia coalfields, where the miners and steel workers, disgruntled by the lack of support from their own union, the United Mine Workers (UMW), had begun to turn to the OBU. The OBU's most colourful organizer on the east coast was an American actor named Ben Legere, a socialist and IWW supporter from California, and Russell came east to join him. At one tense rally, "in an old broken-down skating rink where the galleries were collapsing and hitting the floor," the two stood together in the boxing ring that served as the stage, trying to get their message across to a truculent crowd of OBU supporters and their Communist opponents. As Legere hammered away at "Communist lies," the infuriated crowd began to riot, but Russell — "shaking in my damn shoes, I'll tell you that!" — shouted down the troublemakers by the sheer force of his reputation. "I was only out of jail a little while," he explained, wryly. "You were a little Jesus, you know, and they wouldn't touch you." In the end, however, the UMW won back the defectors.

Then in 1925 the Glace Bay miners' strike exploded in a summer of unprecedented violence. Strike funds were limited, and the miners, their families slowly starving, turned their rage against company stores and mine installations. Provincial and company police retaliated viciously; people were beaten and killed, homes burned. The militia was sent in to quell the battle with machine guns and bayonets. Throughout all this warfare the uncertified OBU could only stand by and offer moral support, with Russell exhorting the miners to "Win your fight first, change cards afterwards." The men returned to work with nothing to show for their season of defiance, and the OBU's efforts went down to defeat with the strikers' lost cause.

For about eighteen months longer Russell insisted on maintaining an office and an organizer in New Glasgow, reluctant to surrender the Nova Scotia territory. Then several part-time organizers, paid according to the number of new members they recruited, were caught bilking the distant Winnipeg office by sending in false reports, until at last even Russell had to concede failure. The east coast undertaking was quietly closed down.

Russell now devoted much of his time to organizing the unorganized, the restaurant and hospital workers and others who were of little interest to the major unions. Under his direction the *OBU Bulletin* took up the cause of the unprotected women workers, and particularly the young immigrant women who were hired by restaurants for board and room and a small monthly wage, who worked long hours seven days a week, and then had to pay for their uniforms and laundry and whatever mistakes they might have made. One girl, the *OBU Bulletin* accused, was charged because she gave a customer an extra piece of butter.

A six-day week and a minimum pay rate were on the statute books. In an effort to have the law enforced, the OBU took on the restaurant owners, and the *OBU Bulletin* ran an exposé of the filthy behind-the-scenes conditions in the city's eating establishments. At one café a strike was called and pickets established, and in the ludicrous melee that resulted the owner threatened to shoot, a cook threw a pot of hot soup, a waiter was taken to hospital, and the issue went to court. The workers got their minimum but no more, and the OBU gained nothing but the further distaste of the general public.

A federal election in September 1926 brought Bob Russell once again into the political arena. He had scoffed at the Independent Labor Party when it was assembled in 1920, and had opposed its candidates in two previous elections. Now he ran under the ILP banner in the Winnipeg suburb of St. James, and was once again soundly trounced.

The OBU had consistently turned down proposals from the IWW to join forces. Now it made overtures to A. R. Mosher's Canadian Brotherhood of Railway Employees, a breakaway union from the Trades and Labor Congress Mosher called a unity conference in Montreal, also inviting the small Canadian Federation of Labor and its several affiliates, and in March 1927 the deal was struck. Eight unions, the largest of them the CBRE, were brought together as the All-Canadian Congress of Labor; the OBU, in the end, provided only sixteen hundred members. One OBU representative was named to the executive, and four others to several committees, and the agreement was ratified in May by the fifth annual OBU convention, the first in four years.

There were further losses for the OBU. In 1926, the union had considered investing the *OBU Bulletin*'s lottery surplus in the left-wing publishing firm of Charles H. Kerr, of Chicago, but when Russell tried to enter the United States he had been stopped at the border because of his prison record, and the deal fell through. A two-year legal battle began in 1927 to have an OBU cardholder reinstated by the CNR; it cost the union thousands of dollars, and the case was dismissed by the Privy Council. The lottery had now ceased to be a lucrative source of income; it was dropped in 1928, although the paper itself continued publication for several years more. By the summer of 1929, aggressive recruiting for the OBU was no longer feasible, and the one remaining organizer was removed from the payroll. The summer camp survived into the thirties, a welcome holiday spot for the shrinking OBU community. Eventually, the OBU building at 54 Adelaide Street was sold for taxes.

Remainders

By 1929, OBU activity was confined to Winnipeg, and although a call might still come from some stubborn enclave, Russell was no longer catapulted from one end of the country to the other. For Peggy and the Russell children, teenagers now, there was more time to spend with Dad, more time for the small pleasures of life. Now Bob could go skating with the kids, or snowballing, or to Assiniboine Park for a picnic. He had acquired a car, and sometimes they drove out to the Locks, to Lockport, north of the city, where the Red River drops into Lake Winnipeg. Occasionally, Bob would go off to Scanterbury, the Indian reserve off the Grand Beach road, for a day's fishing with his former attorney, then his political opponent, and now his friend, E. J. McMurray. Bob's old cronies came often, to gather around the piano with Peggy and harmonize. A Scottish ballad was always grand, but many times their voices would ring out in some rousing ditty from the little red songbook of the Industrial Workers of the World.

"My dad loved heather, and Scottish music, and a good dram of Scotch whisky," Margaret Sykes remembered. New Year's Eve, the traditional Scottish Hogmanay, the family always spent with friends in Elmwood:

It would start at midnight, and they'd spend maybe five or six hours having dancing, food, and singing. . . . We went first-footing, you know, and you usually carried a lump of coal, if you had it, and a bottle of scotch. And a dark-haired man had to be the first to cross the threshold. And then, if the car hadn't frozen up, we'd be coming home at eight o'clock in the morning, past the old City Hall, with the clock on top. . . .

During the Great Depression of the thirties, his daughter said, Bob and Peggy Russell helped where they could, buying food for those who had none. Bob carried on as secretary of the Winnipeg Central Labor Council, occupied with routine union business, his door always open to acquaintances who dropped by. Of the OBU's grand vision of an all-embracing industrial union and perhaps even a world association of the entire working class, only some hotel, bakery, and restaurant workers were left, and to the end, the employees of the street-railway system, privately owned by the Winnipeg Electric Company.

Russell's sights were now concentrated on this one substantial OBU contract. The utility claimed to be losing money and applied to be relieved of paying about four hundred thousand dollars per year in taxes. Because his own members' wages were in danger of being cut, Russell appeared before a legislative committee, incongruously arguing for a tax relief for a capitalist enterprise. His old adversary, John Queen, now mayor of Winnipeg, was outraged and said so publicly. In retaliation, in the November civic election campaign of 1936, with Queen running for reelection, Russell urged the unions not to support the ILP candidates. Partly as a result of the dissention in the labour ranks, Queen was defeated.

After World War II broke out, Russell was appointed to the Manitoba War Labor Board. He spent a short time as plant supervisor in a London, Ontario, steel mill operated by his son-in-law, and then was asked to take on an assignment for the federal Unemployment Insurance Corporation. The job entailed considerable travel once again, and Peggy found herself alone too frequently. In early 1944 the Russells returned to Winnipeg, and Bob went back to his desk in the Labor Temple on James Street.

An uneasy affiliation continued between the OBU and the All-Canadian Congress of Labor. Always at odds with the decisions of the central executive, and determined to retain the separate identity of his own union, Russell repeatedly explored other alliances, to no end. In 1955, the American Federation of Labor and the Congress of Industrial Organizations merged as the AFL-CIO, and the OBU applied to join on an equal footing, as a national body. Russell and two colleagues attended the founding convention of the Canadian Labour Congress the following April in Toronto, and on the last day of the meeting, the president-elect, Claude Jodoin, introduced the old unionist to an applauding assembly.

As for the terms of the merger, however, the OBU accepted provincial status only, and agreed to allow its various units to come under the jurisdiction of the corresponding unions affiliated with the CCL. The terms were ratified at a Winnipeg Central Labor Council meeting in Winnipeg, and on 6 June 1956, the OBU came to an end.

Russell remained as executive secretary of the Winnipeg and District Labor Council, Canadian Labour Congress. Honoured now for his service to labour, and his reputedly revolutionary past now forgotten, he received government appointments to the Manitoba Labor Relations Board, the Fair Wage Board, and the Apprenticeship Board of the Department of Labor, among others. The former "Red" now sat on committees of the Cancer Research Board and of the Community Chest; a professed atheist, he became a member of the Religion-Labor Council of Manitoba. He joined his former colleague, Dick Johns, in developing plans for vocational education in Winnipeg, and travelled to Ontario with Johns to obtain the equipment for the new Technical-Vocational High School. A testimonial dinner for him was held by the Law Society. In 1961, to mark his fiftieth year in the Canadian labour movement, over four hundred guests paid four dollars a plate to honour Bob Russell at a dinner in the Marlborough Hotel.

A year later, on the day the Russells returned from a visit to a granddaughter in California, the veteran labour leader suffered a stroke. He recovered partly, but a short time later his retirement as secretary of the Labor Council was announced. If Mr. Russell wished, the council president said, he would continue to act as paid advisor for unions and labour organizations. Remembering the palmy days of the *Bulletin* lottery, people shrugged that Bob Russell probably had put away a lot of money — buried in his back yard, the rumour said. "He didn't have a cent," his daughter said. "He fought for the men and got them pensions, but he never set up anything for himself."

By this time the labour party, now the CCF, had made gains in Winnipeg, with a strong representation on city council, but the unionist had little use for the labour politicians now in office. For all his own elevation to a degree of civic prominence, he retained always the common man's suspicion of officialdom and of union men who rise in the world and line their own pockets. "Today the struggle is, who's going to be the officers, the big brass jobs," he grumbled, after his own retirement, "because big brass jobs have become something to it. You take the salaries being paid to some of these guys — $12,000 and $14,000 a year. In those days they would have thought the President of the United States didn't even get that money. . . . Some of them are going around with some big cushy jobs with big fat salaries, and forget that they were once in the shops, or should be in the shops yet."

On Labour Day 1964 Robert Boyd Russell received his "Address of Appreciation" from the Manitoba government, "In recognition of the long and devoted service to the cause of the Labour movement in the Province, his wise and farsighted leadership and counsel, and his many and notable contributions to the general welfare of the city"; and for the last time he rode in the place of honour at the head of the annual Labour Day parade. His daughter took him to see the smart new Union Centre on Portage Avenue, and then, exhausted, he went home.

He died on September 25. Funeral services were held at the Union Centre, conducted by the Reverend P. M. Petursson, of the Unitarian Church.

On April 4, 1967, the cornerstone for the R. B. Russell Vocational High School, on Dufferin Avenue, was laid by Manitoba Premier Duff Roblin; and the school's official opening took place on October 28. At the opening ceremonies Mrs. Russell was present, with her daughter Margaret and her son David, as well as Education Minister George Johnson and Winnipeg School Board chairman William Norrie, and a plaque honouring the labour leader was presented by the Winnipeg Labor Council.

Several years afterward, in 1978, the intensive care unit at the Children's Hospital received a gift from the Winnipeg and District Labor Council, an eighty-three hundred-dollar multiple parameter physiological monitoring unit, in honour of the late R. B. Russell. The money, it was explained, had been raised ten years earlier at a centennial ball in the old Royal Alexandra Hotel, toward furnishing an entire ward in memory of the labour leader. Unfortunately not enough money could be collected to complete the project, and it was decided to donate the monitoring unit instead.

Fanning the Flames
George Armstrong, Roger Bray, Richard Johns

George Armstrong

Once the general strike was over, three of the men on the authorities' list of dangerous conspirators left little evidence to justify their once formidable reputations. George Armstrong was considered by many to be the finest orator in the Socialist Party of Canada; impressive in his exposition of Marxist principles to the edgy crowds milling about in Market Square, he achieved only a brief and undistinguished moment in political office, and within a few years was all but forgotten. Roger Bray marshalled the deep discontent of the demobilized soldiers of World War I, and his troops parading in military discipline through Winnipeg streets seemed poised to challenge law and order in the country they had served. But their anger, it soon became clear, was only a footnote to the ongoing social revolution signalled by the strike, and most of the charges against him failed to convince even the jury at his trial. Dick Johns was perceived as the lieutenant of the notorious Bob Russell, responsible for the alarmingly radical policies of the OBU, and found himself branded as a seditious conspirator. Instead he left his mark on his city as a teacher and builder, the architect of an enduring program of technical education.

The Orator of Market Square: George Armstrong

"George was never good at the rough-and-tumble of Labor Council debates," said his friend and former colleague, Alex Shepherd. Five or six minutes were all that the impatient, knowledgeable union delegates to a council meeting would allow a speaker, and Armstrong, said Shepherd, was rather long-winded, and got involved, and did not always make his point. "But put that man on a soap-box in Market Square, and give him an hour, and he could . . . get a big hand from the crowd."

A master carpenter, George Armstrong had arrived in Winnipeg in 1905, and had come to the fore almost at once as a most effective speaker and union organizer. A socialist to the core, he had joined the local branch of the Socialist Party of Canada, holding fast to its basic Marxist tenet that the working class would inevitably take possession of the reins of world government, and he let no opportunity pass to urge his fellow workers to speed the process.

Born in 1870 on a small farm near Scarborough, Ontario, and the youngest of four children, George was descended from United Empire Loyalists, the British subjects who had fled the United States for Canada during the American War of Independence; among the nine men eventually brought to trial for their role in the 1919 upheaval, Armstrong was the only native-born Canadian. Married to Helen Jury, the daughter of a firebrand socialist tailor in Toronto, and herself destined to become a thorn in the side of the establishment, he worked at his trade in the East until employment became scarce, and then tried his luck in the United States for a few years. Then, at the age of thirty-five, he followed his brother Frank to western Canada, bringing his wife and three small daughters to Winnipeg. The Armstrongs' fourth child, a son, was born there.

George became a member of the United Brotherhood of Carpenters and Joiners, Local 343, and in short order its business agent and delegate to the Trades and Labor Council. The United Brotherhood was an affiliate of the American Federation of Labor and of the Canadian Trades and Labor Congress, but like many of his mates Armstrong was dissatisfied with the control by eastern Canada. The construction trades, however, were dominated by the relatively well-paid bricklayers and stonemasons, who were content to follow the moderate policies of the parent Trades and Labor Congress.

Almost equally with his condemnation of the capitalist bosses, Armstrong's socialist ire was directed at those ideologically unsound members of the moderate left who betrayed the cause by their half-hearted programs of reform. When the Manitoba Labor Party was founded by a group of trade unionists, moderate socialists, and middle-class reformers, with Arthur Puttee one of the leading figures, the SPC damned it out of hand. This assembly of labourites, liberals, single taxers, and other cranks, said the statement in the *Western Clarion*, "must be a case of the immaculate conception," since "Puttee, political pimp and spineless animal though he is . . . could not [otherwise] have gathered such an aggregation."

There was dissension within the SPC as well. In the immigrant North End of the city, the party's radicalism had initially attracted some of the newcomers from eastern Europe. Within a short time, however, the doctrinaire absolutism of the SPC lost some of its lustre for many of these "foreign" members, and a defensive resentment of its dominant English-speaking leadership spread among them. In the provincial elections of 1910, the North End members rejected their executive's choice of George Armstrong as party candidate in their constituency, and they also refused to accept a second proposal of Herman Saltzman, an east-European like themselves. Instead, they compromised on a parachute candidate from Brandon, and Armstrong ran in west Winnipeg. Neither was elected.

This campaign also saw the first entry into the political arena of Fred Dixon, running for the Manitoba Labor Party in the adjacent riding of Centre Winnipeg. Making little impact in his own constituency, Armstrong had seemed to dog Dixon's footsteps in the campaign, abetted by Bill Hoop, both intent on demolishing the popular reformer as a "lackey of the Liberals." Dixon's narrow loss because of the split labour vote infuriated his supporters; at a Trades and Labor Council session, Puttee denounced the SPC subversion as "the most despicable piece of political work which has been done in the labour movement in Canada." For the Socialists, it was a triumph: they boasted in the *Western Clarion* that "we dealt Puttee a good blow," and called on all true socialists to "destroy the Labor paper and the Labor Party."

The dismal showing of the SPC in the election sent many of the North End members into affiliation with the Social Democratic Party, a rising force in the area, and the Social Democrats even succeeded in organizing immigrant carpenters in the North End, invading Armstrong's own territory. The SPC cooperated briefly and reluctantly in the 1913 civic elections with the newly formed Labor Representation Committee, and the chosen candidate, Richard Rigg, won a North End seat on city council, but on the whole an adversarial truculence marked their interaction with other members of the left-wing community.

In the 1914 provincial elections the SPC was back in form. It fielded a candidate against Rigg in Winnipeg North, and against the pro-labour Liberal, Tom Johnson, in Winnipeg Centre Seat A, and it nominated George Armstrong for Seat B, opposing Fred Dixon. Once again the popular reformer's broad alliance of progressives made him a target for the Socialist Party, and once again Armstrong turned up repeatedly at Dixon's campaign rallies, to heckle and taunt: Dixon's single tax philosophy was so much mumbo jumbo, his proposed electoral reforms, the referendum and the recall, undemocratic and nothing but rubbish, and above all, the acceptance by a labour candidate of support from the capitalist Liberals sheer heresy, a betrayal of the working class. From British Columbia, fellow Socialist Bill Pritchard agreed that mere reforms were a waste of time, and the attack on Dixon "a great thing with the Party."

Puttee commented in *The Voice*, with remarkable restraint: "Years ago it was all right to adopt a doctrinaire, impractical attitude, but the days are drawing near in which it will be possible to elect working-class representatives in large numbers. No more resources should be wasted in comparatively fruitless demonstrations."

Dixon won his seat decisively, with a comfortable margin of fifteen hundred votes over his nearest rival. Armstrong, with an ignominious 953 votes, dismissed the victor as "just a sentimentalist, that's all." He ran against Dixon once more, and once more lost, in the 1915 election that followed the defeat of the Roblin government. Interestingly, another failed candidate in this election was A. J. Andrews, who was to act as chief prosecutor in the General Strike trials.

In the depression that undermined the western Canadian economy just before World War I, Armstrong's carpenters, always among the lowest on the construction workers' wage scale, were particularly hard hit. Union members could not pay their dues or lost their jobs altogether, and it was not until 1916 that Armstrong, by now the acknowledged carpenters' leader, could report to the Trades and Labor Council that his members were once again finding employment. Even then, carpenters' wages during the next two years increased by only nine percent; by comparison, the electricians' scale went up twenty-two percent, and the labourers, always the least paid, added twenty-nine percent to their wage packet. A virtually continuous series of walk outs in the various sectors of the construction industry added to the labour unrest in the city.

Under the stresses of wartime, radical activists were spurred on to intensify their efforts, redoubling their attack on the injustices of existing society. George Armstrong was in his heyday in his regular weekend and evening appearances in Market Square, reviewing labour battles at great length for a receptive audience, setting forth impressively complex arguments, rousing his listeners at last to a peak of justified fury. He was "a rough and tough kind of speaker . . . always handing out the Marxist line," Fred Tipping remembered many years later. A big man, with a voice to match and a forceful manner, Armstrong's fact-filled style appealed to many of the industrial workers. If he tired, and he sometimes did, the crowd might occasionally be treated to the diverting spectacle of having Mrs. Armstrong rush into the breech, with her shrill and even more intense brand of anti-capitalist vituperation.

George's fund of information made him a favourite lecturer in the SPC's educational program, and he conducted classes in socialism for many years at the party's headquarters on Smith Street, across from the Marlborough Hotel. At the meetings of the Trades and Labor Council, again, as socialists like Russell and Johns clashed acrimoniously with moderates like Heaps and Queen for control of policy, Armstrong could be counted on to bring an endless array of arguments and examples to bear on particular decisions, striving to rein in his flamboyant style, returning doggedly to the socialist scorn for any misguided attempts to ameliorate the capitalist system:

We don't want to be instrumental in improving it in any way; what we're out for is the downfall of capitalism, and the institution of a new order of society, which would be socialism.

When Prime Minister Borden cautiously introduced his National Manpower Registration program, the Trades and Labor Congress directed its members to support the war effort; but in Winnipeg an increasingly radicalized Trades and Labor Council, driven to the left by Armstrong, Russell, and Johns, told workers to ignore the registration cards.

Meanwhile, by 1918 the union movement itself was undergoing further fragmentation from within, as Russell and Johns and the others pushed their OBU toward fruition. As angry as any of the western unionists at the snubbing they had received at the Quebec Trades and Labor Congress conference in September, Armstrong was nevertheless head of the United Brotherhood of Carpenters and Joiners' local, and could not or would not join in the plan to sever connections with the Congress. As a delegate of his union he attended the Western Labor Conference in Calgary early in 1919 at which the OBU took shape, but he rejected the move to secede as a backward step, undermining the strength and influence labour had already achieved. In British Columbia, fellow Socialist Party members R. Pettipiece and E. T. Kingsley concurred with his opposition; in Winnipeg, Social Democrats Ernie Robinson and Dick Rigg raised the same objection; and other prominent labourites such as Queen and Heaps and Ivens questioned the logic of the move at a time when the labour movement was already under great stress.

Armstrong's demagogic popularity made him a natural choice for the speakers' panel at the soon-to-be-infamous Walker Theatre meeting. With a lengthy display of erudition, seconding Comrade Bill Hoop's motion denouncing the federal government's persistent use of orders-in-council, he drew a comparison between present-day labour conditions and the situation in medieval England after the Black Plague swept the country. Unexpectedly, perhaps, the diehard revolutionary paid tribute to the British constitution, respected by the whole world, he said, for its protection of the rights of minorities, but he insisted that inequities had developed, and the rights of the vast working-class majority had been displaced in favour of the powerful controlling minority. The Socialist Party of Canada, he said, was sometimes accused of being an enemy of authority; that was not so, but authority had now "passed from that position where it derives its power from the government of the nation to where it maintains itself by physical force." Amplifying this rather convoluted exposition, digressing irresistibly into parallel examples, but gauging the temper of his audience with practiced skill, Armstrong arrived at his oft-repeated conclusion: existing government, in Canada or elsewhere, was no longer legitimate and its authority must be challenged.

At the Majestic Theatre rally that followed, under SPC auspices only, Armstrong expressed the full range of his opposition to the existing social and economic order. The recent war, he proclaimed, was capitalism's method of aggrandizing itself at the expense of ordinary people:

During the four years of the war, the wealth of Canada increased from eight-and-a-half billion to nineteen-and-a-half billion, in spite of its being the most destructive period in the world's history. What better scheme has our ruling class for the future to increase the nation's wealth, than that just past? . . . The greater the wealth in capitalist society, the larger is the percentage of its population in absolute poverty.

187

With his characteristic discursiveness he invited his listeners to examine for a few moments the origin and nature and history of property ownership in Canada and the United States, and the relationship between the enormous increase of wealth and the "wage slaves" that produced that wealth, and then he reached the point and purpose of his discourse. "All forms of property," he proclaimed, "are torn from the hide of the workers. . . . Your interest as workers is in opposition to all forms of property . . ." — and the audience of workers roared its agreement.

A hotly divisive fury erupted in the Trades and Labor Council ten days later, when the maneuvering of the two rival factions came to the surface. The council moderates, the Socialists charged, had deliberately sabotaged their arrangements to stage the second rally at the Walker Theatre, and further, the use of the meeting hall in the Labor Temple had been denied to them by their own supposed comrades. Someone had thrown a monkey wrench into the plans, the radicals stormed. There was a confused argument about a ten-dollar deposit which the theatre management had or had not accepted, and Armstrong accused the secretary, Ernie Robinson, of being personally responsible for the treachery. Some council members demanded that Armstrong be expelled for a year for his attack on the secretary.

The mainstream press gave full play to the infighting among labourites and the disruptive tactics of the radicals, inside the council and out. Alerted by George Armstrong's frequent and always contentious appearances at union meetings, at political rallies, in the free-for-all of Market Square, and his blatant urging of a revolt against capitalist oppression, the police added the noisy unionist to their list of suspects under surveillance, in their mounting fear of a Bolshevik onslaught.

When the call went out in the spring of 1919 for a general sympathy strike, many construction workers were already off the job, and the carpenters were among the first to back the machinists in their war with the ironmasters. It was obvious to the authorities that Armstrong, the pugnacious orator of Market Square, was at the heart of the trouble.

While Helen Armstrong swung into action to look after the desperately vulnerable female workers, George circulated among large groups and small, urging the strikers to hold fast, reminding them again and again of the injustice perpetrated by the existing system on ordinary people. For his constant visibility, the Citizens' Committee of One Thousand singled him out for special attention, sneering in its publication, the *Citizen*, that he was "another notorious 'Red' " who had incurred the righteous wrath of the returned men for his Bolshevik support of the Russian Soviet.

For all his soapbox prominence, however, George Armstrong played only a minor role in the organization and the conduct of the general strike itself. As the carpenters' representative, he was a member of the large, inclusive General Strike Committee, but he did not serve on the Central Strike Committee nor did he appear among the major negotiators.

Under the impression that recent arrivals from Europe were fomenting the trouble among otherwise peaceable Canadians, Ottawa had put through a series of hasty modifications to existing immigration laws and the Criminal Code, making possible the detention and deportation without trial of all such undesirables, and had already shipped out a number of "aliens" on a variety of charges. Now, as the Winnipeg affair dragged on without resolution, the Borden government moved to turn the same mechanism on the strike leaders. A last-minute adjustment to the legislation extended the deportation penalty to dissidents of British birth, and the arrests were ordered.

George Armstrong was at home, asleep, when the police moved against their quarry in the small hours of Tuesday morning, June 17, and he resisted arrest only long enough to telephone the police station for verification that the warrant was authentic. The Armstrong house on Edmonton Street was ransacked and yielded a gratifying collection of suspicious printed material, the property of both husband and wife, but not the cache of revolutionary arms the agents had been certain they would find.

There was some confusion at first about the identity of the individual arrested on Edmonton Street. Early news reports listed "George Armstrong, street car motorman" as one of the alleged felons, and there was indeed a union member named Armstrong, an entirely inoffensive street-railway employee. Subsequent accounts clarified the alleged lawbreaker as the George Armstrong who acted for the United

Brotherhood of Carpenters and Joiners. There was an even greater embarrassment for Borden and his cabinet when they discovered that Armstrong could not be deported, as threatened, because he was Canadian-born, and a United Empire Loyalist to boot. Further, the remaining nine men for whom warrants had been issued as strike leaders all held British passports, and there was so widespread a protest at the proposed government action that the idea was quietly shelved in favour of formal court procedures.

The strike broken, the city's dispirited workers returned to their jobs, if vindictive employers accepted them back; and for the alleged leaders the anxious process of bail hearings, release from prison, arraignment, and return to prison, dragged on throughout the summer. By September they were free again, awaiting trial.

George and Helen Armstrong travelled to Hamilton in the fall, to attend the annual Trades and Labor Convention. The mood of the western contingent was still defiant; rather recklessly, in view of the charges against him, George proposed a resolution calling for "the immediate withdrawal of [Allied] troops from Russia," and urged the Trades and Labor Congress to "go on record endorsing the Soviets as administering affairs to the best interests of the working class."

In the collective trial that began early in 1920, following Russell's conviction, E. J. McMurray was retained to defend Armstrong, Bray, and Johns. Denying the charge of seditious conspiracy on behalf of all his clients, McMurray took the high road, invoking British justice and the right of free speech. "Penitentiary, " he said, "was never meant for men like these. These men were meant to adorn universities and legislatures, and would have done so, had they not chosen nobler work." More practically, he argued that there could be no conspiracy between men of such diverse opinions: ". . . how could an International representative conspire seditiously with the OBU?" he asked rhetorically, elaborating on the differences between Armstrong of the Carpenters' Union and Johns, the insurgent OBU organizer. Moreover, he pointed out, sedition entailed interference with the welfare of the state, and there was no evidence that an attack on the state was intended. As for Armstrong himself, McMurray maintained that "the Crown just wants him out of the way because he is . . . a thinker."

Judge Metcalfe would have none of this. In his instructions to the jury, he labelled Armstrong as "of the soapbox variety of Socialist," and "one of the 'Reds,' who, with Russell . . . had control." Armstrong, said the judge, spoke at the Walker and at the Majestic and at other meetings; he had committed sedition in that he was responsible for much of the dangerous propaganda distributed by the Socialist Party of Canada. The jury brought in a verdict of guilty, and Armstrong received the common sentence of a year at the provincial prison farm.

Out of this entire disheartening episode there was one benefit for George Armstrong: the political office he had sought unsuccessfully half a dozen years earlier. In the 1920 provincial elections, when the Socialists reluctantly agreed to add their candidates to labour's unified slate, Armstrong picked up votes on the second and third and fourth counts from the overwhelming victory of the reformer he had constantly attacked. With his portion of Dixon's excess votes, he did not quite achieve the required ten percent of the total ballot, but won by attrition, the eighth labour candidate to be named to a city seat in the provincial House, and the only SPC candidate to make the grade. The prisoners were released on February 17, 1920, and Ivens, Queen, and Armstrong ceremoniously took their places in the legislature as the people's choice.

Fear of the "Reds" was still alive. The liberal and astute *Free Press* editor, John W. Dafoe, asserted his concern that labour now held twenty-five percent of the seats in the legislature, "and perhaps with one exception" — presumably Dixon — "all the labour members are 'Reds'." Dissension over the Communist call to world alliance had ripped apart the Socialist Party, and many comrades broke away to join the new Workers' Party of Jacob Penner. Rethinking his initial opposition to the OBU, Armstrong indicated his approval, but the United Brotherhood of Carpenters and Joiners remained an AFL affiliate. He served only the one term as MLA, until the next election in 1922. In the weary reaction to the excitement of the strike, fewer people came to hear the verbal fireworks in Market Square, and there seemed little prospect for future political success.

Times were hard again in the building trades, and thousands of highly skilled workers left Winnipeg to look for work in the United States. As for the Armstrongs, there was not enough income now either for

George or for his three sons-in-law. After eighteen hectic years in Winnipeg, it was time to go. The entire Armstrong family, the parents, the son, the daughters and their husbands, pulled up stakes and moved across the border again, to Chicago, and the anonymity of an American metropolis.

Some years later, George and Helen returned to Canada, to retire to Victoria, but they grew restless, and relocated to California, only sporadically in touch with their old comrades. Helen died there in 1947. George lived on in Concord, California, until his death in February 1956, at the age of eighty-six.

Their son, Frank, returned to Winnipeg, settling with his wife, Catherine, in the suburb of St. Vital. Carrying on in the tradition of his parents, he was active in the labour movement, and in the late sixties served as a vice-president of the AFL.

Roger Bray

Veterans and the Strike: Roger Bray

Roger Bray was one of the thousands of Canadian men who enlisted in the armed forces at the outbreak of the war out of sheer desperation, because they could find no other way to provide for themselves and their families. Born in Sheffield, England, he became a butcher; and as a devout Christian he served as a Methodist lay preacher for some six years, drawn to the church's earnest commitment to helping the disadvantaged. He discovered, as he said, that "Christianity was not the means of correcting social injustice," and espousing socialism, he was attracted into the labour movement. In 1903 he left England for Winnipeg, and worked at his trade until the pre-war depression made meat a luxury on workers' tables, and he could no longer obtain work. Despite his pacifist convictions he felt he had no choice but to respond, in 1916, to the recruiting campaign for the armed forces. "I had no job," he explained simply, "and a large family."

Short and slight and none too robust, he was classified as "B-2," not suitable for frontline duty, and served out his enlistment in England. When he came back to Winnipeg on the last day of December 1918, the contentious Walker Theatre demonstration had just taken place, tempers were flying among union men and left-of-centre party members, and the count down had begun to the explosion in May. Bray's own political sympathies had not altered. "The war," he remarked, "didn't correct social injustices either."

With all the vast changes that had taken place in Canadian society during the four years of the conflict, the country was ill-prepared to absorb its returning soldiers into the peacetime economy. The federal government floated various plans for "reconstruction," all hotly debated in the press and in union halls, and generally condemned by the left as inadequate. Many veterans found it difficult, if not impossible, to return to their old jobs at an office desk, or behind a shop counter, or on a factory line. Women were now employed in positions formerly considered a male prerogative, and at wage rates considerably lower than employers would have had to pay men; and, most infuriatingly of all, the "slackers" who had remained safely at home now appeared to be firmly ensconsed in the best jobs and getting ahead, while those who had served their country were forced to begin again, even more disadvantaged than when they had first enlisted.

Most visible among these usurpers of the fighting men's rights were the hated "aliens," so many of whom had prospered, despite popular suspicion and hostility, in the wartime industrial expansion. "We are opposed to the alien," proclaimed F. W. Law, the secretary of the Great War Veterans' Association, the major veterans' organization, "and will be opposed to him until such time as he gets out of the country."

At the end of January 1919, after the SPC's mass meeting at the Majestic Theatre, a second rally at the Majestic was announced, to deal with the provocative subject, "The Causes of the German Revolution." This time the theatre management was warned that a party of returned soldiers planned to break up the meeting, and the venue was hastily shifted to Market Square, the classic home of Winnipeg's dissenting agitators. On the appointed day, January 26, as the labour faithful assembled, about two hundred veterans in marching order descended on Market Square, looking for the meeting's speakers. The crowd fled, and when no speakers appeared the veterans marched down King Street and on to the SPC office and meeting hall.

As most of the demonstrators milled about outside, some of the men broke into the premises, smashed furniture, heaved books, papers, and a piano out the window, and set fire to the debris in the street, to the cheers of the onlookers. Still not satisfied, the soldiers continued to riot that day and the next, turning their frustration on "aliens." They wrecked Sam Blumenberg's dry-cleaning shop on Portage Avenue, and then demonstrated at the Swift packing plant against the company's employment of the foreign-born.

With similar disturbances occurring sporadically throughout the country, Russell and Bill Hoop tried to make common cause with the veterans, but the prospect of such an understanding alarmed the authorities even more. A. B. Perry, the commissioner of the RNWMP, decreed that "the veterans must be kept out of the clutches of these Socialists and Bolshevik agitators."

Not all the returned soldiers were inclined to vent their frustration against the labour movement, its radical parties, and its unions. In Winnipeg, membership of the Great War Veterans' Association included both officers and enlisted men, employers and employees. More than half the members came from a working-class background; many had been union members before their enlistment, and their sympathies lay with the strikers. When the general strike shut down the city on May 15, the GWVA was thrown into immediate chaos, and divergent accounts emerged of the sequence of events that followed.

At a tumultuous meeting on May 23, it was reported, a pro-labour faction led by a burly ex-sergeant, Jack Moore, succeeded in reversing an anti-strike resolution into a declaration of full sympathy with the aims of the strikers. Law, as secretary, issued a statement repudiating the course taken by the militants and declaring the association "unequivocally on the side of constituted authority as against Bolshevism." A compromise policy of strict neutrality may or may not have been accepted, but at least two of the officers present, F. G. Thompson and J. O. Newton, began — or had already begun — to rally anti-strike veterans in defence of law and order. Testifying later at the trials, Thompson declared that he had been instrumental in placing a veterans' representative on the Citizens' Committee of One Thousand.

There was stalemate within the organization, and the pent-up animosity of the soldiers against established authority erupted into the open. On the evening of Thursday, May 29, Moore's veterans, now with Roger Bray moving into the leadership, came together for a three-hour meeting, determined to bring matters to a head by a show of organized militancy and obtain a fair settlement of the workers' demands.

The next morning a parade of two thousand veterans marched down Kennedy Street to the legislature, many still in military uniform, and confronted Premier Norris and his cabinet with their grievances and their demands. It was unwise, Bray declared, as spokesman for the delegation, to require a pledge from the police not to join a union; and it was totally unacceptable to take the regular force off the streets, as had been threatened, and replace them with military police, instituting martial law. City council had given in to coercion by the Citizens' Committee of One Thousand, he charged; the order should be repealed to avoid trouble. And would the premier therefore call the solders "Bolsheviks" or "aliens," he inquired truculently, with an angry rumble from the men behind him. Norris hastily assured him that he would not. Then, said Bray, the press must be required to end their campaign of vilification against the strike leaders, who held similar views, and the term, "English and Scotch anarchists," a racial and political smear, must be stopped.

Finally the delegation presented the premier with the veterans' proposal to resolve the impasse: special legislation must be enacted, either by the federal or the provincial government, to make collective bargaining compulsory in every workplace in the province. They would return, they said, on the following day, and would expect an answer. Norris called in the legislative reporters and informed them of the development.

On the Saturday morning once again a contingent of ex-soldiers quick-stepped to the legislature, the Union Jack proudly unfurled at the head of the march, a crowd of sympathizers and the merely curious falling in behind, to reiterate their demand for collective bargaining. Norris had his response prepared. To the boos and catcalls of the delegation, he declared that the sympathy strike must be called off before conciliatory talks could be undertaken or legislation considered.

Bitterly, Bray reiterated the troops' resentment of the egregious influence of the Citizens' Committee of One Thousand, and the treatment being meted out to ordinary people, veterans and workers alike. Returned men, he pointed out, had demonstrated their loyalty at the front in order that the government might continue to exist, and the loyalty of the police, many of them veterans themselves, was beyond question. "The boys," he cried, "want you to represent the people, not that bunch of financial barons in the Manufacturers' Association." Call off the Citizens' Committee, he exclaimed, not the sympathetic strike.

Furious at the rebuff, the veterans regrouped and, led by Bray and Moore, they marched out of the legislature grounds to Main Street and the city hall, where a council meeting was in progress. They jammed the visitors' gallery dangerously, until Mayor Gray, afraid that the structure would collapse under their weight, adjourned the session and offered to meet the demonstrators outside. Standing on the city hall steps, he denounced the strike, and was shouted down by the crowd. Aldermen John Queen and Abe Heaps spoke of their efforts to ensure that the just demands of the workers were met, and the crowd applauded and cheered. A number of the returned men addressed the crowd in the impromptu forum with a blunt, direct message: they would march until the strikers were granted their rights.

March they did, parading down Portage Avenue on the following Monday, jeering as they passed the T. Eaton Company, at Donald Street, and the *Free Press*, just off Portage Avenue on Carlton Street, both of them considered bastions of the establishment, with spectators looking on from both sides of the street and hanging out of windows. Then they moved on to the legislature, where a large crowd waited to join the demonstration. Thousands pushed into the building, until no one else in the heaving mass could get in, and the committee in charge of the delegation hurried to impose discipline. Bray ordered the chamber cleared and only bona fide veterans were permitted to reenter, and the Union Jack proudly led the soldiers onto the floor of the legislature, to the patriotic cheers of the assembly.

Calling for complete order and courteous attention to all speakers, Bray presented a prepared resolution. The prime minister had ruled, he said, that the right to collective bargaining was in the provincial not the federal jurisdiction, and therefore, be it resolved that we herewith demand such legislation at once. Also that we demand the withdrawal of the ultimatum by the Provincial Government to its employees. And further, that in the event of the Government not complying with our demands, we call upon the Government to resign.

Smoothly conciliatory, Norris thanked the men for their peaceable and gentlemanly presentation, and assured them that he had appealed to the press for "moderation and fairness." As for their specific demands, he said, "the government must proceed along constitutional lines," and the elected representatives of the people would have to be consulted. He had turned over to city council all the issues under civic control, and the legislature would duly consider the matters in its domain. Collective bargaining, he maintained, could only be arrived at by mutual agreement, not by legislation; he himself did not object to strike action by employees, but he was opposed on principle to the sympathetic strike.

Bray kept his temper long enough to thank the premier for his attention, but fired a parting shot. It was for the government to decide whether to come over to the side of the workers, or to side with "that shameless bunch of profiteers," the Citizens' Committee; the veterans would be back again, he warned, to press for a special legislative session on the emergency, and if that was denied, they would demand the government's resignation. Unappeased, the veterans marched to the St. Boniface city hall, just across the Red River, to make the same demands; then raising banners proclaiming, "We Stand for 35,000, not 1,000," and "Britons Never Shall Be Slaves," and "Down With the Profiteers — Up With the People," they marched back to the headquarters of the Citizens' Committee, in the Industrial Bureau on Water Street. Finding no one on the premises, they tore down the committee's banner and dragged it to city hall, promising, "We'll call again in the sweet by and by," and ended their demonstration with a rally in Victoria Park.

The Central Strike Committee had worked hard to keep people off the streets, not to provoke the authorities, and there were well-founded fears that the veterans' belligerency would lead to violence. Nevertheless, welcoming these volatile but impressive allies, the *Strike*

Bulletin informed its readers that at a meeting on Tuesday evening, June 3, the Great War Veterans' Association had passed a resolution to support the strikers. It was further reported that a majority of those present had voted to expel all former army officers from the association, limiting membership to enlisted men.

At the trials Lieutenant Thompson testified, instead, that he had resigned his membership on the spot, appalled by the coalition being forged by Bray and Moore, in violation of what he insisted was the agreed-upon neutrality of the GWVA. A lawyer and a Mason, and headed for a successful career in politics, he had been told by "some of the boys," he said, that at the protracted demonstration on the Saturday afternoon there were "what they call Bohunks or Austrians in the crowd," and he determined that it was imperative to prevent people from "being led off . . . the way that the Russian system was going."

At the outset of the strike, Mayor Gray had threatened that martial law would be imposed if the city continued out of control, and there was a series of exchanges on that score between Winnipeg and Ottawa. General Ketchen, of Military District No. 10 Winnipeg, mobilized part of the militia, and the possibility was raised that the 27th Battalion, then en route back to Winnipeg from overseas duty, would be kept in service to deal with the emergency. The battalion's Colonel Harold Riley telegraphed his advice not to proceed with the plan: so many of the soldiers, he warned, had relatives among the strikers that it would be unwise to attempt to use them as strikebreakers, unless there was an urgent necessity to enforce law and order. The 27th was demobilized on arrival in the city, with only a few men volunteering for special duty; but a consignment of Lewis guns had been surreptitiously delivered to MD 10, to be used in case of need.

Joined by Lieutenant James Dunwoody, who had been brought to the city to train a unit of mounted "Specials," Thompson and Newton put together their Returned Soldiers' Loyalists Association. The daily newspapers carried a large advertisement on June 4, paid for by the Citizens' Committee, pledging the resolve of the new group to protect the life and property of "Mr. Employer," and "[make] Canada safe for Canadians." The movement, said the manifesto, will speedily clear Canada of the undesirable alien and land him back in the bilgewaters of European Civilization from whence he sprung and to which he properly belongs. . . .

CHOOSE BETWEEN THE SOLDIERS WHO ARE PROTECTING YOU AND THE ALIENS WHO HAVE THREATENED YOU.

A countermarch took place, under a huge banner: "We Will Maintain Constituted Authority, Law & Order . . . Down with the High Cost of Living . . . To Hell with the Alien Enemy . . . God Save the King!" The anti-strike paraders paid their respects to the premier and the mayor, offering their unqualified allegiance. Mayor Gray was reported to have responded, "It is like a drink of new wine to hear such expressions of loyalty." When the police arrested one of the Loyalists for carrying a gun, the labour press alleged, Mayor Gray, his coattails flying, ran down the street after the constable and his prisoner, demanding the man's immediate release.

The same evening over four thousand pro-strike veterans held a protest rally in St. John's Park, in the city's North End. Roger Bray spoke, his small frame dwarfed on the speakers' platform. A gang of "paid thugs," reported the *Western Labor News*, tried to force its way to the podium and "get" Bray; whereupon a group of about twenty women from the audience surrounded him, and dared the hoodlums to "come and get him now!" The men, said the paper, fled to waiting cars, shouting that they would "get him yet."

In the next few days, pro- and anti-strike veterans' formations continued to crisscross the city, and confused would-be adherents of one side or the other blundered into the wrong demonstration, or could be heard asking, "Which parade is this?" At one such march, staged without the permission of the Strike Committee but at the insistence of the veterans, there was an incident that Fred Tipping chuckled at, years later: "I saw an elderly woman, with the lid of a garbage can held like a shield, attack a mounted policeman. The horse reared and the fellow slid off. He was captured like a prisoner of war and led off to the Labor Temple."

The mayor declared a ban on parades, but the soldiers continued to hold what they called "silent parades." A drive began to recruit Loyalists as a "Home Defence Force" against the "alien menace," and Loyalist volunteers were sworn in as "Specials," ready to serve the Citizens' Committee of One Thousand in its self-appointed task of patrolling the allegedly rebellious streets. "We had to occupy the fire halls and police stations, and things like that," one volunteer Special remembered, and there was a generous supply of liquor always on tap, to keep the recruits from straying. In opposition, the *Strike Bulletin* waxed lyrical in its praise for the perfect order of Roger Bray's "returned boys," in their peaceable "march for justice . . . stepping blithely along behind the old flag to the skirr [sic] of the pipes and the roll of the drum."

At the Soldiers' Parliament in Victoria Park on Monday morning, June 9, General Ketchen complimented "the boys" on the "orderliness and discipline" of their parades, and then the beloved "padre" of the Canadian army, Canon F. G. Scott, assured them of his absolute support for their aims — even if "some capitalist hit him on the head with a gold brick," the *Western Labor News* said. That same day, however, the city council and the police commission dismissed the recalcitrant members of the police force and hired specials, at six dollars per day, and Deputy Police Chief Chris Newton replaced the chief, Donald Macpherson. Lieutenant Thompson took credit for this coup, testifying, "We put it to the police commission hot and heavy . . .this damn police force . . .is not doing a fair job, and we want it out or there is going to be real trouble. . . ." Even as the Soldiers' Parliament convened, a squadron of mounted "Specials" wielding truncheons, many of them Loyalist Veterans, charged into a mass of strike supporters who refused to disperse.

A meeting took place between representatives of both veterans' factions and delegates from the Central Strike Committee; Thompson declared that both parties were in agreement on "the alien question" and "collective bargaining," but that the strike was the work of "the Red element and the OBU." Roger Bray, said the *Citizen*, was a notorious "Red"; he "poses as a returned fighter, but . . . never saw the firing lines, and [he] told Premier Norris in cold blood on June 2, 1919, that he was a Bolshevist and out for the establishment of Soviet Government in Winnipeg." Bray claimed that "our delegation now represents nearly all returned men, and we have the backing of a majority of the people of Manitoba."

There were concentrations of provincial police in the city, and units of the militia at the barracks. Veterans were challenged, "Are you citizens or strikers?" At Special Police headquarters, liquor was dispensed freely to potential recruits, and participants in the Soldiers' Parliament found they were being shadowed. Rumours of impending arrests began to circulate in the press and on the street.

When the authorities closed the net on the strike leaders, Roger Bray was included with the rest. His home was entered and searched; and once again stressing the innocence of these victims of police brutality, the *Western Labor News* added the poignant detail that the sleeping children were turned out of bed in the futile search for seditious literature or concealed weapons. Said the *Citizen*, always ready to deride the dissidents, the arresting constables reported that Bray fainted when the police woke him up, and wept all the way to the station.

Left without their leader, the pro-strike veterans carried on under Jack Moore and others. Calling a meeting in Market Square on Friday, June 20, they agreed to hold another "silent parade" the next day, to meet with the federal government's emissary, Senator Gideon Robertson. Six thousand people turned up that afternoon, soldiers and civilians, and the police move against this perceived menace sparked the shocking violence of "Bloody Saturday." Five days later, the great, unprecedented labour action was over.

Roger Bray had been named a member of the large General Strike Committee, although his role was limited. His veterans had maintained a forceful pro-strike presence, even in the waning days of the workers' enthusiasm, and he himself had repeatedly declared his allegiance to labour's aims against the rapacious "bosses." Embraced by the radical socialists, he had even been drawn into the OBU battle against the traditional union movement. When the OBU formed its Winnipeg Labor Council in August after the strike, Roger Bray was elected vice-president.

His trial yielded no new evidence against him, and Judge Metcalfe, addressing the jury, was inclined to discount some of the charges, and as much as told the jury so. Bray, he said, "was not serving two masters. There is no doubt about that":

He was a member of the Strike Committee, and he became very active. He led the soldiers in their parades, and he demanded from the premier that the strike should be settled according to the demands of the strikers. . . . The *Strike Bulletin* had several articles concerning Mr. Bray, and what Mr. Bray did. But to be fair to Bray, he would seem to have no connection with the matters charged, except such connection as you may infer from the Winnipeg Strike itself.

Accordingly, the jury found him "not guilty" on all counts except the rather belittling one of merely "committing a common nuisance," and he was sentenced to six months in jail.

Released in August 1920, to a difficult and disrupted labour market, he was taken on as full-time organizer for the OBU. But the new union movement was already on the decline, and by 1923 that job came to an end. Subsequently, Bray tried his hand at a number of occupations, including market gardening, but left for Vancouver in the thirties, to become an organizer for the CCF. Eventually, he made his living raising flowers, specializing in gladioli.

His daughter, Mrs. E. McKinnon, carried on in something of her father's spirit, making a brief political appearance as CCF candidate for municipal office in St. Boniface.

Richard Johns

The Useful Arts: Richard Johns

Dick Johns joined Bob Russell in Lodge 122 of the International Association of Machinists in June 1913, coming from a background not unlike Russell's. Born in Cornwall, England, in 1888, he had left school at the age of fifteen to take a course in metal work at a polytechnical institute, and having acquired his papers of certification had worked in a number of metal shops. His introduction to socialism came through the writings of Robert Blatchford and the Fabians — George Bernard Shaw and Sidney and Beatrice Webb — and his initial political orientation was in the gradualism of the British Labour Party. In 1909 he left Britain for Denver, Colorado, because work was scarce at home, but he quickly discovered that the American West was not receptive to his brand of fairly radical politics, and he moved again, to Winnipeg. There, he had heard, jobs were plentiful in the CPR shops.

The pre-war depression had already set in and the railways were laying off employees, but Johns had become a highly skilled machinist, a toolmaker, at the very top of the metal-trades hierarchy. Married and with a family, he fared much better than most of his union mates, maintaining a reasonably steady income. Fred Tipping remembered him in those years as "handsome and genial . . . the boy with the smile," and as "a fiery orator who could hold an audience spellbound by his eloquence." He was also a bit of a dandy, his friends thought, quick to shed his work clothes at the end of the day and turn up at union meetings in a well-pressed suit, with stiff-collared shirt, precise tie, and immaculately polished shoes.

Johns rose quickly in the trade union ranks, becoming his union's delegate to the Winnipeg Trades and Labor Council, and when Division 4 of the IAM was formed, one of the leading representatives of the railway shopmen. Removed thereby from the noise and dirt of the shop floor, and required to travel a good deal, he held it a point of honour, as did Russell, that his salary was no higher than the wages of the men he represented. The labour tensions in those difficult war years intensified his opposition to the status quo, and he became a member of the aggressively Marxist Socialist Party of Canada. Together with Russell, and backing Russell's blunt forcefulness with his own quick intelligence, he made a name for himself as one of the Trades and Labor Council's insistent leftists, pushing that body toward ever more decisive action.

At the same time as he rose to prominence in the union movement and in the Socialist Party, the need of the country's wartime industry for skilled craftsmen called into service Johns's outstanding proficiency at his trade. He was technically without academic accreditation, but he was hired in the fall of 1917 and for the next two years to teach evening classes in industrial arts at St. John's Technical High School, in the city's North End. Ironically, his ability to train craftsmen for industry, thus serving the militarism he hated, may well have kept him out of the manpower draft.

As advocate for his machinists' union Johns won the trust and admiration of his mates for his unstinting efforts on their behalf, while as a Socialist he fought for the empowerment of all working people. When Arthur Puttee raised his self-damaging criticism of the chain reaction strikes of spring 1918, the young radical responded furiously: "The time is not for compromise . . . . You have the right to demand anything that you have the power to enforce. In the city of Winnipeg we have the might; let us use it." An inveterate writer of letters to the editor and a correspondent of the *Machinist's Bulletin*, he flayed city alderman Frank Fowler for his amendment to the proposed agreement with the striking civic employees, requiring them to sign a no-strike pledge; and his comment reflected a distinctly Marxist class-consciousness:

> There are only two groups in society . . . and Fowler has merely acted as the mouthpiece of the propertied class. The workers of Winnipeg have met Fowler's challenge in high style by exhibiting a new proletarian morality in their solidarity during the sympathetic strike.

Following the rout of the western delegates at the Trades Congress meeting in Quebec, the struggle in Winnipeg's Trades and Labor Council between the moderates and the extremists became overt in the council elections of December 1918. Russell vied for the presidency and Johns for the vice-presidency, and both were defeated.

Dick Johns was not one of the speakers who took the stage at the fateful Walker Theatre rally, and the *Western Labor News* reported only briefly on his comments at the Majestic Theatre, while reproducing the arguments of Russell and Armstrong at length. Comrade Johns, the paper indicated, dealt with the reconstruction policy of the Manufacturers' Association, and "appealed to the workers to get hold of all the working class literature, for . . . bloodshed could be avoided only by an educated working class."

More ominously, at the Trades and Labor Council meeting at which the animosities of the two rival factions were thrashed out Johns was sufficiently incensed to predict, apparently, actual bloodshed. In Europe, he said, the workers were fighting in their own ranks, and the infection was spreading to Winnipeg. The council was terrified of the word "revolution," he sneered, but the socialists would soon achieve the control they sought: "We are fighting for ideals, and... we will be fighting with guns before we are through." Whether the coming battle would take place in the council meeting-room or in the city's streets was not entirely clear.

At the Western Labor Conference in March 1919, Russell once

again dominated the proceedings with his compelling scheme for a powerful union of all working people, free of the timidity of the entrenched eastern Trades and Labor Congress. In his wake, Johns denounced the Congress "machine," its denial of all the West's proposals for reform and progress and its compliance with the federal government, and advocated total secession from the TLC–AFL. Named to head the all-important policy committee, he presented the assembly with its seven-point plan for the organization of the OBU: a "Central Committee" and provincial subcommittees, an initiating referendum among all union members, a committee to carry out "the necessary propaganda," and a levy on unions to provide the necessary funding. Johns was then elected one of the five members of the Central Committee, Russell was named to take charge of the Manitoba campaign, and the authors of the breakaway union returned to their respective territories to put their plans into operation.

Committed to the replacement of craft unions by the all-encompassing OBU, Johns was still involved in the business of his own machinists. As tension mounted in Winnipeg in late winter 1919, negotiations were in progress between the National War Railway Board and Division 4 of the running trades. In the middle of April Johns left for Montreal to demand improvements in his union contracts. The East, he reported, was more than ready to come into the OBU, and he pursued the cause wherever unionists could be gathered to listen. Thus he had no part in the rush of events in Winnipeg that spring. When the strike was declared he was still in Montreal, spending his days negotiating wages and working conditions, his evenings urging the merits of the new industrial union. He wrote enthusiastically to Victor Midgley that if the strike was successful, then promoting the OBU would be easy.

Spared the cloak-and-dagger nighttime raid in which his fellow "conspirators" were captured, Dick Johns turned up at the arraignment on July 3, to the surprise of the police, who had apparently not troubled to serve the outstanding warrant, and was released on bail with the others, without actually having been arrested. As a known organizer for the OBU, he was labelled a "Bolshevik" by the Citizens' Committee of One Thousand, and the *Citizen* on June 4 reported his various pronouncements, with some apparent embellishment. A revolution was coming, he was said to have warned, and labour would soon be fighting with guns in their hands in the streets of Winnipeg, just as Russian fought Russian in Petrograd. . . . [He was] not anxious to spill blood, but if the occasion arose he was prepared.

Charged with conspiracy, like the others, he was duly brought to trial six months later, and defended along with Armstrong and Bray by E. J. McMurray. Judge Metcalfe's remarks to the jury summed up the case against him:

> Johns was a member of the Socialist Party of Canada, and spoke at the Walker Theatre meeting and Majestic Theatre meeting, where socialistic propaganda was distributed. He was . . . a "Red" like Russell, and the "Reds" had control of the Trades and Labor Council. He and Russell were the official delegates from the Trades and Labor Council to the Calgary Convention. He received the second highest number of votes [to] the Central Committee that was appointed at the Calgary Convention. Johns, while not in Winnipeg at the opening of the Winnipeg strike, was in the East organizing, and wrote letters to Russell, two of which were found in Russell's possession at the time of his arrest, showing his activities along the same line — that is, propaganda of unrest . . . of discontent.

He served his one-year sentence quietly, in good company, at the provincial prison farm. Bill Pritchard, like himself an SPC member, remembered afterward their long walks together and their wide-ranging discussions of the world's postwar problems. As well, said Pritchard, Johns was an amazing craftsman. When a bearing in a pump car at the farm broke down, he fashioned a perfect replacement out of a piece of hardwood, and it worked long after they were all released.

At thirty-three, then, his penalty discharged, Johns needed to assess his position. The fire had gone out in working-class Winnipeg, the radical left was divided over the Communist chimera, the OBU was faltering and not likely to recover. Having given full measure for the cause he believed in, he had won little popular support when he allowed his name to stand on the labour slate in the 1920 provincial elections.

Nevertheless, no longer opposed to attempting to reform the system, he broke with the Socialist Party and his old friend, Bob Russell, and joined the Independent Labor Party. He needed to take thought about his own future, but he was blacklisted now from coast to coast as a troublemaker, and despite his superlative skills he found no employer willing to give him a job.

But the man's very evident ability had won him friends among well-placed labour sympathizers. As Fred Tipping told the story, Johns's plight came to the attention of Ted McGrath, a member of the school board and later the deputy minister of Labor in John Bracken's government; and McGrath, in turn, appealed to Dr. McIntyre, the superintendent of Winnipeg schools. Both agreed, "We must find him some work." Johns was given the full-time job of keeping the mechanical equipment in two high schools in running order, working as instrument-maker, millwright, and general machinist, from 1922 to 1927. As well, in 1922 and 1923, he taught some night classes in industrial arts at St. John's High School.

Observing Johns, McIntyre began to urge him to further his own education and take up teaching as a career, and offered to help. Twice a week, Fred Tipping reminisced, Johns went to Dr. McIntyre's home to be coached:

> Dick lived in Elmwood and he would do maintenance and repair work at Kelvin Technical High School, and he would walk from his home to school, a distance of six or seven miles. He would waste no time, and read from texts as he walked to school in the morning, and read from texts as he walked the long miles back in the evening, and that was how he got his education.

He obtained his matriculation very quickly, including French and Latin, and, taking a teacher-training course at the Normal School, earned certification as a professional instructor in industrial arts. In 1927, he became a full-fledged member of the teaching staff at St. John's Technical High School.

By the thirties, the students enrolled at that ground-breaking North End school were the lively, self-confident children of some of the strikers who had walked the picket lines in 1919. They knew Mr. Johns only as the likable guy down in the shops department, someone who was rumoured to have some kind of faintly unhappy past history, and who was obviously regarded with special consideration by their revered principal, J. G. Reeve.

Not content with what he had already achieved, Dick Johns earned a bachelor's degree in education from Colorado State College, in 1934, and accumulated further credits until he was just short of a master's degree. In 1936-37 he served as night school principal at St. John's, and the following year he was named director of Urban Youth Training, and vocational guidance officer for the province. A new youth training school opened in 1938, with Johns as its director and principal. Then he was promoted to the position of director of technical education, and superintendent of all the province's day classes in shops, arts and crafts, domestic science, and commercial courses. He left his classrooms and was given a loving farewell by his students and fellow teachers.

During these extremely busy years of teaching and administrative work, Johns pursued his professional training with constantly recharged vigour. In summer sessions he took courses at the University of Manitoba in the philosophy, objectives, and methods of technical education, and in practical arts for rural schools at the Normal School. He turned his attention to vocational training for adults, studying the field from the psychology of learning to job analysis.

The years after World War II brought sweeping changes to the labour market, and the realization that the province's traditional institutions of higher education, geared to academic achievement, were no longer appropriate. A Committee on Technical and Vocational Education was appointed, with William Ivens as chairman and a number of labourites and pedagogues, including Johns, as members; its report, after a lengthy study, recommended the creation of a "technical and vocational training institute . . . sufficiently diversified to meet the need of rural as well as urban students" in an increasingly mechanized world. Dick Johns was entrusted with the responsibility of designing the new curriculum and of hiring and training staff; together with his old friend Bob Russell he sought out and obtained the latest and best in systems and equipment.

Past animosities long forgotten, the *Free Press* celebrated the vision of Dick Johns for the country's youth, quoting his explanation that the three Rs would be replaced by "three H's, hand, heart, and head":

Education will combine liberal and useful arts, learning will be humanitarian as well as utilitarian. The hand is used in any manual trade; the head is used in conjunction with the hand, the heart is connected with job pride, with feeling and thinking.

Built under Johns's supervision, the Manitoba Technical and Vocational Training Institute, on Notre Dame Avenue, opened in 1951, with Johns as principal. The name was later changed to the Technical and Vocational High School, or familiarly, Tec-Voc.

In 1953, at the age of sixty-five, Dick Johns retired, to the accolades of his associates and students, current and former, and with a last, uplifting fragment of verse to assess his own life and career:

Give me to fashion a thing,
Give me to shape and to mold.
I have found out the song I can sing;
I am happy, delivered, and bold.

Unable to remain inactive for long, Johns ran as an independent for the school board, in a North End seat, and was elected in 1956 and again in 1957. Once again his voice was raised in frustrated protest at the slow pace of reform. Within a short time of its inception, the Technical Institute, his design, was failing to live up to its promise. It was to be modelled on Toronto's advanced Ryerson Institute, but instead it was no more than a trade school, he charged: it had not achieved its most important objectives, training technicians beyond the high school level and producing advanced instructors in technical fields. There was no leadership, he insisted.

Still fighting for the disadvantaged in society, he argued forcefully as well for special attention to "slow learners," pointing out that IQ scores were no guide to a child's untapped potential: "Just because a child fails to shine at his homework doesn't mean he won't shine later. . . . Some have verbal ability, others reasoning ability, and others have other potentials."

211

He had joined the CCF, and was elected school trustee for two more years on the party ticket. Now in his seventies, however, Dick Johns had little patience for party discipline and the compromises of practical politics. There were persistent rumours of dissension in the ranks, and in February 1960 he resigned from the party, giving no reason for the move. The secretary of the North End branch commented, officially, that there had been "differences of opinion" over a representative's "duties and responsibilities." Johns served out the remainder of his term as an Independent, and did not reenter the race.

At loose ends, he left for Victoria, to be near his daughter, Mrs. J. R. Wilson, his grandchildren, and his great-grandchildren. His son, Edward William, had settled in Hamilton.

Dick Johns died in Victoria in 1970, at the age of eighty-two. Newspaper reports of his death identified him as the last survivor of the group of labour leaders who had been jailed during the Winnipeg General Strike, "when the Russian revolution had stirred the world."

In Winnipeg today, Tec-Voc has greatly expanded its facilities and its curriculum, still striving to achieve the goals of its creator.

Women at the Barricades

Helen Armstrong

Women's Work

"Hello Citizen!" read an item in *The Voice* for April 19, 1901. "Let us tell you what you are paying your $50.00 a year to the Bell Telephone Company for." Sixteen "Hello Girls" had deserted their switchboards at nine o'clock that morning, on strike against what they called "a wretched sweatshop regime," and were using Arthur Puttee's sympathetic columns to explain their cause:

> For sitting in a chair from 8:30 am to 6:30 pm and watching intently every moment the instrument before them, which posi-

tion they cannot leave for an instant without being relieved, the girls get for the first three months the splendid stipend of $15.00 per month, after which if they prove efficient it is $20.00 per month, the maximum pay. After long service it is $24.00 per month. [The employers] have an intolerable system of fines. They demand two weeks' notice on leaving, and reserve to themselves the right of instant dismissal.

But added to these inequities, said the women, was the final straw of "a new manageress . . . a perfect tyrant," apparently with the authority to torment the operators to the utmost. The dispute ended in short order, having called attention to a problem, if little else. Complaints about unfair wages and impossible working conditions for women employees appeared frequently in the left-leaning *Voice*, but the action taken by the telephone operators in 1901 was one of the earliest instances of an organized attempt by women to enforce a labour demand.

A tentative notice in an October 1902 issue of *The Voice* reported a meeting to explore the possibilities of forming a "Women's Protective Union" to save domestics from exploitation, and cited several dreadful stories to demonstrate the need: the "Fort Rouge lady" who paid a woman one dollar for working from 9 a.m. to 9 p.m., the woman from "south of Portage Avenue" who agreed to a dollar for a day's work, and then deducted twenty-five cents for dinner, the "North-End housekeeper who would not pay a woman while she waited for the water to get hot." On the following January 23, *The Voice* announced that the new Women's Protective Association would serve as an employment bureau for domestic workers of certified efficiency, and had agreed upon an eight-hour day and a fair rate of 12 1/2 cents per hour for light domestic work, 15 cents for heavy washing. The organizers hoped to include all women hired for housework by the day — laundrywomen, needleworkers, maids — and membership reached a total of thirty-nine by April. But interest could not be sustained, and the association gradually ceased to function.

Beginning well before the turn of the century, a sizable number of Winnipeg women had been employed in the city's expanding industries as well as in domestic service, many in the garment trade, others in printing and bookbinding, and in food services, as cooks and waitresses.

Some, like E. Cora Hind, had gained entry to the business world by becoming "typewriters," learning to operate the newly patented office device, and increasing numbers of alert and personable young women were finding work at the manually operated telephone exchanges.

Organizing these women workers, industrial and commercial as well as domestic, presented a particular problem. While the underground economy of cottage industry had always entailed an unrecorded amount of female labour, the presence of women in the workplace was in a sense invisible, obscured by the prevailing conventional belief, deeply embedded in the social mores of the time, that a woman's place was in the home. Even as reform-minded and supportive a publication as *The Voice* advised women in 1899 that they would have better homes, better education, and a better chance to marry if they did not compete with men for jobs.

Middle class and working class alike, it was understood that a husband or father was the family breadwinner. A young woman "worked" until she married; a married woman took a job outside her home only under the direst of necessities, and then she could undertake only the kind of employment that her family responsibilities would permit. Despite the innumerable instances where a woman was entirely self-supporting or the sole support of her family, women tended to enter and leave the labour market as their family circumstances changed. Thus, while the total number of women in paid employment at any one time increased steadily, the composition of that work force was largely transient, and the union movement gave no serious consideration to the special difficulties of female workers.

Most women seemingly concurred in their domestic role, and even progressive arguments might convey that traditional message. In 1898 Cora Hind addressed the men of the Winnipeg Trades and Labor Council, urging their support for the principle of equal pay for men and women in the same occupation. Having become an energetic suffragist and advocate for women's welfare and an influential columnist in the *Free Press Weekly*, Hind argued that if wage scales were equal, employers would prefer to hire men, and females would be excluded from occupations such as watchmaking and cigar-making. These trades were particularly objectionable, it was generally believed, because they required the use of substances that might harm women's primary function as the mothers of the race. Hind shrewdly designed her argument to appeal to the men's self-interest, but it unintentionally marginalized women workers. The underlying assumption, shared by both speaker and audience, was that women's role in the workplace was secondary to her biological function.

Unionization had a slow beginning in the occupations in which women predominated. An 1895 item in *The Voice* lists one woman's name among the newly elected officers of a journeyman tailors' union, and two years later there was a failed attempt to organize a group of women laundry workers. By that time the men's union movement was well advanced, and the Trades and Labor Council had already been established.

Then, in 1899, three of the women at the Emerson and Hague clothing factory were fired, and fifty of their co-workers struck the plant, demanding reinstatement and an equitable wage settlement. Out of this concerted action came Local 35 of the United Garment Workers of America. In the light of the pioneering suffrage activity in the Icelandic community, it is interesting that the members of this first recorded industrial union of women workers in Manitoba were predominantly Icelandic.

The strike at Emerson and Hague was never settled. With the help of the Trades and Labor Council, the strikers found other employment, and the council voted to give the gallant "girl workers" the honour of leading the May Day parade that year, a practice that held for a number of years after. A vigorous recruiting drive brought union organization to all but one of Winnipeg's garment factories by 1905, and a second local came into being in 1906, this one reflecting part of the city's remarkable ethnic mix in its British, German, and Jewish membership. One meeting, *The Voice* reported, was addressed by "representatives of the foreign socialistic societies."

Industrial relations in the garment trade were as fractious as in the rest of the city's economy. A clothing manufacturer attempted to fire some of his experienced workers and replace them with cheaper trainees; the entire staff walked out. The Scotland Woollen Mills were prevented from firing some union activists and induced to come to terms with the union. Several months later, the company did fire sixty union members, both men and women, without explanation, and in the violent melee that followed the police arrested twelve men. Interestingly, no women were charged, although "the girl workers" were reported to be alarmingly aggressive on the picket lines. At the King of the Road Overall factory, in 1908, the owners attempted to declare an "open shop," and one hundred operators, mostly women, struck the plant. A benefit concert and a "boxing contest" raised money for the strike fund, *The Voice* reported. When Winnipeg's street-railway was struck in 1910, the Manitoba Clothing Company landed the contract to make uniforms for the "replacement workers"; the employees refused to sew for "scabs," and joined the motormen on strike until the dispute was settled.

The garment workers campaigned enthusiastically for the Label League, urging customers to look for the union label, trying to persuade storekeepers to stock only union-made goods. By 1911 Local 35 had grown strong enough to appoint a full-time business agent, and elected Maggie Tweedy to the position. A third local was formed, with ties to the Social Democratic Party. Despite the membership figures, of course, the turnover among the garment workers was high, as marriage or family obligations pulled women out of the workforce. In this industry, where women workers predominated, a disproportionate number of men still served on the union executive, and the Trades and Labor Council registered its concern over the infrequent attendance of garment-worker representatives at council meetings.

By 1906 Ada Muir was arguing in *The Voice* that more women's unions must be formed, and women must come together in a single umbrella organization, to fight as one for better working conditions. Muir had come from England with her six children, and had gained a platform for reform through her column in the *Grain Growers' Guide*. At her initiative the Women's Labor League was organized in 1910, to educate women about the advantages of the trade union movement, to promote "equal pay for equal work," and to campaign for the vote. As well, the league was to concern itself with such characteristically "women's" issues as better hygiene and household management and the eradication of liquor and prostitution.

In practice, the early Labor League found it could do little to encourage the formation of women's unions. Rather, it seems to have been most active in cooperating with suffrage groups in their battle for women's rights. Shortly after its inauguration, *The Voice* reported that Ada Muir, representing the Women's Labor League, had joined a suffrage delegation to the legislature, together with Dr. Mary Crawford of the University Woman's Club, and Mrs. Nellie McClung and Mrs. Duff Smith of the National Council of Women and the Woman's Christian Temperance Union (WCTU). After a few years, however, Ada Muir left the city, and the Women's Labor League activity diminished.

Suffragists and Seamstresses

On the surface, the exhausted seamstresses toiling for a pittance in basement sweat-shops or the domestics timorously enduring their long hours of unregulated service had little in common save gender with the relatively comfortable, middle-class women who spearheaded the suffrage movement in Manitoba, as elsewhere. The most articulate among the suffragists often worked hard at a profession, earning their own bread and butter, like the self-aware journalists of the Women's Press Club, and in that sense they were also "working women." Having achieved some independent standing, however, these women now fought for the recognition that was their due, both economically and politically. They demanded the right to be heard in the decisions of society's electoral system and the right to manage their own possessions. Neither the ballot nor such middle-class issues as the Dower Law and the Married Women's Property Act had any obvious bearing on the hand-to-mouth existence of the working poor.

The feminists of the late nineteenth and early twentieth centuries, however, envisioned a world in which the nurturing values of home and fireside would be paramount, putting an end to war and to the exploitation of the weak by the powerful. Perceiving from the outset that the devaluation and disenfranchisement of women deeply affected human relations in general and the position of working men in particular, suffrage groups courted the labour movement, and received the support — though not invariably — of labour organizations and labour parties. As Lynn Flett was to exclaim at a "Women's Sunday" meeting of the Labor Church early in 1919, when labour unrest in Winnipeg was coming to the boil, "The women's struggle is linked with labour's; both fight economic bondage, but women have the additional burden of male domination!"

For about two decades, while women's unions were inching toward a foothold in the labour movement, the cause of women in the work force was championed by a succession of women's suffrage groups, whose agenda included the improvement of social conditions from a specifically women's perspective. In March 1895 a delegation of three women from the Equal Suffrage Club addressed a meeting of the Winnipeg Trades and Labor Council. Leading the delegation, Winnipeg's pioneer woman physician, Dr. Amelia Yeomans, offered the now familiar suffragist argument that grown women should not be treated as children, but she also pointed out that labour had a vital interest in women's suffrage. The shamefully low wages paid to women workers, she said, undercut union efforts to raise their members' pay; if women were allowed to vote they would have the influence to enforce equality, and the entire working class would benefit thereby. The chairman of the meeting assured the visitors that most working men sympathized with their cause, and *The Voice* published their presentation in full.

A loosely reciprocal support continued. In 1897 the Canadian Trades and Labor Congress endorsed women's suffrage, and following Cora Hind's representation on wage parity the Winnipeg Trades and Labor Council included women's suffrage on its municipal agenda. The Winnipeg Labor Party officially endorsed the cause, and heard a passionate lecture in support by Charles Hislop, the city's first labour alderman and husband of one of the women active in the Equal Suffrage Club. When the club repealed its women-only by-law, in 1901 Arthur Puttee was elected third vice-president, and *The Voice* continued to promote the suffrage cause. In 1910, the Women's Press Club joined the battle for the vote, and the Manitoba Labor Party included women's suffrage in its platform.

In 1903 Winnipeg's small corps of professional women was increased when Dr. Mary Crawford arrived to open an office, specializing in the diseases of women and children. She succeeded Amelia Yeomans as president of the WCTU; she joined the University Women's Club, and was elected president; she campaigned vigorously for the franchise. Dr. Crawford's practice was chiefly in Winnipeg's immigrant North End, and she became immersed in the social problems she encountered there, particularly in the plight of the women. Far too many children, she found, were being born in primitive and often unsanitary conditions, to families too poor to support them adequately, and malnutrition and disease handicapped these children for all time. Joining forces with James Woodsworth's volunteers at the groundbreaking All People's Mission on Stella Avenue, Dr. Crawford visited the district's mothers in their homes and taught classes at the Mission on birth control and child care, on hygiene and nutrition. She appeared as a regular Sunday afternoon lecturer at Woodsworth's People's Forum, illustrating her talks with lantern slides to make sure she could be understood by people whose English was halting.

Like Crawford, a number of suffrage activists in the interconnected membership of the city's leading women's organizations were swept into the heartbreaking work at the Stella Mission: the Beynon sisters, Francis and Lillian (later Mrs. A. V. Thomas), Cora Hind, Nellie McClung, Harriet Walker, co-owner with her husband of the Walker Theatre. When the Political Equality League came into being in 1912, Lynn and Winona Flett joined, and several progressive-minded men were welcomed into the ranks, including Fred Dixon and George Chipman. The ties between the suffragists and the labour movement continued: the Equality League backed Dixon in his successful 1914 election campaign; Lillian Thomas and Nellie McClung took the rostrum at an election meeting for the labour candidate in the working-class suburb of Transcona, to argue that giving women the right to vote would safeguard the home and protect the workers' interests as wage-earners.

As one of its first crusades, the Equality League resolved to remedy the deplorable conditions in the factories employing female workers, and Mrs. McClung, in all her high-powered self-confidence as an acclaimed novelist, took on the entrenched Conservative government of the province and its adamantly anti-suffragist premier, Sir Rodmond Roblin. He revered all women, Sir Rodmond constantly insisted; "gentle women," he had called a delegation that waited upon him at the legislature, to press for the franchise: "queen of the home, set apart by your great function of motherhood." As for giving these "ladies" access to the ballot box, he was afraid, he had said, that "my friend Mr. Rigg"

Nellie McClung

— Richard Rigg, the labour activist — "might shortly come to us for the extension of the franchise to servant girls, on the plea that servant girls have as good a right to vote as any other class of women."

Roblin's ingrained chivalry toward "ladies," simultaneously complimentary and denigrating, placed him at a disadvantage with McClung and her fellow Equality League members, when they insisted he must observe labour conditions for himself. Against his will he allowed Mrs. McClung and her friend Mrs. Nash to take him on an inspection visit to a basement sweatshop, all the while protesting, in his luxurious, new-fangled motorcar with its vase of fresh carnations, that working-class women "did not expect to be carried to the skies on a flowery bed of ease." As he came down the filthy stairs to the dimly lit garment factory, the stench of sweat and the overflowing toilet made him reach frantically for his white handkerchief. He reeled back from the noise of the machines and the sight of the sickly, sallow-faced operators amid the dust and debris of their materials, exclaiming at the "hell-hole" into which he had been enticed. How dare respectable women like Mrs. McClung and Mrs. Nash, he demanded, "ferret out such utterly disgusting things!" The hell-hole, and others of its kind, remained.

By 1914, when Nellie McClung made this stormy attack on male complacency, wage scales were still notoriously low in predominantly female occupations like the garment industry, and there was virtually no regulation of working conditions. As early as 1900, the Manitoba Factories Act had restricted the employment of women and girls in factories to no more than forty-eight hours per week, but it was not until 1914, after repeated complaints about violations, that a supervising inspector was designated, and Ida Bauslaugh became the first woman named to that position. As for the retail trade, where many women found work, a 1914 survey of women employed in Winnipeg's department stores reported that most were over eighteen years of age, and those of reasonable experience were paid a minimum of nine dollars a week. Younger women, classified as "learners," might get as little as five dollars, and the report glossed over a range of tolerated violations.

It took World War I with its demand for more and still more hands at the machines to establish women as a permanent and visible sector of the wage-earning work force. As industry expanded, women filled the vacancies in some of the traditionally male occupations, to the decided dismay of some of their male co-workers. The machinists' Bob Russell reported an invasion of women into the Montreal shops of the CPR, and warned that "Calgary is prepared to go to the length of calling a strike if women are not removed in fifteen days." The *B. C. Federationist*, in April 1916, predicted that the thousands of women now taking men's jobs would not readily surrender their new independence, that the capitalist class wanted to exploit this cheap labour, and that the government, in giving women the vote, would make sure that the men discharged from the armed services did not get their jobs back. By September 1918, with thousands of discharged soldiers already trying to regain a place in the labour pool, the postal clerks and carriers demanded that women be excluded from employment as long as returned men were available for the positions. The Political Equality League, now reincarnated as the Political Education League, formally protested this proposal to the postmaster-general and the Winnipeg Letter Carriers' Association.

By the end of World War I women made up an estimated twenty-five percent of Winnipeg's work force, most of them in low-paying jobs with little protection: sewing-machine operators, in factories not very different from the sweatshop that Nellie McClung had inflicted on a resentful Premier Roblin; store clerks, bakery and confectionary workers, waitresses; and uncounted numbers of women hired as live-in or daily domestic servants. In business offices, where Cora Hind had been a pioneer "typewriter," the clerical staff was now predominantly female (as one observer remarked, "the skirt [had] replaced the pant"), and a small army of "Hello Girls" now sat at the telephone switchboards.

As a principle, pay equity between men and women had been urged at least as long as Cora Hind's appeal to the Trades and Labor Council, but never actively negotiated either by organized labour or by employers. In 1914 a survey by the University Women's Club had determined that a single, self-supporting woman required a minimum wage of ten dollars per week, but that many women received much less, and the disparity remained. That the estimate of a minimum requirement was based on the needs of a woman without dependents is significant: since the family breadwinner was assumed to be normally a man, the negotiations for men's pay rates were based on the consideration of a "family wage," sufficient to sustain a household, but no such measure was relevant for women. Women, it was commonly assumed by union negotiators and employers alike, were basically supported by their fathers or their husbands, and a wage differential was quite in order.

By the last years of the war, inflated prices had made the prevailing pay rates for women wholly inadequate, and demands for proper regulation escalated. Women could not sustain themselves on their meagre wages, the argument was sometimes advanced, and some might even yield to the blandishments of the infamous white-slave trade. As for the appalling working conditions in some of the factories, concerned voices in the labour press and elsewhere continued to worry about the deleterious effect on women employees' reproductive health.

Despite the sea-change that society had undergone, the notion persisted that women's presence in the work force was anomalous, even among liberal reformers known for their progressive support of women. Addressing the Soldiers' Parliament on "Ladies' Day," during the general strike, James Woodsworth must have seemed at his visionary best as he predicted a day when women would take their place beside men, not as dependents or inferiors, but as equals, and that a better relationship would result, based on equality and love. But even as he made it clear that a lower wage scale for women undermined men's earnings, he was protectively concerned for the women who had been, as he said, "drawn from their homes" for an insufficient return: his subtext was again that for any woman, working outside the home under any circumstances was most unfortunate. Nevertheless, the Liberal Party in 1919 endorsed the principle of pay equity, and Woodsworth was able to report in his speech that "equal pay for equal work" was one of the provisions of the World War I Peace Conference.

Toward a Minimum Wage for Women

Not the least of the disruptive forces gathering toward the upheaval of 1919 in Winnipeg was the heightened militancy of several key women's unions, and the increased participation of radical women in the battles for labour advancement. For most of these politically aware women the only available role was supportive, backing male candidates for election to public office, raising funds by the approved feminine method of teas and bazaars, or — no less important — acting as unofficial assistants to husbands immersed in public affairs. If Lucy Woodsworth understood that her responsibility toward her husband was to maintain his home in all its sanctity, Katherine Queen was an informed and knowledgeable socialist. She became a member of the Social Democratic Party in her own right, like her husband John, working assiduously for the party as her husband gained prominence. Winona Dixon retired from her business career when she married, but continued to appear on public platforms to champion the social reforms she supported. In the labour ranks, a number of union women achieved a kind of temporary notoriety as organizers or on the picket line, and one in particular commanded a lasting attention from the bemused press.

Helen Armstrong first came to public notice when she appeared at her husband's side during his unsuccessful election campaign against Fred Dixon in 1914. Stumping on street corners with George, topping his declarations with arguments of her own, taking on his hecklers with an intensity that entertained the onlookers as much as it provoked them, she canvassed boldly for votes; and, when he lost, she was as vociferous as George in denouncing the iniquity of all the people who had sold out to the Liberals to put Dixon in office.

Having been married in Toronto, the Armstrongs had come to Winnipeg with their three daughters in 1905; their youngest, Frank, was born in 1907. By 1914, Frank was in school, the girls were growing up and could take on some of the household responsibilities, and Helen now had more freedom for the political involvement that was in her blood. She had absorbed her fiery radicalism in her father's Toronto tailor shop on Bay Street, where she herself had been trained as a "tailoress." There, while Alf Jury, her father, worked at his cutting table or at his sewing machine, radical socialists habitually gathered to debate the fine points of Marxism and to decide on strategy. Any proposals that could not pass the test of Alf's absolute principles, party faithfuls remembered, would be rejected out of hand. Identifying totally with working people, his daughter fought their battles for the rest of her life.

The Women's Labor League had been dormant for several years, but it sprang to life again in 1917, with the support of the Dominion Labor Party, and with Helen Armstrong as president and Gertrude Puttee, wife of *The Voice* publisher Arthur Puttee, as vice-president. Katherine Queen became a member. Taking as its mandate the support of existing women's labour unions and the extension of union solidarity to unorganized women, the league applied for membership in the Trades and Labor Council, and was accepted. On May 4 the council officially welcomed Helen Armstrong and two other women as Women's Labor League delegates. Meanwhile, spearheaded by its redoubtable president, it began to provide vigorous support for union action in the predominantly female trades.

In February 1917 Winnipeg's "Hello Girls," six hundred strong, banded together to form a union, affiliated with the International Brotherhood of Electrical Workers, to press their case against Manitoba Government Telephones. Their hours, they protested, were at the employers's will, so that an operator might be required to work an exhausting double shift, and their wages of thirty-five dollars per month were wholly inadequate for the inflated cost of living in wartime. Demanding a minimum of forty dollars per month and regulated hours, the telephone operators staged a three-hour strike on May

1 to call attention to their problem. The general public was largely in sympathy with the women, and a board of investigation found in their favour. An eight-hour day was established, with forty dollars the monthly minimum pay, with graduated increases to a maximum of sixty dollars, and additional overtime. The victory marked a signal advance in the unionization of women workers.

In March 1917 Helen Armstrong presided over the founding of the Retail Clerks' Union, and by June the union and the Labor League were involved in a strike against the F. W. Woolworth Company's Five, Ten, and Fifteen Cent Stores. There were fifty-two women behind the counters in the two Portage Avenue "Fifteen Cent Stores," where working-class Winnipeg shopped for small items of personal and household needs. On duty five days a week from 8:30 a.m. until 6:00 p.m., and on Saturdays until 10:00 p.m., the clerks were paid as little as six dollars per week, not enough even to maintain a single woman with no dependents. The Retail Clerks' Union was making no headway in inducing the company to raise the minimum wage to eight dollars and to grant a half-day holiday, and with the backing of the Labor League the employees struck the two stores.

Picketing was organized, and Helen walked the line, indomitably bolstering the spirits of the young women with her own determination, defying arrest, shoving back at the police constables who tried awkwardly to disperse the clamorous women. As their union representative, she confronted the Woolworth's authorities at the negotiating table; and perhaps even more important, because the women had no means of their own, she harangued and cajoled the Trades and Labor Council and other sources to put together a substantial strike fund, enough to cover each striker's missing wages. Resorting to the same tactics that employers regularly used against union demands throughout this period, Woolworth's obtained an injunction against picketing and offered to deal with workers individually, but would not negotiate with their union. A ten-thousand-dollar fine was declared against the Retail Clerks' empty treasury.

A capacity meeting at the Walker Theatre endorsed the strong position taken by the women and denounced the ban on peaceful picketing; and a meeting at which George Armstrong and Bill Hoop spoke collected $205 "for the girls." There was no movement on the part of the employers, however. They replaced the rebellious workers with others, and the Woolworth stores' operation continued. Defeated, the women gave up, although Helen Armstrong's fundraising had been so successful that there was still some $250 left in the strike fund.

Pressured finally to take action, the provincial government of T. C. Norris moved to consider instituting a minimum wage for women. A report on women workers was commissioned by the Board of Labor, and although its coverage of Winnipeg's industrial economy was far from complete, it revealed the need for a drastic overhaul of pay rates and working conditions. If $10.00 per week was still considered sufficient for a single woman's survival, as it had been in 1914 before wartime inflation, the overall average pay rate for women employees was considerably less, and there were some shocking cases of exploitation and hardship: a woman earning $8.00 per week, who could not afford winter underwear; a young candy-factory worker earning $5.00 per week; a laundry worker who could not pay her doctor's bill or her board and room on her $5.35 a week.

Both the Manufacturers' Association and the Trades and Labor Council had been asked to present proposals to the commission for an appropriate minimum wage for women, and the submission of the Manufacturers' Association had included a sample annual clothing budget for factory girls. Once again Helen Armstrong was prompted to pour out her derision in a scathing letter to *The Voice*:

No furs provided for thirty below, merely a scarf, and this advocated by men who appear in beaver coats, otter caps and warm overshoes, to say nothing of many of them being deposited at their places of business in private cars about 9 or 10 o'clock instead of 7:30 or 8. Is it because of their superior ability, or is it some form of special privilege?

The bill that was finally passed by the provincial legislature in March 1918 did not establish the expected uniform minimum wage. Rather, it called for the appointment of a Minimum Wage Board, to set the rates piecemeal, industry by industry. Both the Manufacturers' Association and the Trades and Labor Council were asked to supply lists of nominees for the new board, out of which one man and one woman were to be chosen from each group, to be presided over by an impartial chair-person. On the labour list were the names of Helen Armstrong, a Mrs. Webb, and Lynn Flett, Fred Dixon's sister-in-law. Flett was chosen to sit on the board, perhaps because by this time Armstrong had become notorious for her bad-tempered intractability.

The decisions of the Minimum Wage Board bettered the pay scale and working hours in some fields, notably for waitresses and office workers, but by and large the approved rates fell far short of the time-honoured "family wage" for men. Moreover, the board allowed employers to argue for concessions in the case of young and inexperi-enced workers, and for other reasons. In supporting the protection of women workers by a separate minimum wage law, the labour move-ment itself had tacitly concurred with the principle that a woman employee was generally single and without dependents, and only tem-porarily in the work force. Helen Armstrong had campaigned for an across-the-board minimum wage in all industries, and she commented sharply, with considerable acumen, that a minimum soon became the maximum, perpetuating old inequities.

Women Against War

If Helen Armstrong was in her time unusually active in labour politics, constantly invading male territory to attack both mainstream politicians and her own left-wing colleagues, she was also particularly sensitive to the needs of the women and children on whom labour action redound-ed. In the summer of 1917 George Armstrong's Carpenters' Union went on strike with the other construction trades; and while George and his mates wrangled with the building contractors, his wife made the problems of the strikers' families her concern. She came to their homes to make sure they were provided for, she delivered food where it was needed and brought milk for the children, and she also found time to join the picket lines — where her vociferous encouragement, from a woman, often embarrassed the men.

Armstrong's determined zeal on behalf of the downtrodden struck a responsive chord in a socialist of a very different stripe. From Roaring River, in the Swan River district of Manitoba, Gertrude Richardson was now regularly reporting on the Canadian scene to the *Leicester*

Pioneer, back home in England. A devout Christian, she believed passionately that Jesus himself taught the rejection of the power structure that oppressed the little people of the world, in his day and in her own; and like the apostles of the Social Gospel she maintained that the only true Christianity was an active compassion for all suffering human beings, and a commitment to the cause of social and economic justice. Notwithstanding the absence of any evidence of a matching piety on Mrs. Armstrong's part, Richardson became her admirer and supporter, offering her English readers the assurance that in this distant western province of Manitoba there were dedicated souls striving to bring about the new Jerusalem.

In her deeply emotional prose, Richardson told her readers about Helen Armstrong, and about the intervention of this "very striking personality" at the head of the Women's Labor League in a dispute between the railways and some of their foreign-born employees. Imprisoned on charges of breach of contract, the "aliens" had left behind families with no means of support. Having visited Stony Mountain to see for herself the conditions in the penitentiary, Armstrong reported furiously to the Trades and Labor Council that the inmates were being "marched around like cattle," and demanded that the council take immediate action. Mrs. Armstrong, said her friend, agitated so fiercely on behalf of the needy women and children that the authorities were forced to make some provision for their sustenance while the men were incarcerated.

By 1917 the conscription battle was in full swing, and Mrs. Armstrong, said Gertrude Richardson, "often stood alone between the soldiers and the anti-conscription men, and refused to move." Totally opposed to conscription, like most of the radicals in the labour movement, Armstrong fought angrily against those misguided members of her sex who succumbed to false patriotism. In August 1917, the press reported, a women's mass meeting in the Central Congregational Church was called to demonstrate patriotic support for the policy, and both Katherine Queen and Helen Armstrong made a point of attending, to register their own disapproval and that of many other women.

"We, the women of Winnipeg in mass meeting assembled," the proposed resolution began, presuming to speak for all the women; and the two dissenters disrupted the set programme by demanding an amendment, to read, "We, some of the women of Winnipeg. . . ." Katherine Queen pleaded with the assembled mothers and sisters and wives to use their influence in the cause of peace:

> Three of my brothers are dead, and my brother of eighteen years is called to the colours. . . . The men who make the war have not suffered. You never touch the people who make war. While you women have a chance to end war you never take it.

Despite her entreaty, patriotic sentiment prevailed. The amendment was swept aside and the resolution passed as presented, but with a feminist call for the conscription of women as well as men, and of labour. The meeting also proposed that money and resources be conscripted to the country's need, a call that echoed the frequent demand of the labour movement.

Helen Armstrong continued to appear in Market Square and at street-corners, and to direct an indefatigable stream of letters to the newspapers, driving home the radical condemnation of capitalism and all its ways. In September 1917 *The Voice* published a tirade condemning the Tories' calculated decision to grant the federal vote only to women with close relatives in the forces, in a move to win votes on its conscription policy. "Absolutely undemocratic from every point of view," she called it, not to be "tolerated for a moment by the people":

> Either give every woman the right of franchise or none. It is just another evidence of the Borden outfit gone military mad and they ought to come out plainly and say military service is the qualification for the ballot. What a spectacle for a moribund, last gasp group of incompetents to dare to legislate away the ballot of Canadian citizens!

One cold December day in 1917 the Tories sponsored a rally of the Next-of-Kin Committee at the Walker Theatre. Balked in her earlier effort to subvert the support for conscription, Armstrong brought her friend Laura Watts, another Labor League member, to stand with her outside the theatre, intercepting people as they arrived, condemning their disgraceful display of ignorance, exhorting them to recant, handing out pamphlets. Some of the ladies, much offended by the insolence

Francis Beynon

Dr. Mary Crawford

Winona Flett

Cora Hind

Mrs. John Queen

Gertrude Richardson

Lillian Beynon Thomas

Dr. Amelia Yeomans

of these unmannerly women, telephoned the police, and six burly officers swooped down in a patrol car. Mrs. Watts escaped, but Mrs.
Armstrong was carted off, to be charged with "distributing rubbish,"
detained for few hours, and then released without further action. The
"rubbish," said *The Voice*, deploring such abrogation of a citizen's rights,
was a treatise on the diplomatic origins of the war, by John S. Ewart,
Canada's leading constitutional lawyer.

The woeful inadequacy of plans to provide for discharged soldiers
provoked another protest from Helen Armstrong in *The Voice*, seething
with radical class resentment:

It is more than I can understand how anyone, the "capitalist
class" especially, that remains at home, or have the well-paid
positions and the least dangerous in the service, have the nerve or
dare ask a man to go out and risk his life, and when he returns,
calmly request him to hand in his uniform, and in exchange hand
him out a miserable pittance that will reduce a once self-respect-
ing citizen . . . to a miserable pauper, dependent on either charity
or friends.

If pacifism on philosophic grounds was common in the pre-1914 liber-
al-labour community, Katherine Queen's plea and Helen Armstrong's
anger seemed to mirror a particularly feminine response to the carnage,
an almost bodily trauma at the annihilation of the children whom
women cherished and nurtured. "Mangled, torn, blinded, maddened,
slain, are the victims of this inhuman strife," shuddered Gertrude
Richardson in one of her columns; " . . . there is nothing left — no
hope, save the pent-up forces of the world's motherheart."

The war and the conscription issue had, however, opened deep fis-
sures in the women's movement. To the dismay of an untold number of
her admirers, Nellie McClung had come down on the side of king and
country and the primary importance of pursuing the war effort.
Publicly declaring her approval of Borden's policies, she advised the
prime minister that only "English and Canadian" women should be
entrusted with the franchise; "alien" women could not be expected to
support the war, and the right of English-speaking women was para-

mount. For Gertrude Richardson, already devastated by the descent of nations into bloodshed and madness, this pronouncement by a woman she admired came as one additional cause for despair. Driven by an ecstatic vision of all humankind united in a God-inspired world of peace and plenty, she described with agonized tenderness the distress of the "aliens" she encountered on a train-ride to Winnipeg. "Sometimes I wonder," she told her readers in the *Leicester Pioneer*, "if Christ was an alien. . . ."

Francis Beynon was as shocked as Gertrude Richardson by the outbreak of international violence, if less extravagant in her writing, and she denounced wartime restrictions on the rights of individuals and of minority groups. Always an advocate for the dignity and worth of the country's ethnic minorities, she was angered by the harassment of "aliens" at home and by the treatment accorded to honest dissenters from mainstream opinion, and as the women's editor of the *Grain Growers' Guide*, she had begun to sound a note of increasing disaffection and dissent.

In concert with a wide range of liberal activists, she hailed the Russian Revolution as a hope for the eventual government of the world by the common man, and she declared her admiration for the German socialist, Karl Liebknecht. She condemned the "fervent patriots . . . who are getting rich out of sweated labour and war profiteering," and denounced their hypocrisy in professing to be shocked by the lack of patriotism in "the man who is living just a little below the breadline and the girl who has to go out on the street to eke out a living." Challenging the federal government's move toward conscription, she echoed labour's demand that the wealth of the country must be conscripted as well as its men, but she distrusted ideological commitment to socialist absolutes, insisting on the necessity for immediately possible reforms, however small.

By 1917 her editor, George Chipman, had come to support the government policy, and there was constant friction. She left the paper that had been her career and her voice, and joined Lillian and Vernon Thomas in New York.

Run-Up to Confrontation

By the last years of the war, tensions and dislocations in Winnipeg were moving toward their inevitable climax. In May 1918 the telephone operators walked out again, in support of the striking civic workers — teamsters, electricians, water works employees, office clerks — for higher wages; and the *Western Labor News* mocked the blundering efforts of the volunteer, upper-class women it called "the daughters of the wealthy" to keep the exchanges running. The Labor League scheduled a meeting of all women workers to hear William Bayley speak on "Women Workers in Britain," and at a Trades and Labor Council session Helen Armstrong demanded that men stay home that evening so that their wives could attend.

Offended by the aggressive intervention of the Labor League, the mainstream National Council of Women sent a letter of protest to the Trades and Labor Council. Helen retorted contemptuously that these were the very women who had set the police on the picketers in the Woolworth's strike. The Council of Women, she pointed out, had called on the government to conscript all men for military service at the same time that it had busied itself with petitions for the protection of the country's sparrow population. "Kill the men but save the sparrows," she snorted. As for the volunteer women's threat to take over the switchboards, the entire Trades Council hooted in derision.

That spring of 1918, Helen Armstrong had been organizing the city's housemaids, and in April she had been elected president of the new Hotel and Household Workers' Union. The month of June saw both George and Helen off to the twin cities of Fort William and Port Arthur; he helped organize a local of the United Brotherhood of Carpenters, while she addressed a capacity audience of the Women's Trades and Labor Auxiliary on labour activity in Winnipeg and on the work of the Women's Labor League. Regrettably, it was reported, Mrs. Armstrong could not stay to attend the regular auxiliary session because she was required back in Winnipeg to testify in court on behalf of a member of the Housemaids' Union.

Dominant wherever she went, Armstrong's relationship with her own Labor League executive could be contentious. On at least one occasion, balked in her efforts to impose policy, she offered her resignation and had to be persuaded to withdraw the offer. Having secured a place for herself alongside of the men on the executive of the Trades and Labor Council, she had announced in February 1918 that she would attend the scheduled fall meeting of the Trades and Labor Congress, representing the Women's Labor League, to raise women's issues, and she attacked William Ivens for failing to publish her comments in the *Western Labor News*. The Political Education League called a convention for October 1918 and invited the local Council of Women to participate; Helen Armstrong lashed out at inviting a group that had furnished "female scabs" in the telephone operators' strike the previous spring.

The Walker Theatre meeting that December met with Helen Armstrong's absolute support, and she had her Labor League pass a resolution echoing the radical left's censure of the Canadian government for its anti-Bolshevik actions. In February 1919 she denounced the Minimum Wage Board for wasting public money and demanded once again that the Trades and Labor Council campaign for a flat minimum; in March, however, her own Women's Labor League reversed its stand and endorsed the board's proceedings — more evidence of growing internal strife. Relinquishing the presidency to Mrs. Webb, Armstrong carried on as corresponding secretary. She was one of the relatively few women to attend the founding conference of the OBU, and to battle for her share of time in the raucous debates. In April she helped organize the biscuit-factory workers, and in May she brought together the laundry women into one union and the knitting-machine operators into another. Harassed by the police and occasionally detained for brief periods, she earned her record in the hidden police files.

In the weeks before the strike, as the certainty of a work stoppage became clear, a number of Winnipeg companies had developed strategies to subvert the action. One small firm sent a friendly letter to each of its female employees, offering praise for her anticipated "loyalty," and enclosing a two-dollar bill. The *Western Labor News* pointed out the irony that even with this obvious bribe, the wages that the women would earn that week were still below the legislated minimum. The T.

Eaton Company attempted to bring in a group of "replacement work-ers" from Toronto, but could get them no farther than the Manitoba border, the *Western Labor News* reported, because railway workers refused to carry "scabs." On the morning of the strike, however, the store offered several key members of its largely female staff the unheard-of increase of four dollars per week, if they would stay on duty; but, said the paper, the solidarity of the women held.

On May 14, the day before the general sympathy strike was sched-uled to begin, and after Russell's machinists had failed to come to terms with their "ironmaster" bosses and all negotiations had broken down, the "Bread and Cake" workers, mostly women, walked out to enforce their own wage demands, shutting down all but one of the city's confec-tionery plants. The Strike Committee had called for a work stoppage at eleven o'clock on the morning of May 15. At seven o'clock that morn-ing, the "Hello Girls" became the first to abandon their posts. The departing shift pulled the plugs on their switchboards and left, and no operators came to replace them. The silencing of the city had begun.

Helen's Girls: The Labor Cafe

The strike divided even the working community against itself. For some families the walk-out meant the loss of a precarious lifeline, for others a chance to earn a desperately needed dollar. The *Winnipeg Tribune* made a point of playing up the furious attack perpetrated by a striking employee of the Club Café on a young woman on her way to work there. The café owner, the story reported, commented with great indignation that the woman had lost her husband in France, and had to work to provide for herself and her three-year-old child. Granted the unfailing anti-strike bias of the mainline newspapers, the sorry little incident was repeated many times over, as women, and men, clinging to a marginal existence, were glad to seize any job offered.

As a group, single, self-supporting women workers had a special problem. Living on their own in rented rooms, barely getting by on their subsistence wages, many of them were suddenly left without a roof overhead or money to pay for food. Not all women workers by any means were unionized, but in the general industrial paralysis that descended on the city, many women not officially on strike were thrown out of work. In line with the Citizens' Committee's plan of action to keep business going, the YWCA had announced, on the day before the general strike was scheduled to start, that it would provide temporary shelter, free of charge, to any woman who lived far from her place of work. The offer served little purpose, and as the distress of hundreds of women became evident, the YWCA extended its offer to include "any girls, strikers or not, who are temporarily in want on account of the strike."

For her part, Helen Armstrong, fiercely protective of her "girls," charged into action with a far more comprehensive aid package. With the backing of the Central Strike Committee, the Women's Labor League organized a food service, with Armstrong in charge, and the proprietor of the Strathcona Hotel, Mr. Rosenthal, placed its dining room and kitchen at their disposal. It operated there for ten days, until, pressured by the Citizens' Committee, the owner withdrew his permission to use the facilities. Armstrong promptly found bigger and better quarters at the Oxford Hotel. The Labor Café, as it came to be known, expanded more vigorously than ever, and in the middle of June moved once again, to the Royal Albert Hotel.

Women strikers were provided with three meals a day, free of charge; if a woman was in danger of being evicted from her room, the Women's Labor League provided money for the rent, and a small cash grant was also available, if necessary. Men, too, needed the food service, if they were picketing downtown, miles from home, or if they were reluctant to deplete an already meagre family table. They were expected to pay or to make a contribution, and if they could do neither then a ticket issued by the Relief Committee entitled them to a free meal as well.

Funding for the food kitchen was a major undertaking. Badgered by Armstrong, the Relief Committee provided support, but most of the help came in an extraordinary outpouring of mutual sympathy and concern from the thousands of working people already hard-pressed by the lack of a wage packet. The Modern Dancing Club held a benefit dance, and by nickels and dimes the collection plates at union meetings throughout the six weeks of the strike filled to overflowing. William

Ivens's Labor Church proved a particularly reliable source of contributions, as the charismatic preacher exhorted his flock to ever greater effort for the love of God and their fellow human beings. Women volunteered for kitchen duty, turning out as many as fifteen hundred meals each day, and the *Strike Bulletin* ran repeated requests for sandwiches and for staples such as tea, coffee, and sugar.

The telephone operators once more were in the thick of the labour action. Within days they claimed to have shut down every telephone exchange throughout the province, despite threats that strikers would be refused employment after the affair was settled. Once again, as they had done before, a bevy of the city's well-to-do young ladies offered their services as "Hello Girls," in response to the call of the Citizens' Committee for volunteers; but this time the telephone company also resorted to more serious measures.

When some two weeks had elapsed without a settlement, the company advertised for "experienced telephone operators," and specified salaries up to a maximum of seventy dollars per month, well above the established pay schedule. They succeeded in enticing back a number of employees, and they also accepted enough novice volunteers to fill out a skeleton service. There were problems, however: the women "scabbing" at the switchboards were frequently subjected to harassing telephone calls, and some of the untrained volunteers broke down under the overload of the demand for service. In the end, the operators-for-a-day were handsomely rewarded, with pay cheques beyond the advertised rates.

For some women, then, the sudden vacuum in the employment market meant an opportunity to enjoy the novel experience of an interlude operating a telephone switchboard or pumping gas at a service station. For the first time women appeared in numbers on the front line of the battle, and on both sides of the fray. When the call went out for volunteers to distribute the *Western Labor News* and its *Strike Bulletin*, some lively young women leapt at the chance to become temporary "newsies," and announced airily that it took only a smile and a cheery greeting to carry off the streetcorner assignment. When, however, the strike-bound mainline newspapers tried to get their publications out in the same way, the women hawking the regular dailies were assaulted by strikers — led, the *Tribune* reported, by the "notorious" Helen Armstrong. On May 30, there was a disturbance at the Canada Bread plant, and charges of disorderly conduct were laid against three people, two men and Helen Armstrong.

Some of the city's smaller stores remained open, their employees not union members. Aiming to "close up tight every wholesale and retail store in the city," as the *Western Labor News* proclaimed, the clerks' union announced an organizational mass meeting for women workers on May 20, and it continued to hold women's rallies, addressed by George Armstrong, by Alderman Heaps, and others. Helen Armstrong made a well-publicized appearance before one retail establishment at five o'clock in the morning on May 26, confronting employees as they came to work, urging them to join the union and the strike; and at nine o'clock she informed reporters that she had signed up a good number of new union members and would continue the vital crusade. The Bakery and Confectionary workers met regularly, despite efforts to lock them out of the rooms they had rented in a bank building on Main Street.

Armstrong's own allies in the labour cause could find her aggressiveness disruptive. Defying the ban on parades, Roger Bray's pro-strike veterans marched to their meeting on Saturday, June 7, to be met by Helen Armstrong, demanding that she be permitted to address the assembly. There was an instant altercation, with some of the men in charge urging that this labour activist be heard, and others insisting that the soldiers-only rule be observed, that "other elements" be excluded. She was removed from the rostrum — manhandled, according to Gertrude Richardson — and not allowed to speak. A few days later, however, the soldiers gallantly declared their "Ladies' Day," in Victoria Park, and "at the invitation of the committee in charge," the *Strike Bulletin* reported, "a large number of women and girl strikers occupied seats of honour near the central platform," to hear Woodsworth prophesy that the day of emancipation for women was yet to come. In response, said the *Strike Bulletin* , "many girls and women shouted, 'We'll fight to the end!' "

Women Warriors

For the public at large, as well as for the warring factions, a most astounding revelation was this unexpected militancy of the striker women, both the workers and the wives and daughters of the men on strike. The Strike Committee realized very quickly the crucial importance of the women, and actively cultivated their support. On May 20, the *Western Labor News* quoted the president of the Trades and Labor Council, James Winning, who lavishly praised their "wonderful forbearance":

> Mothers have gone to the corner store and returned without milk, and have gone home and said, "Stay with it, John. The women will do without milk, and we will make some shift for the kiddies, but you must win."

Behind the very public and visible moves and countermoves of the strikers and their employers, the wives in the working-class households grappled with their own anger and frustration. For a woman struggling to feed and clothe her children, bread and milk and shoes were at stake in the endless, unavailing union negotiations, and when the general strike cut off the trickle of already inadequate wages it was the woman's responsibility to make do, somehow, to set food on the table for six long weeks. The Central Strike Committee repeatedly assured the strikers and their families that help was available, that no worker need suffer, and the Relief Committee under Alderman Abe Heaps struggled to deal with the most desperate cases, but the records of strike transactions reflect little of family tensions behind closed doors. If the strikers maintained a steady resolve until nearly the end of the ordeal, no small part of their stamina was certainly due to the backing of the women at home.

The mainline newspapers, on the other hand, at first presented women's doings with a certain airy condescension, making light of the whole affair, and then, as the strike wore on, with outrage, as if the unforeseen female ferocity made working class insubordination all the more unnatural. The *Citizen* included Helen Armstrong in its early list of the individuals responsible for the civic unrest, declaring, "she has

241

spent some years in an insane asylum." There is some evidence that Mrs. Armstrong may indeed have been hospitalized at one time for psychiatric illness; her family, interviewed many years later, would not comment. Apart from Nellie McClung's tart remark, however, on a subsequent occasion, that men's vaunted chivalry is only extended to women who do not need it, the diagnosis of insanity has served as a classic means to denigrate insubordinate females.

The mainline press reserved a particular kind of horrified disdain for female contributors to the civic disorder. Just before the May 15 deadline for the start of the strike, a light-hearted *Tribune* story had reported a run on grocery stores, describing "the ladies" trundling home supplies in baby carriages and coaster wagons, until "the beds [were] covered with carrots and the bathrooms filled with onions." Winnipeggers would be eating very well during this period of inconvenience, said the paper, encouraging a bland indifference to the very real hunger of many working families. But incidents began to multiply of women harassing nonstrikers on their way to work, and on June 2 a large crowd on Arlington Street stoned a vehicle driving "replacement workers" to one of the department stores.

By June 6, the *Tribune* was reporting what seemed to be an organized campaign by the women of Weston and Brooklands, the working-class western district of the city, to prevent employers from carrying on business as usual. Three department store wagons attempting to deliver orders in the area were attacked and smashed, their contents destroyed, and their drivers with their special guards warned to stay away. "We will murder you," one woman was alleged to have threatened, "if you attempt to make deliveries in this district again."

In retrospect, what now seems rather amusing is the apparent inability of the police to deal with a physical assault by "the tender sex," at least initially. No arrests were made in the Arlington Street or the Brooklands incidents, and attempts to investigate the matter were blocked, said the *Tribune*, by the hostility of the women. "I wouldn't advise any man to go out there," the hapless detective commented plaintively in the Brooklands case; "his life is in danger if these women find out that he is at work, or had been working during the strike."

And throughout the entire action, Helen Armstrong was everywhere, taunting scabs, shoring up the morale of women picketers, defying the police, leading by example. At the Canada Bread Company, on May 30, there was a confrontation between picketers and management; the plant manager, Arthur Riley, was charged with disorderly conduct together with another man, and Helen Armstrong, the noisy ringleader of the bakery workers.

By June 6, Mayor C. F. Gray found it necessary to prohibit all parades and public assemblies. On Main Street near the city hall, on the previous day, a scuffle had taken place, and eleven people had been arrested and charged with disorderly conduct and inciting strikers to riot. Three were women, Miss Ida Kraatz, Miss Margaret Steinhauer, and the ubiquitous Mrs. Helen Armstrong. Their cases were remanded and apparently not pursued. Some days later, a minor riot developed at Portage and Main, and another woman, Mrs. Pete Braster, was one of those charged with unlawful assembly. The belligerent women of the Retail Clerks' Union and their supporters tangled with the renegades trying to get into a department store to work; Matilda Russell was the one woman among the seven persons charged with intimidation.

When the authorities finally moved to break the back of the strike by nullifying the leaders, on June 17, Helen Armstrong's husband, George, was prominent among the malefactors captured in the night-time raid. By now her amazon prowess was a frequent topic in the daily press, and an excited early version of George's arrest had Helen holding the officers at bay, insisting, "You cannot get him out of this house until [Police] Chief Newton tells me you have a right to." Said the report, she ran from her home to the North End Police station, to telephone the chief for his personal certification of the warrant, and only then "went home and formally released her husband to the officers." The Armstrong home on Edmonton Street was some miles from the North End, and Chief Newton was also reported at the Russell home at that moment. A more sober account, later, indicated simply that the police were not admitted until Mr. Armstrong had spoken to the chief of police.

Incidents involving women multiplied as the frustrating weeks wore on. On the morning of June 21, Mayor Gray once again proclaimed the ban on unlawful assembly, with a special warning for venturesome females: "Any women taking part in a parade do so at their own risk." There were any number of women, however, milling about with the rest of the angry crowd between the city hall and Portage and Main on that memorable afternoon, including one who reportedly fainted when the shooting began, and one whom the *Tribune* held up as an egregious example of unwomanly viciousness. In the thick of the surging crowd, said the paper, one man noticed a woman with a baby, and advised her to find a safe place for herself and her child, only to be met "with such a vile outburst of profanity that the well-intentioned man beat a hasty retreat."

It was a woman, said the *Tribune*, who set fire to the streetcar that day — although, of course, most of the females involved in these disgraceful events, the paper maintained, were foreigners, part of the "alien" conspiracy to undermine Canadian society. Police records gave the names of the four women arrested on Bloody Saturday as Irene Heir, Eliza Restall, Christina Ross, and Clara Westman.

By the last days of the strike, the police had begun to press charges more vigorously against the unmanageable female troublemakers. On June 25 Ida Kraatz and Margaret Steinhauer were indicted for assaulting two *Tribune* employees selling the paper on the street, and fined five dollars apiece, but Helen Armstrong, charged with them for "counselling to commit an indictable offense," was detained until bail could be set by a judge in the Court of King's Bench. She was in jail on the morning of Thursday, June 26, when the Winnipeg General Strike came to its ignominious end, and on June 27 the *Tribune* reported that she was still being held "owing to the refusal of the authorities to grant bail," a measure deemed necessary to protect Winnipeg from "the dangerous Helen Armstrong." She was in good company, said the *Western Labor News*: the editor, Fred Dixon, had surrendered to the police. Armstrong was released on June 28.

The Kindness of "Ma" Armstrong

In the disheartened aftermath of the great labour stand Helen Armstrong's "girls" fared badly. Manitoba Telephones announced immediately that not all of its former employees would be re-hired because a number of the available positions had now been filled, and that all employees would now be required to sign a pledge not to participate in a sympathetic strike. Rehired workers would lose their seniority; they might be required to accept a demotion, and their wages would be adjusted according to their length of service. The retail clerks lost ground as well. Many of their members were unable to regain a footing in the disrupted labour market and nothing had been accomplished to improve the lot of factory workers. In the bakery and confectionery plants, union organizers seemed to be specifically targeted, and Helen Armstrong told irate tales of candymakers being put to work cleaning toilets when orders were slow. Union recruiting dwindled, although a Brooklands and Weston branch of the Women's Labor League was inaugurated early in July.

The vital Labor Café remained open for about a week after the end of the strike, and then the Trades and Labor Council ordered it shut. Helen Armstrong took the floor at the council, to demand that some provision be made for the many women who had loyally responded to the strike call and who were now being refused jobs by vindictive former employers. Armstrong herself, the *Western Labor News* reported, had been struggling to help these women, but could not cope with all the problems, and proposed that the council hire a woman to take charge, to assist them in finding living accommodations and work.

Joining the campaign to raise money for the strike leaders' defence fund, Helen Armstrong travelled east in August, addressing meetings in Toronto and Hamilton. She was well received by labour supporters, but the mainstream newspapers played up her truculence as "the Wild Woman of the West." The Women's Labor League raised five hundred dollars for the defence fund, and Armstrong was among the speakers at a mass meeting to protest the continued incarceration of the strike leaders awaiting trial. At the Trades and Labor Congress in Hamilton, George and Helen Armstrong were among the delegates who tried, unsuccessfully, to galvanize the conference into a more radical stance, and on her return Helen Armstrong told the *Labor News* that she had "had enough of the effete East" and of the conservative Congress.

For all her highly visible offenses against the status quo, Helen Armstrong was not brought to trial as one of the alleged conspirators bent on destroying orderly society, rather as if radical dissent by a woman could not be taken seriously. In early December, with Bob Russell's trial underway, she was acquitted of the outstanding charge against her of intimidation. In the subsequent proceedings against George and the others, however, her name was raised so frequently by exasperated counsel for the prosecution, that the litany of her misdemeanours, hardly applicable to the case at hand, made Fred Dixon register a disarmingly reasonable protest.

With her husband in jail, Helen Armstrong did what she could to keep the unjust fate of the labour martyrs before the public eye, and above all to reinforce the sagging spirits of the families they had left behind. In their troubles, the wives of the convicted men clung together. Many years later Russell's daughter, Margaret Sykes, still remembered the companionship of Katherine Queen, who lived across the street, and the kindness of "Ma" Armstrong, utterly indomitable in her defiance of oppression.

It was not an easy time for the small Queen children, as Gloria Queen-Hughes well remembered:

> We used to go down to Vaughan Street [jail] and see him, and to the prison farm at Shoal Lake. . . . My mother got a letter from my dear old grandmother in Scotland; "Katie," my grandmother wrote, and my mother was crying, "I cannot believe that my John has done anything wrong." And . . . he hadn't done anything wrong. He had been standing up for a philosophy, a way of life, and he got put in jail for it. We were as proud as hell of him, thanks to my mother. She said, "Don't forget, your father is in jail not because he had committed a crime, but because he is a political prisoner. Be proud of it." And we are.

Continuations

By the end of the war Gertrude Richardson no longer believed in the exclusive virtue of women as peacemakers, and had discovered, in "the great soul of the New Humanity," that "not only women, but men have great, tender hearts, strong, courageous souls, beautiful minds." She rejoiced in the achievement of the Russian Revolution, and became active in the Women's Social Democratic League; and some of the left-wing terminology that helped convict the leaders of the Winnipeg General Strike began to creep into her reports: "A very successful social gathering at the home of Comrade Mrs. Loeb, . . . a good number of Comrades and friends being present. . . . Comrade J. Connor told us about the work of the Canadian Freedom League. . . . " She corresponded with William Ivens, and deplored his dismissal by the Methodist Church. She corresponded with the American socialist writer Upton Sinclair, who sent her a copy of his new magazine exposing the treatment in the United States of conscientious objectors.

On a visit to Winnipeg in May 1918 Gertrude Richardson was met at the train by Helen Armstrong, and she stayed at the Armstrongs' home, talking with them about the glorious new society that socialism would inevitably create. She delivered an address at the Labor Temple on "The New World Motherhood Women's Crusade," with Mr. Dixon and Reverend Ivens in the audience, and had dinner at the home of Arthur Puttee; and in response to many inquiries, Mrs. Armstrong held a reception for her after church on Sunday evening.

Back home in Roaring River, Richardson was intensely distressed by the turmoil of the general strike and shocked by the arrests and the subsequent trials. The war and its aftermath had left thousands of children homeless and adrift in Europe, and she spent hours at her sewing machine, turning out clothes to be sent overseas through church organizations for child relief. By 1920 or 1921 she was writing less and less, and her active community life was now past. A psychiatric illness she had suffered in her youth resurfaced, and she was admitted to the Brandon Hospital, where she spent the remainder of her years. Her death there, in 1946, was noted in a brief obituary in the *Swan River Times*, making no mention of her writing or her community work.

Francis Beynon remained in the United States, apparently disillusioned by the failure of organized groups to bring about a workable solution to the world's problems, and falling back on the hope of a spiritual regeneration, a redemptive change in individual human beings. She died in 1951.

In Winnipeg, by 1919, the Women's Labor League had gradually become something of an organization in name only, synonymous with Helen Armstrong. Its ties to the Dominion Labor Party had continued, but while the party president, Fred Dixon, unfailingly supported women in their quest for the franchise and for equal pay, Helen Armstrong had little use for his brand of well-mannered reformism, and had crossed swords with him on a number of occasions. Nevertheless, when the party was considering its candidates for the unified labour slate in the 1920 provincial elections, Helen Armstrong was one of three women nominated. Subsequently the nominations appear to have been declared void, although a tactful account in the *Western Labor News* asserted that the women had withdrawn in favour of the jailed labour leaders.

Reports of Helen Armstrong's attempts to correct social inequities continued to appear in the press. She complained that women sent out to a prospective position by the Employment Service Office were often turned away, told to come back the next day; at least, she said, these hard-pressed women should be given their carfare. She chaired a public meeting to protest the government's cuts in the mothers' allowance. She charged that there were serious problems with the Social Welfare Commission, and, dissatisfied with the report of an investigating committee, she undertook to look into the matter herself.

In 1923 Helen Armstrong was a candidate in Ward 2 for a seat on the Winnipeg City Council, her nomination endorsed by six women. With no campaign funds to speak of, she ran no advertising, and polled an unimpressive 533 votes against the almost four thousand that elected labourite Thomas Flye.

After this, with George's difficulties in earning a living and the lack of progress on the labour scene, there was little to keep the Armstrongs in Winnipeg. The three girls were married now, and the entire family — George, Helen, the daughters and their husbands, and son Frank — moved to Chicago. Mrs. Armstrong was now in late middle age, her public fighting days effectively over. When George retired, the pair tried settling in Victoria, B.C., and finally chose Concord, California.

By 1922, labour had established its beachhead in the Manitoba legislature and on the city council, as well as in Ottawa, and John Queen had hitched his own rising political star to the fortunes of the new

Independent Labor Party. Katherine Queen had been a member of the Social Democratic Party, at the forefront of its women's activities, since the time, as she said, that socialists were "comrades of danger, poverty, and scorn." Socialism, her close friends understood, was for her "a religion, a philosophy, a heart's desire." A determined activist in the Women's Labour League, she had fought beside Helen Armstrong against conscription and for the enactment of adequate minimum wage laws, and now she joined her husband as a member of the ILP.

The Women's Labor League dissolved, and in the new political arena Katherine Queen helped organize the Labor Women of Greater Winnipeg, a broadly left-of-centre group with a membership of perhaps thirty or forty. Operating characteristically as a kind of women's auxiliary, the Labor Women swung into action during elections, holding bazaars, teas, and whist drives, selling labour buttons and "dollar bonds," to raise campaign funds for labour candidates. Under Queen's presidency, the group fought for mandatory physical examinations before marriage, for birth control clinics, and for equal employment opportunities and equal pay for women.

A humanist and a humanitarian like her husband, Katherine Queen was instinctively responsive to the daily problems of ordinary people. She organized widows' groups, helping them to obtain mothers' allowances, and she lent a hand to young people's associations, encouraging them to assert their particular needs in society. John was instrumental in establishing a Labor Sunday school in the working-class suburb of Brooklands, and Katherine took her turn teaching there. As her husband's political career developed, in the city council, as mayor, and in the legislature, she functioned endlessly as his aide, answering the incessant telephone calls, dealing with as many as possible of the myriad daily problems, trying as he did to alleviate some of the difficulties of the poor and the unemployed. In 1931 she represented the Winnipeg West-End ILP at a labour conference in Calgary.

In September 1933, just as the labourites in Winnipeg were preparing for the annual civic election campaign, as the nominations of John Queen for mayor and Gloria Queen-Hughes for school trustee were about to be announced, Katherine Queen died of pneumonia. Her funeral services were held at the Fort Rouge Labor Hall, attended by friends and political foes alike. At her own request, her casket was draped in a red flag, reaffirming in death the socialist principles that had informed her life.

Helen Armstrong's passing, in California in 1947, was apparently unnoticed by the Winnipeg newspapers. An obscure figure in most histories of the turbulent strike years, she has been identified as one of the two women among the fifty men in an archival group portrait of the General Strike Council.

In some small way, perhaps, the Winnipeg General Strike did serve as a watershed for politically minded women, and particularly women of the liberal-left, marking their recognition as valid candidates for public office. In the aftermath of the strike, Rose Alcin ran as a socialist for the Winnipeg School Board. She was elected by a reliable labour vote, and served one term, 1920–21. It remained, then, for the next generation of political women, like Gloria Queen-Hughes and Grace Woodsworth MacInnis, to continue the battle.

An Idealist in
the Political Arena

*James Shaver
Woodsworth*

Student Minister

James Shaver Woodsworth, the eldest of the six children of Reverend
James and Esther Shaver Woodsworth, was born in 1874 at
Applewood, the homestead of his Shaver grandparents, in Etobicoke,
outside Toronto. Devout Methodists and intensely proud of their
British heritage, the Woodsworths raised their family in the ideals of a
strenuous Christianity, striving to achieve the utmost in service and
self-discipline. In their eldest son particularly they instilled a sense of
his solemn responsibility toward God and toward the less fortunate
among his fellow human beings.

251

The elder Woodsworth was first assigned to a number of rural churches in Ontario; then, in 1882, he was appointed superintendent of Methodist Missions for Western Canada. The family came west to Manitoba, settling first in Portage la Prairie and then in Brandon. From this outpost of civilization the superintendent took charge of the Indian missions and the scattered Methodist churches from the head of the Great Lakes to the Pacific coast, and for thirty years he assiduously crisscrossed his vast territory, first on horseback, sleigh, and canoe, and then by rail, as the silver network of track reached out over the prairies and across the mountains.

Reverend Woodsworth was absent from home much of the time, leaving his wife in charge of the family, and for young James a pattern seems to have been set. Inevitably, as the oldest of the children, he assumed some of the household authority, supervising his brothers and sisters in their various duties and earnestly attempting to lighten the load for his mother. He was not an easy taskmaster, one of his siblings later remembered; as exacting of the others as he was of himself, he demanded absolute perfection in their chores.

During young James's last year of high school, the Woodsworth family spent three months back east, and he took the opportunity, as his diary noted, "to see the principal cities in Ontario and Quebec." Eaton's store in Toronto, he recorded, was "like a great and complex machine," and a tour of a fire hall "an exciting experience." Sternly, he set down his judgment on an art exhibit: "It is a pity such prominence is given to Criminal Characters." He listed the public edifices he saw, the churches he visited, the sermons he heard. The surrounding countryside struck him as very pretty, but he thought the religious life of the community rather wanting, and the Sunday school dull. In the early spring of 1891, the family returned to Brandon, and James completed his high school at Brandon Collegiate.

That fall, at seventeen, he left home to enroll at Winnipeg's Wesley College, which his father had helped to establish. He found Greek difficult, played football well enough to make the college team, and was elected Senior Stick. Forced always to be frugal, he took a season off to earn enough money for his final year by teaching at a rural school, and graduated in 1896 with a bachelor of arts in the Department of Mental and Moral Science, with a gold medal in philosophy. Then, dutiful to the path his parents had envisaged for him, he elected to enter the Methodist ministry, and undertook a two-year stint as student-probationer in the farming areas near Brandon.

Wesley College in the 1890s was not yet the centre of theological radicalism it was to become a few years later, when Salem Bland taught the anti-capitalist dogma of the Social Gospel, and nothing in James's experience had as yet seriously unsettled his Methodist faith and his middle-class values of respectability and industry. Travelling by horse and buggy from one meagre prairie hamlet to another, like his father before him, James now came face-to-face with rural poverty and hopelessness at its worst, and with the unfair distribution of wealth, and the first stirrings of uneasiness began to appear in his letters and his diary.

In one slovenly shanty he found a farmer and his wife and their twelve children, none of them attending Sunday school because they had no proper clothes, and with a five-week-old baby at its mother's breast. "Yes, twelve living," he wrote his mother, "I dared not ask the number of the dead. . . . Woman was going about with bare feet and an old waist and a skirt or petticoat failing to connect by some inches." Twelve years earlier, the young student minister learned, the man had bought a binder for $250; with interest accumulating, he had already paid back $400, another $80 was still owing, and there was debt on most of his other implements. Thoroughly beaten down by his circumstances, the man could only admit to the preacher that he knew he was not "living as he ought to," but "if he goes to Hell he will try not to blame God for it." James was appalled by the dirt and degradation and ignorance, but he could only exclaim in bafflement that the farmer must surely, somehow, have "sufficient will or backbone or courage or *something* to do what he knows to be right."

By the second year of his student ministry, he had begun tentatively to consider that there was "a great deal of truth" in the envy and resentment of the poor, "the comparatively uneducated class," toward the well-to-do: "when a man is struggling away making a bare living and sees others living in luxury from profits made in business transactions with him, he is apt to think there is something wrong."

Something was vaguely wrong in the vocation into which he had entered with such eager confidence. Even as he laboured at his pastoral tasks, he confided to his diary that a well-turned sermon or an enthusiastic prayer meeting had left him dissatisfied, feeling that "I was not walking in the spirit as I had promised to walk. . . . I have been almost ready to draw away part of the sacrifice already presented to God. May I never fall away." In the summer of 1898 he left for Toronto to enroll in the divinity program of Victoria College. (Despite his doubts, the congregation at his farewell sermon had numbered over one hundred.) "I will endeavour," he wrote in his diary, "to regain systematic habits of study and prayer, and try daily to follow 'in His steps.' "

In Toronto, two of James's cousins, Clara Woodsworth and Charlie Sissons, were also attending Victoria, and boarding on Avenue Road, and James joined them there. There was also another young lady in residence at the house, a friend of Clara's, dark-haired Lucy Staples, the twenty-four-year-old daughter of a pioneer Methodist family near Lindsay, Ontario. The four young people found each other's company most congenial, and the fall and winter months sped by in a pleasant round of engrossing studies and agreeable outings. If something further had begun to blossom, if Charlie was greatly taken with Lucy and James thought Clara decidedly attractive, the two young women were not inclined to go beyond a companionable friendship, and their would-be admirers accepted the constraint. James earned his bachelor of divinity degree and then made plans for his first foray into the wider world, a season at Oxford and a taste of the Old Country of his family history.

Arriving in Oxford in October 1899, Woodsworth registered for lectures in philosophy and theology at Mansfield College. England intrigued him, the pretty countryside, the curiously different customs, and above all, the extraordinary experience of standing where his great heroes of literature and history and religion had once stood. With his characteristic seriousness of purpose, he made his intentions clear. His aim, he said, was not sightseeing or even mere book-learning, but "to study life rather than do places. To gain as many points of view as possible — more specifically to see what may be helpful later. To get a fair idea of the principles of the religious and educational and social problems and work, and to try to understand the spirit which characterizes the whole system."

English Methodism, he was disconcerted to find, did not seem to enjoy the same high standing that his church did in Canada: there was little or no Methodist presence at the university, for example. Back home he had lectured fervently to the Woman's Christian Temperance Union on the evils of drink and smoking, and here Methodists both smoked and drank. His faith had taught him a profound, ineradicable opposition to all warfare; he had objected to Canada's sending troops against the Boers in Africa, and now was shocked to find open recruiting in Britain. Conversely, he had grown up on the prairies accustomed to hunting for food, and he could not fathom the high moral stand that English Methodists took against the upper-class sport of fox-hunting. James was acquiring some unexpected exposure to "life."

Most horrifying of all was his first introduction to the sordid misery of the English slums. In December he spent two weeks at Mansfield House, the settlement house run by the college in London's East End. The surrounding streets appalled him, the drunken men, the slatternly women, the gin palaces, in one of which he noticed a mother feeding liquor to her small baby. He saw women who had eaten nothing all day working at sewing buttonholes for "ha'penny a hole," and he reacted with a wrenching pity to the prostitute who accosted him from a dark doorway, "offering to the passing stranger the dregs of her womanhood." As part of the community service that Mansfield House provided, he helped serve a ragged crowd of schoolchildren a meal of soup and bread, and was torn between disgust at the children's greed and the pathos of their pleas for "just a little more of the thicker soup near the bottom."

He visited the "splendid" city of Edinburgh and saw the same slums as in London. He visited the Midlands, and found the area grim and depressing. "Mile after mile of great chimneys," he wrote home, "the whole country one irregular, ugly town, with blazing furnaces, great earth mounds, ash heaps, smoke everywhere, sky dull, earth dirty beneath." He crossed the English Channel to Paris, where he was astonished at the number and size of the rooms at the Palace of Versailles: "Many would make splendid little churches," he thought.

Back again in London, he commented, "No wonder the poor are envious of the nobility," and his letters to his father reiterated his doubts about his intended life's work, adding, "What a need there seems to be in the world for someone to go about doing good."

Grace Church, Winnipeg

In London, a letter was waiting to inform James Woodsworth that he had received an appointment as Methodist pastor in Carievale, Assiniboia, the present Saskatchewan — "I'm afraid I don't even know the name Carievale," he confessed — and he was formally ordained on his return to Canada in 1900. His one-year term in Carievale was followed by a year at Keewatin, near Rat Portage, now Kenora, in northwest Ontario.

Once again James found himself in a state of great spiritual conflict, increasingly questioning the theological truths taught by the church, and he confided his unhappiness in letters to Charlie Sissons. "Next Sunday is Easter," he wrote: "Think of doubting the Resurrection and then having to stand in a pulpit! The position is utterly false. It drives me half-crazy at times to think of it." And again: "My future course is not yet clear. . . . I have never been in such trouble as I am at present. . . ."

Above all, he was lonely, and Charlie suggested that "a loving wife might help." Sadly, James responded: "I haven't the slightest doubt that a home would be a very great help — how a man does long for companionship. . . . Still, there is little likelihood that any such good fortune is to be mine." In that delightful year in the Avenue Road house, he had indeed fallen in love with Clara Woodsworth, but his affections had not been returned, and he had no thought for anyone else. His theological uncertainties deepened, he wrote Charlie, and he began to feel "driven by some inevitable force to a kind of intentionalistic Unitarianism." In this state, he said, he was thankful "that no wife is involved in my — shall I say it — approaching apostasy."

He offered his resignation to the church, but was refused. Instead, in 1902 the Methodist Conference appointed him to a junior pastorship in Winnipeg's fashionable Grace Church, at the then princely salary of one thousand dollars per year. In contact now with such prominent and wealthy Methodist citizens as James Ashdown, the hardware merchant, and James Aikins, the corporation lawyer, he taught Sunday school, organized clubs and classes, and in the absence of the senior minister he conducted the services and preached from the pulpit.

Meanwhile, Lucy Staples had gently but firmly turned down Charlie Sissons's courtship, and with some generosity the rejected suitor wrote to James that Lucy had hinted at her inclination toward the young minister. James was considerably surprised. He had never thought of Miss Staples, he replied, "in any other light than that of a very intimate and dear friend. . . . I certainly could never have had the assurance to imagine . . . that she might think of me otherwise." A desultory and rather formal correspondence with Miss Staples ensued, until the fall of 1903, when James returned to Toronto after an absence of four years. Encouraged by Charlie Sissons, he went on to Lindsay, where Lucy Staples taught at the collegiate. There was, by his own account, a flash of electrifying illumination; he proposed and was accepted. And an ecstatic Woodsworth — a rather insensitive Woodsworth, considering Charlie's lovelorn state — poured out his delight in a letter to his cousin: "It is a wonderful experience to look deep into a woman's eyes and know that you are loved!" The marriage took place on September 7, 1904. Charlie was best man, and the bridesmaid was James's first and unrequited love, Clara Woodsworth.

The young couple moved into the Grace Church parsonage, and the joys of domestic life filled their letters to their families. James's happiness brimmed over when their first child, Grace, was born, on July 25, 1905, and he beheld his Lucy in her new role as "little mother."

Safely ensconced in his affluent, comfortable charge, Woodsworth's uncertainty about his calling continued to grow, and his sermons began to expound an explicitly Christian socialism. To strive for the purity and the redemption of one's own soul and offer charity to the poor was not the whole of a Christian's duty, he urged. God requires the utter rebirth of society, the conquest of the world for Christ:

It is right to help the sick; it is right to do away with filth and over-crowding and to provide sunlight and good air and good

food. We have tried to provide for the poor. Yet have we tried to
alter the social conditions that lead to poverty? . . . Christianity
is not merely individualistic, it is socialistic. . . . The work of the
church is not merely to save men, it is to redeem, to transform
society. Jesus spoke very little about saving souls — He spoke
often about the establishment of the kingdom.

Sternly Reverend Woodsworth called the businessmen among his
parishioners to account, challenging them to remember the teaching of
the gospel in their dealings with their employees. Christian love
required them to protect the weak, to provide a fair wage. If profit was
the guiding principle of the marketplace, Christian ethic demanded
service without thought of gain:

I am here to condemn as unChristian the spirit that refuses to
acknowledge the responsibilities which are involved in power. No
Christian lives to himself. His abilities, his wealth, his business
are all held in trust and must be used in the master's
service. . . . The Christian is often called upon to do things that
won't pay and to keep out of things that will pay. Business interests must be subordinate to higher things. . . .

Equally, he argued, trade union efforts must go beyond the demand
for higher wages. Fired by the vision of a society in which capital and
labour would cooperate in a redemptive harmony, he proposed that
industry should use its power to improve the lives of the people, and
that labour should strive to further the interests of business. The concept of human society as an organic, interdependent whole was to
remain at the heart of his philosophy.

In the summer of 1905, after the birth of the baby, Lucy was ill and
needed the care of a nurse. Tired and in poor health himself, James had
become sufficiently unhappy about his position at Grace Church to ask
for a leave of absence.

In 1906, eleven-month-old Grace was left with Lucy's family in
Cavan, Ontario, while James and Lucy travelled in Europe with James's
father and sister Mary. After several months, Lucy came home, and

James went on to tour the Holy Land, returning just before Christmas. Charlie Sissons, then teaching in Revelstoke, British Columbia, wrote him about a temporary position available there, filling in for a sick minister, and with considerable hesitation, James applied and was accepted, and left for Revelstoke. Lucy, who was pregnant again, stayed on at the Cavan homestead, where a second daughter, Belva Elizabeth, was born on May 2, 1907.

Mission to the Downtrodden

After the stint in Revelstoke, Woodsworth was once again determined to resign from the Methodist ministry. In June 1907 he appeared before the Methodist Conference armed with a lengthy letter outlining how little of the church's discipline he could now support, how much received Christian doctrine he could no longer honestly profess. Once again, however, quite possibly out of regard for his father, the Methodist Conference rejected his resignation, choosing to salvage their pastor by offering him the kind of task that would be close to his heart, helping the poor and the downtrodden.

Woodsworth was sent to take charge of the Maple Street Mission in Winnipeg, near the CPR station in the impoverished North End, where an immigrant population fought for survival on unfamiliar ground. The plight of the people appalled him, as he had been horrified by the degradation he had observed in the London slums. In keeping with his commitment to an activist faith, Woodsworth brought his family west once again, to live among the people he had undertaken to serve, and two years later he accepted the even more demanding assignment of superintendent of the All People's Mission, on Stella Avenue.

Under Woodsworth's direction the settlement house brought together a group of concerned volunteers, trying to provide the people of the area with some escape from the drab desperation of their lives. There was a kindergarten for small children, while in another classroom their mothers tackled the impenetrabilities of the English language, or attended cooking classes designed to teach the best use of limited resources. There was a swimming pool in the basement for boys and girls for whom bathing was a rare luxury. There was a library, and language classes at night for working men. On Sundays there were church services, and Sunday school for the children, with lantern slides and hymn singing.

The work was all-consuming, draining Woodsworth's energy in the round of board meetings, Sunday school teaching and supervision, Fresh Air Camp consultations, playground associations, visits to homes in his constituency, committee meetings concerned with overcrowding in tenements, and overseeing the teaching of English, so that the foreign-born could apply for and hold jobs. Occupied seven days a week from early morning until late at night, he worked as director, preacher, fund-raiser, social animator, community facilitator, and as liaison with outside agencies. In the process, as he laboured to accommodate the diversity of customs and beliefs in his constituency to the Canadian reality, and to provide some material help, he gravitated increasingly toward political involvement.

Resolutely Woodsworth set himself the task of bringing the problems of the Russian, Polish, and Ukrainian immigrants to the attention of the public, its civic leaders, and the government. He pointed out that juvenile crime was fostered by slum living conditions, and he worked for the establishment of a juvenile court to help young people in trouble, rather than subjecting them to the punitive rigours of the adult judicial system. He supported the Juvenile Delinquents Bill then before the federal parliament, and achieved a measure of success in 1908, when Winnipeg became the first city in Canada to set up a juvenile court under the new legislation.

Increasingly aware of the wider issues his concerns entailed, Woodsworth discovered that nearly one-third of Manitoba's children did not attend a school of any kind, and he spearheaded the drive for a compulsory education law in Manitoba. Partly as a result of Woodsworth's pressure and influence, the Public Schools Act was finally amended in 1916, clearing the way for legislation making public school attendance compulsory. He urged the need for playgrounds and supervised recreation for the children in deprived areas, to keep youngsters off the streets; and in 1913 the Winnipeg civic administration took on the task of building and overseeing the city's parks and playgrounds.

Beyond these specific pursuits, some of Woodsworth's most fundamental assumptions were unsettled by the impact of the "foreigners" he
worked with at the All People's Mission. Culturally rooted from earliest
childhood in the British tradition, he feared that the flood of immigrants would turn Canada into a non-British nation, and the concept of
a multi-ethnic Canadian identity had not yet come into being. In a
democratic nation, he held, citizens are united in a common core of
values, and he was concerned that not all the heterogeneous peoples
jostling for a place in a developing Canada displayed the requisite traits
of energy, enterprise, self-sufficiency, intellectual capacity — the basic
values, indeed, that his own background had inculcated and he himself
embodied. These newcomers, he believed firmly, would be best served
by helping them conform to Canadian ways, and assimilation was the
best way to preserve and further democracy.

At the same time, his Christian ethic, permanently embedded in his
thinking, impelled him to accept all people as equal in the sight of God,
and he considered it his duty to persuade Anglo-Canadians to rise
above their arrogant superiority and exclusiveness. The conflict and
contradiction appear frequently in the book Woodsworth co-authoured
in 1909 with A. R. Ford, *Strangers within Our Gates*. Pleading that
Canadians must understand the newcomers and help them acclimatize,
he argues that "other languages, customs, and religious ways have their
value." The value of foreign ways, however, must be subsumed in the
indigenous culture, as with unconscious arrogance Woodsworth follows
his plea for toleration with the assurance that, patiently and benevo-
lently, the foreigners can be weaned from the old loyalties and accultur-
ated in the new. During Woodsworth's tenure at the All People's
Mission, the Methodists acquired ownership of a Polish Catholic
church in the area, and he set about tactfully encouraging the "illiterate
peasants" of the congregation to dispense with their superstitious trap-
pings of candles and crucifixes and patron saints. The "new," refined,
Canadian way of worship was better.

In his book's final chapter, "A Challenge to the Church,"
Woodsworth makes a strong plea to the church to lead in the task of
building citizenship. Accordingly, he initiated a program in the fall of
1910 that was to become one of his most influential achievements. The

"People's Forum," first held in the old Grand Theatre at Jarvis and Main streets, began as another effort to integrate new Canadians into the general community, but it grew into an experiment in community cooperation, a curriculum of adult education, and a platform for the expression of liberal opinion.

Sunday evening concerts, usually featuring the talents of the various ethnic groups in Woodsworth's constituency, became a regular cultural event, and on Sunday afternoons a lecture took place on a subject of popular interest, often illustrated by lantern slides, and always followed by lively discussion. The audience might hear Reverend Salem Bland speak on "Canada and the Empire," or Winona Dixon on "The Challenge of the Franchise." F. J. Dixon, MLA, enthralled his listeners with his vision of "The Parliament of Man," Professor W. F. Osborne informed them about "The Railway Situation in Canada," and among the many other guest speakers was John W. Dafoe, the highly respected editor of the *Manitoba Free Press*.

Woodsworth's second book, *My Neighbor*, published in 1911, expressed his rapidly developing secularism, and his belief in the need for social change. Now an uncompromising foe of privilege, he emphasized the interdependence of all the people within the social organism. "The welfare of one is the concern of all . . . we are members of one another," he pleaded.

Committed now to a radical approach to improving the condition of the underprivileged, *My Neighbor* considers cooperatives, public ownership, the association between socialist principles and the regeneration of mankind. The author still has a modicum of hope that the church might regain its social leadership, but his confidence is in labour and trade unions. Unionism, he points out, has already accomplished much. Factory acts, the reduction in the hours of labour, and the establishment of a standard rate of wages have been brought about largely through union pressure, so that "In the final adjustment of the conflicting factors of the industrial situation and the social reconstruction that must inevitably take place, trade unionism will undoubtedly have a leading place."

Woodsworth had now been appointed to the Winnipeg Trades and Labor Council as the delegate of the Ministerial Association. Among the innumerable reports and case histories he prepared of the various families within his scope, his 1913 study of the family of a painter in the railway shops captures the problem of the underpaid wage-earner in trenchant detail:

> Income averages $60 a month. . . . Has wife and six children, none old enough to work. Rent, $23 a month for six-roomed house in very poor locality, beside railroad track. . . . Lights, 50 cents to $1.97 during September. Water, $2.10 a quarter. Coal, four tons, at $11, $44 (in winter, $70), wood, almost three cords at $7. . . . Groceries, $20 to $25 (wife bakes her own bread, can not afford to buy cow's milk). . . . Some children without shoes. Wife does her own sewing. Her own clothes and those of her children were "made over" from old clothing obtained from "missions". . . . Wife does some dressmaking: averages $2 a week. . . . Tried boarders but no money in it. . . . Little girl's eyes had been bad. Had been examined at hospital . . . given glasses. Eyes grew worse. Consulted specialist at $10. Specialist said child should not have had glasses, and would be permanently blind. Now in an institution at government expense. . . .

These were the unfortunates who claimed the concern of the Methodist pastor. By now he regarded himself as a moderate socialist, finding a new direction for his Christianity in the teachings of the Social Gospel. He had written a series of articles for *The Voice*, under the pseudonym of "Pastor Newbottle," taking all the churches to task for their preoccupation with their own existence as "corporate, property-holding, office-perpetuating institutions," and for their failure to address their true calling, bettering the world; and in an essay in the Methodist *Christian Guardian* he had arrived at an unequivocal conclusion:

> there is no satisfactory way of protecting the poor and the less able from the exploitation of the rich and clever except public ownership, and only through community ownership can there be secured to the poor all things necessary to a proper, healthful and happy human life. . . .

Internationally, trouble was brewing, as World War I loomed on the horizon. Opposed to violence of any sort, Woodsworth was grievously disillusioned by the failure of virtually all the mainline churches to take a moral stand on the issue of warfare. By 1913, he had been working at the Stella Avenue Mission for seven years, and had finally become convinced that the Methodist Church would not back his pacifist position, nor was it prepared to concern itself adequately with the pressing social problems in the community. For himself, he realized, dealing with the immediate needs of the poor was only a stop-gap solution; he had to broaden his activities. In May 1913, James Woodsworth announced his intention of resigning from the All People's Mission at the end of the church year in June.

His family had now increased, with the birth of Charles in 1909 and Ralph in 1910. Like James's mother before her, Lucy had grown accustomed to shouldering the major share of the domestic responsibilities and the guidance of the children, while her husband poured out his energy for the common good, to return exhausted to his own fireside. Looking back on those formative years, James's daughter, Grace, begins her biography of her father with a perceptive sketch of life with the man they called "Father," never "Daddy," with love and with awe: "At home or a thousand miles away, he was the keystone of the family arch, the centre around whom we grouped our living. His dominant personality made it so. Furthermore, he was buttressed by Mother, who felt that this was the natural order of things."

Vivacious and outgoing where James was austere and formal, Lucy stood behind her husband through all his struggles with his beliefs, and the demands his principles placed on her household. A constant sounding board for his concerns, his evolving theories of social reform and his dwindling ties with the Methodist Church, she found time to help with the work at the All People's Mission, teaching immigrant women English and instructing them in nutrition and hygiene, and she participated in the early birth control movement in Winnipeg. Intelligent, educated, energetic, her sphere was the home.

A Pacifist in War Time

Woodsworth went from the All People's Mission to become secretary of the newly formed Canadian Welfare League. Officially launched by the Canadian Conference of Charities and Corrections, in Winnipeg in mid-September of 1913, the league undertook a broadly defined program, to study Canada's deepening social problems, reaching out to the community with the help of concerned citizens as well as professionals. There would be close cooperation with universities and other educational institutions, with government agencies, industrial bureaus, and religious groups. The Canadian Welfare League was later expanded to include like-minded members across Canada.

Woodsworth's plan for a social service centre with a comprehensive mandate appeared to have become a reality, enabling many individuals and organizations to channel their efforts through one coordinated, "organized helpfulness." His duties included raising funds for his own salary as secretary and for travelling and operating expenses, and his office became a centre for socially conscious community activists. Those who were unable to visit in person, from Halifax in the east to Victoria in the west, exchanged ideas by correspondence, and the Woodsworth children did their bit when they visited their father's office, Grace remembered, by licking the stamps for his replies to the endless stream of letters.

In constant demand as a lecturer, Woodsworth spoke in meeting halls and one-room schoolhouses throughout the West, unfurling his enormous charts, explaining the origins and cultures of the new immigrants flooding into the country, striving to weld his audience into a unified force for a better Canada. On the road now much of the time, he shared with Lucy his elation at the success of a People's Forum meeting, or the lavish praise of a socially prominent benefactor; or with visionary extravagance he allowed himself to dream that a great new moral and social movement was under way, and that his own arduous toil in the service of that new truth was "something like the work of John the Baptist."

In the fall of 1915 he spent a prolonged period in Montreal, delivering a series of lectures at McGill University on Canadian immigration problems, and making other vital contacts. Occasionally he admitted that he was overreaching himself, but plunged ahead for the sake of his larger objective. "I am working a bluff on these university people," he wrote Lucy. "The Philosophical [Students] Society has asked me for a paper. I don't know anything about philosophy or psychology — I would like very well to meet this group — so I think I'll accept — and I have been wondering if I can only get time to read a book or so on Social Psychology. . . ."

Woodsworth's pacifism was well received in Quebec. Pleased and rather amused, he wrote Lucy that *Le Devoir*, the paper of the French-Canadian publicist, Henri Bourassa, had called him "the first English-speaking Canadian that has gotten hold of 'our' ideal for Canada. . . . Rather dangerous from *Le Devoir*," he commented. With some sense of daring, he made contact also with the Jewish community in Montreal, again describing the occasion in a letter to his wife:

At night attended as guest of honor the Montefiore Club — the fashionable Jewish club. . . . And I'm asked before I go, to speak in the Temple Emmanuel. I think I'll do it. . . . I suppose I'll come in for some criticism. But if I have any message which they are willing to hear, why not? Then in this particular case we can always meet objections by suggesting that the founder of Christianity preached in the synagogue.

The work of the Welfare League seemed to prepare Woodsworth for his entry into politics, and perhaps even laid the foundation for the eventual Co-operative Commonwealth Federation. Early in 1916, however, the president of the Canadian Welfare League notified the organization that its activities could no longer be funded, since the requirements of war had dried up the source of its support. For the secretary, fortunately, the loss of employment was mitigated by his appointment to a related post: the three prairie governments jointly set up a Bureau of Social Research and named Woodsworth as secretary. Most satisfactorily, there was every prospect that in this new context he could continue the work he had begun in the old.

The venture was short-lived. Painful as Woodsworth found the war in Europe, and particularly the churches' willingness to act as recruiting agencies, he had more or less refrained from open criticism. In December 1916 he received a letter from R. B. Bennett, the future Tory prime minister, then director of the new National Service Registration, asking for the help of the secretary of the Bureau of Social Research in promoting the conscription-related scheme. Instead, Woodsworth declared his opposition emphatically in a letter to the *Manitoba Free Press*. He questioned the justification for the policy of registering men for army service, and echoing the demand of anti-war labourites, he insisted that the conscription of wealth must precede any conscription of men. Finally, he issued a call to Canadians to resist any future policy of what he called "forced service."

Abruptly, within a few short months of its inauguration, the Bureau of Social Research also ran out of funds. Woodsworth had already appeared at more than a hundred lectures and meetings, and just before his letter to the *Free Press* had presented an account of his term in office as bureau secretary. The report was never published. Instead, the secretary was summoned to appear before the responsible cabinet minister, and asked to curb his unacceptable stand on the war. With his characteristic refusal to compromise on principles, Woodsworth responded that it was his duty to express his beliefs freely, and he was summarily dismissed, as of January 31, 1917.

Woodsworth was now in his forty-third year and at the height of his intellectual powers, but the future looked bleak. With the onset of the war, his new Canadians had become "aliens" in the eyes of a patriotic public, and strife had developed between the various ethnic groups. At the end of the 1916–17 season, the People's Forum in Winnipeg closed its doors, defeated by wartime xenophobia. James's father had died on the day before the Social Research Bureau closed, depriving the son of a beloved friend and close confidant. With the birth of Bruce in 1914 and Howard in 1916, there were now six children in the family, and both Lucy and James were ill and tired. To their surprise and sorrow, many of James's former associates and acquaintances now ostracized him, but husband and wife discussed the consequences of their stand and agreed that the need to speak out against the evils of war was paramount. Badly in need of a respite, they packed their belongings, took their small savings, and headed for the west coast, for a seven-week stay in Victoria.

In this crisis, the Methodist Church once again provided an option. Still apparently unwilling to relinquish their unhappy pastor, the local Methodist Conference agreed to have him take charge of the Howe Sound mission, and the Woodsworths moved to the small settlement of Gibson's Landing, British Columbia, in June 1917. There were about 140 families in the area, white people, aboriginals, and Asians, in a twenty-five mile coastal strip including several small islands, and Woodsworth sought out both Methodists and non-Methodists, on foot and on horseback, and by boat over the open waters of the Sound, once again discovering a constituency of the poor and the marginalized.

Isolated on the "Hill," apart from the generally English-speaking inhabitants of Gibson's Landing itself, a group of Finnish people had settled. Most of the men were away from home for at least part of the year, in the army or working with pick and shovel in the interior, and the women and children lived as they could, with a garden and a flock of chickens or a cow or two. These new Canadians, Woodsworth reported to the Methodist Conference, had turned their backs on the corruption of the Russian church they had known back home, and on church worship in general, and had became, he said, "materialistic socialists." More than ever convinced that only by a community effort could the poor surmount their difficulties, he became a member and an energetic supporter of the cooperative store established by the Hill folk, greatly annoying the businessmen of Gibson's Landing by his endorsement of an intrusive competitor.

He held regular classes at the parsonage to teach the Finnish women English, and at the Howe Sound school he organized Friday night community lectures, which drew an attendance of thirty to sixty people from all sections of the community. Much like his People's Forum, the lectures ranged from school matters and agricultural and neighbour- hood problems to the women's movement, from socialism and social reform to sexual hygiene. During the federal elections, the school forum provided each candidate with a rostrum, and there were several outside speakers, including the socialist Bill Pritchard. Woodsworth's reputation had preceded him, and he continued to make no secret of his opposition to war. Some of the people at Gibson's agreed with him, but others were antagonized by his stand, especially when he refused to allow war bulletins to be read from his pulpit.

The work at Gibson's Landing did nothing to overcome Woodsworth's misgivings about his relationship with the Methodist Church. On June 8, 1918, he submitted his third and final resignation to Reverend A. E. Smith, then president of the Manitoba Conference. He spoke of his disillusionment with a church that was led by men of wealth, making it virtually impossible to foster anything like a proper program of social reform; and above all, he explained, he could not remain associated with an institution that sanctioned war. Therefore, he had no choice but to resign:

> For me, the teachings and spirit of Jesus are absolutely irreconcil-
> able with the advocacy of war. Christianity may be an impossible
> idealism, but so long as I hold to it, even so unworthily, I must
> refuse, as far as may be, to participate in or influence others to
> participate in war. When the policy of the State — whether the
> state be nominally Christian or not — conflicts with my concep-
> tion of right and wrong, then I must obey God rather than man.

Abiding by his unshakeable moral principles, he had forfeited his livelihood, and needed to find some means to earn money for his family. Lucy and the six children stayed behind in Gibson's, and James went to Vancouver to look for work. There were no teaching positions open and no jobs in the shipyards, but at the longshoremen's office he encountered E. E. Winch, the union secretary and later the CCF MLA for Burnaby, who had chaired a People's Forum meeting in Winnipeg two years earlier. Winch thought that Woodsworth, slight though he was and never robust, would probably be able to manage the heavy dockside work, and pointed out the added advantage that he would be free to take time off and to speak his mind on whatever he pleased. At sixty-five cents an hour, then, for an eight-hour day, the ex-minister was hired to work on the Vancouver docks.

More than a little taken aback to find himself toiling among the coarse labouring men whom he had championed and encouraged, he described the scene in the hiring hall for Lucy: the union men playing cards while they waited to be assigned, and the casual, non-union labourers clustered outside, hoping for a chance to earn a few hours' wages. He had much to learn, he wrote Lucy that night: "I have a new theory as to why the men describe themselves as working *stiffs!*" Of course, he said, this was an excellent way to get an insight into labour conditions, "but think of you as the wife of a common labourer — a casual labourer at that! — a docker!" Lucy replied that she was proud to be the wife of a docker and the mother of his children.

On the Docks

Sticking grimly to his task, Woodsworth did indeed experience labour conditions on the docks from the inside, and in a newspaper article he described the back-breaking monotony of a longshoreman's day:

> Back and forward — loaders to pilers — pilers to loaders. Is it any wonder he looks at his watch? Ten-thirty, the morning is half gone, anyway. Backwards and forwards, loaders to pilers, pilers to loaders. The pile of salmon cases grows slowly — it is twenty cases wide, twelve high, and before night it will be twenty deep. . . . Back and forth — loaders to pilers, pilers to loaders. . . . "Twenty minutes," says a fellow trucker as he passes. . . . Twenty minutes till noon — and freedom.

Woodsworth won his union card, and earned $491.50 for a winter's work, while back at Gibson's Landing Lucy taught school and added another $177 to the family's purse. The children made do with cast-off clothes from their family and friends, but Lucy managed somehow to find the money for dental care and for music lessons.

Material necessities were not allowed to take precedence over principle. The longshoremen's union had passed a resolution in sympathy with the Russian Revolution, and when Woodsworth discovered one day that the boat he was helping to load carried munitions, to be used by the Allied forces in Siberia against the revolutionaries, he walked off the job, forfeiting his day's work and pay. Much to his chagrin, very few of the twelve hundred longshoremen followed his example.

As the struggle between the western radicals and the eastern-based Trades and Labor Congress gathered momentum, an article by Woodsworth in the *B.C. Federationist*, in August 1918, lamented the fact that "class-conscious Socialists under their various national flags are at each others' throats," and endorsed the worldwide unity of labour toward socialist goals. The war, he argued, had accelerated change, and while he disapproved of many entrenched left-wing theories, he embraced "the great underlying principle stressed by Marx, viz., the collective ownership and democratic control of the means of production. Men may differ widely in theory," he added, "and yet unite to fight a common foe." And finally, although he proclaimed with visionary fervour that the workers' revolution was at hand, that a new heaven and a new earth were being born before their eyes, he expressed his abhorrence of violence as a means of change. The gradualist model of the British Labour Party, he maintained, supported his belief that there could be political change by democratic means, a bloodless revolution, a revolution without tears.

In general, the article outlined Woodsworth's lasting approach to practical politics. He approved of larger and more inclusive industrial unions, since industry itself was becoming larger and more concentrated. Supporting trade unionism, he was not opposed to industrial action by workers, including the mutual support of all unions in a sympathy strike. He saw labour organization as part of a wide movement that encompassed not only unions but the Socialist Party of Canada as well, and possibly also included farmers and academics, progressive-minded citizens from all walks of life. The foundation was being laid in his mind for a democratic national political structure, and already evident was the perception that was to become his hallmark, that striving for the immediately practicable was not inconsistent with the pursuit of long-term goals.

Winch had invited Woodsworth to live in his home, and more important still, he introduced his guest to the socialist movement in British Columbia and to its leadership. Continuing to write in the *B.C. Federationist*, the official organ of the B.C. Federation of Labor, Woodsworth helped organize the Federated Labor Party of British Columbia, which promoted a coalition of workers, farmers, and middle-class progressives, and he spoke regularly at the Sunday night meetings held by the FLP in downtown theatres. In the spring of 1919, recognized as the party's leader and still working as a longshoreman, he accepted the invitation of the Reverend William Ivens to make a lecture tour of western Canada, to arouse workers and their organizations to the need for social change.

Jailed

Woodsworth was on the train from Prince Rupert when he first heard that labour action had been called in Winnipeg and had rapidly escalated to become a general strike. Continuing with his itinerary of lectures, he arrived in the now strike-bound city on the appointed day, June 8, and was immediately swept into the conflict.

Ten thousand strikers gave the distinguished visitor a rousing welcome at the meeting sponsored that day by the Labor Church in Victoria Park. Woodsworth told the strikers that their action had worldwide significance, and that workers must protect their own interests and gain their ends by banding together. He said that while this was not a strike for the One Big Union, he himself favoured the OBU. Canadian business, he insisted, must realize that workers were now determined to recover for themselves the wealth from natural resources that properly belonged to them.

Woodsworth had neither the lyrical eloquence of Dixon nor the flamboyance of Ivens nor the dogged, plain-spoken appeal of Russell; his style was pure intellectual conviction, sincerely and straightforwardly delivered. He had played no part at all in the preparation for this general strike, and despite his theoretical approval of the action, with his inherent instinct for order he had reservations about its advisability and the likelihood of its succeeding. Nevertheless, he was dismayed by the hostility in the city, fomented as it was by government officials and by the press, and in the crisis his sympathy was with the workers and his loyalty absolute. The right man in the right place at the right time, he was co-opted to the Central Strike Committee and undertook his assigned responsibilities with his customary diligence.

Indefatigably, he addressed audience after audience, at the Labor

Church, in union halls, and in Victoria Park, pleading always for reason and moderation, and pointing to the moral culpability of society as a whole. The general public, he argued in the *Western Labor News*, blames the strikers: "why not blame the employers whose arrogant determination has provoked the strike?" And further, he continued, with characteristic rationality, "Why not, rather . . . attempt to discover and remove the causes that have produced the strike and will produce, if not removed, further and more disastrous strikes?"

Taking over as the editor of the *Strike Bulletin* after the arrest of Ivens, he ensured the continuation of the vital information sheet, until his own time ran out. On the Monday evening, June 23, after Bloody Saturday, he was stopped on the street, arrested, taken to the city jail, and charged with seditious libel.

At Gibson's Landing, the news from Winnipeg threw the Woodsworth family into turmoil, although Lucy and the older children had been well aware that James's principles would take him into danger. Even five-year-old Brucie knew why his father had been put in jail, and Grace, now almost sixteen, moved immediately to protect him. All about the house were her father's books and papers on economics and on socialism, any of which might be considered evidence to back up the charge of seditious libel, and she was terrified that the Mounted Police would come and search. With a friend, she recalled many years later, she slipped out of school and ran home.

> We took the old tin bread box and lined it with oilcloth. Into it we put every book which, in our judgment, could be used to bolster up a charge. We took the ones on socialism, those on war and peace, a few containing vigorous sermons, even some with red covers — if their content were controversial. Then, in the mid-afternoon quiet, we stole away to the woods with our burden . . . careful to break no twig or leave other traces of our passing. Under a great fallen log we buried our bread box, covering it with the moss and dead leaves we had displaced. . . .

There the awful menace lay concealed, until Woodsworth returned home months later, and his daughter led him proudly to the hiding place.

273

Lucy herself, despite her anxiety, remained unshakeable in her support of her husband and his cause. "I really believe," she wrote to her sister-in-law Mary, "that James could do no other than he has done without compromising the truth." Firmly she acquiesced in his values and accepted the consequences of his principles:

With James, I have ceased entirely to wish for luxury, ease, comfort or advantage for us, yes, or for our children, while countless thousands never do and never will, under the present system, get a chance for ordinary, decent living. You see, since James has been a longshoreman, I have seen that those who work with him can never get enough money to clothe and nourish their children, and to provide for dentistry, surgery, high school or university education, music, travel or indeed the delights of a few hours every day of carefree leisure. We like all those things intensely. . . . We have thought that remedial measures would bring in the day [of reform]. Now we have lost faith entirely in these, and have come to believe intensely that when people realize it, the competitive system will be replaced by the co-operative.

If there is a trace of wistfulness here for the small amenities her family would never know, Lucy would never allow herself to admit deprivation or regret.

As for James himself, his incarceration on Rupert Avenue, and later his five days in the provincial jail on Vaughan Street, evoked no grief or shame, but rather a heightened sense of mission, and perhaps even of martyrdom. In his papers is an evocation of his first night behind bars:

My cell was furnished with a washdish, a lavatory seat and a bed (iron frame covered with a sort of linoleum). I prepared to try to sleep, no pillow, not a stich of covering. Try it on the bare floor! I thought of that poem of Govenetti's in which he sits on the same bench with drunkards and prostitutes, and thanks God that it is not polluted by any priestly smell! If the world is divided into the sinning and the sinned against, I fancy that the jail people will come into the latter class and I must take my place with them.

274

At the rally outside the city limits, on the Sunday after all the strike leaders were released on bail, Woodsworth addressed the crowd defiantly celebrating their heroes, and in a letter to Lucy he described the spirit of the people, the "sense of brotherhood," the "yearning for a better order," the Presbyterian elder who prayed "that God would bring repentance to the profiteers."

With the other indicted strike leaders that summer and fall, Woodsworth undertook a speaking tour for the Strikers' Defence Committee, travelling as far east as Montreal and as far west as Victoria. He spoke at forty public meetings and at countless smaller gatherings, and gave repeated interviews.

He also found time to ask, "What next?" in a series of five articles in July and August for the *Western Labor News*, amplifying the social philosophy that was to remain at the bedrock of his belief. As a proponent of the non-Marxist left, he espoused universal public health services, such as medical and hospital care, with social insurance covering accident, sickness, and old age. He advocated unemployment insurance, and public ownership of certain industries, such as transportation, communication, and mines and natural resources; all credit would be a public utility, and, of course, all natural resources would belong to the commonwealth. On the other hand, he was not against commercial enterprise. Family farms and small commercial enterprises, he proposed, would remain in private hands, but great wealth should be subject to the deep taxation of income and inheritance. And finally, paramount to Woodsworth's philosophy was his firm belief that women must take their place in society not as dependents or inferiors but as equals, so that a better relationship could be achieved, based on mutuality and love.

The following spring he travelled west on another strenuous speaking tour on behalf of the now imprisoned labour leaders. On the way he did some work for the OBU, meeting with some of the organizers, and in the little mining town of Bienfait, Saskatchewan, he had a brush with the provincial police and the Mounties, who were bent on preventing the union men from speaking to the workers. The experience left him with a lifelong abhorrence of company towns — "a dictatorship over people's lives," he called them.

For her part, Lucy had written to James on December 28, expecting that after Russell's conviction James, too, would be convicted:

I do think it highly necessary that you should fight to the last gasp just to try to let people see how far we are from freedom. I only wish I could be there to hear you. Never mind if you don't come off with flying colors. It is something to take your stand upon plain, simple truth and stand or fall by it alone. So be of good courage.

James Woodsworth was never brought to trial, nor were the charges against him ever formally withdrawn. Prominent in the slate of offences compiled against him were two passages from the Old Testament, from Isaiah, that he had cited to dramatize his arguments. "Woe unto them that decree unrighteous decrees," the ancient prophet had thundered, "that widows may be their prey and that they may rob the fatherless." Even more to be condemned as revolutionary, it appeared, was Isaiah's visionary plea for an equitable society:

And they shall build houses and inhabit them, and they shall plant vineyards, and eat the fruit of them. They shall not build and another inhabit; they shall not plant and another eat; for as the days of a tree are the days of my people, and mine shall long enjoy the work of their hands.

If his mother had not taught him his Bible verses, Woodsworth commented wryly, he would never have got into trouble.

In September 1920 he returned once again to British Columbia. The family had moved from Gibson's Landing to Vancouver, where they bought a house — "the only house my parents ever owned," Grace remarked — and James Woodsworth made his first attempt at electoral office. In the provincial elections that fall, he ran for the Federated Labor Party, together with Tom Richardson, a one-time labour member of the British House of Commons, and W. R. Trotter, a member of the Typographical Union. On a straightforward socialist platform, each polled about seventy-five hundred votes, but all three were defeated.

Woodsworth spent the winter of 1920–21 doing educational work for the labour movement in B.C.

Once again the problem of earning a living loomed large. In the spring of 1921 he accepted a position as secretary of William Ivens's Labor Church, at fifty dollars per week, and returned to Winnipeg. He taught classes in industrial history and economics, and on Sundays conducted large public forums.

But his appetite had been whetted by his run for office in Vancouver, and the political route seemed to him the best way to bring about a change in society. In the federal election of 1921 James Woodsworth ran in Winnipeg North Centre as the candidate of the new Independent Labor Party of Manitoba. His role in the strike had greatly enhanced his popularity, and with the backing of a capable group headed by Dixon, Ivens, and Tipping, and with support from labour as well as from a sizable number of middle class voters, James Woodsworth won his seat in the House of Commons.

The new MP was jubilant. On election night a wildly enthusiastic crowd hoisted their candidate up on a dray and paraded him in triumph down Portage Avenue, stopping for speeches and still more speeches to delirious supporters. "You see," James wrote to Lucy in Vancouver that night, "the bakers and bread drivers and street-car men — all seem to regard it as something of a personal victory, and it is a victory for the people." Lucy replied, "So you have been successful and in the very scene of your supposed disgrace two-and-a-half years ago! This is indeed a strange world."

Negotiating Labour's Social Agenda

Woodsworth's first reactions to the Ottawa scene were paradoxical, a clue to the complexity of his character. Traditionally, the opening of Parliament was marked by a grand, formal governor-general's reception for members and other dignitaries and their ladies, evening dress required. Lacking the necessary finery, many of the farm members in the Progressive Party declined the invitation, scornfully pointing out the disgrace of this extravagant entertainment when thousands of Canadians lived in dire poverty. Woodsworth attended, explaining rather lamely that he "happened to have the equipment, purchased in the days when I was young and foolish, or at least younger and more foolish," and that he wanted to see the show. Inherently patrician by background and by nature, he had consciously chosen a diminished lifestyle, but the elegant ball retained its attraction. Mingling with the sleek and successful businessmen and the officers in their military regalia, observing "the diamonds and silks and bare backs of overfed society women," he denounced the system "that gives to the few the places of power, and consigns the many to unrelieved drudgery and impotent longings."

Six days after the House opened, Woodsworth made his maiden speech, challenging his peers with a radically new conception of the role of parliamentary responsibility:

> I submit that this Government exists to provide for the needs of the people, and when it comes to a choice between profits and property rights on one hand, and human welfare on the other, there should be no hesitation whatever in saying that we are going to place the welfare considerations first, and let property rights and financial interests fare as best they may.

Canada's rich natural resources, he said, now the monopoly of a few individuals and corporations, must be used to benefit its citizens. It was government's duty to provide employment for the labour force, and unemployment insurance must be a prime consideration.

Now more than ever Woodsworth saw high finance as the super-monopoly that controlled all other monopolies in the country, and through these webs exerted a stranglehold on the lives of the people. When the Bank Act was debated in 1923, he read off a list of the industrial interests held by the directors of banks: textiles, breweries, implements, transportation, food, real estate, and more; and the implications of Woodsworth's facts and figures silenced the House. Tirelessly, he pressed for the fundamental changes he perceived as the basis for social change: public ownership of the country's natural resources, transportation, communication, and finance and banking — and the constitutional independence from Britain that would make such reforms possible.

Convinced that the BNA Act was a major obstacle to progress because it enshrined the status quo, he began to urge the patriation of the Canadian constitution from its British repository, a measure he would not live to see fulfilled. Canada, he said, "has attained constitutional unity before she has developed a national ideal." His early sentimental attachment to the British heritage now faded, he believed that Canada possessed a unique opportunity to achieve its own special, humanitarian destiny, in the face of major difficulties: the vast expanse of the land itself, the divided authority between Ottawa and the provinces, the overwhelming influence of its neighbour to the south. A barrage of criticism and ridicule met the Labor member's proposal, and Woodsworth withdrew his motion on the constitution.

The neophyte parliamentarian also manifested a talent for the political process. In the new administration Mackenzie King's Liberals had replaced the wartime union government, with the Tories as the opposition. Seated with Woodsworth was his Labor colleague from Calgary East, William Irvine, and there was also a bloc of sixty-five Progressives, an association of dissident Liberals and representatives of farm groups in western Canada, Ontario, and New Brunswick. The two labourites were invited to join the Progressive caucus, but they chose to remain separate, their interests, they held, not identical to those of the farmers. As William Irvine quipped, "Mr. Woodsworth is the leader of our group, and I am the group." Within a short time, however, Woodsworth attracted other Progressives, including Ontario's Agnes Macphail, the first woman member of Canada's parliament. Voting with the two Labor MPs and recognizing Woodsworth as their leader, the informal association became as known the "Ginger Group" of the Commons, eloquent, knowledgeable advocates of specific measures for social reform.

Winnipeg Centre, now called North Centre, returned James Woodsworth to Ottawa with an emphatic majority in the October 1925 election, and he settled his family back in Winnipeg, first at 76 Chestnut Street and then at 60 Maryland Street.

Nationwide, the tally for the Liberals in the new House of Commons was just short of disastrous: only 99 seats, to the Conservatives' 116; and King himself, having gone down to defeat in his own riding, was forced to direct the affairs of his party from outside the Commons chamber, while he negotiated for a safe seat. William Irvine had been defeated, but Woodsworth was joined in the Commons by A. A. Heaps, for Winnipeg North. There were several Independents, and twenty-four seats were held by Progressives, only some of them likely to vote with the Liberals.

King assessed his situation, calculated that with Labor and the Ginger Group he would have a tentative edge, and elected to form the new government. In this extreme instance of minority government the two Independent Labor Party members rather unexpectedly held the balance of power, and they developed their advantage into a technique that would serve them well at this time and in the future.

As early as 1919 the Liberal Party at its national convention had approved a resolution in favour of a program of social legislation, including unemployment insurance, medical insurance, old age and widow's pensions, but with the cautious qualification, "in so far as may be practicable, having regard to Canada's financial position." The one concrete proposal out of this far-reaching endorsement, the old age pension scheme, had been recommended by a 1924 parliamentary committee, but had stalled in the House over the division of responsibility between Ottawa and the provinces: Quebec vetoed the scheme, always on guard against any encroachment on provincial rights.

Now, as the Liberals struggled to hold their position in the precariously balanced Commons, Woodsworth and Heaps made their move. They addressed a courteous letter to Mr. King, with copies to the leader of the Opposition, Mr. Meighen, and the leader of the Progressives, Mr. Forke, making an offer with an implied warning: the two labourites and the Ginger Group would vote with whichever party was willing to implement the long-delayed pension scheme. If the Liberals did not comply, the government would be brought down.

The wily Mr. King was not yet ready to commit himself. The member from Winnipeg North Centre had amply demonstrated his legislative skills, and he was immensely popular with much of the restive Canadian labour movement; a cabinet position might make Mr. Woodsworth an ally rather than an adversary. Charles A. Bowman, a confidant of Mackenzie King's and then the editor of the *Ottawa*

Citizen, conveyed an invitation to the two Labor members to attend a private dinner at Laurier House, the prime minister's elegant residence, and the possibility of a mutually beneficial appointment was broached.

King had not, however, sufficiently calculated the strength of principle in the labour leader. As Bowman confirmed in a subsequent letter to Grace MacInnis, Woodsworth turned down the labour portfolio, saying that there were members of the cabinet who would never agree to the measures he advocated. For all his desire for cooperation within the social organism, Woodsworth would not accept office under a politician who served the interests of the industrial elite, and whose sincerity he doubted.

Further negotiations with the Liberal leader followed behind the scenes, while rumours flew and the Conservative opposition pushed noisily to unseat its shaky opponents. Matters were brought to a head on January 28, 1926, when an Independent member challenged the government to clarify its intentions. Still without a seat in the House pending a by-election, Mackenzie King responded by letter, with as unequivocal a commitment as that cautious politician ever permitted himself to make: the government would indeed "introduce at this session Legislation with respect to Old Age Pensions." As for the additional items that Labor had urged at their meetings, King's roundabout phrasing came only slightly short of an absolute promise. "Having since taken up the proposed amendments with the Ministers concerned," he wrote, "I feel I am in position to assure you that legislation on these matters will also be included in the course of the present session."

In turn, Woodsworth indicated that the Labor members would support the Liberals, a sufficient number of Progressives fell into line, and the session proceeded, cantankerously. The government presented a pension bill, with Abe Heaps prominent in its preparation and in the debate; it was passed and sent to the Senate for approval.

Often described by his detractors as an impractical visionary, Woodsworth had succeeded in matching Mackenzie King at his own game, striking a deal with his ideological opponent without sacrificing his ideals. The strategy, he recognized, was effective and necessary:

We believe in opportunism and compromise in securing practical reforms, but never when they involve the abandonment of the hope of attaining the ultimate goal, or the sacrifice of vital principles. Without losing sight of our ultimate object, we believe in taking advantage of every opportunity to better our conditions. In this way we attain a stronger position from which to carry on the fight.

Successes and Failures

By early summer the government's time had run out. Determined to stop the Liberals in their tracks, the Conservatives had exploded a bombshell in February, evidence of widespread corruption in the customs department. An investigative committee was appointed, and confrontation was postponed, barely, again with the help of Heaps and Woodsworth. In June the investigating committee brought down its report, confirming the allegations of scandal: a roaring underworld trade in illegal liquor was going on across the border to the thirsty, Prohibition-bound United States, while Canadian customs officials were paid off and looked the other way.

Characteristically, the highly ethical Woodsworth was outraged by his country's complicity in this sordid tale of rum-running, gang warfare, and human depravity, and denounced the corruption roundly in the Commons. Here was an instance, however, when ethical principles collided with practical considerations. As Woodsworth's seatmate Abe Heaps shrewdly understood, a Liberal defeat would replace King, who promised reforms in exchange for cooperation, with Meighen, no friend of working people, who as the interior minister in 1919 had ordered the suppression of the general strike. Woodsworth tried to temporize, transparently proposing a further investigation. He was hooted down, and a non-confidence motion put to the House. Against his moral judgment, Woodsworth supported the Liberals, the motion was defeated, and the government once again staved off extinction.

Time after time that June a Liberal motion passed and King stayed in place only because the two Labor members kept their side of the bargain. King managed to put through some relatively minor changes demanded by the labourites in the Immigration Act and the Criminal Code, limiting the right of arbitrary deportation, and sent these on for ratification by the Senate. At the end of the month, choosing to take his chances on a new election and a new mandate, he asked the governor-general, Lord Byng, to dissolve parliament — and initiated a constitutional crisis. Arguably exceeding vice-regal authority as some observers conceived it, Byng rejected the prime minister's recommendation for dissolution and called upon the Conservatives to form the government. Meighen took office on June 28; and on July 1 the Liberals demanded a vote on the legality of the move, charging that the governor-general had unconscionably attempted to override the will of the Canadian people. Heaps and Woodsworth supported King, the Progressive bloc split. By a single vote, Meighen's government was defeated, and the rancorous session finally ended.

In the election that followed, on September 14, 1926, the Liberals were returned to office with a sufficient plurality of 116 seats, and the configuration of the Commons changed. Woodsworth held his own seat without difficulty, while in the neighbouring Winnipeg riding Abe Heaps overwhelmed his opponents, and in Calgary William Irvine regained his seat. Beyond this small gain, however, Labor and the Ginger Group no longer had the upper hand.

Some momentum for change still continued. The Old Age Pension Bill had been rejected by the Senate; now reintroduced in the Commons with some revisions, it passed again, and this time achieved Senate approval, becoming law on March 31, 1927. The plan would be administered by the provinces, the cost shared equally with Ottawa. Not universal in scope, it provided only a monthly pension of twenty dollars to citizens seventy years of age and older, and its worst provision, one that Woodsworth objected to strenuously, was a means test. Nevertheless the achievement paved the way for the social legislation still to follow, and the beginning of Canada's social safety net. "The measure," said Woodsworth, "was far from ideal, but we accepted it as the best at present attainable."

Beginning in 1928 Woodsworth also won headlines in another area of social reform, the divorce process. Most of the provinces had jurisdiction over this matter, but in Ontario and Quebec a divorce could only be obtained through a private member's bill in the House of Commons. A costly procedure, because witnesses had to be brought to Ottawa to testify, it meant, in effect, that only the well-to-do could afford this legal redress for their marital misfortunes. It was also time-consuming, since each petition required three readings in the Commons and three in the Senate, and the backlog in both houses was threatening to divert attention from other legislation.

In April 1928 Mackenzie King tried to slide a file of seventy-five divorce petitions through the House with no more than a cursory reading. Morally offended by the offhand indifference with which the legislators treated their task, Woodsworth gave notice that he would henceforth insist on individual attention to each case. "Woodsworth Objects to Sacred Tie Being Broken in Chunks," read the headline in the *Toronto Telegram* the next day, and the story continued derisively:

The little Winnipeg preacher got up on his hind legs and howled. He declared that this divorce legislation was being treated too lightly by the Commons. Some day he was going to demand the House go into details on one of those bills. Then it might be necessary to ask the lady member to leave, to clear the galleries, and to ask Hansard to cease to function.

The "lady member" was Agnes Macphail, by now a confirmed supporter of Woodsworth's policies. An unexpectedly strong backing for his stand on divorce came from the public, and especially from women's groups, and a great many women crowded the visitors' gallery a few days later when a divorce bill was next debated. Woodsworth demanded to know whether there were children to be considered, whether the women had some means of support, and even whether there was a health factor, whether the man in question had not transmitted a venereal disease to his spouse. (The *Toronto Globe and Mail* reported that Mr. Woodsworth's remarks "bordered on the indelicate," but that none of the "ladies" left the chamber.)

Catholic Quebec was immovable, but beginning in 1928 Woodsworth repeatedly placed on the order papers a "Bill to Provide in the Province of Ontario for the Dissolution and Annulment of

Marriage," and he repeatedly challenged each private bill for divorce, holding up the business of the House while he asked for more information about the case. Finally in 1930, either persuaded by Woodsworth's eloquence or weary of his persistence, the House passed the legislation to allow divorce courts in the province of Ontario, by a satisfactory margin of one hundred to eighty-five.

There were failures, however, in the further effort to implement labour's social and economic agenda. As early as 1923 Woodsworth had unsuccessfully urged national control of Canada's water power, to develop and preserve the resource, and in 1926, once again without success, he introduced a motion urging public ownership not only of water power but also of coal mines and other natural resources. His argument was forthright, to the point: "If power is monopolized, the nation is monopolized." Again in 1928 Heaps and Woodsworth had tried and failed to keep Manitoba's Seven Sisters Falls from privatization. Now in 1929 the Beauharnois Light, Heat and Power Corporation of Quebec applied for permission to develop a hydroelectric power plant on the St. Lawrence River, and King made it clear that he intended the decision to be made by order-in-council, not in the House of Commons. Woodsworth moved that "no disposition of natural resources under the control of the Federal Government shall be effective until ratified by Parliament," but the motion was flatly rejected. On March 8, 1929, an order-in-council turned the great waterway over to the Beauharnois company.

From the outset, there were rumours of trouble in the agreement. The Liberals were defeated in the next election, on July 28, 1930, and replaced in government by R. B. Bennett's Conservatives. Woodsworth himself was returned, as he would be in every election until his death. Bennett immediately convened a parliamentary committee, including Robert Gardiner of the Ginger Group, which found that the Beauharnois Company had contributed $864,000 to both the Liberal and Conservative parties, with the larger share going to the Liberals. The details of this bribery shocked Woodsworth, and confirmed him in the realization that the capitalist system breeds corruption. He rose in the House to denounce not only the individuals involved and the magnitude of the scandal itself but also the economic system that fostered and condoned such wrongdoing. "My closing warning," he said, "is that capitalism is on trial and that democratic institutions are on trial."

The Co-operative Commonwealth Federation

Woodsworth's comprehensive philosophy had now taken shape. A declared socialist, advocating ultimately the nationalization of all means of production, he rejected Marxism, not least because of its emphasis on class warfare and violent revolution. While he was ready himself to make headway toward his goals by politically expedient means, he harboured an abiding suspicion of the Communists, condemning them as cynical opportunists, aiming to replace capitalist tyranny by a Marxist dictatorship. The change in society must come about democratically, he wholly believed, by the combined will of the people as expressed through the legislature. To this end, the cooperation between labour and farmer representatives in the House of Commons now had to reach beyond Parliament; it was necessary to build a national movement in which farmers, workers, small businessmen, and professionals could work together, toward a transformed, humanitarian social order.

At their convention in 1932 the United Farmers of Alberta extended an invitation to all interested progressive groups to join in discussing the establishment in Canada of a cooperative commonwealth, and a conference was slated for the summer. Woodsworth attended the conference to promote the idea among the delegates, and on March 2, 1932, he moved a provocative resolution in the House of Commons:

> that the government should immediately take measures looking to the setting up of a co-operative commonwealth to which all national resources and the socially necessary machinery of production will be used in the interests of the people and not for the benefit of the few.

As was to be expected, the motion received the support of Labor and the Ginger Group only, and failed even to come to a vote, but notice had been posted of a development to come.

On the afternoon of May 26, 1932, a meeting was held in the Ottawa office of William Irvine, attended by Woodsworth, Heaps,

Angus MacInnis, and Agnes Macphail; by Robert Gardiner, the president of the United Farmers of Alberta, and by M. J. Coldwell, the president of the Saskatchewan Labor Party. Also present were several young academics from the universities of Toronto and McGill, who had in January of that year formed the League for Social Reconstruction. Plans were discussed to form a national organization, to be called the Commonwealth Party, with J. S. Woodsworth as acting president. Agnes Macphail was to represent Ontario, M. J. Coldwell would speak for Saskatchewan, and Robert Gardiner for Alberta; and the organization would encompass Manitoba's Independent Labor Party and British Columbia's Socialist Party of Canada.

In a further response to the call of the UFA's 1932 convention, western labour and farmer organizations met in August in the Calgary Labor Temple, to lay the foundation of the new, socialist-oriented political movement. The delegates included men and women, tradespeople and farmers, professionals and unionists, a number of small business operators and a larger number of unemployed — a broad sampling of the ordinary citizens of good will in whom Woodsworth placed his trust. A name was chosen, the Co-operative Commonwealth Federation, with an explanatory addition, "Farmer-Labor-Socialist"; and an eight-point provisional program was adopted:

1. Establishment of a planned economy;
2. Social ownership and control of financial institutions and natural resources;
3. Security of tenure for farmers;
4. Extension of social security legislation;
5. Equality of opportunity, regardless of sex, nationality, or religion;
6. Encouragement of co-operative enterprises as steps to the attainment of the co-operative commonwealth;
7. Socialization of all health services;
8. Suitable work or adequate maintenance to be provided by the federal government for those unemployed.

J. S. Woodsworth was the unanimous choice for president, and Norman F. Priestley, the vice-president of the UFA, was named secretary. The four western provinces were represented: Angus MacInnis for British Columbia, William Irvine for Alberta, George H. Williams for Saskatchewan, John Queen for Manitoba; and Ontario's A. R. Mosher, of the Canadian Brotherhood of Railway Employees, added a powerful union presence.

In preparation for the CCF conference in Regina, slated for July 1933, Woodsworth asked Frank Underhill, president of the League for Social Reconstruction, to help expand the eight-point outline into a comprehensive programme. The resulting Regina Manifesto specifically included such attainable goals as family allowance, health and welfare insurance, and workers' compensation — precisely those concessions to human need that the absolutist radicals on the left dismissed with contempt as serving only to lull the proletariat and delay the inevitable revolution. The manifesto also concluded, however, in a firm statement of the new party's ultimate goal:

> No CCF government will rest content until it has eradicated capitalism, and put into operation the full program of socialized planning which will lead to the establishment in Canada of the co-operative commonwealth.

Transcending entrenched dogma, Woodsworth's address to the delegates at the Regina conference held out the concept of a growing, dynamic new socialism, characteristically Canadian and open to the infinite possibilities of an expanding world:

> Undoubtedly, we should profit by the experience of other nations and other times, but . . . I believe that we in Canada must work out our own salvation in our own way. Socialism has so many variations that we hesitate to use the class name Utopian Socialism, and Christian Socialism, Marxian Socialism and Fabianism, the Latin type, the German type, the Russian type — why not a Canadian type?

A democratic commonwealth of people from all walks of life, joined together in a harmony of cooperation to build its own unique model of the future: the new party mirrored in its name the vision of its founder.

Civil Liberties and the Communists

For James Woodsworth and many others, the depression of the 1930s provided bitter proof that the established economic and social order was indeed bankrupt, leading inevitably to ruin, and unable to afford most people the opportunity to achieve a decent way of life. Relief programs could not cope with the overwhelming numbers of applicants for help, soup kitchens sprang up everywhere, doling out their meagre rations to the desperately hungry, and the common anger and despair found a ready voice in the fulminations of extremist agitators, both of the left and the right.

Woodsworth himself was labelled a "Red" and a "Bolshevik" in the right-wing press across Canada, and in Quebec he was called an outright Communist: he had advocated shocking social changes and had expressed his opposition to long-cherished ideas about flag-waving patriotism. From the extreme left, in this charged atmosphere, Woodsworth's idealistically conceived party came under persistent and concerted attack.

Banned under the War Measures Act and operating quasi-legally as the Workers' Party, the Communists throughout the twenties and into the thirties and after fought a pitched battle against the more moderate parties on the left, in their successive incarnations. Savagely competing for the support of the working classes, they hurled unbridled invective indiscriminately against supporters of the status quo and against advocates of reform. For Woodsworth, now almost venerated in liberal circles, the Communist newspaper cultivated a special venom, branding him a "social fascist" and a "faker," among other epithets. "This slimy pacifist," trumpeted the *Worker*, reporting a Kiwanis Club meeting addressed by Woodsworth, "bleated out a lot of vague (but dangerous) banalities of a general character but when he got down to cases he soon showed his hand. . . . He is either a fool or a liar." Woodsworth read a selection of these comments into Hansard in April 1931.

That year Conservative Prime Minister R. B. Bennett revived the ban on Communists and reactivated Section 98 of the Criminal Code to allow the summary imprisonment of all such "undesirables." Section 98 was one of the pieces of legislation that Woodsworth and Heaps had been trying to have amended, but the provision remained on the statutes. Both Liberal and Conservative administrators argued that the Immigration Department must have the power to remove these people, but Woodsworth countered that although he had no objection to deporting undesirables, they must not be deported without trial. "I am pleading for their rights," he had argued in the House of Commons in 1929,

> not because I love communism or because I am co-operating with communism, but because I have at heart the old teaching of our childhood days, namely that the British citizen has certain inalienable rights, and I believe that those rights should be preserved.

"Freedom of speech," he said, "has always been the proud boast of Great Britain." On a number of occasions the Commons had approved a repeal amendment, only to have the measure vetoed in the Senate — which Woodsworth, like Heaps, sought to abolish.

Before the end of 1932 eight prominent Communists, including their leader Tim Buck, were arrested and imprisoned in the Kingston penitentiary. The Workers' Party then challenged the Regina convention of the CCF to unite with them in mass demonstrations to free the "class prisoners," their comrades. The convention refused. Woodsworth declared that political action through Parliament would be more effective than agitation or a show of force, and proceeded accordingly to raise the issue in the Commons time after time, championing the right of his detractors to speak their minds. Under the provisions of the much-hated Section 98 and the Immigration Act, Woodsworth charged, the government simply deported people whose opinions they did not like, and there were cases where labour organizers were refused admission to Canada, even for brief visits.

True to principle, Woodsworth continued to protest these and other violations of basic civil liberties and minority rights. In 1934 the Liberal government of British Columbia passed legislation to deny the vote to all Doukhobours and their descendants in perpetuity; and Woodsworth denounced the disenfranchisement of any Canadian citizen, introducing an amendment to remove the proposed discrimination from the Franchise Act. Out of a House of 245, the amendment was defeated by a vote of 56 to 27 — leaving 162 members, Woodsworth said bitterly, who were not concerned with civil liberties and had not troubled to vote at all.

In the federal election in the fall of 1935 the Tories were defeated, the Liberals resumed office, and seven CCFers were elected to the House of Commons. J. S. Woodsworth, A. A. Heaps, and Angus MacInnis were returned, joined by Grant MacNeil and J. S. Taylor of British Columbia, and by two future CCF party leaders, M. J. Coldwell and T. C. Douglas of Saskatchewan. Once again they were supported by Agnes Macphail, who later became a member of the CCF. A small but powerful presence in the country's highest legislature, the new party had now become an acknowledged addition to Canada's two-party system.

With the backing of his colleagues, Woodsworth condemned the discrimination against Asians in British Columbia. Speaking to a resolution introduced in 1936 by Angus MacInnis, he protested the treatment of the Japanese as "a subject race . . . trying to earn a precarious living while excluded from a great many occupations, and with a rankling sense of injustice because they are not granted full rights of British citizenship." Repeatedly, he exposed the activities of fascist and anti-Semitic organizations, becoming the country's outstanding defender of civil liberties.

In Quebec, under Premier Maurice Duplessis, the 1937 so-called Padlock Law permitted the closing of any building used by Communists, and made the dissemination of Communist ideas punishable by imprisonment. Woodsworth's group fought to have the measure declared within the authority of the House of Commons, where this attack on freedom of speech could be blocked. It was not until 1957 that the Supreme Court of Canada declared the Padlock Law unconstitutional, an infringement on federal jurisdiction over criminal law.

The defence of radical endeavours by Woodsworth and his party did nothing to appease the calculated animosity of the Communists toward the moderate left. As the CCF gained in prominence, the Workers'

Party pursued its strategy of attempting to force a "united front" on the party of moderate socialism, with the transparent intention of acquiring domination over the entire left-of-centre movement. The rise of fascism in Europe and the response from homegrown sympathizers alerted the left to an imminent danger to all their ranks, and within the CCF there were many who insisted on a joint effort with the radical Marxists to combat the threat from the rabid right.

Woodsworth resisted the pressure categorically, and under his leadership the CCF national council went so far in 1934 as to suspend the provincial council of the Ontario CCF because its labour section was in favour of collaboration with the Communists. Resolutely he continued to hold up the image of a special destiny for the Canadian people:

> The CCF advocates peaceful and orderly methods. In this we distinguish ourselves sharply from the Communist Party which envisages the new Socialist order as being ushered in by violent upheaval and the establishment of a dictatorship. The decision as to how Capitalism will be overthrown may not lie in our hands . . . [yet] in Canada we believe it is possible to avoid the chaos and bloodshed which in some countries have characterized economic and social revolutions.

The dedicated pacifist had retreated behind a profound trust that his country could somehow be spared a violent confrontation with social evil.

Crisis of Conscience

For the Woodsworth family the thirties brought some well-earned satisfactions. J. S. Woodsworth, the man of peace, at fifty-seven years of age was seconded in August 1931 to work for the League of Nations secretariat. James and Lucy toured Europe for four months, and while James served as observer at the League of Nations assembly, Lucy attended the sessions of the Women's International League for Peace and Freedom. James visited the Soviet Union, and proposed that Canada develop trade relations with the Russians, to the benefit of both countries. Returning home, tireless as ever, he crisscrossed Canada to deliver a total of 212 lectures and addresses in 1932 alone. In the biography of her father, his daughter Grace records the comment of Angus MacInnis: "If J. S. heard of three Eskimos in the Arctic Circle who wanted a meeting, he'd be off to them on the next train!"

These years saw further changes and expansion of the family's activities. In 1932 Grace Woodsworth and Angus MacInnis were married. Angus, who had first been elected to the House of Commons in 1930 as an Independent Labor member for Vancouver South, was to serve under the leadership of his father-in-law until James's death, while Grace became her father's secretary and, for a time, the honourary secretary of the CCF group in the House of Commons. She was to follow her father and her husband into politics, as a British Columbia MLA from 1940 to 1945 and an MP from 1965 to 1974. With the younger children also pursuing their own careers, James and Lucy found time for more travel and relaxation. In 1934 they visited China, Korea, and Japan, and in 1936 they managed nine days at Gibson's Landing.

For the Woodsworths, however, as for families around the globe, normal living was soon to be disrupted. With the outbreak of the Spanish Civil War in 1936, it became clear that the world was about to be thrust once more into the horrors of bloody warfare. Woodsworth's sympathies lay with Spain's elected republican Popular Front government of anarchists, socialists, and communists in their battle with the insurgent Falange, the fascists, but he insisted adamantly that Canada should take a position of complete neutrality and isolation. All that he could offer the republican government was moral support, and in February 1938 he cabled his best wishes on behalf of his party: "May struggle of Spanish people soon end in victory and democracy triumph." Democracy did not triumph. Generalissimo Francisco Franco defeated the republican army early in 1939, and Woodsworth's response was only to demand that the Canadian government pressure France to protect the flood of refugees from Spain.

As Hitler tightened his grip on Germany, hundreds of thousands of German citizens sought refuge elsewhere, and fascist groups across Canada spread the Nazi doctrine of race hatred. Aroused as always by tyranny and violence, Woodsworth spoke out against the purveyors of fascism; and in May 1938, in the company of his colleague, Abe Heaps, he asked the prime minister to appoint a special cabinet subcommittee on the refugee problem.

Passionate humanitarian though he was, however, Woodsworth could not bring himself to differentiate between his ideological foe, capitalism, and the looming threat of Nazism; Adolf Hitler was no worse for him than the capitalist exploiters of London or Paris. Just after Germany seized Sudetenland from Czechoslovakia, he expressed his views in the *Manitoba Commonwealth*:

> Must we not concede that larger empires fear the growing power of Germany? If we get rid of this re-incarnated "Beast of Berlin" would we get rid of the dangers inherent in imperialism? Did the last war settle anything? Does the threatened war offer any hope? Have we not in our sane moments declared that war is an inevitable outcome of our present system of capitalism with its glaring inequities and injustices? Are we to scrap our Socialist beliefs? And for what?

He had been cool to the League of Nations at first but later supported it because he considered it an instrument of peace. An idealistic internationalist, he believed that there must be a global organization leading to a world parliament of nations, and that if such an organization embraced all countries without exclusion it could maintain the balance of peace, by economic sanctions if necessary. In the end he became convinced that the league was a tool of imperialism, used by the major powers to force territorial settlements, and he withdrew his support.

Withal, there were some reservations and perhaps even some inconsistencies in his assessment of other supporters of non-violence. He expressed his admiration for Ghandi, but declared that he could not endorse Ghandi's methods, that Ghandi's campaign of mass civil disobedience would lead to destructive civil strife. He admired the basic tenets of the Doukhobours, and when he broke with his own church he even considered going to live in one of the Doukhobour colonies, but he took a critical view of the protest tactics of their radical wing, the

Sons of Freedom: their women's disrobing, their burning of buildings. These methods, he said, were the pacifism of fanatics. Essentially a man of order, he could not countenance disorderly behaviour.

Increasingly isolated in his stance now, as liberal opinion the world over marshalled behind the need to stop Hitler, he remained resolutely pacifist. As a member of parliament, he was torn between his principles and his responsibilities, but he could only repeat his arguments again and again, and anguish over his moral dilemma:

I believe that among the many causes of war the economic are the most fundamental, especially in modern times. Capitalism, social injustice, imperialistic expansion and war are inseparable. In my judgment war will not end until we destroy capitalism, with its social injustice and imperialism. . . . As an individual I refuse to participate or to assist in war, yet I am a citizen of a country which still relies upon force, and as a public representative I must vote on alternative military policies.

Appalled by the killing fields of World War I, he had defined the personal creed of nonviolence that he retained for the rest of his life. Now, in September 1939, as the inevitable came to pass and Canada followed the mother country into the war against Nazi Germany, Woodsworth spoke to the House of Commons of one last despairing hope:

I have sometimes thought, if civilization goes down in Europe, as it may go down, that in America there may be at least the seeds left from which we can try to start a new civilization along better lines.

Three days after Canada's official declaration of hostilities, on September 10, 1939, the extent of its involvement still not clear, an emergency call brought together the national council of the CCF from every province except Prince Edward Island, augmented by provincial presidents and secretaries. Gathering in a committee room of the Parliament buildings, they sought to decide the party's stand on the conflict.

J. S. Woodsworth chaired the three-day meeting. He appeared strained as he explained the seriousness of the decision they would have to make, and his own opposition to participating in a war of any kind. As the old leader well knew, most of those present had reached the conviction that the fascist and Nazi aggression had to be met head on. A committee of six was appointed to draft a statement of policy for approval by the council. Woodsworth made a final attempt to influence his party's decision, presenting a motion seconded by S. J. Farmer, "that this Council refuse to endorse any measure that will put Canada into the war." The motion was not put to the vote, perhaps to avoid a direct rejection of the party leader, and the committee struggled on to draft an acceptable compromise statement.

In the end, a compromise emerged, approved by a vote of fifteen to seven: a declaration that the CCF favoured Canada's participation in the war, but only to the extent of economic assistance to Britain and her allies. Bound by his principles, Woodsworth could not support it. M. J. Coldwell, then national chairman, conveyed the CCF position to the House of Commons, and when Woodsworth rose to speak, it was as a lone defender of a lost cause, bereft of the party he had created and led. War, he said once again, was the negation of freedom and democracy; it could never be won except by adopting the selfsame tactics for which the enemy was condemned:

> As one who has tried for a good many years to take a stand for the common people, personally I cannot give my consent to anything that will drag us into another war. . . . We laud the courage of those who go to the front; yes, I have boys of my own, and I hope they are not cowards, but if any one of those boys, not from cowardice but really through belief, is willing to take his stand on this matter and, if necessary, to face a concentration camp or a firing squad, I shall be more proud of that boy than if he enlisted for the war.

Grace and Angus MacInnis both supported the war, and in 1942 Howard Woodsworth, the youngest in the family, was to join the Canadian Tank Corps.

Understanding Woodsworth's agonizing crisis of conscience, Prime Minister King paid him a generous tribute:

> There are few men in this Parliament for whom in some particulars I have greater respect than the leader of the Co-operative Commonwealth Federation. I admire him, in my heart, because time and again he has had the courage to say what lay on his conscience, regardless of what the world might think of him. A man of that calibre is an ornament to any Parliament.

A few days later, Woodsworth spoke again in the House, and for the last time. The die was cast, a terrible juggernaut had been set in motion, and the weary leader could only remind his listeners of some universal values that must somehow survive:

> I would hope that through all the restrictions and privations which necessarily must come in a war, the principles of liberty, the principles of free speech and the principles of a free Parliament . . . may be upheld to the very end of the war — however long it may last.

Yet in spite of his stand, Woodsworth's credibility in his constituency held. "Woodsworth's Seat Is Safe," read the headline in the *Winnipeg Tribune*, after the federal election in the late spring of 1940. A loyal following had returned him to the Commons, although his friend and colleague, Abe Heaps, had been defeated. In failing health, out of step with his party, he suffered a stroke and collapsed at a caucus meeting. In July, partly recovered, he was able to join the CCF members of the House at a small dinner party celebrating his sixty-sixth birthday, and then he left with Lucy on the journey home to Winnipeg.

The house at 60 Maryland Street was empty now, no longer thronged with people engaged in lively discussions. When the CCF convention met in the fall of 1940, in Winnipeg, James Woodsworth was absent for the first time, too ill to attend. His right hand paralyzed, he dictated a letter of resignation to Lucy, suggesting that the CCF members of the House might well choose their own leader.

Unanimously, the convention named Woodsworth honourary president, and by the will of his constituency organization he remained the elected member of parliament for Winnipeg North Centre.

When the harsh prairie winter set in, the Woodsworths made the difficult decision to uproot themselves once again. They dismantled the house, distributed among the children the treasured mementoes collected over a lifetime, and left for the milder west coast. Several months of rest seemed to improve James's strength, and in the fall of 1941, with Lucy in attendance, he travelled once again to Ottawa, to take his seat at the opening of Parliament. He could not sustain the effort, and only a few days later the train carried him and his wife back west, across the country he had loved and served, a country now bristling with wartime belligerence.

James Woodsworth died on March 21, 1942, in Vancouver. The family took the urn containing his ashes out to sea on his son Charles's boat, and midway between Jericho Beach and Spanish Banks they scattered his remains, as he had requested, and sank the urn into the deep waters.

The Art of the Possible

Abraham Albert Heaps

The Immigrant North End

Winnipeg's North End began to acquire its definitive polyglot character in the last years of the nineteenth century, when the Canadian government's campaign to attract new settlers to the West brought a flood of immigrants from Europe. Some came from Great Britain, from the Scandinavian countries, and from Germany and Austro-Hungary, and a large number from czarist Russia: Poles, Romanians, White Russians, Ukrainians, drawn by the federal government's promise of free land, and even more by the abiding hope of a brighter future.

For the people in the Slavic hinterland, the drive to escape an intolerable existence at home was especially urgent. There masses of peasants struggled for a livelihood, labouring on land they did not own, in awe of their aristocratic absentee masters but bitterly resentful of the overseers who enforced the rapacious tax demands. The majority of these new arrivals from eastern Europe were unlettered country folk; "sturdy peasants in sheepskin coats," they were called by Clifford Sifton, the minister of the interior in the Laurier government. Others, notably those from Ukraine, came to the new world with some experience of urban society, of labour organization and political activism.

Singled out for particularly harsh treatment under the czarist regime were the Jews. Anomalous outsiders subject to repressive laws, they were restricted to certain provinces within the so-called Pale of Settlement, forbidden to own land, and the frequent targets of their non-Jewish neighbours' fury and frustration. By the turn of the century, a Jewish community was developing in Winnipeg, beginning with the arrival in 1882 of several hundred men, women, and children in flight from eastern Europe. These early settlers were largely tradition-bound, intent on preserving their faith and their familiar customs; their adamant refusal to work on Saturday, for example, proved a recurring source of irritation to employers.

After the abortive Russian Revolution of 1905, however, a far more worldly generation of young Russian Jews arrived in the city, eager to embrace a "modern" lifestyle. With more secular education, on the whole, than the earlier group, some had broken from the confining religion of their parents and declared themselves "free-thinkers." Some were fired by the dream of a return to Zion, a restoration of the scattered Jewish people to full nationhood in the land of their biblical forefathers; and some argued for a Jewish cultural identity within the larger general community. There were socialists among them, born out of the grim battle against czarist tyranny, and even a small group of philosophical anarchists, opposed to any authoritarian limit on individual freedom. By the time Abe Heaps arrived in 1911, the Jewish North End had changed markedly from its unworldly, self-enclosed beginnings. Still self-consciously outside the mainstream, it was becoming an increasingly secular community, with an active labour component.

Most of the diverse new Canadians who poured off the colonist trains in Winnipeg spoke no English, and came with nothing more than their scanty personal possessions and a willingness to work. Some did indeed acquire a few prairie acres, but many remained in Winnipeg, to swell the ranks of the work force that the teeming city demanded. They crowded together with others like themselves in the unkempt streets north of the CPR tracks, a multi-ethnic enclave of many cultures and disparate voices, bringing with them the suspicions and hostilities that prevailed in their native countries. Relations among them were uneasy. Individual neighbours on the same street, speaking different tongues, sometimes developed a cordial friendship, but as a rule the groups kept aloof from each other, and the general population, the "English," regarded all these people with instinctive distrust.

If the late twentieth century has come to regard "racism" as unacceptable, at least in public pronouncements, ethnic animosities were taken for granted in Winnipeg's early history, as elsewhere at the time. In public oratory as in private conversation, racial jokes provided a staple source of hilarity, often quite without conscious malice. The high-minded Fred Dixon, always an ardent champion of human dignity, titillated a Labor Church meeting in 1919 with his tale of the "darky" who wanted to join a fashionable white church but was kindly told to "go home and pray over it":

"Well, sah," replied the coloured man, "Ah prayed an' de good Lawd, he says to me, 'Rastus, Ah wouldn't bodder mah haid about dat no mo'. Ah've been trying to get into dat chu'ch mah-se'f fo' de las' twenty yeahs, and Ah done had no luck.'"

In this class-conscious put-down of the rich and fashionable, "Rastus" and his quaint lingo merely added to the fun, and neither Dixon nor his audience were likely aware of the offense to human dignity.

So endemic were racial stereotypes, so acceptable to the common understanding, that the victims themselves sometimes played that self-abasing card. Reporting on the Majestic Theatre meeting in the hectic preliminary to the 1919 strike, the *Western Labor News* drew attention to the laughter that greeted Sam Blumenberg's ingratiating comment on his own unmistakable origin, that "the map of Palestine was written on his face, and on his nose was the mount of Zion," a reference to the instantly recognizable popular caricature of the hook-nosed Jew.

Ethnic tensions continued for many years to colour labour relations in general and North End politics in particular. Allied with the

Winnipeg branch of the Social Democratic Party of Canada, which increasingly attracted a broad range of moderate socialists, separate ethnic groups hived off, none very comfortable with the "English" who dominated the party as a whole, or with each other. The numerous Ukrainian socialists came together to form their own Ukrainian Social Democratic Federation, with *Robochy Narod* as their newspaper; a Russian "language local" pursued its parallel but separate activities; a Jewish local coalesced, and a Lithuanian local and a Finnish local; an "English" local, considerably smaller, continued to function.

More disruptively still, when World War I broke out, a patriotic suspicion of the "foreigner" appeared as ingrained among working people as among their well-established employers. For all labour's proclaimed vision of the universal brotherhood of man, a demand for severe restrictions on immigration was to surface regularly in the union movement, particularly during times of economic stress.

Leeds to Winnipeg

Abraham A. Heaps came to this complex society from England. His parents had fled oppression earlier, emigrating from Russian Poland, and Abe was born in Leeds, on December 24, 1885. At ease in the language of his adopted country and fully accustomed to life and work in an industrial city, he was something of an anomaly in Winnipeg's foreign-born enclave. Yiddish was the mother tongue in the tenement flats on Nile Street in Leeds, where the family lived in the city's Jewish ghetto of Chappel Town, but out on the streets and at the Gower Street Board School the children played and learned in English. In Winnipeg's North End medley of accents, Heaps's Yorkshire diction would sound very "English."

Young Abe was bright, and had done well enough at school to be offered a scholarship for further study, but like most working-class boys he ended his formal education after seven years. At thirteen, he became an upholsterer's apprentice in Leeds, contributing his two shillings six-pence a week to the family's support. He qualified and obtained his papers, tried for a year or two to operate his own upholstery shop, and then joined the work force at Shilansky's Furniture Store in Water Lane.

Abe's grandmother ran a boarding house, where three young actresses stayed when they were performing in Leeds. The Morris sisters were members of a touring theatrical company that played the provinces, and occasionally even London; their family had lived in England for four generations. The landlady's slight, rather shy grandson was already planning to immigrate to Canada, but he courted Bessie Morris with eager persistence, promising to send for her as soon as he had made a start in the new world. She agreed to wait.

A two-week Atlantic crossing, in steerage, and a seemingly endless train ride halfway across an empty continent brought the young uphol-sterer to Winnipeg. The CPR needed skilled tradesmen and Abe Heaps found work almost at once in the railway coach shops. He joined Local 49 of the Upholsterers' Union and, always an insatiable reader, spent his free time attending one after another of the popular self-edu-cation classes offered by the city's labour groups. Within the year he was elected as his union's representative to the Trades and Labor Council and had secured for himself the post of official statistician. Union activity brought him into contact with other British-born unionists, including two who became his lifelong friends, the street-railwaymen's John Blumberg and the barrel-makers' John Queen. The three had in common the experience of the well-established British labour movement, and all three became members of the city's Social Democratic Party.

Two years after he left England, Abe Heaps had found his niche in the labour movement of his new home. He sent for Bessie Morris, trav-elling to Montreal to meet her. They were married there in 1913, and he brought her back to a small frame house on Burrows Avenue in Winnipeg's North End. By that time an energetic Jewish community was well-established, with synagogues, social and mutual aid organiza-tions, after-school classes for children, a Yiddish weekly newspaper, and a spirited Yiddish amateur theatre. Bessie Heaps neither spoke nor understood Yiddish, however, and her fluent English set her apart from most of her "greenhorn" neighbours. There was nothing for her among the enthusiastic Yiddish thespians, and with Abe away a great deal she spent many hours at the piano in her living room, playing by ear the songs she remembered from home. Abe was in the middle of a contest for political office when their first son, David, was born on May 31, 1916.

Into the Civic Arena

Well-spoken and knowledgeable, Abe Heaps was quickly recognized as a promising candidate for public office. His first foray into civic politics ended in defeat. In 1915 he entered the race for alderman in Ward 3 North, a mainly Anglo-Saxon working-class area, and lost by 554 votes to W. T. Edgecomb. Undeterred, he tried again in the next year's aldermanic contest, as the standard-bearer for the Social Democratic Party in Ward 5, the heart of the Jewish North End.

In the bid for the "Jewish" vote, two other Jewish candidates were pitted against Heaps, Alter Skaleter for the Conservatives and Maurice Triller for the Liberals, and a furious battle erupted, as bitter as only a family quarrel can be. The adversaries trumpeted the merits of their own policies and disparaged their opponents' competence and honesty in one public meeting after another, as noisy crowds jammed the district's popular Jewish meeting halls: the Hebrew Sick Benefit Hall on Selkirk Avenue, or the Talmud Torah School auditorium at the corner of Charles Street and Flora Avenue. The voters were inundated with leaflets, and there were charges and countercharges in the columns of the *Israelite Press*.

Canada was in the throes of the conscription controversy, and national registration of manpower had been instituted in the spring of 1916. Like virtually all his labourite colleagues, Heaps was a pacifist on principle, and he made his opposition to the war a central issue in his campaign. He was to continue after the election speaking out against the European involvement: on December 23, at a North End mass meeting, A. A. Heaps, John Queen, and George Armstrong, among others, joined the labour chorus to denounce "conscription of manpower without conscription of wealth," and were held up to scorn in the popular press. This stand against World War I would be raised against Abe Heaps years later, during World War II.

Heaps lost the 1916 election to Alter Skaleter by fifty-nine votes. The margin was narrow, and suspicions began to fly when a breakdown of the tally revealed that Skaleter's heaviest vote had come from a poll where the clerk was his own son. Not to be duped, Heaps set about investigating the voters' list, and found the evidence he needed: among those who had "voted" in that one particular poll were some individuals no longer living in the province, and others long dead and buried — all told, at least as many as the margin by which Skaleter had won. Triumphantly Heaps charged his opponent with election fraud and handed his findings over to the civic authorities. An official investigation confirmed the charge, and Skaleter resigned in the spring of 1917. A by-election was held, and Heaps defeated a Communist candidate, John Nowacki, by 314 votes.

John Queen had been elected alderman as well, and the two Social Democrats found themselves fighting the labour battle on city council. Winnipeg's civic employees had been arguing for an adequate wage increase since the early days of the war, without success, and unrest was high. In 1917 the women employed by the Manitoba Government Telephones staged a three-hour strike to call attention to their plight: working fifty-two hours a week, they made as little as five dollars, and never more than seven. The Trades and Labor Council petitioned the provincial government to enact a minimum wage of ten dollars a week for women, and Heaps raised the issue in city council, supported by Queen. In the face of growing labour pressure, the Norris government accepted the figure demanded by the Trades and Labor Council, and introduced Manitoba's first minimum wage legislation. A bare beginning, it applied only to female workers in Winnipeg and Brandon and did not cover employees of municipal, religious, charitable, or political institutions.

By April 1918 the civic office workers, water works employees, and electrical workers had all been engaged in months of fruitless negotiations for a raise, with Heaps and Queen urgently pleading their cause. But the municipal authorities insisted that restraint was required in wartime, and would agree to grant only a temporary bonus, with the rather nebulous promise to negotiate a new wage scale once the war was over. Thoroughly exasperated, ninety employees of the light and power department walked out on May 2, and when the city council continued to turn down the union demands, sympathy strikes of other civic departments were called, on May 7. For their part the telephone operators had already joined the city yardmen in strike action, on May 6, and the CPR machinists had announced their willingness to answer a general strike call.

Throwing their support behind the strikers, Heaps and Queen

addressed a mass meeting on May 9. Heaps, soft-spoken and eminently reasonable, appealed to the Trades and Labor Council to consider a cooling-off period of sixty days, or even thirty, time to work out a careful solution. In city council the next day he pleaded with his fellow aldermen to consider the interests of their constituents and not those of the Board of Trade, and he proposed the appointment of a committee to meet with the strikers. Reluctantly, council agreed, naming Mayor C. F. Gray, A. A. Heaps, and three other aldermen, and appointing Arthur Puttee as chair.

The Puttee committee quickly drafted an agreement that outlined provisions acceptable to the strikers: union recognition, improved wage schedules, and in the case of any further dispute, a sixty-day arbitration period before either a strike or a lockout was permitted. Presented with the committee's report, however, on May 11, city council added an amendment that nullified the concession of union recognition and collective bargaining that the committee had recommended. Over the furious opposition of Heaps, Queen, and other aldermen, both labour and non-labour, a narrow majority voted to require civic employees to sign a no-strike pledge, to submit all demands to arbitration, and to accept the settlement of their current strike by a board of conciliation.

The strikers refused to surrender the fundamental bargaining tool of all unionists, the right to strike. Other unions responded, and a city-wide general strike seemed imminent. Winnipeg's alarmed business establishment marshalled a Committee of One Hundred, a precursor of the following year's Committee of One Thousand, to restore civic order and force an agreement, and Ottawa sent Senator Gideon Robertson to intercede.

At Heaps's urging, a settlement was finally achieved, restoring most of the provisions of the Puttee report, although with reservations. The city administration approved the reinstatement without penalty of all its striking employees, but it insisted that firemen must refrain from striking except in the most extreme circumstances, and that the brigade's officers must be excluded from union membership. Heaps warned that limitations such as these would surely lead to more dissension.

Crisis and Coercion

In the months that followed, sporadic strikes and lockouts erupted continuously in Winnipeg, and the rivalry within the union movement itself added to the unrest, as Bob Russell's One Big Union began to take shape. John Queen contributed spectacularly to the verbal excitement at the Walker Theatre meeting in December, but Abe Heaps was not there, an absence that would later prove of some importance.

Time and again, as labour turmoil escalated toward the explosion in May, Alderman Heaps struggled to convince the city fathers that a comprehensive solution to the postwar dislocations in the economy could only be found in consultation with both labour and business. He was still pleading with the Trades and Labor Council for cooperation and moderation when municipal employees in Winnipeg, Assiniboia, and St. Boniface voted overwhelmingly to join Russell's machinists in a walkout, only too ready to demonstrate their own grievances as well as their sympathy with their fellow unionists, and the unprecedented call for a general strike went out.

By the evening of May 15 the city council had a major crisis on its hands. City services abruptly ceased. Telephone and telegraph operators left their stations, the postal service closed down, streetcar operators took their cars to the barns and went home. The city police and the fire department, the waterworks department and the electricians were prepared to walk. The Citizens' Committee of One Thousand swung into operation, aggressively bent on taking control into its own hands.

At the request of the Central Strike Committee, the police stayed on duty. The firefighters offered to keep an emergency crew in service. There were hasty discussions with the waterworks employees, who agreed to maintain enough pressure in the system to provide households with a minimal supply. Countercharges erupted: that some households above the ground floor could not get water, that hospitals were endangered. The supply of bread and milk became an issue, and when the delivery wagons once again appeared on the streets, bearing the placard, "By Special Permission of the Strike Committee," there was another chorus of alarm that these Bolsheviks were indeed proposing to usurp the legitimate government.

As days wore on without a settlement, bringing real hardship especially to the lowest-paid among the strikers, the Strike Committee set up an assistance program, with Heaps in charge. Already a member of the city council committee responsible for overseeing the civic welfare program, Heaps was desperately overworked, dealing with over two hundred cases a day.

City council met continuously, trying to maintain some semblance of authority, but always under pressure from the Citizens' Committee of One Thousand not even to negotiate until the rebellious workers returned to their jobs. Six days after the strike began, on May 21, Senator Robertson, now the Labour minister, arrived once again in the city, with the minister of the Interior, Arthur Meighen, sent by Prime Minister Borden to put a speedy end to the "Bolshevik" disturbance. The two emissaries met in frequent consultation with Premier Norris, with General Ketchen of Military District No. 10, with members of the Citizens' Committee, with groups of employers, but they would not confer with the Strike Committee or with the labour aldermen on the city council.

Vehemently backed by John Queen, Heaps pleaded for reason and flexibility, pointing out that by its adamant stand the Citizens' Committee was blocking a settlement, and thereby endangering civic life. A strike, he told the council, was like a fester on the human body, and force was no remedy. Still steadfast in his belief in orderly change, he warned a full city council and an overflow gallery on May 30 that it was time for the business community to realize that labour must be accepted as an equal partner in the economy.

The Citizens' Committee began publishing its own information sheet, the *Winnipeg Citizen*, and invited the public to pick up copies at the various fire halls; the labour aldermen pushed through a motion forbidding the use of the fire stations for that purpose. Again at the insistence of the Citizens' Committee, the city administrators turned down the firefighters' offer of stand-by services; and then, concerned about the danger of fire, council banned the use of fireworks for the duration of the strike.

Council meetings were anything but orderly, with the labour aldermen almost invariably pitted against the rest. A *Tribune* reporter was to testify later that on at least one occasion an angry disagreement degenerated into a near fist fight, and Heaps and Queen were shoved into the adjoining vault and held there until the session was over. Although the Strike Committee did not encourage mass demonstrations, crowds assembled regularly in front of the city hall, and Alderman Heaps frequently left the council chamber to encourage, reassure, and calm the citizenry, speaking from the imposing stairway at the building's entrance.

On June 5 discussions with the restive police force finally collapsed, and over the anguished protests of Alderman Heaps and other dismayed members of council, Mayor Gray was authorized to hire special replacements. The normally conciliatory Heaps demanded that the police commissioner be removed for conducting the negotiations without informing council. Mayor Gray threatened not to allow any more strikes of civic employees. Over the opposition of Heaps and Queen, on June 9, council approved a motion to require all civic employees to sign a no-strike pledge, and threatened to dismiss all strikers out of hand. John Queen demanded that the mayor resign. The city was in an uproar.

By June 17, more than a month after the strike began, and with nothing to show for the effort, the unprecedented labour action had begun to falter, and the authorities made their move. When the police sped through the sleeping city with their arrest warrants and pounded on Abe Heaps's door, they found to their surprise both Heaps and John Queen. Both were hustled away in waiting cars, first to the North End police station and then to the penitentiary. The Heaps home was ransacked in search of subversive material. The following week, the Central Strike Committee capitulated.

"Aliens and Radicals in Our Midst"

For the new Canadians in Alderman Heaps's North End ward something far more was at stake in the defeat of the general strike than union recognition and higher wages. These "strangers within our gates," as Woodsworth called them, benignly unconscious of his own racist condescension, had become the targets of intense suspicion at the outbreak of the war, and four years of increasing social turmoil had exacerbated the problem into an overpowering xenophobia. At the end of the war the problems of returned men trying to get back into the work force brought the additional charge that "foreigners" were taking jobs away from "real" Canadians. In January 1919 a band of unemployed veterans destroyed Sam Blumenberg's dry cleaning shop on Portage Avenue, after forcing his wife to kiss the flag, and then rampaged down the Jewish shopping district of Selkirk Avenue in the North End: they were venting their frustrations in the time-honoured fashion on people they perceived as "other," as parasites and traitors.

Inevitably the "Red Scare" that swept the continent after the 1917 Russian Revolution targeted the stranger. Fanned by the avid sensationalism of the press, "Bolsheviks" were feared everywhere, among German immigrants because they were the kin of the newly defeated enemy, among all those seemingly indistinguishable East Europeans, and most particularly among the Jews, always seen as troublesome, always disliked; and Winnipeg's North End, of course, visibly housed a dangerous concentration of such "enemies of the realm." As the *Winnipeg Telegram* informed its readers, with a grand indifference to mere fact or even probability, "not only are Bolshevik leaders Jewish, but Polish, Lithuanian and Galician Jews have German blood in their veins."

For much of the Canadian public, constituted authority and private citizen alike, the unprecedented Winnipeg General Strike was the final proof of revolution in the making. Unsuspecting Canadian workers and the "ignorant, foreign-born masses," said the rumour mills, had been duped into participating in this subversion. On May 19 an advertisement in the *Manitoba Free Press* by the Committee of One Thousand offered an explanation that some readers were only too ready to believe: "aliens and radicals in our midst" had instigated this revolt masquerading as a strike; and the solution appeared a few days later in the same paper:

They have to go, bag and baggage, back to the happy homes in Central Europe which vomited them forth a decade ago. Their place must be taken by a clean, decent Canadian workman, preferably by men who fought for this country.

For most of Abe Heaps's constituents, the suspicion and hostility of the host community was a daily challenge, and the fear of deportation considerably more than a distant threat.

Ottawa responded to the turmoil in Winnipeg by hastily enacting legislation that permitted the deportation without trial of all foreign-born agitators. The police sweep that began in the early hours of June 17 gathered up five "foreign-born" in addition to the prominent strike leaders who were charged and later tried. Three were Jewish: Moses Almazov, Michael Charitinoff, and Samuel Blumenberg; two were Ukrainian: Mike Verenchuck and Oscar Schoppelrei. All had acquired some minor notoriety in their communities as radicals, but none had taken any part in the planning or direction of the strike. Radical ethnic groups in the North End were raided, their newspapers closed, and their officers interrogated.

When bail was arranged for Heaps and his colleagues, three days after their initial imprisonment at Stony Mountain, no such provision was made for the "foreign-born." They remained in jail, the injustice of their treatment the subject of much righteous indignation on the part of labour supporters. Eventually, as the much-publicized trials of Russell *et al.* got underway, the public lost interest in the "other" alleged conspirators, and they disappeared into the margins of history. In the end only one, Schoppelrei, was deported — to the United States, his actual birthplace — on a technicality relating to his immigration. Blumenberg and Almazov were allowed to leave voluntarily for the States, and the other two dropped out of sight.

In the political career of Abe Heaps, the elected representative of a largely "foreign" North End, the problems of newly arrived Canadians, their rights before the law and their precarious acceptance by the ruling majority, would become a central concern, inseparable from his political commitment to a more equitable social order.

For Justice and the Rule of Law

The release of the accused strike leaders had been accompanied by a rather half-hearted injunction to "keep the peace," refraining from all further agitation, but Heaps made his intention clear, speaking for all. "We will not keep silent while awaiting trial," he declared, "because of the campaign of vilification conducted against me and the others," and he participated in the drive to raise money for the defence fund.

In Toronto on July 8, he informed the *Star* that the group's purpose was to seek help for the "aliens" still being held under the Immigration Act, and a week later six thousand people came to Queen's Park to hear him make that appeal. In Montreal's Parc Maisonneuve he told several thousand listeners that the authorities contemplated appointing a special immigration commissioner to hear the case, and he warned that such an attempt to bypass statutory proceedings endangered the inviolable principles of democracy. Law and order, he said, were imperiled when the Winnipeg City Council replaced the police force with bands of special constables, many of them brought in from as far away as Montreal. Whisky, he said, was especially provided to these thugs, and "I saw men and boys playing dice and drinking whisky on the main streets." In Glace Bay, Nova Scotia, the mayor declared a civic holiday "in honour of the visit by Alderman Heaps."

Back home again, addressing a protest meeting at Victoria Park, Heaps drew a chuckle with a trace of his characteristic understated wit. "It is unusual," he said, "for a Winnipeg alderman to have been inside three different jails in one year, but I feel privileged to have had the opportunity."

The Crown singled out Bob Russell to be tried first, with a fairly obvious purpose: proof of Russell's guilt would lead, by association, to the conviction of the others indicted, even those like Queen and Heaps who fought against the OBU leader for his splintering of the union movement. Heaps spent day after day in the courtroom, assiduously following the proceedings and taking careful notes of the points of law involved. In the November city elections, with their cases still pending, both Heaps and Queen were reelected once again to city council, and the end of January brought them and their co-defendants before Judge Metcalfe.

Initially, Heaps and Queen engaged A. R. Bonnar as their attorney, but from the outset both undertook to examine witnesses themselves and question the multifarious evidence brought against them. As the trial proceeded, first Bonnar and then his replacement, W. H. Trueman, succumbed to the strain and withdrew from the case, leaving them to conduct their own defence.

In his characteristic fashion, Heaps's meticulous dissection of the confusion of facts and inferences presented by the Crown proved greatly effective. Coolly, reasonably, he demonstrated the illogicality and the implausibility of the attempt to involve him in matters in which he had no part or which he actively opposed. He had attended neither the Walker Theatre meeting nor its sequel at the Majestic Theatre; he was no friend of the OBU — which was, however, he pointed out, a legitimate labour organization; and if as a member of the Trades and Labor Council he had done his best to help the strikers, he had been so busy with the constant meetings of city council, with as many as seven committee meetings a day, and with the work of the relief committee, that he could not possibly have found time to engage in the conspiratorial scheming that was supposed to have lurked behind the strike. As his co-defendant Bill Pritchard later remembered, "he went around to see that people had the things they needed"; and at the trial, said Pritchard, "he told a beautiful but pathetic story about how he dealt with the troubles of the women and the children, the aged and the handicapped."

It was the Citizens' Committee, Heaps insisted, that had turned a legitimate labour action into a violent civic disturbance, and Mayor Gray had yielded completely to pressure from that self-appointed agency. Still, when the mayor took the stand, he offered some testimony, perhaps unwillingly, in the defendant's favour. Heaps, he admitted, had indeed been present at all the exhausting sessions of council and its committees, and he had also worked most helpfully to settle the civic workers' strike of 1918. And it was true, said the mayor, that the labour alderman had repeatedly warned against the use of force, pleading that only by getting at the root cause could the problem be solved.

Most striking of all in Abe Heaps's presentation was his repeated insistence on the rule of law. He had prepared for his day in court by studying British and Canadian labour law, and he marshalled his arguments with clarity and skill. During the anxious deliberations of city council after the outbreak of the strike, he told the court, he had reminded his fellow aldermen of the inviolability of constitutional authority. He had pointed out that the entire city council thought that a sympathetic strike was a proper form of labour action, and he himself had suggested that the tension might be defused if such actions were given legal status. With unwavering belief in the rule of law, he protested the irregularities perpetrated by inept government tactics: after his arrest he had been denied bail by Judge Metcalfe; a British citizen, he had been threatened with deportation; three of the Crown prosecutors, Andrews, Pitblado, and Sweatman, were also active members of the Citizens' Committee of One Thousand, and the official presence in this court of these partisans of a body hostile to the strikers constituted an unacceptable conflict of interest, damaging to the impartiality honoured by British law and to the legality of the entire case.

In all the exhaustive searches that had been conducted, Heaps argued, nothing incriminating him had turned up, no subversive documents in his own home and not even a mention of his name in the mountain of paper the Crown was offering in evidence. Not one of the witnesses had heard him say anything subversive except, perhaps, for denouncing the "slavish pact" that the employers were trying to force on their workers. Sergeant Reames had testified that Mr. Heaps had been seen at the Industrial Bureau: Heaps agreed that he had indeed been there, meeting with Mr. Andrews and the Citizens' Committee in an effort to resolve the strike. Not only was the entire notion of an intended Bolshevik revolution a preposterous fiction, a feverish dream, but together with other genuine trade unionists he had steadfastly fought against Communist influence in the unions. Now to be lumped together with his opponents, to be called the worst of the lot, boggled the mind.

There were no rhetorical fireworks in Heaps's presentation, only the commonsense scrutiny, piece by piece, of some very shaky allegations, and a statement of his own politics of moderation. Rather to his surprise, he found that the spectators in the courtroom responded warmly to his unassuming manner and slightly self-deprecating wit. "He told funny stories in a very serious way — that was Abe Heaps," recalled Pritchard, and Abe played to his newly discovered audience with obvious pleasure. "I don't mind being called a nuisance," he said, deriding the last, all-purpose charge laid against him, "but to be called a common nuisance is one too much."

Two weary months after the group trial had begun, Judge Metcalfe sent the jury off to deliberate their decision, after a six-hour summing up. Hedged round by legal precedents and authoritative judicial comment, his instructions to the twelve good men and true were unmistakable: the accused as a group had indeed committed the misdeeds imputed to them. About Heaps he could not be quite as absolute, although he did his best:

> Heaps was a member of the Trades and Labor Council. The Trades and Labor Council assisted at least, aided at least, abetted at least — and did they also counsel and procure the taking of the strike vote? Why hedge about it? . . . Heaps was a member of the [strikers'] Relief Committee. He was a member of the Strike Committee. He spoke and voted at the city council in favour of keeping the water pressure low, and generally in favour of the attitude of the strike leaders. . . . Like rancid butter, does it not leave a dark taste in your mouth . . . ? He was secretary of the Strike Committee, which tries to disclaim responsibility for everything. . . . Will a man serve one of . . . two masters? And, if so, which did Heaps serve?

There was, the judge conceded, some area of doubt, and the jury would have to decide, after careful consideration.

The jury, on March 29, brought in a verdict of guilty on six of the defendants. It found Abraham A. Heaps not guilty, to the cheers of his supporters in the crowded courtroom and his own enormous relief. Yet there was a sense of loss, also, in the conviction of the others. "I do not feel elated over my acquittal," he told reporters in the jostling crowd waiting outside. "I would rather have been convicted along with the rest."

Released from his long ordeal, he threw himself into the continuing campaign for the release of the convicted prisoners. In Calgary, on April 5, he told an audience of almost fifteen hundred people that the labour martyrs were victims of a monstrous oppression:

> If I have done nothing wrong, these men have not. If they are guilty, I am guilty. If I am innocent, they are innocent. And if they ought to be in jail, I ought to be with them. As they left they said, "We are going down now and are going to do our bit, and we hope you'll do yours."

The position of the Crown, he told his listeners, was untenable. According to Judge Metcalfe, he said, the workers had a right to strike, but it was illegal to exercise that right — it was illegal even to propose a new form of government. For Alderman Heaps, who had served his political apprenticeship in the British labour movement, the proscription was grotesque. As evidence of his guilt, he said, the Crown had brought in the manifesto of the British Labour Party, so that "if Judge Metcalfe is in Great Britain when the Labor Party comes into power, he will probably indict the whole nation!"

City Council to House of Commons

Heaps was reelected in successive years to city council, where his competence in the management of facts and figures made him an invaluable member of the council's finance committee. Appointed head of the Winnipeg Public Utilities Commission in 1923, he proposed a plan for the establishment of a public transportation system, and argued cogently for its contribution to the quality of civic life. He continued as an active member of the Trades and Labor Council, working to repair the ground it had lost in its internal strife with the OBU, and he participated enthusiastically in the founding of the new Independent Labor Party. At the same time, recognized now beyond his own immediate circle as a knowledgeable and articulate authority on labour affairs, he contributed a weekly column to the *Winnipeg Tribune*, making time in an already crowded schedule. His income, always extremely modest, had suffered during the strike and the subsequent trial, and he opened a small insurance office, to help support his growing family. A second son, Leo, was born in July 1923.

Heaps made his first attempt at federal office in October 1923, running against the incumbent in Winnipeg North, E. J. McMurray, the same attorney who had acted as counsel for some of the accused in the strike trials. A prominent Liberal, McMurray had defeated Socialist Bob Russell and Communist Jacob Penner to take the seat in 1921, when a Liberal government replaced Borden's Conservatives, and he was now Mackenzie King's solicitor-general. During his term of office, however, a scandal in a bank with which his law firm enjoyed a large overdraft had damaged his integrity, and he had considered it necessary to tender his resignation and submit to the judgment of the electorate. A by-election was called.

It became apparent immediately that this contest in an ethnic and predominantly Jewish constituency had political significance beyond its immediate boundaries. Montreal's prominent Jewish MP, the Liberal S. W. Jacobs, KC, arrived in the North End expressly to campaign for McMurray, joining the local community's M. J. Finkelstein, also a Liberal and a lawyer. In addition, a special telegram from Mackenzie King extended best wishes to his good friend, Mr. McMurray, and pointedly reminded the Winnipeg North voters that it was in their interest to have their own representative in the cabinet. Rally after rally urged Jewish voters to support McMurray and the Liberals as the party truly sympathetic to the concerns of the Jewish citizens of Canada.

Immigration policy was the central concern in this campaign, not only for Jewish citizens but for almost all the recently arrived "foreigners," whose families and friends, left behind in the ruins of post-war Europe, clamoured for admission to Canada. A post-war order-in-council banned the nationals of former enemy states from admission, including of course the most desperate refugees from the upheaval in Russia. Another required that an applicant come directly from the country of birth; anyone fortunate enough to have escaped to a temporary shelter elsewhere was automatically disqualified. A third order, in 1920, demanded a landing fee of $250 a person, a staggering, impossible sum for a destitute refugee. On most of these counts the kinfolk of most North End residents, Jew and non-Jew alike, were hopelessly excluded.

Even labour was divided on the advisability of offering refuge to fellow human beings who might threaten the livelihood of Canadian workers. Fred Dixon's friend and ally, S. J. Farmer, declared flatly that he was opposed to opening the door to an influx of immigrants until the country's economic situation improved. William Ivens agreed, willing only to make an exception to permit the unification of families. In the Manitoba legislature, on the other hand, John Queen moved a resolution calling for the free entry of all Europeans with relatives in Canada. It was defeated.

Sam Jacobs had pleaded in the House of Commons for the lifting of the inhuman immigration laws, only to have his fellow Liberals proceed to tighten them. Nevertheless he told the Winnipeg North voters that the government in power was still the best hope for a change in policy, and that McMurray, a cabinet minister widely known for his generous sympathy for the underdog, was still the best man to trust with the difficult task. On election day bad weather kept many voters at home, but the Liberals assembled a fleet of automobiles to get their supporters to the polls, the Jewish press reported. McMurray was returned to office, taking 5649 votes to Heaps's 2843.

The voters' confidence in the Liberal government was not rewarded. Although Jacobs pursued the fight in the Commons, he made no headway with his colleagues, nor did McMurray's presence in the cabinet prove effective, and Canadian immigration policy continued as exclusionary as ever. By 1925, when the next general election was called, the North End electorate had become disenchanted with establishment promises.

Heaps was again the unanimous choice of the ILP to contest the seat in Winnipeg North, adjacent to Woodsworth's riding of Winnipeg North Centre, and once more against the Honourable E. J. McMurray. In addition to the immigration question, both Heaps and Woodsworth campaigned on the issues that would form the foundation of their platform for years to come: legislation to advance the cause of labour and safeguard the rights of the common man; old age pensions, health and unemployment insurance, a minimum wage act. They cited the inability of both old-line parties to deal with the country's economic problems, pointing to the shameful treatment of the Nova Scotia coal miners, gunned down because they demanded a living wage for themselves and their starving families. Further they demanded the repeal of the Criminal Code's Section 98, which in effect legalized imprisonment without trial at the discretion of the government in power, abrogating a citizen's fundamental civil rights.

When the votes were tallied, A. A. Heaps had won by a majority of about a thousand. William Irvine had been defeated, however, so that Heaps replaced him beside Woodsworth in the federal House.

A Presence on Parliament Hill

In the House of Commons Heaps's common sense pragmatism meshed well with Woodsworth's high socialist principles. He entered into Ottawa's political chess game with the skill of a veteran, ably seconding Woodsworth's protracted negotiations with Mackenzie King to support the Liberals in return for a measure of social legislation. Telling the tale of King's discreet Laurier House dinner with the two labour MPs, Charles Bowman indicated that he had advised the prime minister, when Woodsworth declined a cabinet portfolio, "Mr. Heaps would be a practical asset to the Government as Minister of Labour." There is, however, no objective confirmation that the offer was actually made to the member for Winnipeg North.

Heaps himself may have helped to draft the old age pension bill that King presented to parliament in March. Supporting the measure, the self-taught statistician placed before the House the results of his study of pension plans in the United Kingdom, in Australia, in New Zealand, arguing persuasively for the benefits to the entire country of a humanitarian provision uniform in all the provinces. In reply to the Conservatives' charge that implementation of such a measure would cost the taxpayers an outrageous twenty-three million dollars, he had statistics to prove the relative economy of the scheme and the efficiency with which it could be administered, and he pointed out that Canadian labour was solidly behind the scheme. (He did not need to add that labour commanded a great many votes.) Over the vociferous objections of the Conservatives, the pension bill was pushed through the House and sent on for ratification by the Senate.

On issue after issue, Heaps provided the clarification of his thorough research. Woodsworth proposed the nationalization of Canada's coal and water resources; in support of public ownership, Heaps eagerly explained the merits of Winnipeg's municipally controlled electrical power system, tabling statistics to show that Winnipeg consumers paid half the rates charged by the privately owned utility in Montreal. In the budget debate he attacked the Conservative notion that high tariffs were necessary as a means to protect Canadian jobs. Business, he said, did not need tariff walls in order to flourish — witness England's booming automotive industry. Bringing figures from Quebec and from as far away as Japan to show that import restrictions often went hand in hand with egregiously inadequate wage scales, he denounced the shameful mistreatment by Canadian industry of its employees: the annual earnings of the average Canadian worker, he informed the House, had risen barely $200 between 1917 and 1923, from $760 to $959, while industrial profits had multiplied. A sound economy, he insisted, required that the interests of working people be assured, by collective bargaining for higher wages and better working conditions.

The two labour members of parliament also had the satisfaction in this session of having the covert dealings of the Conservative government during the general strike brought to light. Peter Heenan, a former Labor member of the Ontario legislature and now a Liberal MP, reported to the House that he had found evidence of extensive military preparations against the strikers. Moreover, following the middle-of-the-night arrests of the leaders, Borden and his cabinet were belatedly uncertain about the legality of the operation, and a flurry of anxious communications had passed between Ottawa and Military District No. 10. Heenan tabled a confidential telegram from Arthur Meighen:

> Notwithstanding any doubts I have as to technical legality of arrests and detention at Stony Mountain I feel that rapid deportation is the best course now that arrests are made and later we can consider ratification.

The Conservatives indisputably had been bent on deporting the troublemakers, knowing that the authorizing legislation had not been ratified, and choosing quite deliberately to proceed.

Glorying in this opportunity to set the record straight, Heaps rose to condemn Meighen and his cabinet, now His Majesty's respected Opposition, for having deliberately forced the confrontation in Winnipeg to violence and bloodshed, and most of all for having violated the very precepts of the constitution they had sworn to uphold. Without the knowledge of the House, he charged, a list of men intended for deportation had been prepared, "because they had certain ideas which are distasteful to the powers that be." A high-handed procedure, he called this, unworthy of a British institution, a betrayal of the very spirit of British law, and certain to fail:

> Worthwhile ideas will continue to live and grow more in favour with the people. Ideas that are not worthwhile will die without any unnecessary action by any public authority. . . . When men are arrested and thrust into jail because they hold certain ideas . . . the authorities who do so are merely strengthening these ideas among the masses of the people in this country. . . . There was never a penitentiary built strong enough to contain within its walls ideas which are worthwhile.

For the "foreigner" from Leeds, the disclosure was a vindication, albeit belatedly, of his faith in the democratic ideal.

In the matter of the customs scandal, his pragmatic advice to stick with the Liberals had prevailed over Woodsworth's moral scruples, but in the convolutions of the political process that followed, the reforms Heaps and Woodsworth had bargained for were defeated, at least temporarily. The Senate turned back the immigration and Criminal Code amendments and declared its absolute condemnation of the pension plan; if this "socialistic" scheme passed, said Quebec Senator C. P. Beaubien, "the obligation of the children to look after their father and mother and grandfather and grandmother goes by the board." Reform would have to wait.

Heaps went back to his riding to campaign once more on the concerns he shared with his constituents: a more humane immigration policy, unemployment insurance and a pension scheme, public ownership of public services; and he specifically advocated the abolition of that bastion of entrenched power, the Senate. In the matter of immigration he could also report a concession, of sorts: for one year Robert Forke, the minister of immigration, would allow free entry to three hundred Jewish refugees each month, limited to persons with relatives in Canada.

Election day, September 15, 1926, saw Abraham A. Heaps returned to office, this time with an enormous majority. His Liberal opponent polled only slightly more than half the number of Heaps's votes, and the Conservative lost his deposit. Heaps rejoined Woodsworth and the reelected William Irvine in the House, but King had won the majority he needed, and the crucial value of the labour votes had disappeared.

Nevertheless the persistent campaign to make some provision for the country's elderly had achieved its results. When the Old Age Pensions Bill reappeared on the agenda of the new House, Heaps once again took the lead in its favour. To the continued objections of the Quebec members, permanently alert to any intrusion on provincial jurisdiction, he marshalled his formidable arsenal of information and logic to demonstrate that a nationwide scheme was essential, and that the larger share of the cost must be borne by the federal government. His arguments prevailed at last. The bill passed the House and the Senate and became the law of the land.

A Friendship and a Chair

For Abe Heaps, these first few years in his country's highest assembly had proved to be something of a revelation. A child of one ghetto and the chosen representative of another, he had discovered that his diligently acquired knowledge put him in the company of the nation's powerful elite, and that his voice was being heard. He believed utterly in the democratic principle, taking the patrician R. B. Bennett to task on one occasion for extolling the significance of wealth in a public figure:

> I do not think that wealth gives or ought to give priority to anyone who holds a responsible position in public life in the Dominion of Canada. I think he is doing an injustice to a good many members of this House who are not so fortunate as to be possessed with any wealth at all.

Just as genuinely, however, he admired the able men he encountered in the seat of government, including Bennett himself. Essentially diffident and without the adversarial truculence of Russell or Pritchard, he had won the friendship of some of his political opponents as well as his colleagues, and he savoured his new relationships enormously.

Most interesting was the rapport he developed with the prime minister. For King and later for R. B. Bennett, the Winnipeg North MP provided a window into the thinking of a working-class electorate remote from their own experience; and the reserved Mr. King in particular seems to have been disarmed by Heaps's open interest in other human beings. Perhaps also the reverence with which the man from the North End regarded the work of government may have stirred a hidden idealism in the battle-hardened Liberal politician.

The quality of the relationship between these two is illustrated by an episode retold by a number of historians. With the other privileges of office, King had come into possession of an old chair that had belonged to his illustrious Liberal predecessor, Sir Wilfrid Laurier. Its frame scratched and its upholstery tattered and sagging, it stood in the prime minister's chambers, a relic of the past amid the swirl of government business. During the 1927 session Heaps called on Mr. King and noticed the curious object. King explained its origin and Heaps, fascinated, offered his own services to restore the chair to its former elegance.

He took the chair away, worked on it in his free time, and returned it meticulously repaired and gleaming in black leather and polished wood. King was obviously touched, and his obligatory note of thanks to "My Dear Heaps" brimmed over with affection for a kindred spirit:

It was a very kind thought on your part to offer to do this work as a labour of love. I feel that few, if any, tributes to the memory of Sir Wilfrid could be finer than this one you have thus paid. The work done is that of an artist, and the thought which inspired it that of a true patriot and poet.

In June, after the session ended, King sent another "My Dear Heaps" letter. He had enjoyed their talks during the session, said the prime minister, and he appreciated Heaps's "helpful co-operation," and the Laurier chair would remain one "with which hereafter we shall each share an association. . . ."

Part of the Commons tradition that unites political adversaries, the chair even acquired an unlikely rival claimant. Curiously, Grace MacInnis's biography of her father, James Woodsworth, offers a description of that labour patriarch seated in "the big leather chair that had once belonged to Sir Wilfrid Laurier and that A.A. Heaps, upholsterer by trade, had recovered for his Labour colleague." A showpiece now, the chair was re-upholstered in 1942, and once more in 1982. Now consigned to an East Block museum room, it has passed into history, with the men whose lives it touched.

Unemployment Insurance: Stalemate

If Mackenzie King was moved by the gift from the Winnipeg North member, his political judgment remained as circumspect as ever. Opening the new session in February 1928, the speech from the throne ranged over a wide area of policies, but did not acknowledge the need for new social legislation.

Much help was needed as the twenties ended to deal with the problems of an economy lurching to a halt, and the provinces, unable to cope with the mounting costs, turned again and again to Ottawa for funds. Only too aware of the human suffering that statistical reports obscured, the member from Winnipeg North pleaded for more federal involvement and a more generous financial contribution. As social democrats understood, however, in a profit-based and unregulated economy unemployment is perennial, and must be addressed by a coherent national system of unemployment insurance. Merely stop-gap measures would not do.

The campaign of the labourites to provide this comprehensive coverage was repeatedly rebuffed by the argument that these matters were under the jurisdiction of the provinces and the municipalities; as in the pension debate, Quebec in particular was stringently protective of its autonomy. King appointed a parliamentary committee to investigate the issue, and although by House rules Heaps had no official standing on this committee, in an extraordinary variation of procedure he was invited to participate.

The Canadian Manufacturers' Association argued that unemployment in Canada was "natural," and that industry could not be saddled with insurance costs. Heaps argued that on an average wage of only eighteen dollars a week a Canadian worker could not afford an insurance deduction, and he cited the examples of England and Switzerland, both with efficient labour insurance programs of long standing. Both the Trades and Labor Congress and its rival, the new All-Canadian Congress of Labor, indicated their support of a national system, and Quebec's Catholic Federation of Labor approved. The commission's findings, tabled in the House in June 1928, moved the adoption of a national unemployment insurance program, with compulsory contributions by the employee, the employer, and the federal government. Still Mackenzie King delayed, maintaining that government regarded the report's motion as "simply an expression of opinion . . . and not as one embodying any obligations to the Federal administration."

By the next parliamentary session the problems of the unemployed and of the poor and hungry across the country had become even more critical. Another committee was appointed, with the question of health insurance now included. Still the argument was raised that provincial approval would present a grave obstacle. The government was not inclined to proceed, and the measure was allowed to disappear silently from the order papers.

Once again Heaps presented to the Commons his carefully documented case for unemployment and health insurance. Once again Ernest Lapointe, as cabinet minister from Quebec, repeated the same objection, that such matters were under provincial, not federal, jurisdiction. In the House Heaps exploded in frustration:

> If pigs or cattle in a province of this Dominion became sick, our Department of Agriculture would send expert after expert and spend federal money freely in order to find out the cause of the illness. . . , but when human beings are suffering, we are told that it is not a federal question. I should like to know how long a human being has not been considered an equal to a cow or a pig. . . .

Unwilling or unable to deal effectively with the growing crisis, the Liberals had lost parliamentary support. In March 1930, the Conservatives defeated the government on a motion of non-confidence, the House was dissolved, and an election was called.

The 1930 Election

Heaps went home to Winnipeg North to shoulder the now familiar task of organizing and raising funds for an election fight. Voting habits in the constituency had by now hardened into more or less predictable patterns. The old-line parties, Conservatives and Liberals, retained a limited following among the respectable establishment community leaders, but supporters of the left dominated, in all their variety of convictions and disagreements. In the years following the Russian Revolution, the Communist party had established a beachhead there, its noisy agitation attracting a degree of attention out of proportion to its small numbers. Sworn enemies of mere socialism, the Communists fought the moderates of the Independent Labor Party at every turn.

Ethnicity further complicated ideology. Socialists voted for Socialists, Communists for Communists, Conservatives and Liberals for their own, but there was also a "Ukrainian vote," a "German vote," a "Jewish vote," as the various North Enders still clustered together in mutually exclusive societies. For Abe Heaps there was a reliable turnout at the polls of trade unionists and committed ILP supporters across the ethnic spectrum, but his electoral base came from the Jewish community, the "Jewish vote." Language still divided much of the North End electorate, and potential voters were specifically targeted from the platforms of their own schools and meeting halls, or through the ethnic press.

In the rough-and-tumble politics of the era, it was not uncommon for the well-funded Liberals or Conservatives to buy a foreign-language newspaper for the duration of a campaign, drive home their election message, and then sell the paper back to the owner for a nominal sum. Capitalizing on the inexperience of newcomers, ethnic ward bosses might trade favours for votes, or ensure the nomination of a particular politician by stacking a party meeting with new members conveniently supplied with paid-up memberships. Whether out of greater integrity or because they had less money than their establishment opponents, left-wing parties refrained from such practices.

The campaign in 1930 emerged as a particularly ugly effort by all Heaps's opponents to break the sitting member's hold on the riding.

Certain that they could not win, the local Liberals did not enter a candidate but threw their pool of votes behind the Conservative, Dr. M. R. Blake, reasoning that the Communists would then draw off enough labour votes to defeat Heaps. From Toronto the Communists parachuted in as their candidate Leslie Morris, the editor of their weekly, the *Canadian Tribune*, and directed a stream of vitriolic abuse at the socialist enemy. By his record in Ottawa, they sneered, Abe Heaps had proved himself "a servile lackey of the capitalists," among other epithets.

In the district's weekly newspaper, the *North-Ender*, a nasty editorial attacked Heaps's character and his record, implying that he had used his parliamentary position to line his own pockets. Heaps served the paper with a suit for libel and forced the publisher to print a retraction and apology. Undeterred, the Conservatives repeated the *North-Ender's* charge, and further branded Heaps as a "slacker" for his pacifism during World War I. And behind the official platforms and the statements designed for publication, ethnic antagonism simmered, anti-Semitic hostility ran deep.

Nevertheless, despite all these concerted efforts to unseat him, Heaps had once again kept the confidence of his electoral base, both by his prominent advocacy of labour interests and by his consistent and well-reported efforts to liberalize the country's immigration laws. Election day, July 28, 1930, saw him returned to office, having won nearly two thousand votes more than the Conservative and over four thousand more than the Communist. Nationally, the Liberals lost, the Tories swept into office, and R. B. Bennett became prime minister of Canada.

Principles and Practice: the Mature Legislator

As a long-standing member of parliament, Abe Heaps found he needed to devote much of his time to routine constituency business, and to the individual concerns of his constituents. A druggist applied for a sub-post office; the Post Office Department inquired officially whether the local MP was aware of any objection to the appointment. A university student asked to be recommended for any civil service position, in

Ottawa or back home. Elderly residents, without proof of age, needed help in qualifying for the old age pension. A relief recipient, in these desperate years, pleaded to be given a job — any job. On a purely commercial matter, the Pardiss Co-operative Society of Tel Aviv, Palestine, asked the member from Winnipeg North to obtain preferential treatment for the entry into Canada of its oranges and grapefruit; and after protracted negotiations, the requisite dispensation was arranged.

Most difficult of all were the cases where special pleading was required to override the letter of the law. A rabbi from a distinguished rabbinical lineage in Europe had been granted permission to immigrate to Canada only if he agreed to leave his disabled daughter behind. Now, living in Winnipeg's North End, he begged Mr. Heaps for help in having the exclusion lifted, so that the young woman might join her family: her affliction was incorrectly diagnosed by the European doctor, he argued. Mr. Heaps took steps to explain the matter in the appropriate quarters; his discreet intercession finally succeeded, and the rabbi's disciples gladly provided for the new member of his household.

Serving as member of Parliament required that Abe Heaps maintain two homes, one in Ottawa and one in Winnipeg. Travel between the two cities, by train, took three days, and Heaps was away from home for many months of the year. By the 1930s the family had moved from Burrows Avenue to somewhat better quarters on Polson Avenue, but Bessie Heaps found the Winnipeg winters difficult, and for years the two boys and their mother spent the winter months in California. Both boys attended school in Santa Monica, and when David graduated from high school, he enrolled at the University of Southern California.

At the same time, despite his limited salary, Abe Heaps cultivated a deep interest of his own in fine art. Self-taught, he began a modest collection, filling the walls of his office and of his room in the house where he boarded. On one occasion he presented his friend Mr. King with a small English landscape in oil, and received a lyrically sentimental response from the old campaigner. In 1932 he donated twenty paintings to the new Winnipeg Art Gallery, then located in the Auditorium, the present Provincial Archives.

Now a seasoned politician, Abe Heaps had become an impressive spokesman for left-of-centre causes, able to move with some assurance among a variety of people: statesmen, union activists, newspaper reporters, and his own ethnic constituents. The nemesis of any member of the House who rose to speak without adequate preparation, he had something of a photographic memory, an almost infallible capacity to produce the appropriate information on demand.

He was "sharp, quick on the uptake," commented Don Aiken, a one-time editor of the *Winnipeg Tribune*, recalling Heaps as a visitor to his parents' home in the 1930s. "He had this narrow face and a mop of black hair. You got the impression there were two things going on: one was a recording device, and two was a responding device. He would respond immediately, pointedly, precisely — I admired him tremendously for that ability." Heaps's ability also impressed Prime Minister Bennett, and in the give-and-take of parliamentary debate the imperious Tory showed himself remarkably willing to listen to comment and criticism from his labour opponent. Bennett found Heaps's analysis incisive and his proposed solutions useful, if generally at odds with his own.

Apart from his consistent pursuit of social legislation, Heaps took both the Liberal and the Conservative governments to task on several issues that would have a familiar ring for future Canadians. Canada's independence had been recognized at the last imperial conference, he pointed out in 1928, but in the matter of the new Soviet Republic the Liberals had once again automatically concurred with the mother country's foreign policy, breaking off diplomatic relations. Further, still on the constitutional question, Heaps objected strenuously to the undemocratic powers bestowed upon the Canadian Senate, and long before the second chamber's function had become a matter of public discussion he demanded that it be abolished.

Even more immediate was his concern about American economic domination. The rich resources of the Canadian northland, he argued, were increasingly being exploited by American capital, and there was no union protection for workers in the mushrooming company towns where American industrialists were allowed to build their economic empires. "We have bartered away many of [our] resources for a mere pittance," he exclaimed, and, in the familiar biblical phrase, the Canadian people, he said, must not become "hewers of wood and drawers of water" for United States capital. American imperialism, he warned, had shown its face in Mexico and Nicaragua.

When Woodsworth brought together his Co-operative Commonwealth Federation in 1932, in an effort to combine farm and urban labour under one political banner, the platform of the new party included measures that both Heaps and Woodsworth had ardently championed, but Heaps was uneasy about the alignment of interests. No longer the theoretical socialist of his immigrant years, and ready to make pragmatic compromises to gain his ends, he had become uncomfortable with Woodsworth's almost messianic zeal to unite all humanity in a quest for a moral society. First and foremost a trade unionist, he sensed that the farm elements now being recruited to the new party were essentially conservative, their concerns at odds with labour's needs. Moreover, he rather distrusted the intellectuals whom Woodsworth had attracted; for all his success on the national scene he remained diffident about his own lack of formal education. His son Leo recalled that as an MP his father was frequently asked to handle legal matters, but when he inquired about the possibility of entering the University of Manitoba Law School, he was turned down because he had only a grade-school certificate. Nevertheless, unwilling to disrupt the unity of Canada's federal labour party in its new and extended formation, Heaps threw his lot in with the CCF, joining its leadership corps.

The Thirties

In the disarray of the thirties, and paradoxically under a Tory administration, labour's social agenda began to make further headway. When the 1930 session opened Heaps urged the administration to come to the aid of the municipalities, many of them bankrupt and unable to help the desperate men and women on their relief rolls. Bennett concurred, and some twenty million dollars was allocated for the purpose.

By the second year of the Conservative administration, the appalling conditions of the Great Depression had put the country's economic order on trial, and the desperate need for some basic social legislation could no longer be ignored. On April 29, 1931, Heaps moved and

Woodsworth seconded a resolution once more calling on the government to consider "the immediate establishment of a federal system of insurance against unemployment, sickness and invalidity." This time the prime minister himself endorsed the Labor proposal, although he amended the motion to make the federal role "contributory," limiting federal responsibility. There the matter remained for the time being, studied and restudied by parliamentary committees.

Beyond these limited and stopgap measures, however, the Tories clung to their basic remedy of high tariffs, proposing to build a protective wall around Canadian industry to shore up its faltering viability. Methodical as always, Heaps brought facts and figures to show that the imposition of tariffs did not improve business but merely contributed to the already serious problem of overproduction. It was monstrous, he said, that goods of all sorts lay idle in warehouses, while people across the country were denied the necessities of life:

the more bread we have the more breadlines there are. The more clothes we manufacture, the more people there are without clothes. The more homes we build, the more there are looking for shelter. The more wealth we produce, the greater is the poverty.

Take the opposite approach to the one proposed by the government, Heaps insisted, bringing a formidable array of statistics to prove his point. Reduce the work week, improve wages and working conditions: only in this way could people afford to buy the goods that were now clogging the country's warehouses, only in this way could a stagnant country come to life again.

Homeless men began to appear in increasing numbers on residential streets, knocking furtively at doors to beg for a meal or a place to bed down. Armies of the unemployed gathered and demonstrated in the streets of Canadian cities. Waiting at a soup kitchen in Winnipeg, in 1933, a tattered collection of jobless men rose up in fury at the system that had reduced them to beggary, and occupied the building, threatening to burn it down. Alderman John Blumberg, a friend of Abe Heaps and John Queen, was acting mayor at the time, and he stood his ground against the demands of the police and the military that he read the Riot Act, to quell the insurrection by force. Instead, he ordered the food depot to serve an augmented meal, and he forced Military District No. 10 to make available a sufficient number of cots and blankets, to provide some rest for the homeless indigents. There was no riot, and the prevention of bloodshed remained for Blumberg one of his proudest achievements.

By contrast, Bennett's answer to joblessness and the radical protests it spawned was an authoritarian rigour, smacking of penal dictatorship. Work camps were established for unemployed single men, and legal measures were once again invoked against "aliens" and "agitators." Two sections of the Immigration Act, still in effect, permitted the summary deportation of any "undesirable" person of foreign birth, and Section 98 of the Criminal Code defined as seditious any organization that advocated a forcible change in government, and made membership in such an organization or the distribution of its literature subject to a stiff prison sentence. These measures were now put into operation to solve an economic problem as well as a political one.

Since joblessness in a naturalized citizen could well be construed as undesirability, the Conservative government began to deport people simply because they were on relief. During the five years of the Tory administration several thousand people were forcibly removed under this edict. It was dangerous to be both "foreign-born" and impoverished, and many a destitute family suffered in secret, terrified of the consequences if they applied for public assistance. Eight Communist leaders were jailed, and some eighty people were deported as Communists, most of them of Central European or East European origin. Heaps had, of course, been the constant target of some scathing Marxist invective in the campaign of the extremists to destroy all social-democratic organizations, but he joined Woodsworth vigorously in demanding their release and the restoration of their rights.

The country found some relief from its troubles in a wave of black humour directed against its ineffective prime minister. Bennett appealed to all good Canadians to bring down an "iron heel" against this menace — and earned for himself, in left-of-centre circles at least, the mocking title of "Iron Heel Bennett." Car owners who could no longer afford to buy gasoline hitched their vehicles to horses, and called their absurd contraptions "Bennett buggies."

It was not until 1935, with the Bennett regime nearing the end of its mandate, that an Unemployment and Social Insurance bill came before the House of Commons. Far short of what Heaps, Woodsworth, and their labour colleagues considered adequate, it made no provision for that part of the work force most in need of protection, casual labourers, and it attempted to skirt the question of federal/provincial powers by identifying Ottawa's participation as a "grant." The bill was approved in the Commons, with Heaps continuing to object that more must be provided, but years elapsed before it actually became law. Predictably, both the Supreme Court of Canada and the Privy Council of Great Britain struck down the measure as an infringement of provincial rights: a constitutional amendment was required, giving Ottawa the necessary powers. Canada would only acquire a system of national unemployment insurance in 1941, after the political career of Abe Heaps had come to an end.

As for the reduction of the hours of work, labour's equally fundamental demand for reform, one of the last acts of the Bennett government, in 1935, was to propose a forty-eight-hour work week. Again the measure failed to satisfy the exacting analysis of Abe Heaps, who brought his figures to show that only by requiring a thirty-hour week could unemployment be solved and a balanced economy achieved. Such an enormous shift proved unthinkable, of course, and the measure passed as presented, establishing at least the principle of federal control. With his mandate running out, Bennett made an overt bid for public support by calling for additional social reforms, for health insurance and for the progressive taxation that Heaps and his colleagues had been demanding, but five years of the "iron heel" had served only to inflame the anger of the dispossessed further.

In the spring of 1935, a ragged band of the unemployed began to form in the West, and to move across the country toward the capital, joined by hundreds more as they went, determined to make Ottawa do something about their plight. Walking, riding the rails, hitching rides with any willing motorist, finding a meal or a bed wherever they could, harried by police, their single-minded persistence seemed to confirm

Bennett's fear of a radical insurrection. In Parliament, Heaps and Woodsworth repeatedly warned against the use of force, but when the "On-to-Ottawa March" reached Regina, ironically on July 1, Dominion Day, it was confronted by a combined contingent of federal and local police. In the fracas, several people were hurt and one man was killed.

The Tory regime was ending in disarray. In the fall of 1935, Canadians once again went to the polls.

A Rescue Denied

Across the Atlantic Hitler had consolidated his power and initiated his policy of extirpating the non-Aryan taint from the German *Herrenvolk*. The Nazi campaign against its own "undesirables," and especially the Jews, had begun. As the first scanty reports of persecution filtered out of Germany, the world's statesmen continued to maintain, on the surface at least, business as usual, but in Abe Heaps's largely Jewish constituency, as in Jewish communities the world over, there was an immediate, horrified recognition of the portents. Since the twenties Canadian policy had admitted barely a trickle of would-be immigrants, and now the need to rescue hundreds of thousands of human beings from certain death had become imperative. The immigration issue dominated the North End's 1935 election campaign, as Heaps's record and his inability to achieve any significant results were attacked by both his opponents.

The Communists pitted their leader, Tim Buck, against their hated social-democratic rival, and deployed their usual arsenal of campaign invective. The Conservatives, this time, refrained from fielding a candidate, clearing the way for the Liberal, Colonel C. S. Booth, a lawyer and a hero of World War I, who returned to the argument that had defeated Abe Heaps in his first run for federal office: a Liberal representative, because he belonged to the party in power, would best represent the interests of this constituency. In the event, however, the loyalty of Heaps's North End held. Heaps regained his seat with a majority of four thousand votes over his Liberal opponent, and five thousand over the Communist. Mackenzie King's Liberals swept Bennett and the

Conservatives out of office, winning 181 seats to the Tories' eighty-nine; and for the CCF, Tommy Douglas and M. J. Coldwell came onto the national stage.

In the new Liberal parliament, Section 98 was finally repealed, ending its criminalization of radical opinion, and there were some additional improvements in social legislation, but no movement at all on immigration. Heaps had been pleading for the admission to Canada of the homeless and the dispossessed since 1926, when Mackenzie King needed help to sustain his shaky government, and he had continued his efforts year after year, alone or with others, without appreciable results. In 1933, when a national plebiscite proclaimed Adolf Hitler chancellor of Germany, he had made a trip to Europe and Palestine to see for himself what was happening, and on his return home he had sounded the alarm from public platforms and from the floor of the House of Commons. In a Europe threatened by Hitler's National Socialists, he told a mass meeting in Winnipeg, there was no future for the Jews, and he offered a thoughtful analysis of the possibilities of settlement in Palestine.

In 1935, two Jewish Liberals also won federal seats, S. W. Jacobs of Montreal and Samuel Factor of Toronto, and they held out the hope that their party's return to power would prove a breakthrough. All three held conversations with Liberal cabinet minister Thomas Crerar, whose Mines and Resources portfolio included immigration, but without results. As frantic refugees from Hitler's Germany clamoured for asylum in Canada, they were met with a chilling silence from the Canadian government and its Department of Immigration.

Hitler's drive to engulf Europe began to take shape, Britain went through the motions of negotiating terms with the *führer*, the United States declared its neutrality; and as the inevitable world conflict approached, Mackenzie King temporized, equivocal and noncommittal, pleading the delicacy of Canada's position in view of United States neutrality. And behind the scenes the build-up of military hardware accelerated, in a race against time. The possibility of war entrenched James Woodsworth more firmly than ever in his highly principled opposition to violence of any sort, and under his leadership the CCF repeatedly denounced the arms race and the war psychology it created.

Heaps called Mackenzie King to account, in an eloquent speech in February 1937, demanding that Canada come forward to call for a world conference on peace:

> Should we not . . . make our contribution toward creating an atmosphere of peace among the nations of the world? Should we not try to do something to banish the fear of war from our midst, and strive toward creating that much desired peace sentiment?

In hindsight, in the light of the inexorable advance of the Nazi drive, his appeal now seems as well-motivated and as unrealistic as the ethical ideals of his party leader.

There was still time, however, more than two years before the actual outbreak of hostilities, for public diversions and for family pleasures. King George VI was crowned in May 1937, and as a parliamentarian of long standing A. A. Heaps received his official invitation to attend the festivities, with a special commemorative medal accorded to Mrs. Heaps. The family travelled overseas, joined by David Heaps from France where he was studying at the Sorbonne, to revisit Leeds where Abe's sisters still lived, and to enjoy the cosmopolitan excitement of ceremonial London. Still thoroughly British at heart, Abe was obviously pleased by the royal pomp and circumstance, but as a good socialist he insisted on making a gesture of class protest: he refused to wear the formal top hat and tails, but appeared instead in a dark business suit, the festive attire of his working-class peers.

The fall of that year saw the beginning of a difficult change in the Heaps family's existence. Bessie Heaps, long ailing, was diagnosed with an increasingly debilitating malignancy, and Abe brought her and their younger son, Leo, then in high school, to live with him in a third-floor walk-up apartment in downtown Ottawa. Bessie endured a year of suffering, dying at the age of forty-nine, on November 12, 1938, with her husband and her two sons at her bedside. Mackenzie King stood among the mourners at the funeral and accompanied the family to the Jewish cemetery in Ottawa; and none too well himself, he trudged up the three flights of stairs to pay his condolence call on his friend.

Heaps had been named CCF party whip, but his efforts to marshall support for a humanitarian response to the refugee problem continued to prove futile. In 1938 Woodsworth joined Jacobs, Factor, and Heaps to present a cabinet committee with a modest scheme to admit five thousand Jewish refugees over a period of five years. All costs would be borne by the Jewish community, and the newcomers would not be settled in Quebec, where they were clearly not welcome. The proposal was rejected.

In May of that year an interview with the prime minister himself succeeded in obtaining a promise from King to set up a cabinet subcommittee to consider the issue. A committee was named, but there were no practical results. Mackenzie King's chief advisor on immigration, Frederick Charles Blair, was convinced that Canada was being "flooded with Jewish people," that "none is too many," and King himself now believed that the admission of Jewish refugees into Canada would destroy the country's ethnic balance. These views were shared by most of the members of the Liberal cabinet. Undaunted, Heaps continued to introduce motion after unsuccessful motion to have Canadian admission policies ameliorated.

Hitler marched into Austria in March 1938, and several thousand more Jews became refugees. In July, President Franklin Roosevelt brought together the representatives of more than thirty nations at Evian, France, in a conference on refugees; but warned by Blair and by O. D. Skelton, the under-secretary for external affairs, that attending the conference would place Canada under obligation to admit numbers of Jews, King responded that Canada would be willing to participate in negotiations, but would "reserve fully the decision as to the future policy on the subject of immigration."

By November, after his wife's funeral, Heaps at last had to admit betrayal by his friend the prime minister, and he showed his distress in a letter protesting King's adamant stance. At least eight members of the cabinet, the letter noted, were willing to allow a "reasonable" number of refugees into the country. While almost every nation had agreed to accept a "limited" number, Heaps pointed out, Canada's regulations were "probably the most stringent in the world," and arbitrarily applied: "If refugees have no money, they are barred because they are poor, and if they have fairly substantial sums, they are often refused admittance on the most flimsy pretext." Then he allowed himself to deliver a guarded accusation:

> The existing regulations are inhuman and unChristian. . . . I regret to state that the sentiment is gaining ground that anti-Semitic influences are responsible for the government's refusal to allow refugees to come to Canada.

King did not reply and when, incredibly, Thomas Crerar announced on December 1, that he had had a change of heart and was ready to recommend admitting ten thousand refugees, neither King nor his cabinet would consent. Australia agreed to receive fifteen thousand refugees over a period of three years; Heaps wrote King that this humanitarian act on the part of another Commonwealth country made him ashamed to be a Canadian.

Nevertheless, despite repeated frustration, Heaps continued to maintain that the only proper course open to the Jewish community was through the accepted channels of high-level negotiation. In April 1938, the *Israelite Press*, always one of Abe Heaps's staunchest supporters, had published an interview with Heaps in which he assured his constituents that "the question of refugees is in good hands," and insisted specifically that all negotiations must be kept extremely discreet. According to Mr. Heaps, the paper reported,

> Competent Jewish representatives are in constant contact with the government in Ottawa on the problem of Jewish refugees from Germany and Austria. . . . [Mr. Heaps] asked us to convey his earnest recommendation to all Jewish community leaders to avoid going public with the problem, and to refrain from approaching the government on the subject, because it may only aggravate the situation.

Discreet diplomacy, behind the scenes and with the utmost tact, was the considered policy of the Jewish establishment, the designated community leadership, such as the Canadian Jewish Congress, the Zionist Organization, and the B'nai B'rith, out of an age-old instinct to keep a low profile and avoid antagonizing their non-Jewish neighbours. But the Jewish community itself, by and large, had found a new self-confidence, and was becoming restive under this enforced restraint, as Heaps's own warning to King obliquely suggests. There was a groundswell of protest against the inadequacy of polite representations in the face of daily reports of the horror overseas, and radical-led groups like the clamorous Anti-Fascist League won more and more approval. An editorial in the *Hebrew Journal* of Toronto warned Jewish leaders that rather than "avoid going public" they must indeed "launch mass movements [of protest]." If Jews continue to play the game of secret diplomacy, the writer argued, "we play into the hands of our enemies."

It was as if the reforming energy that had propelled Abe Heaps into his country's highest legislature had now abated, or had settled into a familiar, repetitive pattern. He still had old friends in Winnipeg, but few ties to the North End and to its changing mood. Schooled in the tradition of legislative debate, now a friend of the great and near-great, and like Woodsworth out of tune with the growing belligerence of his constituents, he could only continue on his earnest, reasonable, unavailing course.

The policy of the Liberal government was finally made explicit in a confrontation between Heaps and Fernand Rinfret, the secretary of state. An item in the *Montreal Gazette* for January 21, 1939, reported that Rinfret had assured his constituents that government restrictions would remain, especially against "that element which is assimilated with difficulty among the English and French in our country." The reference, capping a long history of Quebec anti-Semitism, was unmistakable.

In the House, eight days later, Heaps attacked Rinfret, accusing the cabinet as well as the minister of "harsh and brutal language . . . devoid of sentiment and humanity." The Liberal government, he charged, had made promises to the Jewish people that were never kept. King's response was blunt: no door would be opened to refugees by his administration. Heaps's lifelong faith in the democratic process had been betrayed.

The outbreak of war in 1939 ended the political career of A. A.

Heaps. Modifying only slightly Woodsworth's absolute opposition to militarism, the 1937 convention of the CCF had gone on record as rejecting "imperialist wars," and despite internal disagreement this policy held. Heaps had never been comfortable with Woodsworth's utopian vision of a commonwealth of working people, peaceably cooperating, and now he fought openly within the CCF against the party's failure to recognize the magnitude of the Nazi threat. As late as September 1939, however, the party's national council responded with mixed signals to Britain's declaration of war: for Canada's involvement in the war but against sending troops to fight, endorsing the provision of economic aid to Britain but refusing to join a national unity government to pursue the war effort.

When a federal election was called in early 1940, it was relatively easy to discredit Abe Heaps in the light of his party's indecision regarding the validity of the battle against Hitler. His traditional "Jewish vote" was alienated, and even his pacifism in the first World War told against him. His Liberal opponent, once again Lieutenant-Colonel C. S. Booth, now seemed best suited to pursue the war effort, as the candidate of the party in power, and this time the disruptive tactics of the Communists succeeded. Leslie Morris, the *Canadian Tribune* editor, drew off enough labour strength, and on March 28 Abe Heaps went down to defeat by 1,643 votes.

Letting Go

Retired from active service in the political arena, Heaps continued to pursue fine art as a hobby and an occupation. He acquired more paintings, sold a few, and put together another small collection. It was rumoured that the Liberal government offered him several positions: a seat in the Senate, a cabinet post as minister of labour, a top civil service position. During the war he served as a grain expediter at the Lakehead, and became decidedly unpopular among the local citizens when he insisted on conscripting draft-exempt hockey players to help in the loading operations. After the war he assisted the Liberal government of the ever-durable Mackenzie King in setting up the old age pension program, and he was also appointed to the Unemployment

Insurance Commission, another of the programs he had fought for and helped to win.

In 1947, at the age of sixty-two and after a lifetime of soldiering in the ranks, Abe Heaps was married again, in Manchester, England, to a textile manufacturer's widow, Fanny Almond. The couple settled in Montreal, where both had friends, and Heaps took a job in the dress industry as an arbitrator of labour disputes, at one hundred dollars per week. He needed the money, he said, because his resources were limited. But he soon tired of the conflict between his sympathy for labour and the realities of the cutthroat marketplace and, even more, of the triviality of almost all the disputes he had to settle, after his role in national affairs, and he gave up the position.

Early in 1954 he had a minor heart attack and was warned by his doctors to limit his activities, but he carried on much as usual. Both his sons were pursuing their careers elsewhere, David with the Ford Foundation in the United States and Leo as a journalist in Canada. He had friends everywhere but few close ties, and he began to think of returning to his boyhood home. He had been back to England several times, and now he decided on an extended visit, to be with his relatives in Leeds, to look up old cronies in the Labour Party. David saw him off on the boat in New York, on a bright, sunny day.

In Bournemouth, on April 4, 1954, Heaps had his second and fatal heart attack. The family was telephoned, but arrived too late, just hours after Abe's death. Deciding that Abraham Heaps would be buried in the city where he was born, his older son made the necessary arrangements and collected his father's few belongings. Abe's funeral and interment took place in Leeds, with Fanny and his two sons in attendance. "He had," David said, "few assets at the time of his death."

From Winnipeg, the city clerk sent the Heaps family the text of a resolution adopted by council, expressing "its deep sorrow at the death of ex-Alderman Abraham Albert Heaps," and adding that "during all of his public career, Mr. Heaps's paramount consideration was the welfare of his fellow man."

In the city he served there is now only a single public reminder of the immigrant from Leeds, ex-alderman, ex-member of parliament: the A. A. Heaps Building on Portage Avenue. Housing some provincial government sections, it was dedicated in 1988, when the reins of office were held by the New Democratic Party, the successor to the CCF. Abe Heaps's silent memorial remains in the record of his achievement: the Unemployment Insurance Commission, and, with Woodsworth, old age pensions, and what eventually became the Canadian public health system. As one observer remarked, "much of the improved quality of life we take for granted grew from the quiet speeches and fact-filled arguments of Abraham Heaps."

Writing in the *Canadian Encyclopedia*, Allen Seager sums up the career of this "class-conscious socialist":

His wit and deep humanity earned him few real enemies, but they included [Conservative] Arthur Meighen . . . and [Communist] Tim Buck. . . . Heaps's tireless efforts as the most credible economic critic in the Commons during the 1920s and 1930s contributed to the passage of vital though limited social legislation by Liberal and Conservative governments. His most keenly felt failures were his unheeded warning in the 1930s about the dangers of fascism and his desperate lobbying on behalf of anti-Nazi refugees.

A Socialist Reformer in a Capitalist World

John Queen

Trade Unionist and Social Democrat

In the fall of 1915 the members of Winnipeg's Social Democratic Party met to consider their slate for the annual civic elections. Fred Tipping was there and Jacob Penner, still retaining his SDP membership, and there were others, all active in party affairs. Unfortunately, as Tipping remembered years later, regulations required that a candidate for office be a registered property-holder, and not many active Social Democrats owned any property.

Then, said Tipping, someone thought of John Queen, "silent John."

Genial and soft-spoken, the big Scotsman rarely raised his deep-pitched voice in debate, but he had been a dependable party member for years. John had a huge mortgage on his house, on Ross Avenue near Bob Russell's, but he was eligible to run, and the committee promptly nominated him. Queen won his seat on city council that year, the first of a continuing series of election victories in civic and provincial politics. There was one other labour alderman on the fourteen-seat council in 1916, but in the following year there were six, now including also Arthur Puttee and Abe Heaps, and labour's popularity at the civic polls was slowly mounting. Queen's election in 1934 as mayor of the city of Winnipeg would mark a kind of coming-of-age for the labour movement, when the principles of left-of-centre dissent encountered, at a particularly difficult moment, the responsibilities of actual power.

When Queen arrived in Canada at the age of twenty-four he was not a socialist, according to his daughter Gloria. Back home in Scotland, he had told her, it was amusing to join in the game of heckling street corner socialists as they earnestly propounded their panaceas for the world's ills, but there were more important considerations. His father had begun as a coal miner in a mining town near Glasgow, but had branched out into a small retail store, and lost everything because he extended credit too freely. He had then taken a job with the Singer Sewing Machine Company and had done well, but the experience seemed to have left him obsessively concerned with ensuring his security and that of his wife and ten children.

John was born on February 11, 1882, and attended public school in Dunfermline. Apprenticed to a cooper or barrel-maker at the age of twelve, he remembered his father as interested only in religion and making money. The elder Queen belonged to the rigid Plymouth Brethren sect, and regularly used the rod on his children for their souls' sake. His son grew up with a lifelong abhorrence of war and of physical violence in any form. When young Queen proposed to seek his fortune in the godless wilds of western Canada, his father adjured him never to touch alcohol and never to go to a football game. John made neither commitment. Freed of his father's heavy hand, he would become a free thinker; he never went to church, his daughter said, and he did not send his children to Sunday school. What may have remained of his strict upbringing was a highly developed dedication to principle and an unwillingness to compromise. His daughter was to say, "John Queen would rather be defeated on principle than elected on compromise."

The young Scottish immigrant was headed out somewhere on the prairies, or perhaps British Columbia, when the CPR train stopped for a few hours in Winnipeg on a hot, bright summer day in 1906. Tall, red-headed, sporting a handlebar moustache and a cane, John sauntered out of the station to see the sights. It was Decoration Day and a parade was in progress down Main Street, with soldiers in full dress uniform marching to the skirl of pipes and the blare of brass bands. The holiday crowds lining the sidewalks seemed relaxed and friendly, and everywhere there was talk of business deals and fortunes to be made. Making a quick decision, John took his bags off the train, found a boarding house on Dorothy Street, and another new Winnipegger had arrived.

The cane was left off almost at once, an object of amusement among these breezy westerners, and the moustache had to go when prairie winters hung icicles from its luxuriance. But jobs were plentiful and Queen said he "hardly had to move a finger to get work with the Prairie City Oil Company. And the pay was good, too," he added. As a matter of course he joined the Coopers' International Union of North America, Local 241. The following year a young Highland woman, Katherine Ross, came out from Inverness at his invitation, and the two were married in 1908. Eventually, there would be five children in the Queen family, three daughters and two sons.

Skilled and able, John was quickly promoted from barrel-maker to supervisor at Prairie Oil. At the same time, however, contrary to his own account of lighthearted fun with soapbox socialists, he had certainly come to the new world with more than a passing interest in trade unionism and labour politics. An avid student of the British social philosopher John Stuart Mill — his daughter maintained that she and her siblings were brought up on Mill's treatise *On Liberty* — he had accepted as a foundation principle Mill's dictum that one must aim for "a state of society combining the greatest personal freedom with [a] just distribution of the fruits of labour," a provision that existing property laws denied.

Queen was drawn almost at once into the labour movement in his new home. In 1908, a newspaper notice for a meeting of the Social

Democratic Party in the North End caught his eye, and out of curiosity he wandered in to investigate. He found a very small group of mostly Ukrainian and Jewish labourites, led by Jacob Penner and Fred Tipping, deep in discussion of principles and purposes that meshed familiarly with his own, and impulsively he became a member. The newly formed association had just seceded from the Socialist Party of Canada, objecting to the Marxists' refusal to pursue immediate and specific reforms.

Over the next decade, the Socialists lost ground to the Social Democrats, particularly in the North End, which developed into an SDP stronghold. The group that John Queen had joined became a "Jewish" local, but he remained a member. Her father, explained Gloria Queen-Hughes, had no trace of the common Anglo-Saxon supremacist attitude but "thought of everyone as his equal as a human being. He always had great sympathy for the under-dog — hence his sympathy for the Jews."

Queen quickly became active in his own union and in the Trades and Labor Council. *The Voice* for August 27, 1909, just three years after his arrival, reported that John Queen had been named chairman of the Trades Council committee in charge of Labour Day celebrations. When the Coopers' Union dropped its affiliation with the Trades Council in 1910, Queen was no longer working at his trade, having been fired from his job because he refused to hire people at the lowest possible rate and because he protested his employers' taking advantage of unsophisticated new immigrants. For a time he drove a bread truck for Speirs-Parnell, and then he began selling insurance for Metropolitan Life. At the same time he continued to hold office in the council and to rise in the trade union movement. When the *Western Labor News* replaced Puttee's *The Voice* as the Trades Council organ, Queen became its business agent and advertising manager.

For Working People to Live in Decency

Once Queen assumed office on the city council he developed as a speaker and thinker with remarkable speed, consistently taking an emphatic stand on the bread-and-butter issues that impinged directly on the lives of ordinary people. In his first term, he backed the demand of the Health Department teamsters for a pay increase in the ongoing dispute between the civic employees and the city administration; in his second term he argued that the city's practice of paying its employees once a month made it difficult for families to manage between pay-cheques at a time of rampant inflation, and he insisted that they be paid bimonthly. With characteristic sensitivity to the human element in management decisions, he protested the firing of older workers from the city's street-cleaning crews, when most of them, he said, were "still able to do a good day's work." "The machine was made to conform to man," he often repeated, "not the man to the machine."

Concerned about the cost of public transportation, he presented a motion to disallow an increase in streetcar fares; the motion was carried. He proposed that streetcars collect no fare if no seats were available; the motion was denied. He persuaded the council to obtain permission from the provincial government to purchase a timber tract, so that wood for fuel could be made available to citizens at lower than market prices, and he fought to have the sale of "impure" coal stopped, as a health hazard. He demanded that the city undertake the distribution of milk, to counter the rising cost of dairy products. Intent on remedying the inequities of the taxation system, he called for a graduated income tax, to ease the burden on small wage-earners, and he was successful in having a provincial commission appointed to investigate the escalating cost of living.

A colourful addition to city council proceedings, with his indelible Scottish burr and his flashing wit, he would continue to furnish good newspaper copy, with his demands for "fool emplaiment," so that "workin' paiple" might live "in daicency," in "better hoosin'." Emphasizing style rather than substance, the press began to describe him as "flamboyant."

Not precisely a pacifist but totally without illusion about the horror and futility of war, Queen added his voice to the widespread left-wing outcry against conscription, and he also became an urgent spokesman on city council for soldiers and their families. He charged that pay rates in the armed forces were unconscionably low, and moved that a petition be sent to Ottawa urging a substantial improvement. The motion was ruled out of order. In the summer of 1918, concerned about the plight of his impoverished fellow citizens in the bitter weather to come, he backed a motion to have the Board of Control find the means to supply coal and wood to soldiers' dependents and other poor in the city. This motion was passed, not without some protracted haggling.

In the last year of the war, with its crescendo of strikes and near-strikes, worker disaffection, and the formation of the business establishment's Citizens' Committee of One Hundred, Queen acquired a reputation as a troublemaker. He fought beside Heaps in support of all the strikers' demands, and above all for their fundamental right of collective bargaining; he appeared frequently at strikers' meetings to pledge his support, and he argued vehemently in the council chamber against the repressive measures demanded by business-oriented aldermen. There was now a growing file on him at RNWMP headquarters.

Among the working people whose cause Alderman Queen championed were the restive members of the police force itself, their continuous grievances a cause for concern to the proponents of law and order on city council and on the Committee of One Hundred. The men on the beat, in their brass-buttoned tunics and their helmets like those of the London bobbies, had the same goals of security and greater control of their working lives that motivated other workers. They had banded together in a union, affiliated with the Trades and Labour Council, and requested recognition from the Police Commission; and John Queen moved on October 18, 1918, that the Commission acknowledge the union and conduct its negotiations accordingly. The motion was passed after some difficulty, but unsettled disputes persisted between employer and employed in this union as in others in the Winnipeg workforce.

In a foretaste of what was yet to come, the military had been granted extraordinary powers over civilian life under the emergency conditions of wartime, and instances of arbitrary restrictions irritated both the city police and the general public. A new Labor Temple building was being planned on James Street, with Alderman Queen playing an active role, and a campaign for funds was underway. Citing "public safety" but undeniably aiming to curb labour agitation, Military District No. 10 refused permission for a fund-raising rally to take place on a Sunday afternoon. Outraged, Queen reported this "unwarranted interference" to the Trades and Labor Council on December 13, and at city council he called for urgent measures to curb this curtailment of civil rights and other such government impositions.

The question of authoritarian action by the federal government was high on the agenda of the Walker Theatre meeting only ten days later. In the spirit of his mentor, John Stuart Mill, Queen was quick to defend the personal freedom of the individual and the British respect for constitutional procedures, which Ottawa's persistent use of orders-in-council had negated. Now that the war was over, he declared, there was no excuse for the continued incarceration of "aliens" and other "political prisoners." As the prominently advertised chairman of the event, he called on the working class to demonstrate unmistakably that such violations of civil rights would not be tolerated. In the ears of the police agents taking notes in the theatre, this declaration by the rabble-rousing alderman reverberated as a clear threat of revolution.

Responsive as always to the excitement of a sympathetic audience, Queen rose to the defence of the inspired Russian patriots who had liberated their country from czarist tyranny, and denounced the sending of Allied troops against the "Bolsheviks," and he sealed his fate at the meeting's end by calling for "Three Cheers for the Russian Revolution!" Hardly a Marxist, he believed like so many of his contemporaries, moderates like himself, that in that distant upheaval a new social order had dawned. In the factional bickering that followed the rally and the refusal of the Trades and Labor Council to endorse the Socialist Party again, Queen admitted privately that he might have been carried away by his own rhetoric.

That winter and late spring, Queen struggled on the city council to head off the repressive measures against labour unrest demanded by unsympathetic aldermen. As the Trades and Labor Council fought down the attempted takeover by the Socialists, but began to accept the hitherto extreme notion of a sympathy strike, Queen also was drawn to the left. Russell's OBU was generating a great deal of interest and Queen could only approve of this drive for greater union power, even as he deplored its headlong divisiveness.

An Alderman on Trial

The virtual declaration of a labour war on May 15, 1919, presented an immediate problem with law enforcement in the city. The police union notified the Central Strike Committee that its members were in favour of joining the walk-out; Queen and Heaps persuaded them to stay on the job. Nevertheless, the alarmed police commission issued an ultimatum, ordering every officer to sign a pledge by May 29, undertaking not to enter into a sympathetic strike, or to face dismissal. By the deadline only some two dozen policemen out of a force of several hundred had complied. Pressured by the Citizens' Committee, now reinstated as the Citizens' Committee of One Thousand, the police commission fired its insubordinate constables and replaced the police chief, charging that he was sympathetic to the strikers and soft on the police union's demands. The hastily armed "Specials" began to patrol the streets.

As terrifying rumours circulated, particularly in the North End, that the army was advancing on the city, Queen fought to keep the reins of civic government in the hands of the democratically elected city council, and to persuade council to legislate the recognition of collective bargaining, but Winnipeg edged a step closer to a military takeover. The stage was set for the termination of the general strike by a show of force.

The traumatic early morning arrests on June 17 remained for most of the strike leaders a moment of high drama; for the irrepressible John Queen, his daughter said, it was "the most hilarious day in my life," in its blundering, spy-thriller confusion. Katherine Queen and the children were out at their summer cottage in Gimli, and the Scotsman was staying with his friend, Abe Heaps, on Burrows Avenue. As if in collusion with the overheated human events that May and June, the unusually sultry weather over the city had peaked, the previous evening, in a spectacular tornado, and the two men had watched from their front porch as the roof of the nearby Strathcona School lifted and sailed away over their heads. They were both asleep, late that night, when a thunderous knock at the door brought Queen stumbling down to answer. Several Mounties loomed out of the darkness, with a portentous announcement: "We have a warrant, Mr. Heaps, for your arrest." "Abie," called Mr. Queen, "it's you they want, not me." There was a hasty consultation, and then, "We have a warrant for you too, Mr. Queen," said the police. With due regard for proper procedure, the two alleged malefactors satisfied themselves that the arrest papers were in order, asked permission to dress, and then were handcuffed together and escorted into the waiting automobile, to be taken with the other arrestees to Stony Mountain.

Awaiting trial, Queen kept his seat on city council, and he was returned as alderman in the civic elections that fall. In November, just as Russell came to trial, Queen tried unsuccessfully to have the council rescind its edict of June 9 that civic workers were not permitted to strike, and he presented the first in a long series of motions to eliminate the property qualification from the civic election rolls. Early the next year, before his own trial, he induced council to declare an August civic holiday, giving working people an extra day in the sun.

By the time the proceedings against Queen and his co-defendants were underway in the new year, the presiding magistrate, the prosecutors, the attorneys for the defence, and their clients were all exhausted and tempers were short. Queen's lawyer, W. H. Trueman, tangled with Judge Metcalfe on a point of law, and exclaimed, in flagrant disrespect for the court, "You are an unjust judge!" Threatened with contempt, he withdrew from the case, saying stiffly, "I cannot do my client justice under these circumstances," and Queen was left, like Heaps and Pritchard and Dixon, to carry on in his own defence.

For John Queen the case was transparently one of justice and equity. Apart from his own jeopardy and his disdain for the professional spies whose dubious "evidence" was being paraded in court, he made it clear that he spoke not for himself but for the people he represented. "This is not a trial of seven men as you see them here," he told the jury; "it is a trial of the movements of men." He had been elected to the city council, he said, to give expression to the views of working people, and it was for those views that he now stood before the bar of justice. Once again he denounced the attempt to force civic employees to give up the right to strike: if the worker agrees, he stormed, "hasn't he given over every God-given right that he has and handed himself over to the city of Winnipeg?" And he protested furiously the takeover by the Citizens' Committee of the functions of government, while "there was I, an alderman of the city of Winnipeg, sitting on the City Council in that humiliating position!"

Like most of the defendants, he made the daily pain of the ordinary working person under the constraints of an unfair social and economic system the central appeal in his defence. Where the prosecution pressed home the primacy of the law, Queen's plea was humanity and compassion. "I resent very much," he exclaimed, "men like Mr. Andrews telling the workers they must be thrifty. . . . The worker has to be thrifty when wages are so low. I venture to say that a number of men here spend more money on their automobiles than would keep some families alive." Reported the mainline *Telegram*, no friend of labour, "[Queen] painted a vivid picture of a worker in a shoe factory who was making shoes at a very small wage. At the same time his children were going around with wet feet because he had not sufficient income to buy good shoes for them."

The letter of the law, as read by the prosecution, prevailed in the trial: to advocate the upheaval that went by the name of "socialism" was sedition, to join with others in advancing these ideas was conspiracy. Judge Metcalfe's charge to the jury, in the case of John Queen, was almost perfunctory, and the jury duly found him guilty on all counts. Queen received the going sentence of twelve months at the provincial prison farm.

There was some question of whether Alderman Queen, now convicted of disloyalty to his country, could be allowed to remain on city council, but the law regarding expulsion required a five-year criminal record, obviously not designed to cover these extraordinary circumstances. The provincial election of 1920 reaffirmed the convict alderman as the people's choice: John Queen was returned to the legislature on that year's common labour slate. He did not contest the aldermanic election in the fall. Having served his prison term, he was released with Ivens and Armstrong a month short of the actual sentence, and with them took his place in the provincial house on February 28, 1921, two weeks after the beginning of the session.

Issues and Differences: Queen v. Dixon

"Silent John" was silent no longer, as one of the labourites in the legislature who acknowledged the leadership of Fred Dixon. In the range of political orientation among these newly elected representatives, Queen made his position clear. "The capitalist system is the prime cause of international friction and war," read a motion he introduced early in the session; and again, in a characteristically blunt statement of principle, "While we produce the wealth of the world, the worker continues to live in poverty. It is power that we want. . . . "Actual power was a distant prospect, but Queen became a leading voice forcefully demanding consideration of the working person's point of view.

He attacked the Norris administration for its policy of economic retrenchment, its debt-cutting when it should have been putting money into creating badly needed jobs. He spoke for thousands of disgruntled working people angered by the lavish reception planned for the visiting governor-general, the duke of Devonshire: in hard times, he said, this money should be used rather for the relief of unemployment. He tried and failed to convince the legislators to revise the regulations governing living conditions in mining and lumber camps, and repeatedly he attempted to introduce a bill to allow "peaceful picketing" in labour disputes, only to have the measure turned down. Said the premier, "no such thing as peaceful picketing can exist." And undoubtedly prompted by his recent penal experience, and seconded by Ivens, he asked that the province "give to each person on his discharge from the Provincial Gaol, a sum of $10 in cash, and such clothing as is necessary for warmth and decency." This proposal was approved.

In the international field, he demanded that the provincial Liberals recommend to Prime Minister King the rapid disarmament of the country. He urged the development of trade with Russia, "because Russia needs our manufactured goods, and they need our wheat to feed their people"; and, his motion defeated, he called on the government to send aid to Russia, to combat starvation in that beleaguered country.

Between this forthright stance on the left and Fred Dixon's moderate reformism there seemed to be something less than absolute amity, perhaps because Dixon's willingness to cooperate with the Liberal establishment offended Queen's labour sensibilities, or perhaps because the Scotsman's irreverent sense of humour grated on the Englishman's moral seriousness. By the middle of February 1922, their disagreement on various issues was coming very close to the surface. The government proposed to make certain concessions to people who had bought Crown lands on speculation, and now were unable to meet their payments. Dixon, pursuing his Georgeite opposition to unproductive landholding, presented an amendment, in effect censuring the government and demanding foreclosure, and most of the labour caucus backed his position. Queen openly opposed Dixon: an order to seize land that was in default would strike a blow against small farmers as well as against speculators, he insisted, and in view of the difficult economic situation, no such action should be taken. When the question was put, he pointedly abstained, not willing either to cross his party's policy or to vote against his conscience.

One particular preoccupation of Queen's was regarded with scant interest by Dixon. Intent on providing for his "workin' paiple" a reasonable access to some of life's small pleasures, Queen had repeatedly raised the question in the legislature of an amendment to the Lord's Day Act, to permit the operation of trains to the Lake Winnipeg resort areas on summer Sundays, so that a worker might spend the one free day a week on a family outing. The scheme was bitterly opposed by the Lord's Day Alliance, and Dixon also appears to have retained a strong attachment to the religion he had been taught as a child, so that he could only frown upon Queen's proposed violation of the Sabbath. At any rate, when the Norris government was defeated on a motion of censure in March 1922, and the remaining business on the order papers was by consent of all the parties quickly dispatched, Dixon agreed to eliminate the Sunday Trains bill from consideration. Furious, Queen charged that a Star Chamber of party leaders was at work. The following day George Armstrong tried to get the bill reinstated, but Queen could only muster fifteen votes in its support. Dixon told the press obliquely that he was "getting kind of tired of members putting the same motion time and again."

In the election that followed, the Norris government was replaced by a United Farmers majority, headed by John Bracken. Undeterred by past set-backs, Queen put his two proposals before the new legislature once again. In January 1923, his "peaceful picketing" bill was rejected once again, although Bracken and four cabinet ministers voted to approve. The following month, at last, the Sunday Trains bill passed the legislature, although it still was referred to the Court of Appeals for a judgment on its constitutionality. Court approval did not come until 1924, but the railways jumped immediately at the business opportunity. The inaugural Sunday excursion special rolled down the tracks on June 23, 1923, carrying the first of thousands of day-trippers, for many years to come, to public beaches on both sides of the lake.

In February, it had been announced in the legislature that John Queen, previously sitting as a member of the Social Democratic Party, had joined the Independent Labor Party, and would now be a part of that party's caucus and represent the party in the house. Perhaps only coincidentally, in that same year Dixon's personal problems forced his sudden departure from the political scene, and he resigned from the legislature and the leadership of the ILP. John Queen was named the party's house leader.

For the Public Good: Against the Bracken Administration

Labour lost five of its rural seats in the 1922 election, although Queen, Dixon, Ivens, Bayley, and Farmer were elected. Queen was in his element now in the small but commanding labour opposition. If he had found the Norris regime objectionable, despite its rather laudable record of liberal reform in many areas, the accession of Bracken and his United Farmers provided limitless opportunities for vociferous disapproval.

Bracken's entry into politics from his senior position in the Manitoba Agricultural College was hailed by the *Manitoba Free Press* as the replacement of ideological and party divisions by an unobtrusive and efficient administration. In practice, administrative efficiency called for a stand-pat program, concerned primarily with bringing the province's finances into order by balancing the budget and eliminating allegedly unnecessary expenditures in precisely those social and humanitarian fields that John Queen championed.

Serving on a number of standing committees of the legislature, and most notably on the Law Amendments Committee, Queen distinguished himself for his grasp of the effect that a proposed measure would have on the rank and file of Manitoba's population. As the administration sought to curtail costs, Queen fought for better housing, for the restoration of pay cuts to public employees, and for greater aid to municipalities. He demanded that the government assume its proper responsibility to support education, to build more schools, to train more teachers and raise their salaries. Education, he insisted, was the only way for the working class to raise itself above poverty and slums.

The 1927 provincial election returned Queen to his seat, but reduced the labour representation to three, and brought back the Bracken alliance between farmers and conservatives with an overwhelming majority of twenty-nine seats.

Empowered now by this substantial mandate for its pro-business priorities, the Bracken cabinet proceeded to make its controversial deal with the Northwestern Power Company and the Winnipeg Electric Company to develop the hydropower facility at the Seven Sisters Falls. Assurance had been given that the Manitoba members of the federal House would be consulted before a decision was made, but without reference either to the legislature or to the federal MPs the cabinet granted the Seven Sisters site to the private corporation.

At stake for the labour left, for Queen as for Heaps and Woodsworth in Ottawa, was the principle of public ownership of public utilities, and the even more fundamental question of the democratic role of the people's elected representatives. Queen charged that the people and the province had been sold down the river by the premier and his cohorts. Implying corruption in the choice of the site, he pointed out that the alternative at McArthur Falls would have produced the same amount of power and the same number of jobs, and he demonstrated conclusively, as labourites did repeatedly, that public ownership served the public needs more cheaply and more efficiently. There had been an egregious violation of democratic rights, Queen declared: Bracken had indicated that there would be no decision until an engineers' report on Seven Sisters was received, but only three days later, without bringing the matter before the House, he had signed the deal with the private developers.

The contract with the two private firms was binding, but the issue collided with the interests of the United Farmers in Bracken's coalition, and they withdrew their support, leaving the premier to seek cooperation with the Liberals in order to retain the government. It also led to an interesting confrontation between John Queen and members of his own party.

During the investigation, it emerged that Queen, the very prominent chairman of the Independent Labor Party and outspoken opponent of private ownership of public utilities, was himself the owner of fifty shares in the Winnipeg Electric Company. Understandably embarrassed by this revelation of an apparent betrayal of a fundamental socialist principle, Queen immediately tendered his resignation to the ILP, which almost as quickly rejected the offer. The party's provincial board, said the news release, regretted the chairman's "indiscretion," but continued to have "full confidence" in his service to the working class, and held that his resignation "would not be in the best interests of the party."

Interestingly, the investment that he had made in Winnipeg Electric shares — a rather modest venture, in keeping with his limited resources —was in no sense illegal, and, in fact, would have been regarded as astute and even admirably civic-minded by business interests. There was no actual conflict of interest: he had fought against the advantageous deal for the Winnipeg Electric Company, not for it. That holding shares in a privately owned utility constituted a moral offence in the eyes of at least some ILP members reflects the strong commitment of the left to principle; that the party chose to minimize the problem suggests an increasing recognition of the realities of practical affairs. Queen himself would be in a position within a few years to make good on some of the party's specific proposals, if not on its visionary, far-reaching goals.

In 1930, after Fred Dixon died, Queen was officially designated the ILP leader, having been its chairman since Dixon's departure from active politics. For the next several years, through the provincial election of 1932 and into the continued Bracken administration that followed, he captured an increasing amount of newspaper space by his unrelenting opposition to the government's conservative policies.

After the stock-market crash of 1929, the natural disasters of grasshoppers and drought had further exacerbated the economic collapse on the prairies. By November 1930 there were sixteen thousand people on relief in Manitoba alone, and by March 1934 the relief rolls would peak at over ninety-one thousand. In the legislature, Bracken tried to control the soaring budget by cutting down on such public services, and Queen and his fellow labourites fought just as grimly to protect the assistance given to the most vulnerable members of the community.

Inundated by demands for help, the Child Welfare Board became a frequent target of Queen's condemnation, for its "brutal and callous" treatment of desperate people. It held up applications on bureaucratic pretexts, said Queen, it deducted what it termed the "potential earnings" of any family member from an already meagre allowance, even if no one in the family could find employment. In the budget debate in 1931, Queen brought statistics to show that the monthly allowance for food and clothing for a mother with three dependent children was $37.50, with $6 per month for household expenses. On average, Queen pointed out, twenty-seven cents per meal was allotted a family of four, and in many instances recipients did not even get that amount.

At a 1932 election campaign meeting, Queen charged that all of Bracken's policies had brought business to a near standstill by reducing the purchasing power of the masses to almost nothing. He attacked the provincial government for refusing to allow Winnipeg to levy an income tax, while permitting the city to raise the water rates and to tax gas and electricity, all of which impacted disproportionately on poor people. At another meeting in Brandon he sneered that Bracken had made his great sacrifice in hard times by cutting the allowances to widows and orphans, in order to protect the bondholders and save the province's credit.

Returned to the legislature in the 1932 election, Queen pointed out that the maternity death rate in Manitoba was higher than in any other province in Canada, and he denounced a proposal to "cut out the frills" by eliminating the public nursing service in some rural areas; where such service was not provided, he protested, babies were being born without prenatal care, women's lives were being sacrificed. According to Mr. Bracken, he exclaimed,

> the people have to be sacrificed to maintain interest payments! What does it matter if a few, or many, mothers die? So long as the government can continue to pay interest . . . to those who gather in the interest tolls. . . . It evidently does not matter very much whether a bunch of mothers die so long as money can be sent to the bondholders.

Bracken was to remain in office until 1942, and the conflict with the labour group on principles and policies continued. In the 1934 session Queen gained one small victory, the passing of a statute guaranteeing one day's rest in seven for all employees.

Running for Mayor:
Attack from the Left and the Right

At the end of the twenties, the ILP had become a dominant political force in Manitoba, and taking the initiative had called a western conference of labour parties in 1929, "to arrange common actions and to bring about the entire unification of the labour and socialist movement throughout western Canada." By April of that year, a Calgary and district branch of the ILP had emerged, and the Manitoba group once again took the lead in developing and consolidating a political network among like-minded associations. Hosted in Calgary by farmer, labour, and socialist parties another conference took place in August 1931, which endorsed as its central resolution "the socialization of economic life in the country." Kathleen Queen attended, representing the ILP branch in Winnipeg's West End, and delegates came from the four western provinces and Ontario.

On the national scene, James Woodsworth was actively pursuing his dream of achieving a cooperative commonwealth of working people in all walks of life, and the meeting in Ottawa, in May 1932, of labourite MPs, eastern academics, and others, issued the following year in the founding conference, in Calgary, of the Co-operative Commonwealth Federation. Queen was present, an enthusiastic supporter of the idea, disagreeing on the issue with his good friend Abe Heaps, and he was named to the new party's provisional national council. He also attended the Regina conference in 1933 at which the manifesto of the CCF was proclaimed.

Attempting a return foray into civic politics while he still sat as a member of the legislature, Queen had run for mayor of Winnipeg in 1927, making some pointed political capital out of his continued identification with the working class and his continued residence on working-class Ross Avenue. He had been defeated by Lieutenant-Colonel Dan MacLean, who had served as city alderman. In 1932, reconfirmed as ILP leader, John Queen was once again his party's choice for the mayoralty. The campaign was marked by the virulent intervention of the Communist Party, now led by Queen's former associate in the Social Democratic Party, Jacob Penner.

Since the early 1920s the Communist Party had trumpeted its allegiance to Soviet Russia and the Soviet revolutionary model. It had been ruled an illegal organization in 1931, but had continued to function under a succession of thin disguises. Now in open competition for control of the labour-left, the Communists demanded that the moderates join them in a "United Front" against capitalism and the growing threat of European fascism. The ILP was flatly opposed to the Communist insistence on world revolution, increasingly wary of Russian dominance, and more than suspicious of Communist intentions, and would not be pulled into this dubious alliance.

Now presenting themselves in the civic election of November 1932 under the banner of the "United Front," the Communists fielded Jacob Penner for mayor, in direct opposition to Queen. Penner issued a public challenge to the ILP candidate to face him in debate. Queen refused to be lured into a publicity stunt for the extremists, but replied by letter, releasing copies to the press. He would be pleased to meet Mr. Penner to discuss the nature and activities of their respective parties, he said, but after the election. He would then ask Penner to produce, he said,

> the instructions under which you act . . . which come to you from the Communist International . . . [and] wherein you are instructed to attack those who are on the firing line of the Labor movement . . . to surround them with suspicion, and to distort and misinterpret facts in order to destroy any influence they might have with the workers. . . . In the meantime, if you desire to be taken seriously, your organization will have more regard for the truth in the future both in the papers it circulates, and in its platform.

Queen lost the mayoralty race that year to Webb by a margin of under five thousand votes, arguably the victim of the "spoiler" tactics of the Communists.

In the next year's civic elections, the "Workers' Unity League" announced that Penner would run for the mayoralty once again. However, when their aldermanic candidate in Ward 3, Leslie Morris, was ruled ineligible because he was then serving a prison sentence for sedition, Penner was switched to run for alderman in the North End's

Ward 3, where he regularly derived most of his support, and M. J. Forkin replaced him for the mayoralty.

In the ILP, not yet fully amalgamated with the new CCF, some consideration was given to making Lewis St. George Stubbs the party's candidate. A colourful and idiosyncratic figure on the labour scene since his membership early in the century in the coterie at the Mobius bookshop, Stubbs had recently become a cause célèbre when he was removed from the bench for refusing to jail a man for petty theft: theft on an infinitely larger scale, the judge pronounced, was routinely commited with impunity by the corrupt and powerful capitalist establishment. But the ILP leadership decided, it was rumoured, that the much-publicized former jurist was "too much of a prima donna," and a nominating committee in October named Queen once again.

Mayor Ralph Webb reluctantly agreed to run for an eighth term; making little distinction between his two mutually inimical opponents, he indicated that he felt obliged, specifically, to combat the threat from the left. If he believed John Queen could deal with the city's problems better, he told his supporters, he would vote for him and support him, but "It would be disastrous to place Winnipeg in the hands of the Socialist party . . . [because] there are many planks in Mr. Queen's platform which, if put into effect, would set back the city's well-being."

From about 1919 or 1920, after the high drama of the general strike had subsided, the shadowy members of the Citizens' Committee of One Thousand had continued their watchdog scrutiny of city politics as the Citizens' League, their proclaimed purpose to endorse for public office such candidates as would be certain to safeguard the city's financial interests. It was this group of conservative, business-minded movers and shakers that backed Mayor Webb and a majority of the aldermen.

Central to Webb's campaign was the argument that the city must be bound by its financial constraint, and there was an unsubtle appeal to the racist elements of the "English" majority:

We have to live within our means. . . . The secret of the success of the British people... has always been that their word is good. British people came here and built this city. Their thrift was a virtue. . . . So let us keep up the good old British tradition, and be on the constructive side of the picture . . . and see that our city lives within its means.

"Living within our means," John Queen charged, meant an appalling indifference to the problems faced by the victims of the Great Depression. Webb and the Citizens' League aldermen, he pointed out, had cut back on relief payments and on funds to the school board, choosing to close schools in order to keep up payments on the city debt. Reconsider your options, Queen demanded, do not protect the city's credit at the cost of its people's suffering, and he flayed Mayor Webb and the Citizens' League aldermen for their high-handed insensitivity to the plight of the unemployed. A family of four, he told an election crowd, was expected to live for fifteen days on a $10.89 food voucher, while as an MLA Colonel Webb airily informed the legislature, "We never pretended to give them all they can eat, only what we think is enough for them."

The entire system represented by the Webb administration was inhuman and corrupt, said Queen. "They know that a life without poverty is possible for all," he accused, but "instead of planning a distribution of the plenty available on every hand, these forces are now actually scheming for the creation of a condition of scarcity through curtailed production. . . . If we do not organize to prevent them from carrying out their designs, we are in grave danger of losing what comfort and security in life we have been used to. . . ."

Webb and the Citizens' League prevailed. Queen was defeated again for the mayoralty, by a substantial margin, but predicted that victory for his party, now the ILP–CCF, would come in the near future.

The Communists did not field a candidate in the 1934 mayoralty race, and Ralph Webb retired from the scene, having been assured that the veteran alderman J. A. McKerchar would stand for election — endorsed by the same, longstanding group of anonymous business interests, now calling itself the Civic Election Committee (CEC). John Queen received his party's nomination once again, but only by a majority of four votes, as rival factions within the CCF had begun to question the wisdom of his holding several positions.

His platform restated in unequivocal terms the party's political philosophy:

The social ownership of the means of production, distribution, and exchange is essential to the permanent solution of the problems arising out of social and economic ills.

As for methods of dealing with the immediate problems facing a ravaged city, Queen proposed that "[the federal government] should bear the whole cost of relief and maintain a standard of assistance sufficient to preserve the self-respect of individuals," and that a sewage system should be built immediately under the combined sponsorship of the federal, provincial, and municipal governments, to save the city's rivers from further pollution and to provide a much-needed infusion of employment.

The credibility of old-line practices had begun to erode. A report on the city's finances commissioned by the city council had recommended such vastly unpopular measures as the taxation of essential commodities, an increase in utility rates, the elimination of free tuition in grade eleven and of all free textbooks except to the indigent; and these were widely believed to be the intended policies of McKerchar and the CEC. Faced with the disaffection of an increasing portion of the electorate, the CEC group fought the ILP–CCF incursion with the plea that the city council should be kept free of party politics, and raised the standard threat that the socialists would confiscate all homes and all property for public ownership.

The scare tactics did not work. To the surprise and shock of a great many upstanding citizens, the city went to bed late on that November election night knowing that it had chosen its first avowedly socialist mayor: John Queen had won fifty-three percent of the total ballot, and a tiny majority of 220 votes. The largely middle-class Ward 1 had gone almost two to one for McKerchar, but the working-class electorate of Wards 2 and 3 had sent the labour candidate to the mayor's office.

Taken aback, the *Winnipeg Tribune* sought to reassure its readers: "He will probably make a good mayor, serving the city's interests with ability and carrying the honours and responsibilities of office with ease and grace. His election is not a calamity." In the *Free Press*, a droll and folksy profile of Winnipeg's new chief executive mused that many people wondered whether this man was "the big bad wolf or a fine fellow," but went on to predict that the mayor-elect would remain "John" to one and all:

His neighbours will no doubt get quite a kick out of seeing His Worship's limousine, with liveried chauffeur, roll up in front of the unpretentious Queen home at 1452 Ross Avenue. "There's John going to work," they'll probably say, when they see him taken down to the City Hall in the morning. He'll most likely ride in front with the chauffeur and stop to give friends a lift.

Racism and the Manitoba Defamation Act

Energetic, thriving on the give-and-take of political encounters, more apt to disarm his opponents by wit and humour than to batter them with anger and denunciation, John Queen was "a rare campaigner," his friend and future alderman, Lloyd Stinson, said of him, able to "charm the birds out of the trees with his rich Scottish voice and magnetic personality." As his family grew, he had found that selling insurance did not add enough to the MLA's allowance of fifteen hundred dollars per year, and had switched to selling cars and trucks for Breen Motors. He was equally comfortable swapping tools with the neighbours on Ross Avenue, or trading stories with colleagues under the legislative dome, or joining the weekend commuters to the summer colony at Gimli.

At home, his daughter Gloria reflected afterward, he rarely lost his temper. He would come home from the legislature or some other meeting, often quite late, and make himself a pot of porridge to share with his Scottish terrier, Heather, before going to bed, and he might talk for a while with anyone who was still awake. One night, Gloria remembered, he was obviously distressed as he sat at the table. He had been giving an official a hard time in the Law Amendments Committee for some decidedly less than honourable actions, he told her, but the man was in deep personal trouble. His wife had died and his daughter had committed suicide, "and there he is trying to maintain an impossible position as far as the public is concerned. . . . I had to question him, and make him answer up to the things he's done, but I still feel sorry for him and I didn't like to have to do it."

A compassionate man, and not given to personal animosities, John Queen would not tolerate any suggestion of racial prejudice. Always angered by the casual racism among many of his British compatriots, he had lashed out during his first year in the legislature against Colonel

Rattray, the provincial commissioner of police, for his remark that ninety-five percent of bootleggers were Jews. "In a community where there are so many nationalities represented," he was quoted in the press, "and where we all have to live together, any attempt to stir up race prejudice is a most dastardly thing." Living together was a lifelong commitment for John Queen, and any racial intolerance a moral offence.

The Icelandic community at Gimli played host every season to city families of many different ethnic origins, many of them only recently established in their new country and enjoying their modest vacation luxury. Nearby was the OBU camp, its sports facilities open to the cottagers as well as to the campers, and attracting a boisterous mixture of Jewish and non-Jewish youngsters. Occasionally ethnic tensions marred the serenity of the long summer days.

One young vacationer remembered all his life the tall Scotsman's steely anger on his arrival at the lake one Sunday afternoon, to be told of a casually anti-Semitic remark dropped at the OBU camp by the teenage son of a trade union leader. Confronting the culprit at the camp before all his mates, Queen delivered a stern lecture on the responsibilities of a human being, and demanded an apology to the young people he had offended. Then, still unhappy, he sought out some of his Jewish neighbours and offered his personal regrets.

The new mayor had achieved his position at a peculiarly inauspicious moment in the history of his community and of the planet. Despite frequent encouraging assertions on the part of public figures that economic difficulties were only temporary, the paralysis of the Great Depression seemed, in the midthirties, to have fastened a permanent grip on people, and with particular savagery, perhaps, on the battered prairies. Winnipeg was then the third-largest city in the country, the largest in the region, and the hub of the western Canadian economy; and, as in the crucial postwar year of 1919, it was there and in the rural area surrounding the city that the tremors of seismic change registered their early-warning signs.

In Europe, seemingly remote from the fractious politics of Manitoba, a strange and at times even laughable individual named Adolf Hitler had become the important power in Germany, and his strutting, brown-shirted Nazis were asserting themselves in an extraordinarily unpleasant way, making life difficult for one segment of the German population, the always problematic Jews. Long before the general Canadian population had become aware of an imminent threat to the orderly unfolding of their lives, the Canadian Jewish community had recognized the fascist infection on their own side of the Atlantic. In September 1933, the same year that Hitler became chancellor of Germany, a former British soldier, William Whittaker, launched his Nationalist Party in Winnipeg, proclaiming that the purpose of his paramilitary brown-shirted followers was to get rid of "Bolsheviks and Jews."

The ravages of the depression had provided ample ammunition for the Communists to denounce the capitalist system as evil and moribund, and once again the Red Scare revived, with its attendant ugliness of racial venom. In the 1934 session of the Manitoba legislature, Colonel Webb had advised the lawmakers that "all those who don't like this country . . . [should] go back to the country where they came from," and added ominously, "Some people are liable to think this a joke, but you don't know what I know or see." Once again, as in 1919, undercover agents in Winnipeg were reporting to police authorities that an armed Communist insurrection was afoot, that guns were being imported, and that there were well-developed plans to capture the banks, the Minto Barracks, and the city's utilities. One report described a "man named Friedman, alias Frieda," as the "manager and organizer of the Junior Communistic Association . . . round fresh face with big fat nose . . . a typical Jew." Battening on the same rumours, irate letters to newspapers and to government officials once again demanded that steps be taken to put down these "foreigners . . . who trample our Flag, shoot our Police, burn our Schools," and who take away jobs from good, English-speaking Canadians.

As the Nazis in Germany glorified the image of a resurgent Aryan nation, Whittaker's homegrown fascism found fertile ground in the German-speaking rural areas south of Winnipeg and in the general German community, as well as among the ultra-nationalist Slavic groups. His paper, the *Canadian Nationalist*, began to circulate increasingly in southern Manitoba and into Saskatchewan and Alberta, together with the pro-Nazi, anti-Semitic *Der Courier*, out of Regina, and an array of publications from Nazi presses in Germany. Deliberately provoking trouble, the Nationalists staged parades and held meetings in the ethnically mixed North End of Winnipeg, fiercely challenged by the Communists and by a Jewish Anti-Fascist League. In Market Square, the classic home of political dissent, pitched battles between the two adversaries once again brought out the city's riot police.

Contemptuous of the small but noisy Communist bloc for its Soviet-inspired fulminations, but even more alarmed by the growth of fascism and the spread of anti-Semitism, John Queen was immediately on the alert to the threat against the democratic principles he cherished. The Trades and Labour Congress investigated Whittaker, and in February 1934 Queen demanded in the Manitoba legislature that the attorney-general lay charges of sedition against the local Nazis. He produced the Nationalists' membership card and read into the record its inquiry about the potential recruit's proficiency "in the use of rifles, machine guns, Lewis guns, and other lethal weapons"; and he quoted an article in the *Sturmer*, the Nazi publication from Berlin, that the aim of Canadian organization was to overthrow the existing government and to set up its own strong central government.

To their credit both Winnipeg dailies were unequivocally anti-fascist in their editorials and feature articles, but the local authorities could not or would not distinguish between the Communists and the Nationalists, between the two extremist factions disturbing the peace of the community. Unable to make headway in a direct attack on fascism, Queen and his ILP–CCF colleague in the provincial House, Marcus Hyman, devised a measure to thwart the Nationalist propaganda. At Queen's instigation Hyman presented a bill to the House providing for an injunction against any publication defaming a racial or religious group or inciting hatred against a group; and with a further amendment making the printer's and the publisher's names mandatory on every kind of printed material, the bill passed into law as the Manitoba Defamation Act, the first group libel law in Canada.

Under the legislation Whittaker and his printer were successfully prosecuted for publishing the ancient libel that Jews practice ritual murder, and a connection was established between the Nationalists and German officialdom: it was revealed that the largest shareholder in the *Deutsche Zeitung*, the Nazi organ in Canada, was the German consul in Winnipeg, and that its printer was also the printer of Whittaker's racist sheet. By the same token, the requirement to identify the origin of all printed material endangered as well the voluminous propaganda from Communist sources, and the Communist *Worker* promptly lumped together their social-democratic rivals with the fascist enemy and the hated capitalists: "The social fascists, like Hyman, are assisting the open fascists, like Mayor Webb, in their attacks on the working class. . . . It is a direct attempt to deprive the workers of this weapon of struggle." Still to come was the about-face of the Communists on the subject of Nazi Germany after the Russo-German pact of 1939.

For John Queen the immediate danger was clear: the destructive anti-humanitarian attack on democratic institutions and constitutional change from the rabid, disaffected far right. In Winnipeg's German community, as world events in the thirties plummeted toward disaster, German national pride became indistinguishable from the celebration of Nazi ideology, and German organizations openly disseminated race hatred. Appalled, Mayor Queen would not allow the screen of official nonpartisanship to conceal his condemnation of the fascist obscenity. As mayor, he refused to attend the annual German Day picnic in October 1938, and when he was attacked in the *Deutsche Zeitung* for his refusal, he explained his thinking with acid precision. While he was sympathetic to all the city's many national groups, he told the press, he did not conceive it to be his duty to pay homage to Hitler:

> I am so determined that . . . we are going to retain our democrat-
> ic institutions in this country that I positively refuse . . . to salute
> any form of dictatorship or to give any encouragement to the
> growth of Nazism in this country or any other.

Aware as always of individual sensibilities within the mass, he added, "I do not believe for a moment that the people who are criticizing me form a majority of our German citizens."

As for Jacob Penner, once a Social Democrat like himself, but now concurring with Soviet-inspired machinations and leading the attack from the Marxist left, Queen told friends, as he came to preside as mayor over the city council, that the reelected Communist alderman was his lifelong foe.

Civic Responsibility in Hard Times

Queen's accession to the mayoralty brought renewed pressure within the ILP–CCF to replace him as the party leader in the provincial house. Yielding to his critics, he resigned from the leadership but retained his seat in the legislature, and S. J. Farmer assumed the responsibilities of party leader.

Five former mayors, including Farmer, came to witness the proceedings at the inaugural meeting of the new council early in 1935. For Queen's conservative predecessors the arrival of a labour chief executive must have occasioned considerable scepticism, if not outright trepidation. Farmer, a moderate reformer rather than a committed socialist, had been elected to the office in 1923, but labour had been in the minority then on city council, and he had not had the slim advantage that John Queen now held.

In 1935 the eighteen council seats were evenly split. On the one side were nine aldermen sponsored by the Civic Election Committee, and on the other nine left-of-centre members: six ILP, two Workers' Unity League, and an Independent who normally voted with the labour group. In a deadlock Mayor Queen would have the deciding vote, and with it a possibility of bringing about some of the reforms for which he had long campaigned. Power in the council was invested in its subcommittees, and out of the acrimonious negotiations that initiated council proceedings that year the labour group emerged dominant in the most important subcommittee, finance, and three of the five others.

In that dismal depression year of 1935, however, reform-minded groups in government had little leeway. With business slowed to a crawl, tax revenue was inadequate to meet the fiscal obligations of either the city or the province, at a time when the problems of the needy were making an unprecedented demand on an already depleted treasury. Unemployment was so high that in the ten years between the great stock market crash of 1929 and the outbreak of World War II in 1939, it was estimated that about half the families in Winnipeg were forced to resort to public assistance for a greater or lesser period. The situation was made worse by the influx into the big city of destitute people from the rural areas and even from elsewhere in the country; and the province, drawing the major part of its revenues from the economic activity in its largest centre, had little or nothing left to spare.

Premier Bracken put the problem squarely: in "carrying on Canada's great social experiment" of meeting the needs of destitute people, "governments are travelling an uncharted course. . . . We cannot long carry on the expenditure of large sums of money . . . which we have to borrow." John Queen's response, many times repeated, was that "the life and well-being of men, women, and children is the only thing that counts." Almost his first move in the mayor's chair was to raise the relief allowance by ten percent.

In this national crisis the economic principles of the CCF called for the institution of relief projects, to improve the city's infrastructure and simultaneously to create jobs. Soon after taking office, Queen negotiated with the federal government on the financing of the project he had long advocated, the sewage disposal plant for Winnipeg, and obtained a cost-sharing agreement between the three levels of government. Work began at once, to be spread over three years, and with his instinct for the immediate needs of individual people, the mayor insisted that priority for the new positions be given to workers whose families had been longest on relief. He put forward other proposals for public works — bridges, viaducts, underpasses at railway crossings — all of them met with alarm by the CEC as more evidence of irresponsible spending by radicals.

Queen had been attempting, as far back as 1916 or 1917, to have the burden of taxation more equitably distributed. Under the existing taxation system, he argued, the little shoe-shine boy on the corner was taxed at the same business rate as the huge retail empires, Eaton's and the Hudson's Bay Company, a grotesque disproportion. The city's major commercial establishments, he insisted, were undertaxed. Two chain stores in Winnipeg, between them accounting for forty-four percent of the city's retail sales, paid a total of $3,722 in 1934 taxes; an insurance company was assessed only $4,692; and the eight largest banks altogether added a mere $9,939 to the hard-pressed city treasury.

Vehemently opposed by conservative interests, by the Home and Property Owners' Associations, the Board of Trade, the Retail Merchants' Association, and by the Civic Election Committee members of his own city council, Queen fought a running battle in the legislature to change the tax limits set by the city's charter. He won his case for a graduated tax rate, and an increase of almost eight hundred thousand dollars in business taxes cut the city's deficit and helped ease the burden on small property owners.

In other attempts, Mayor Queen was not as successful. Pushed by demands from the two Communist alderman on city council that the ILP members make good on their ideological promises, the labour group succeeded in having the council pass a motion to remove the tax exemption on railway property, but the measure was blocked by the CPR. A proposal to levy city taxes on provincially owned property was deferred for later consideration.

Nevertheless Queen persisted, coming forward in city council, at the legislature, and at public meetings, to urge support for his vision of a more hopeful existence, even at this time of deprivation. A seasoned politician now, he well understood the importance of the "hand-clapper," as he called it, the appeal to the imagination of his audience, even as he worked at the mundane changes that were within his reach. He talked of free education, better housing in clean neighbourhoods, access for all to the necessities of life. Assessing the new mayor's performance as early as March of his first year in office, a *Winnipeg Free Press* editorial conceded his ability:

> It's hard to know what to make of Mr. John Queen. Sometimes [he] is merely a Scottish haranguer and his speeches are moonshine and wind music. . . . At other times he stirs the heart by putting on what looks like a real battle for the improvement of life in Manitoba. Yesterday was one of those times. Mr. Queen for once was not talking a murky brand of socialism . . . but firing at a target he could see and might hit.

If an infinitesimal shift had taken place and opinion-makers were prepared now to listen seriously to a new approach to the management of public affairs, the old guard was unhappy. There were more intimations of a Bolshevik threat, fed by the campaign of the Bennett government to suppress the Communist Party. Declining to make a second stand against Queen for the mayoralty, ex-alderman McKerchar pronounced gloomily, "Winnipeg has been going back ever since 1919."

Queen was returned to office for 1936 both as mayor and as MLA, and continued the battle. He realized now, however, that overall solutions were not to be found either in the city's council chamber or in the provincial House, but that the federal government must assume a significant role in ensuring the requirements of life for the country's citizens, in a basic constitutional reallocation of rights and powers. He became a dominant force in the Union of Canadian Municipalities, urging the mayors and reeves to insist that the federal government assume responsibility for welfare programs, for civic improvements, for housing, for education, and for the relief of the unemployed.

Still a union member at heart, he made no secret of his convictions in one labour conflict during his second year in office, and was forced to justify his stance and explain his actions. If the celebrated 1919 strike had been, primarily, an effort to obtain for workers the right to unionize, collective bargaining was still in dispute almost two decades later. The Furriers' Guild of Manitoba had adamantly fought to keep a union out of their shops, insisting that their employees were being harassed and intimidated by a handful of radicals. The union called a strike, and the president of the Neaman Fur Company charged in the press that when a delegation of his workers had asked for the mayor's protection from the strikers, Queen had advised them to join the dissidents.

The mayor corrected the record the next day. The Furriers' Guild, he said, had promised to sign a collective agreement if the majority of workers wanted to join a union; and having made that commitment, two guild members had fired thirty-two employees, all active union members. He intended to bring legislation before the provincial House, said the mayor, to penalize firms that would not recognize their employees' right to unionize. "It may be a long struggle," he added, "but we may be sure of winning." Eventually unionization in the fur industry was accepted.

If a socialist mayor might expect to come under fire from business and the mainstream press, an attack from within the labour movement was more painful and considerably more damaging. Against the mayor's steady insistence that private companies must pay their full share into the city treasury, Bob Russell attempted, just before the civic elections in the fall of 1936, to obtain tax relief for the privately owned Winnipeg Electric Company, in order to prevent possible wage cuts for his OBU members there. Queen condemned the now sidelined unionist for his betrayal of principle.

372

Further, as the city's chief executive the mayor himself was now the employer of all the civic workers. Defending their wage packets, the employees objected strenuously to an increase in their pension deductions, and the disagreement escalated. Russell charged that city employees did not have collective bargaining rights; stung, Queen replied that they did. Pointing scornfully to the number of times Russell had been denied public office by the electorate, he countered that the man was anti-labour and did not speak either for the civic employees or the OBU. Russell then circulated a letter to all the unions demanding that support be withdrawn from the ILP candidate.

The spat undermined the delicate majority that had carried Queen into office, and he lost the November election to Dr. F. E. Warriner. Russell was unrepentant. "I don't intend," he crowed, "to allow foxy John to draw a red herring across the trail in this matter, by his attempt to make it a personal quarrel between us."

The hiatus out of civic office was brief. Running against Warriner in 1937, Queen was once again elected mayor, but this time the majority of seats on city council were held by Civic Election Committee nominees. The mayor would have even less influence than before to alter the cast of his city's government.

Relief costs the previous year had amounted to 1.5 million dollars, and a crop failure on the prairies had further undermined the city's shaky economy, dependent on western trade. The city's finances were in so precarious a state that at one point in early January 1938, when Queen resumed the mayoralty, city council came up short on payroll, and had to keep the teachers waiting a day for their salaries.

Pending the report of its Rowell-Sirois Commission on financial relations with the municipalities, Ottawa had agreed to lend Manitoba the money to cover the relief costs, but the province refused to activate the offer, insisting that Winnipeg cut its budget. There was a healthy balance in the city's sinking fund, enough even now to keep its credit rating higher than that of most other Canadian cities, and a commission under economist Carl Goldenberg had recommended that the annual payment into the fund be temporarily suspended. But the powerful finance committee on city council, again controlled by CEC aldermen, would not allow it to be tapped, in keeping with accepted business practices. In a situation reminiscent of Bill Prichard's dilemma as the depression mayor of Burnaby, Premier Bracken threatened to place Winnipeg under an administrator.

Queen had promised, as a matter of conscience, to make no cuts in the relief allowance, and he kept his word, but funds were cut to libraries, school administration, the police commission, and the parks board. The CPR refused to relinquish its tax exemption, as recommended by Goldenberg, but City Hydro was induced to raise its annual contribution by $150,000, and the province agreed to pay tax on its city properties. The unemployment department was merged with the relief department, to increase efficiency; liquor was taxed, water rates were increased, a tax was imposed on light and power; and, over the anguished protests of die-hard conservatives, the mill rate limit for business was abolished and business taxes increased.

Still the economies proved insufficient. Vociferously backed by Queen's old enemy Bob Russell, the street-railway employees agitated for the restoration of the wage cut they had sustained because of the depression, and the civic employees demanded a five percent increase. By June, there was a serious threat of another paralyzing strike, and a most reluctant city council agreed to a modest pay hike, adding to the fiscal problem.

Nevertheless by 1938 there were some signs that Winnipeg's decade-long depression was beginning to lift. By now an accomplished tactician, the mayor had led the campaign to have the headquarters of the newly organized Trans-Canada Airlines located in his city, and the federal government at long last made its decision for Winnipeg, in the strategic centre of the country and the continent. Expansion of the municipal airport began, stimulating the city's economy. More property owners managed to meet their current assessments, and some even began to pay up arrears.

Harassed by the Communists on his left, with their constant pressure to force their "United Front" on the CCF and their persistent gibes that this so-called representative of the working class was nothing but a political opportunist, a "capitalist lackey," and by entrenched conservatives on the right, bent on safeguarding the city's credit rating and preserving traditional controls, Queen had perceived the necessity of a fundamental change in the structure of government, to make democracy work at the grass-roots level. Never giving up his primary principle, that there must be justice and equity in the apportioning of the world's goods, he knew that the ideal society envisioned by John Stuart Mill could only be realized by democratic, constitutional means. Having accepted the responsibilities of elected office, he pursued the political art of the possible, a socialist reformer in a capitalist world, and a subtle shift began to appear in the policies of the political party he represented. Where the Regina Manifesto had proclaimed the ultimate ideals of public ownership, CCF information releases now concerned the provision of present and specific reforms.

Queen's function as mayor of a large city had involved him in a variety of public relations functions, which he undertook urbanely. He made a much-publicized appearance at the regional competition of the Dominion Drama Festival, to promote the city and to advance its bid to become the site of the following year's finals. Accompanied by the head of Manitoba's Tourist and Convention Bureau, he travelled the almost four thousand miles of Highway 75 from Winnipeg to its southern terminus in Galveston, Texas, on an advertising and goodwill tour. He took a trip to California, part business and part vacation, and the hometown papers were gratified to report that the mayor had dined with Winnipeg's favourite daughter, the movie songbird Deanna Durbin, and had met other film notables. He participated in a cross-border goodwill carnival in Detroit Lakes, Minnesota.

Closest to John Queen's heart was a low-income housing development, which Ottawa agreed to help finance. Her father's life, said Gloria Queen-Hughes, was centred on better housing, so that the slums that bred crime and disease would give way to planned communities where working people could live in dignity and decency. Like the proposals of the British Fabians, or the utopia imagined by the socialist artist-writer William Morris, or the rosy village in George Bernard Shaw's Major Barbara, paradoxically founded on the manufacture of munitions, a special housing project would arise in the working-class West End of John Queen's prairie city:

An overseer would be hired to look after the development. Everybody would have their little gardens with flowers growing out of the windows. There would be pathways, and the children would go to school, and would be safe and happy.

Enthralled by the prospect, Queen's daughter remembered, he sat up night after night, poring over the architects' plans.

The dream came to only partial fruition. By May 1938 the first phase of the proposed plan had begun, and a number of affordable housing units were erected. But private real estate developers looked askance at this intrusion into what they considered their own preserve, and within a year or two, as the scheme proved more expensive than planned, further construction stopped.

An end to the city's penury, and real relief for its working people, would come in a form utterly abhorrent to John Queen, the outbreak of the savagery of World War II.

The End of a Career

A two-year term was instituted for the mayoralty, beginning with the 1938 elections, and Queen campaigned for office as much on his personal record of achievement as on the principles of the party he represented. Attacked by one opponent, Travers Sweatman, KC, as a "Red" who was bent on destroying the city, in another reversion to the scare tactics of 1919, the longstanding public servant countered the personal abuse with a dignified reproof: "I like to think that the citizens of Winnipeg, whether they agree with me in politics or not, respect me personally, as well as the position I occupy." He had always encouraged new industries to locate in the city, he said, but the same conditions that had prevailed throughout the continent had affected the growth of Manitoba as well. He was returned to office, as the portents of the coming world conflict became unmistakable.

In the early summer of 1939, Commonwealth ties were reinforced when King George VI and Queen Elizabeth visited Canada. The press made much of the still disconcerting fact that a socialist mayor would be required to present his city's compliments to Their Majesties, that the man who was jailed twenty years earlier for a crime against the state would now shake hands with the monarch. And would His Worship consent to appear in the required formal dress, long the butt of working-class scorn? Joining the game, Mayor Ralph Day of Toronto sent his Winnipeg counterpart the gift of a fashionable top hat. There was no problem. Sure of himself and of his unwavering commitment to democratic equality, and no longer requiring the outward signs of class identification, Mayor John Queen welcomed the royal visitors in impeccable morning dress with the requisite topper, a valid representative of the people carrying out the ceremonial duties of his office.

The now notorious Russo-German pact that heralded Germany's invasion of Poland and the Allied declaration of war consolidated John Queen's absolute rejection of the Communist ideology and his contempt for the local party hacks. Obedient to their single-minded compliance with central Soviet policy, Queen's sworn foes on the extremist left hailed the development as the greatest move for peace that the world had ever seen, throwing into turmoil many of their own followers, and forcing many a well-meaning progressive to reexamine old assumptions. For John Queen the issue had never been in doubt. There was no mayoralty race that year, but he used the election campaign for aldermen and school trustees to pronounce a sweeping judgment on the false prophets who had only injured and impeded the true socialist cause. "The Communist Party is dangerous to democracy," he declared at an ILP rally:

Nothing but dishonesty and hypocrisy has marked their history. . . . After all that preaching against Hitlerism and against fascism, they stand forth again as the apostles of dictatorship. . . . It would be a tragedy if a single Communist candidate was elected to office. . . . This war has started, and there can be no turning back . . . until Hitlerism is a thing of the past.

The moral aversion to bloodshed that had called forth his pacifist stance in World War I had given way before the immediate and actual threat to the human values of liberal democracy and the hard-won gains that the past twenty years had produced. This new world conflict generated little of the unreal public excitement of righteous patriotism, but rather a tense, sombre determination. Unlike Woodsworth, abandoned by his own disciples and ineffectual in the isolation of his absolute pacifist principles, Queen saw his duty, public and private, in the unstinting prosecution of the present war effort and the safeguarding of the society of the future.

Declaring his profound certainty that the men and women now leaving their normal lives behind to serve their country would never again submit to the humiliation of relief handouts, he announced that the city would guarantee seniority rights for all civic employees who joined the armed forces. As mayor, he worked diligently to obtain for his city as large a share as possible of the expanding wartime economy. The aircraft industry grew, contracts for uniforms reactivated the nee-dle-trades factories, the railway yards hummed with activity, a British Commonwealth pilot training scheme was located in Winnipeg, and the city began at last to prosper.

John Queen was reelected by acclamation in 1940 for another two-year term as mayor, and named vice-president for 1941 of the Federation of Mayors and Municipalities. The editor of the *Municipal Review of Canada* commented, "John Queen is something more than the official head of the great western community. He is a reformer with a realistic mind which he puts into action whenever he gets the opportunity."

Those were lonely years, however, for the busy mayor, with no one left in the big family home. Katherine Queen had died in September 1933, just as her husband's party was gearing up for another civic election, and by 1942 his entire family was involved in the war effort. The oldest, Gloria, was in Britain with the Canadian Women's Army Corps, and her husband, Wilfred Queen-Hughes, had been captured and held a prisoner-of-war by the Japanese at Hong Kong. A second son-in-law, Lieutenant A. R. Wise, was reported missing at Dieppe. John Queen, Jr., served in the Royal Canadian Air Force, and Flora, the mayor's youngest daughter, a nursing sister in the navy, had been posted to the west coast.

Having now spent by far the largest part of his adult life in the political arena, having held a seat in the legislature continuously since 1920 and been in the mayor's office seven times, John Queen failed to draw a sufficient number of votes in the provincial election of December 1941, and the next legislature convened without him. He continued his vigorous activities as mayor and remained a strong presence in the trade union movement.

The fate of his son-in-law at Dieppe was still not known in August 1942 when he addressed a convention of pulp and paper unions in

Kenora, Ontario, and some of his grief and anger, never to be resolved, at the system that had reduced the world to such misfortune flared out in his protest:

> Lives are being given for human freedom. What are we really fighting for? . . . When I think of ten years of so-called depression, suffering, misery, and want, when people were denied the opportunity to make a livelihood, my blood runs cold that we should be fighting for a recurrence of that. That suffering and want was unnecessary and a contradiction of this country's enormous resources.

An editorial in the *Winnipeg Tribune* gently reproved the mayor for forgetting why Canadians were fighting the Nazis. As he himself knew, it was unthinkable to contemplate "Canada as it would be if we lost the war." But the mainstream newspaper concurred with Queen's central demand:

> If there is one thing that the people of this nation are agreed upon it is that there shall be no return to the conditions of 1919 and the early Twenties, to unemployment and breadlines for our returned soldiers . . . [and] a recurrence of those conditions of gross hardship and sheer lack of opportunity for a whole generation of young people that characterized the depression of the 1930s. . . .

As rhetoric, the assurance was undoubtedly sincere, but the people of Queen's Winnipeg had now put the depression years behind them, in the artificial euphoria of a united war effort and a comfortable wage packet, and the old socialist theme had lost something of its immediacy.

Queen threw his hat into the ring once more in the civic elections the next fall, contesting the mayoralty against T. C. Knight and Garnet Coulter. Once more, his campaign reiterated the ideals that had won him endorsement time after time. Again he invoked the misdeeds of the establishment, inviting the electorate to contemplate the still uncertain future, at the end of the endlessly weary hostilities:

We cannot have any confidence in the promises of a government for a better world after the war, when that self-same government supports an economic system which places profits ahead of people. . . . The government during the depression allowed people to go hungry, [while] at the same time it was passing legislation to force farmers to grow less wheat, destroying apples in British Columbia while children in Winnipeg and other parts of the country could not get any fresh fruit.

But the electorate, for the most part, was no longer hungry but ready to hear a more optimistic, more encouraging message. Garnet Coulter came in ahead of the socialist incumbent, and John Queen was out of political office for the first time in more than a quarter of a century.

There were no offers of a lucrative private position, no corporate directorships or management appointments, as there might have been for a man of comparable service to a business-oriented political party, but the union movement did have one task for John Queen to undertake, as organizer for the Retail Clerks International Protective Association, returning to the grass-roots endeavours in which he had first been involved.

After the high-level responsibilities of a member of the legislature and a city mayor, the mundane duties of a union organizer could only provide a stopgap, at best, even for as unassuming a man as John Queen. When the mayoralty was next on the ballot, in 1944, he jumped eagerly back into the fray, and once again was turned away in favour of Garnet Coulter. Dispirited, or perhaps only tidying up his affairs in preparation for the next task he might undertake, Queen gathered together his accumulation of papers, the record of an extraordinarily significant period in the history of his city and his province, took them to the city dump, and burned them. When Gloria Queen-Hughes returned from overseas she could only protest too late the destruction of this archival treasure trove.

There was not a great deal of time left for John Queen. He went bowling with friends one Saturday evening in September 1946, and shortly after midnight, looking forward to the next outing, he returned, alone as usual, to the empty house. At four in the morning he awakened his doctor with a laboured telephone call, reporting severe chest pain.

The doctor responded at once, but arrived only moments before John Queen died, at sixty-four, of a heart attack. After a lifetime in public office, the former mayor left an estate of less than ten thousand dollars.

John Queen has been described as a "cooper, bread driver, alderman, political prisoner, legislator, party leader, insurance salesman, automobile and truck salesman, mayor, and union organizer." A compendium of the society to which he gave his unstinting devotion, he remained to the last a social democrat and a hopeful reformer, urging young people to join in labour's great cause: "Even though the reward may be long in coming, it will surely come."

Conclusion

The Winnipeg General Strike of 1919 has become a labour legend, held up as a shining example of courage and determination. It has been lauded, with some justification, as a milestone in the development of the Canadian social safety net, since the benefits that the strikers failed to win, and much greater gains that few of them even contemplated, are now taken for granted. The beginnings of present-day programmes such as universal health coverage, unemployment insurance, old age pensions, welfare legislation were generated by the militants of this period, both men and women; and the active role women played marks a major change in the long evolution of the relationship between the sexes.

The general strike was an untidy happening, arguably spinning out of the control of its leaders, and countered by the authorities with a notable lack of finesse. With the passing of time, the once-alarming radicalism of 1919 no longer commands attention. Both the women's battle for the franchise and the demands of the "Hello girls" and their sisters in the labour force now arouse admiration rather than outrage, if the magnitude of their effort is even fully recognized. Equally, the story of the labour upheaval that brought down on its perceived instigators the full force of the law has passed into the general domain, as it were, now accepted by the general public as a subject for nostalgic reminiscence and a fascinating component of our common heritage.

At the end of the turbulent twentieth century, the political certainties that fuelled the energy of the labour action have all but evaporated.

World-wide, doctrinaire Marxism has crumbled with the demise of the Soviet Union, and the apparently invincible market economy has been modified by an underpinning of social welfare; and in Canada, the left-of-centre party that developed out of the coalition of differences in 1919 has, in its present incarnation, lost its philosophical base, becoming increasingly uncertain of its proper goals. On the feminist front, divergent factions clash in strident opposition. If an ultimate vision of a harmonious and egalitarian existence for humanity in peace and plenty was at any time the common denominator among the dissenters of the earlier age, in all their variously suffragist, reformist, socialist, or Marxist disagreements, utopia has now quite lost its credibility.

On consideration, however, the opposing sides in the strike trials were contending an issue never quite articulated in court, and perhaps only comprehensible in hindsight. As the Crown attorneys hammered home their charge of sedition and conspiracy, it was paramount for the defendants to demonstrate, point by specific point, that the assertion of conspiracy was simply not tenable, and as they outlined their differences they repeatedly denied a common cause. No convincing evidence could be produced that a revolutionary take-over by radical elements had been in the making.

But if instant revolution was at any time anything more than a flickering possibility for radicals like Pritchard and Russell, even moderates like Dixon and Queen were indeed asserting a watershed change in the balance of social power. Demanding as did Queen's guiding social philosopher, John Stuart Mill, that those whose labour produces the world's wealth must share equitably in that wealth, they were also speaking for the political empowerment of the economically disadvantaged. The underlying principle in the arguments of the strike leaders was the right of the working majority to a meaningful voice in political and economic decisions. Not sedition, the destruction of the state, was their purpose, but the fulfilment of its human potential.

The case against the accused, in effect, asserted law and order, or the immutable authority of constituted government, seeking to demonstrate that the traditional structures of society could not be attacked with impunity. As Judge Metcalfe pronounced at Bob Russell's trial, statements that served to fan discontent and disturbances were seditious and could not be tolerated, even if they were true. On the surface of it, constituted authority triumphed, and the dissidents were duly jailed. In the longer perspective the strike, despite its immediate failure, marked a watershed in the devolution of authority in the country. An irreversible shift in power had imperceptibly taken place and the unspoken purpose of the strike had been won, to achieve recognition of the right of the governed to participate in government, in the range of decisions, political as well as economic, that affect their lives. The move of the moderate left into politics represents a de facto assertion of that right. As for the women's movement, the acquisition of the franchise made the exercise of that right at least technically available, for women on the left as for others, on an equal basis with the men.

One interesting pattern emerges from this study of the leading figures of an earlier period. Each of these stories rises to a crescendo of promise, and for some of these people there are some rewards in their own time, some humanitarian social provisions, some recognition in the community. Virtually every life, however, ends in decline and fall, in disappointment and defeat. In a narrow sense, this observation may only amount to a truism, that political development always overtakes and leaves behind the people who were once in its vanguard. Bill Pritchard is interesting in this respect, however. Having opted out of the struggle to improve the lot of his fellow citizens, disappearing out of the public arena, he lived long enough to find himself sought after by a younger generation, for the message he could bring from one troubled time to another. As he himself understood, dissent is eternal, for "to teach the alphabet is to inaugurate a revolution," and at the heart of conscious human existence is an unassuageable hunger for a better world.

This portrait gallery of men and women who took issue with the prevailing mores speaks to some enduring humanitarian values that transcend the passage of time. In his dogged battle for union benefits, Bob Russell was claiming for the ordinary working man what he wanted for himself, a reasonable share of the small satisfactions of civilized existence, beyond the subsistence requirements of food and shelter: time to watch a football game, the peace of mind to join friends in a song, the means to provide children with a space in which to flourish. It was the paramount existential significance of ordinary decencies like these that motivated the drive of the women's movement against drunkenness, disease, and prostitution, against unrealistic wages and insufferable conditions in the workplace, and against the subordination of one part of the human race to another.

Roger Bray's soldiers demanded that they must not be forgotten, in the future their war had supposedly been fought to preserve, and Dick Johns, abandoning fruitless doctrinal loyalty, sought to provide average people with the education and the skills to make an honourable place for themselves in that world. Heaps and Queen, each in his own sphere, devoted their lives to the patient, pragmatic correction of specific inequities. And beyond these bread-and-butter verities, a less definable spiritual need animated the 1919 group of protagonists: for Dixon, the freedom to achieve full self-realization; for Woodsworth, a personal integrity of spirit; and for all an overwhelming need to be part of a organic community and to serve that community.

Dissent is inherent in the human story, a perception always of present inadequacy and failure. If none of these valiant warriors achieved what Nellie McClung called "our heart's desire," it may well be that the goal is infinite, and therefore unattainable. In unquiet times, when received theories offer no support, a look back at some recent forebears may offer an understanding of the needs that must be met, the direction that might be taken, the obstacles that must be overcome — and perhaps most subtly of all, a sense of the unity in diversity that characterizes us all.

For Further Reading

Abella, Irving. *The Canadian Labour Movement, 1902–1960*. Ottawa: Canadian Historical Society, 1975.

———, and Harold Troper. *None Is Too Many*. Toronto: Lester & Orpen Dennys, 1982.

Artibise, Alan. *Winnipeg: An Illustrated History*. Toronto: James Lorimer, 1977.

Belkin, Simon. *Through Narrow Gates*. Montreal: Eagle Publishing, 1966.

Bercuson, David J. *Confrontation at Winnipeg*. Montreal: McGill-Queen's University Press, 1974.

———. *Fools and Wise Men: The Rise and Fall of the One Big Union*. Toronto: McGraw-Hill Ryerson, 1978.

———, and Kenneth McNaught. *The Winnipeg Strike: 1919*. Don Mills: Longman, 1974.

Bland, Salem. *The New Christianity*. Toronto: McClelland and Stewart, 1920.

Bradbury, Bettina. "Women's History and Working-Class History." *Labour/Le Travail* 19 (Spring 1987), pp. 23-44.

Cleverdon, Catherine L. *The Woman Suffrage Movement in Canada*. Toronto: University of Toronto Press, 1950.

Coldwell, M. J. *Left Turn, Canada*. London: Victor Gollancz, 1945.

Ferns, H. S. *Reading from Left to Right*. Toronto: University of Toronto Press, 1983.

Gray, James H. *The Winter Years*. Toronto: Macmillan, 1970.

Hacker, Carlotta. *The Indomitable Lady Doctors.* Toronto: Clarke, Irwin, 1974.

Haig, Kennethe. *Brave Harvest: The Life-Story of E. Cora Hind.* Toronto: Thomas Allen, 1945.

Heaps, Leo. *The Rebel in the House.* Rev. ed. Markham: Fitzhenry and Whiteside, 1984.

Horodyski, Mary. "Women and the Winnipeg General Strike, 1919." *Manitoba History* 11 (Spring 1986), pp. 28-35.

Horowitz, Gad. *Canadian Labour in Politics.* Toronto: University of Toronto Press, 1968.

Jordan, Mary V. *Survival: Labour's Trials and Tribulations in Canada.* Toronto: McDonald House, 1975.

Kealey, Gregory S. "1919: The Canadian Labour Revolt." *Labour/Le Travail* 13 (Spring 1984), pp. 11-44.

Kealey, Linda. "Canadian Socialism and the Woman Question, 1900–1914." *Labour/Le Travail* 13 (Spring 1984), pp. 77-100.

Kinnear, Mary, ed. *First Days, Fighting Days: Women in Manitoba History.* Regina: Canadian Plains Research Centre, 1987.

MacInnis, Grace. *J. S. Woodsworth: A Man to Remember.* Toronto: Macmillan, 1953.

Mardiros, Anthony. *William Irvine: The Life of a Prairie Radical.* Toronto: James Lorimer, 1979.

Masters, D. C. *The Winnipeg General Strike.* Toronto: University of Toronto Press, 1950.

McCallum, Margaret E. "Keeping Women in Their Place: The Minimum Wage in Canada, 1910–25." *Labour/Le Travail* 17 (Spring 1986), pp. 29-58.

McClung, Nellie. *Clearing in the West: My Own Story.* Toronto: Thomas Allen, 1935.

———. *The Stream Runs Fast*. Toronto: Thomas Allen, 1945.

McCormack, A. Ross. *Reformers, Rebels, and Revolutionaries: The Western Radical Movement*, 1899–1919. Toronto: University of Toronto Press, 1977.

McNaught, Kenneth. *A Prophet in Politics: A Biography of J. S. Woodsworth*. Toronto: University of Toronto Press, 1971.

Mills, Allen. "Co-operation and Community in the Thought of J. S. Woodsworth." *Labour/Le Travail* 14 (Fall 1984), pp. 103-120.

———. *Fool for Christ: The Political Thought of J. S. Woodsworth*. Toronto: University of Toronto Press, 1991.

———. "The Later Thought of J. S. Woodsworth, 1918–1942: An Essay in Revision." Journal of Canadian Studies 17, no. 3 (Fall 1982), pp. 75-95.

———. "Single Tax, Socialism and the Independent Labor Party of Manitoba: The Political Ideas of F. J. Dixon and S. J. Farmer." *Labour/Le Travail* 5 (Spring 1980), pp. 33-54.

Osborne, Kenneth W. *R. B. Russell and the Labour Movement*. Agincourt: Book Society of Canada, 1978.

Penner, Norman. *The Canadian Left: A Critical Analysis*. Scarborough: Prentice-Hall, 1977.

———, ed. *Winnipeg 1919: The Strikers' Own History of the Winnipeg General Strike*. Toronto: James Lewis and Samuel, 1973.

Peterson, Larry. "The One Big Union in International Perspective: Revolutionary Industrial Unionism, 1900-1925." *Labour/Le Travail* 7 (Spring 1981), pp. 41-66.

———. "Revolutionary Socialism and Industrial Unrest in the Era of the Winnipeg General Strike: The Origins of Communist Labour Unionism in Europe and North America." *Labour/Le Travail* 17 (Spring 1984), pp. 115-131.

Roberts, Barbara. *A Reconstructed World: Gertrude Richardson, A Feminist Biography*. Montreal, McGill-Queen's University Press, 1996.

Robin, Martin. *Radical Politics and Canadian Labour*. Kingston: Queen's University Press, 1968.

Smith, A. E. *All My Life*. Toronto: Progress Books, 1949.

Smith, Doug. *Let Us Rise: An Illustrated History of the Manitoba Labour Movement*. Vancouver: New Star Books, 1954.

Stinson, Lloyd. *Political Warriors: Recollections of a Social Democrat*. Winnipeg: Queenston House, 1975.

Stubbs, Roy St. George. *Prairie Portraits*. Toronto: McClelland and Stewart, 1954.

Trachtenberg, Henry. "The Winnipeg Jewish Community in the Inter-War Period, 1919-1939: Antisemitism and Politics." *Jewish Life and Times*, 3, 1983, pp. 177-185.

Underhill, Frank H. *James Shaver Woodsworth: Untypical Canadian*. Toronto: University of Toronto Press, 1944.

Usiskin, Roz. " 'The Alien In Our Midst': The 1919 Winnipeg General Strike." *Jewish Life and Times*, 5, 1988, pp. 28-49.

Wiesbord, Merrily. *The Strangest Dream*. Toronto: Lester & Orpen Dennys, 1983.

Woodsworth, James S. *The First Story of the Labor Church*. Winnipeg: Winnipeg Labor Church, 1924.

———. *My Neighbour*. Toronto: University of Toronto Press, 1972 [1911].

———. *Strangers within Our Gates*. Toronto: University of Toronto Press, 1972 [1909].

Index

PRINTED AND BOUND
IN BOUCHERVILLE, QUÉBEC, CANADA
BY MARC VEILLEUX IMPRIMEUR INC.
IN MARCH, 1997